WHAT EVERYONE SHOULD KNOW ABOUT THE 20TH CENTURY

Also published by Adams Publishing:

*What Every American Should Know about
American History*

*What Every American Should Know about
Women's History*

WHAT EVERYONE SHOULD KNOW ABOUT THE 20TH CENTURY

200 Events that Shaped the World

Dr. Alan Axelrod and Charles Phillips

Adams Publishing
Holbrook, Massachusetts

Published by Adams Media Corporation
260 Center Street, Holbrook, MA 02343

ISBN: 1-55850-506-7

Printed in Canada.

J I H G F E D C B A

Library of Congress Cataloging-in-Publication Data
Axelrod, Alan, 1952–
What everyone should know about the 20th century : 200 events that shaped the world /
Alan Axelrod and Charles Phillips.
p.   cm.
Includes bibliographical references and index.
ISBN 1-55850-506-7
1. History, Modern—20th century—Miscellanea. I. Phillips, Charles, 1948– . II. Title.
D422.A94   1995
909.82—dc20   95–41912
                               CIP

*This book is available at quantity discounts for bulk purchases.
For information, call 1-800-872-5627.*

*In memory of
Charles Lamar Phillips, Sr.,
and Ruby Freeman,
brother and sister*

This book would not have been possible without the dedicated help of Patricia Hogan, a clear thinker and a talented editor who helped choose the events and form the writing about those events.

Contents

Introduction

As with our previous work, *What Every American Should Know about American History: 200 Events that Shaped the Nation*, we have tackled the complex history of the twentieth century through a fixed number of events that we use as jumping-off points, as opportunities to describe not only an arbitrarily chosen event but the milieu surrounding an event, with its connections to other events and larger historical trends. Once again, let us say that choosing two hundred events to create a historical narrative is no more artificial than breaking such a narrative into cleverly titled chapters, nor does it prevent one from developing broad themes and discussing major issues.

In a terribly interesting book entitled *The Age of Extremes*, Eric Hobsbawm writes the history of what he calls the "short twentieth century," meaning the span of time between the assassination of Archduke Ferdinand in an obscure Balkan town called Sarajevo in 1914 to the collapse of the Soviet Union and the attendant end of the Cold War in the late 1980s. For Hobsbawm, the twentieth century essentially occurred around the two world wars, whose causes and effects created the social reality that made this century different from the last. There are, of course, other ways to distinguish the unique qualities of the twentieth century. For many Marxist historians, for example, the twentieth century was the heyday of late capitalism, or finance capitalism. For any number of "modernists" early in the century, our times were chiefly characterized by the growing mechanization of the world and the consequent alienation of the individual. Many historians have seen the true face of the twentieth century in the great ideological clashes between East and West. Others have seen it in the growth of massively destructive technologies, and still others have perceived it in the rise of totalitarian governments and the imposition of an administered world. Not a few have noted the inability of legal concepts developed in centuries past to cover adequately the scientific advances of the twentieth century, and many have bemoaned the failure of older religious metaphors to capture the nature of the world as described by modern physics. For many, the twentieth century was a time of constant change, a time when the old verities no longer sufficed, when the old truths had been slain, when seemingly everything, including language itself, was in a crisis; in short, an age of flux, relativity, and anxiety. Still others, more optimistic, see in the changeling century the integration of the human species, primarily through technology, into a global village.

Indeed, one might be forgiven for finding in the twentieth century, with its rapid revolutions and rabid reactions, something that defies an understanding based on historical knowledge (which is really only a discussion, sometimes accurate, sometimes not, of what we think has happened in the past). And it seems hard to ignore the impact of the communications revolution on our daily lives, which makes so much more information so much more widely available so much quicker. In fact, the century is rife with exhortations to give up interpretation entirely, to forget history altogether, and to march headlong into a brave new world. If nothing else, the professionalizing of virtually every field of knowledge, and the attendant code language those professions use, make a general understanding of what is happening in our world and why it is happening so much more difficult than need be. Americans, living in a culture whose very foundation is based on a turning-away from the past, have felt surprisingly comfortable with the cult of the new that developed first among the artists and writers of the twentieth century and then spread far and wide with the help of a publicity-savvy and ubiquitous culture industry. For those of us lucky enough to live in the industrial West, it does occasionally seem that we can escape the consequences of events at home or abroad by simply switching off the machines that tell us about them.

Of course, if we believed that, we would not have written this book. With modern events, as with those more specific to our American past, we should not confuse the event with either its telling or the medium of its conveyance into our lives. If American history does not have to degenerate into a hodgepodge of homilies for restless and distracted youths to avoid like the plague, neither do the events of our own time have to become lessons in civics, or an attack on our moral sensibilities, or the signposts to a future shock trend that we must not miss lest we fall behind the times. The world is an interesting place, by turns thrilling, frightening, colorful, even frustrating, but it never has to be dull. For us, the best way to approach the events of the elusive twentieth century seems to be from an American perspective, since that is the perspective we most naturally share with those likely to read this book, and the one we could make work best in that tricky game of language called narrative. We do not imply that other perspectives are wrong, or that other Americans could not have chosen two hundred entirely different events as their jumping-off point with just as much justification as we have chosen ours. All we say is that the events in this book both shaped our lives and told us something about the century in which we live, a century whose basic character we have attempted to serve up in a popular history that we hope, once again, will be enjoyable to read even as it explains how things turned out the way they did.

Charles Phillips
Alan Axelrod

The United States Goes to War with Spain (1898)

The event: The explosion of the U.S. battleship *Maine* in Havana Harbor on February 15, 1898, whipped up war sentiment to fever pitch and propelled the United States into war with Spain and into a century of involvement in world affairs.

EVER SINCE GEORGE WASHINGTON had warned against "foreign entanglements" in the first Presidential Farewell Address of 1797, many Americans had cherished their isolation, particularly from the ever fractious nations of Europe. Late in the nineteenth century, however, America's spectacular post–Civil War economic growth had resulted in a boom-and-bust economy that was creating great civil unrest and a fairly open if not quite all-out class warfare, which would not truly abate until the 1920s. In the face of growing economic hardship and a series of increasingly violent labor disputes at home, many policymakers in the United States began to look toward imperial adventures abroad to distract Americans from domestic strife and rescue big business from its doldrums.

On the threshold of the twentieth century—when Americans were generally isolationists while the elite of its businessmen and opinion makers were expansionists—General Valeriano Weyler arrived in Havana as Spain's new colonial governor of Cuba, an island no more than ninety miles off the coast of Florida. Weyler's mission was to put down the Cuban rebels who had been fighting Spanish dominion for more than a year. Weyler began by rounding up Cuban citizens and putting them in "reconcentration" camps in order to keep them

from covertly supplying the rebels. This act of tyranny only bolstered the rebels' resolve— and it gave U.S. imperialists the wedge they needed to turn American public opinion against Spain and permit national leaders to embark on the road to world power.

President Grover Cleveland, whatever his personal sympathies may have been, did not want his country to become involved in a conflict between Spain and its Cuban colony, and William McKinley, who succeeded him in 1896, publicly expressed the same sentiments. Yet, as the months of tyranny continued, many people in the United States agitated for intervention. Not only were the Spanish atrocities—just ninety miles off our shores—intolerable, but American business interests and citizens, both plentiful on the island, were at risk. Into the growing national debate jumped two rival newspaper giants, Joseph Pulitzer and William Randolph Hearst, whose *New York World* and *New York Journal* were engaged in a bitter war of their own—a circulation war—and coverage of the situation in Cuba was a highly desirable spoil of that war. The papers outdid each other in publishing sensational stories of valiant rebels fighting cruel Spanish overlords.

At last, in January 1898, as the fighting and riots continued in Cuba, President McKinley dispatched the battleship *Maine* to Havana Harbor in order to protect U.S. citizens. When the *Maine* blew up on February 15, killing 266 crewmen, most Americans blamed Spanish sabotage and called for immediate retaliation. The findings of a naval court of inquiry supported popular opinion, concluding that the ship had hit a submarine mine. (Modern scholars believe the ship actually exploded accidentally, when one of its powder magazines ignited.) Cries of "Remember the *Maine!*"—an echo of the "Remember the Alamo!" battle slogan that had stirred the nation to action during the Texas Rebellion and the Mexican War more than fifty years earlier—were heard throughout the country. In April, McKinley asked Congress for authority to send forces into Cuba. Congress also passed a resolution recognizing Cuba's independence, whereupon Spain, on April 24, declared war on the United States.

The first battle did not take place in Cuba, but in the Spanish-occupied Philippine Islands. Immediately upon the declaration of war, U.S. Admiral George Dewey took his Asiatic Squadron from Hong Kong to Manila Bay. There, on May 1, he fired on the Spanish fleet, destroying all ten ships anchored in the bay without suffering any losses himself. Eleven thousand U.S. ground troops were dispatched to the Philippines where they collaborated with Filipino irregulars commanded by Emilio Aguinaldo to defeat Spanish forces in Manila on August 13.

The fighting war in Cuba was similarly swift and decisive. On May 29, the U.S. fleet blockaded the Spanish fleet at Santiago Harbor, and the next month seventeen thousand troops invaded Cuba at Daiquiri, then advanced on Santiago. The fierce battle for the city was fought at San Juan Hill, which American forces, including Lt. Col. Theodore Roosevelt's Rough Riders, took on July 1. In the meantime, Spanish Admiral Pascual Cervera, under fire from U.S. ground forces and blockaded by the U.S. Navy, resolved to run the blockade. The result was a four-hour battle in which the American fleet completely annihilated the Spanish fleet while suffering the loss of only one sailor.

On August 12, Spain not only agreed to withdraw from Cuba, but to cede Puerto Rico and Guam to the United States. Formal peace talks in Paris also resulted in Spain's selling the Philippines to the United States for $20 million.

Secretary of State John Hay would call the conflict a "splendid little war" that certainly gave the United States instant prestige in the eyes of the world, setting it on a course to become a true world power in the dawning century. Therein lay the splendor of that splendid little war, and therein also lay its burden, which was apparent from the start. Puerto Rico submitted to the establishment of a U.S. territorial government with little difficulty. But conflict between the American military government that President McKinley established in Cuba and Cuban rebel leaders was immediate. There was much talk of U.S. annexation of the island, but this scheme was abandoned in 1902. The United States agreed to Cuban independence, but retained the right to establish military bases on the island and to intervene in Cuban affairs whenever necessary to "preserve" order and maintain Cuban independence. The Philippines also proved troublesome, as nationalist guerrillas, under Aguinaldo, fought the American occupiers. Peace was restored by 1902, but Philippine independence from the United States remained a thorny issue until after the end of World War II, when the islands were granted independence in 1946.

President McKinley did not long savor the victory in Cuba. On September 6, 1901, he was shot by an anarchist, Leon Czolgosz, while attending the Pan-American Exposition in Buffalo, New York, and died eight days later. His vice president, Theodore Roosevelt, assumed office and was elected in his own right in 1904, whereupon he established a policy toward the Caribbean islands and Latin America that came to be known as the Roosevelt Corollary to the Monroe Doctrine. It effectively made the United States an international police force for the region, a role that was destined to expand, for better or worse, throughout the century.

Max Planck Proposes the Quantum Theory (1900)

The event: At a meeting of the Berlin Physical Society on October 19, 1900, Max Planck announced the elements of quantum mechanics, launching perhaps the most successful theory in all of science.

SOMETIMES THE MOST profound events seem to have the least bearing on the "real" world. Max Planck was a German theoretical physicist who taught at the University of Berlin. On October 19, 1900, he proposed a revolutionary explanation for the so-called "ultraviolet catastrophe." Few people, at that end of the last century or this, would know or care about the problem, but for classical physicists it was a bona fide catastrophe, threatening explanations of the structure of reality that had endured since at least the days of Sir Isaac Newton. According to classical physics, there should be an infinite amount of light—energy, radiation—inside a heated cavity, such as a kiln. Why? Classical theory predicted that the particles in the heated walls of the kiln were subject to continuity of process. The particles that vibrated to produce the light would vibrate to an infinite range of frequencies.

The problem was that, of course, nothing of the kind happened. But *why* not? What kept the energy in the cavity from radiating infinitely into the far ultraviolet? Planck worked on the problem for three years, starting in 1897. Suddenly, shortly before the Physical Society meeting, a solution dawned on him. He proposed that the vibrating particles can only radiate at certain energies. These energies would be determined by a new constant, a universal constant, which Planck called an "elementary quantum of action." *Quantum* is the neuter form of the Latin word meaning "how much?" and it described energy given off not continuously, but in discrete pieces, packets, or "quanta." Since violet light had half the wavelength of red light, for example, violet light traveled in quanta that were twice the size—and therefore twice the energy content—of red light.

Planck worked out the relationship between energy and frequency (or wavelength) as a universal constant, an infinitesimally small number—6.63×10^{-27} erg-seconds—that represented the "graininess" of energy. Only those energies could appear that were whole-number multiples of the constant (soon to be christened "Planck's constant") multiplied by frequency. Under most circumstances in day-to-day life this graininess, slight as it is, goes unnoticed, and energy behaves, for all *practical* purposes as if it were radiated in fluid fashion. But in the case of the ultraviolet catastrophe, the graininess has to be taken into account.

Planck did not pursue the implications of his arcane theory, but another German theoretician, Albert Einstein, did. He noted that when light shines on certain metals, electrons are knocked free. This is the "photoelectric effect" that has practical use today in solar cells. However, Einstein observed, the energy of the electrons liberated does not depend, as common sense would suggest, on the intensity of the light, but on its color—that is, its frequency. To explain why, Einstein proposed that light, which decades of science had demonstrated to behave as if it traveled in waves, actually traveled in discrete packets, or quanta. These quanta—or photons, as they are called today—have a certain energy (Planck's constant times the frequency of the light) and transfer most of that energy to the electrons they strike; a brighter light releases more electrons, but not more energetic electrons. The energy of the electrons depends solely on the frequency of the light.

Einstein's work, published in a 1905 paper, took Planck's theory from the realm of mathematical speculation and into the world of physical fact. For physicists, quantum mechanics marks the division between "classical physics"—how reality was explained prior to 1900—and "modern physics"—how reality is explained today. For the rest of the world, it marks the beginning of a current of thought that would, before the century was half through, result in the liberation of unimaginable energy from the atom—energy that could produce more energy, such as electricity to power great cities, or energy that could produce an explosion powerful enough to destroy great cities.

Eastman Kodak Introduces the Brownie Camera (1900)

The event: In 1900 the Eastman Kodak Company began producing a remarkable new box camera called the Brownie. The inexpensive camera made the ability to take photographs available to virtually everyone, transforming what had formerly been a fad among a few artists and a somewhat tawdry enterprise for any number of commercial photographers into a democratic pleasure for the masses. It also made possible a popular new means of preserving personal memories and the historical record: the snapshot.

PHOTOGRAPHY HAD BEEN around for nearly a century, but had been used mostly by professionals until the 1880s. Almost everyone was familiar with the commercial photography studios, where customers sat rigidly still for long periods in order to have their images captured and preserved. Talented photographers, some working for the federal government, had been lugging their cumbersome and expensive equipment around on battlefields and in the wilds of the American West for decades, taking extraordinary pictures of the Civil War, Native Americans, and the splendors of nature. "Art" photographers had long been persuading gullible young women to pose scantily clad in flowing sheets or in nothing at all, and a few artists, like Alfred Stieglitz, had worked at using the medium to produce profound images that would stand the test of time as well as paintings and sculptures. Late in the century, when the Rochester, New York, entrepreneur George Eastman developed the Kodak fixed-focus box camera, a growing number of amateurs took up photography to record the moments of their everyday lives, creating a popular craze for photographs and helping to make the fortune of Eastman's new Kodak Company.

By 1897, however, Stieglitz was proclaiming, "Photography is a fad well-nigh on its last legs, thanks largely to the bicycle craze." Stieglitz was actually celebrating the death of the photography craze, not eulogizing its passing, for he believed that once the fad subsided, photography could at long last become a true art. However, he was wrong on both counts. Popular photog-

raphy would not die out, and photography would nevertheless become a major art form in the twentieth century. The introduction of the Brownie camera ensured the former; Stieglitz himself would be in many ways responsible for making sure the latter became true.

The Brownie was named, one assumes, for its designer, Frank Brownell, though Eastman's use of a little sprite for what we would today call the camera's logo was surely meant to attract young customers. Brownell's point-and-shoot hand-held camera took the "revolution" in photography to new levels. Almost everyone could afford the dollar it took to buy the camera, which produced reliably good pictures without all the professional fuss of focusing lenses and timing exposures. Even a child could use the camera and take a good picture, and Kodak promised to develop the film, which freed would-be photographers from having to purchase expensive developing equipment or master the artful mysteries of the darkroom. More than a quarter of a million Brownies were sold the first year, breaking all records and making George Eastman a truly rich man. In one form or another, the Brownie would remain on the market for almost eighty years, becoming the first example of a great twentieth-century trend, the taking of technological innovations and simplifying them until the products they spawned were easily affordable by the middle class.

The Brownie was followed by such innovations as color photographs, the Polaroid Land Company's introduction of instantly self-developing film (around mid-century), and the hand-held, 8-mm moving-picture camera, then the now-ubiquitous video cameras. The trend itself was not limited to the camera business; it affected everything from automobiles to computers.

Folks called the images they could "take" with the new Brownies "snapshots," and birthdays and bar mitzvahs went instantly from quiet family affairs to great public events that documented the passing of our individual lives.

No doubt the placing of usable cameras in the hands of the masses drove artists like Stieglitz to distraction, but he persevered. Five years after he had gleefully announced the death of the photography craze, the already internationally recognized photographer put together a show of photographic art called, "An Exhibition of American Photography arranged by the Photo-Secession." Formerly, painters had scorned photography because they thought it mechanistic, merely a matter of pointing and shooting, a philosophy that the introduction of the Brownie certainly did little to refute. After Stieglitz's exhibition, however, a new class of photographers entered the staid American art scene and shook things up. They introduced the concept of the photo session, a span of time in which the photographer took the mundane materials of raw reality and transformed them into an art photo. Photo sessions allowed budding photographers to imagine they were practicing an alternative to conventional point-and-shoot photography. The new camera-carrying

aesthetic ideologues aligned themselves with the European painters of the avant-garde and campaigned on behalf of what they called "the new," regardless of medium. The Stieglitz-spawned sessionists opened their own galleries in New York in 1905 at 291 Fifth Avenue in order to display both paintings and photographs *together,* a shocking proposition in its day.

In the course of time, "291" would itself become an institution in the American art world. There, Americans would encounter for the first time the work of some of Europe's contemporary artists and, occasionally, the artists themselves. Among America's own young talents who came, saw, and were conquered were Georgia O'Keeffe and Paul Strand. Stieglitz would marry O'Keeffe in 1924, and he would help to make Strand's work famous, validating in the process photography as an art form. Stieglitz himself would go on to found *The Seven Arts* magazine, helping to start yet another trend: the appearance of obscure "small magazines," read by few, but dictating the course art and literature would take, and influencing the tastes and the life of many.

Both the introduction of the Brownie and Stieglitz's stubborn dedication to the aesthetic potential of photography helped to make the latter an essential part of the twentieth century, not only giving birth to a new art form and a new pastime, but helping to create the necessary conditions for a new profession—photojournalism—and a new kind of periodical—the news magazine.

Theodore Dreiser Publishes *Sister Carrie* (1900)

The event: On November 8, 1900, Doubleday, Page and Company published *Sister Carrie*—effectively suppressed for twelve years—then considered an amoral, unsentimental, and unflinchingly naturalistic vision of American life in the new century.

BORN IN TERRE HAUTE, INDIANA, in 1879, the son of hardworking, impoverished, joyless religious fanatics, Theodore Dreiser received a spotty education and drifted from job to job. Homely and awkward, Dreiser eked out a living writing for various midwestern newspapers. He moved to New York in 1894, where he became a moderately successful magazine editor. At this time, he discovered the works of the great French novelists Honoré de Balzac and Émile Zola, as well as the intensely skeptical scientific writers, Herbert Spencer, Thomas Henry Huxley, and Charles Darwin. Their influences strongly colored his version of American life at the threshold of the new century.

What he saw was a nation driven by raw instinct and populated by men and women who were blindly motivated by a hunger for power, money, and sex. The strong survived and prospered at the expense of the weak. Within this "naturalist" vision there was no room for God, morality, or sentiment. The new nation in the new century ran on raw energy, mechanical as well as biological.

Sister Carrie, Dreiser's first novel, developed many of the same themes found in his best-known book, *An American Tragedy*, later published in 1925 for which he achieved great success and renown. But *Sister Carrie* was reviled by the few reviewers who saw it when its timid publisher, fearful of the censors on the one hand and a breach of contract suit on the other, grudgingly published a small number of copies in 1900. It was the story of a country girl who comes to Chicago, rejects the wage slavery of factory work, takes up with an affable traveling salesman, then runs off to New York with a middle-aged restaurant manager, George Hurstwood, who has stolen his employer's money to make the trip. Hurstwood, having transgressed the rules of society, proves too weak to live in the absence of those rules and steadily declines in fortune, dignity, and health, eventually taking his own life. In contrast, the star of Carrie, whom the morality of the earlier century would cast as a "fallen woman," rises steadily. Young, vital, and eminently adaptable, she discovers in herself a talent for the stage, becomes a celebrated actress, and is rewarded with riches and fame.

Americans have always coveted dreams of success, and, in the nineteenth century, writers like Horatio Alger anointed those dreams in the thick unguent of conventional morality. In a universe presided over by a just God, hard work and virtue would necessarily produce success. In Dreiser's twentieth-century world, success went to those biologically and emotionally equipped for it, and the morality of any particular society, no matter how cherished, was simply irrelevant. The era's small-minded guardians of the public virtue—in the tradition of Anthony Comstock, a morals crusader against obscene literature and a founder of Society for the Suppression of Vice—saw this view as immoral. In reality, it was far more subversive. For Dreiser, people did not choose to fail or succeed or to act "decently" or "indecently." They were driven to act by forces within themselves—Dreiser called them "chemisms"—and right and wrong were largely supplanted by undifferentiated, indiscriminate energy.

This was the essence of Dreiser's message: The new century valued power, period.

It would take another dozen years for the message of *Sister Carrie* to reach a wide readership, for the book was suppressed and neglected until 1912. The successful struggle against the censorship of this masterpiece of American naturalism would lead to the first major defeat of those who, like Comstock, would in the name of a puritanical morality, keep from Americans some of the world's greatest modern literature, including the works of such twentieth-century giants as James Joyce and D. H. Lawrence.

The Chinese "Boxers" Rebel (1900)

The Event: In 1900 China was convulsed by a xenophobic uprising known as the Boxer Rebellion. After quelling the revolt, the European great powers—including a fledgling newcomer to the colonial game, the United States—imposed an indemnity on China. This effectively forced it to yield to European imperialism, bringing about the fall of the last of China's great dynasties, and laying the groundwork for the ancient "Middle Kingdom," as China called itself, to undergo a revolution that would establish the first, frail Republic of China.

HAVING COME LATE into the game of imperialism that European nations had long played, the United States, by the end of the nineteenth century, advocated an "Open Door Policy" with regard to China. In 1899, Secretary of State John Milton Hay communicated his endorsement of the policy to France, Germany, Great Britain, Italy, Japan, and Russia. The Japanese challenged the policy, but the European powers replied that they would comply—if the others did.

Actually, none of the nations involved ever intended to adhere unconditionally to the policy, and the interests of China itself

were largely neglected in arriving at it. This resulted, during the spring of 1900, in an uprising spearheaded by militia units in the north called Yihe Quang (I-ho Ch'üan)—"righteous harmony fists"—a name that yielded the label "Boxers" in the foreign press. It was the violent climax of a movement, active since at least 1898, to rid China of all foreigners. Encouraged by the redoubtable Empress Dowager Tz'u-hsi, the Boxers rampaged throughout China, killing foreigners as well as Christian Chinese and Chinese with ties to foreigners.

In Peking (now Beijing), foreign legations were held under siege. In response, an international force of British, French, German, Japanese, Russian, and American troops entered Peking in August 1900 to lift the siege. Before the expedition got underway, Secretary Hay, fearing that the foreign powers would use the Boxer Uprising as a pretext to abrogate the Open Door policy and carve up China, issued a circular letter on July 3, stating it as the policy of the United States "to seek a solution which may bring about permanent safety and peace to China, and safeguard for the world the principle of equal and impartial trade with all parts of the Chinese Empire."

Despite the noble intentions of Hay's circular letter, after the Chinese imperial court fled to Hsi-an (Xi'an) before the onslaught of the expedition sent to subdue the Boxers, and after the uprising was contained, the Empress Dowager agreed to a protocol in September 1901, calling for China to pay a harshly punitive indemnity totaling $333 million, of which $24.5 million was to go to the United States. China also was compelled to yield to new foreign demands, including the stationing of troops in Peking at the legations and along the route to the sea.

The Open Door Policy to China took into account very little, if at all, the good or sovereignty of the Chinese people. The United States repeatedly acquiesced to violations of the Open Door Policy that invited further incursion into China's sovereignty. The Taft-Katsura memorandum of 1905, between the United States and Japan, laid the foundation for a Japanese protectorate in Korea. The United States also acknowledged Japan's "special interests" in China by means of the Lansing-Ishii agreement of 1917, setting the stage for the 1932 Japanese invasion of Manchuria, which was one of the opening notes in the long overture to World War II. More important, the Boxer affair ended the Qing, or Manchu, dynasty, which was founded in 1644 when warriors swept down from Manchuria and conquered China, and signaled the last gasp of imperial China. In 1911, centuries-old resentments against the "foreign" Manchu (in 250 years, the Manchus had failed to assimilate into Chinese society) grew particularly intense following the destructive civil wars of the mid-nineteenth century and the successive defeats in the Sino-Japanese War of 1895 and in the Boxer Rebellion. The world's most populous nation was now a republic, but its fragility left it ripe for an even more significant revolution—that of Communism.

Marconi Sends a Trans-Atlantic Radio Signal (1901)

The Event: On December 12, 1901, a young Italian engineer named Guglielmo Marconi used a balloon-lofted antenna to broadcast radio waves from the southeastern tip of England to Newfoundland, sending the first directed radio signal across the Atlantic Ocean.

A S EARLY AS 1888, German physicist Heinrich Rudolph Hertz discovered and described invisible, long-wave electromagnetic radiation first called Hertzian waves, but soon dubbed radio waves. A number of scientists were immediately taken with the possibility of using such waves to transmit telegraphic signals over great distances and without wires. In 1890, Edouard-Eugene Branly, a French physicist, developed a radio wave detector that could receive waves at a distance of 150 yards. Four years later, a British physicist named Oliver Joseph Lodge improved the detector sufficiently to allow it to detect signals up to half a mile away. What is more, Lodge actually used the device, which he called a "coherer," to receive a Morse code transmission.

The year after Lodge developed his coherer, two young men, one Russian, the other Italian, independently made a crucial discovery. Attaching a long vertical wire to the transmission source and another to the

receiver immensely improved the strength of the radio signal. The Russian was Aleksandr Stepanovich Popov. The Italian, an electrical engineer, was Guglielmo Marconi. The wires these experimenters used were called antennas, because people thought they looked like the feelers on an insect's head.

It was Marconi who persisted in developing and improving transmitters, receivers, and antennas so that, on December 12, 1901, he was able to make a dramatic demonstration of the potential of radio by transmitting intelligible Morse code signals across the Atlantic. Conceived and gestated in the nineteenth century, radio was born at the beginning of the twentieth, promising a revolution in communications that would profoundly affect every aspect of life in the new age.

The First Nobel Prizes Are Awarded (1901)

The Event: On December 10, 1901, on the fifth anniversary of the death of Alfred Nobel, the King of Sweden bestowed the first five Nobel Prizes, a recognition of accomplishment in science, art, and politics that over the course of the century would come to be regarded as the ultimate professional honor.

SWEDISH TYCOON Alfred Nobel, a failed novelist and playwright and a committed pacifist, as well as a highly successful industrialist and the inventor of dynamite, was shocked when a newspaper prematurely announced his death and called him a "merchant of death" in the obituary. Thereafter determined to leave a legacy of peace, he wrote a will that stunned his expectant relatives upon his death in 1896: 94 percent of his immense fortune should go, he declared, as an annual award to honor a hand-

ful of people around the globe whose work in physics, chemistry, medicine, literature, and peacemaking had "conferred the greatest benefit on mankind."

Nobel's executors spent five years arguing over the rules and finances of the vaguely worded last testament, but by the turn of the century the mechanics were in place. The first Nobel Peace Prize went to Swiss diplomat Jean Henri Dunant for his work at the Geneva Convention and in establishing the International Red Cross and to French statesman Frederic Passy for helping to create the French peace society. The prize in literature was bestowed on French poet Sully Prudhomme; in chemistry on Dutch scientist Jacobus van Hoff for contributions to chemical dynamics and the discovery of osmotic pressure; in medicine on Germany's Emil von Behring for developing immunizations for tetanus and diphtheria; and in physics on the German scientist Wilhelm Roentgen for the discovery of X rays. Each "laureate," so called after the laurel crowns awarded ancient athletes, received some $42,000 in prize money, a small fortune at the time and many times in excess of any comparable prize, and worldwide recognition.

There is little doubt that in science and medicine (the quasi-scientific category of "economics" was added in 1969) the Nobel Prize has been a spur to new technology and discoveries, as well as the overweening ambitions of scientists, doctors, and researchers. Without dreams of winning a Nobel Prize much research may well have been abandoned long before it yielded the remarkable results we have come to expect as a matter of course from twentieth-century science—the discovery of DNA is one of many examples. In literature and in peacemaking, however, the role of the Nobel Prize has been more controversial.

Given Nobel's idealism in proffering the awards, it is hardly surprising that the prize in literature centered on the literature of ideas, a kind of writing decidedly at odds with literary modernism and its obsession with style and form over content. On the one hand, such an emphasis guaranteed that many of those the twentieth century would come to consider the most expressive of its temperament had no chance of becoming laureates—James Joyce, for example. On the other hand, a preoccupation with grand ideas by its very nature ran the risk of making the prize a political football or embarrassingly irrelevant, since ideas—even grand ones—have a tendency to change quickly.

The first literature prize for works in English went to Rudyard Kipling, the poet laureate of western—specifically British—imperialism, whose poem "The White Man's Burden" has come to symbolize the deadly paternalism of an empire. At the time, in 1907, forty-one-year old-Kipling was as immensely popular as a present-day rock n' roll star, the publication of a work by Kipling being considered news worthy of broadcast around the world. And in 1901, to such fanfare Kipling had published *Kim*, his tale of an Irish orphan in India receiving lessons from an aged Tibetan lama that—for all its sympathetic portrayal of Indian mysticism—rested squarely on the justification of colonialism as a moral obligation on Englishmen to spread their superior culture to uncivilized heathens. Within a few short years of receiving the Nobel Prize, Kipling—his personal and political prejudices fundamentally at odds with the leading literary lights of the day—had declined into obscurity, a fate visited on not a few laureates (who today remembers the work of Pearl S. Buck, the first American woman awarded the prize for literature?). By the mid-twentieth century, the French existentialist philosopher and left-leaning man of

letters Jean-Paul Sartre felt compelled to refuse the prize on principle in part because of
its cultural-political implications. The Nobel Peace Prize, the most blatantly political
of the categories, often spawned controversy and anger. Parts of the American establishment joined the right-wing racist fringe
when the Nobel committee bestowed the prize
on Martin Luther King, Jr., after he had openly
opposed the Vietnam War, for example, and
conservative commentators were outraged
when the award went to the formerly
avowed terrorist Yasir Arafat in the wake of
the Middle East peace initiatives.

But for all the political grumbling and

professional jealousy inspired by Nobel
Prizes, throughout the century they grew in
prestige as one of the few international
perks for the sacrifice and hard work of
those who choose to benefit mankind rather
than line their own pockets or chase after
power. And the $800,000 or so now be-
stowed each year on men and women who
accomplish such goals, while less princely
than some state lottery prizes, is nevertheless a fine enough way to spend the proceeds of a fortune built on the destructive
power of an infamous invention conceived
by a repentant late nineteenth-century merchant of death.

Queen Victoria Dies (1901)

The Event: The death of Queen Victoria on January 22, 1901, marked not only the end of the
longest reign in England's history (almost sixty-four years), but also the close of the era named
after her, the Victorian Age, when Great Britain's imperialistic adventures had reached their
high-water mark and—as the Victorian ruling class was wont to boast—the sun never set on the
British Empire.

MORE THAN ANY other nation, Victoria's
Britain ruled the geopolitical world
upon which the twentieth century dawned.
Always a sea empire, Britain had gained
worldwide naval supremacy with Admiral
Nelson's great defeat of the Napoleonic
French at Trafalagar in 1805, paving the
way not only for the period of relative calm
among the great national powers known as
the Pax Britannica but also for the new and
aggressive British imperialism under
Queen Victoria. During her reign, England
completed its century-long conquest of India, which began with the defeat of the
French and the Mughals in 1757 and, fol-

lowing the Indian Mutiny in 1857–1858,
was crowned by the administrative takeover of the government's British East India
Company. Late in the nineteenth century,
Britain oversaw the partitioning of Africa,
ensuring its own dominance of what Europeans then called the Dark Continent in taking control of Egypt and the Nile by 1898.

Born in 1819, Victoria came to the
throne in 1837 determined to hold on to
power at a time when the Crown's political
role had become quite murky. In 1840, she
married her cousin, Prince Albert of Saxe-
Coburg-Gotha, having proposed to him five
days after his first court visit during her

reign. From the honeymoon until Albert's premature death in 1861, she doted on her prince, who became the de facto sovereign. Though the age to which she gave her name idolized mothers and families and though she alone gave birth to nine children (through whom she became grandmother to half the royalty in Europe), she despised pregnancy and childbirth, detested babies, and could not stand to be around children. In an age of reform, she showed no interest in social issues. She stoutly resisted technological change, though new technology and modern inventions—telegraphs, railroads, steam engines—were reshaping the face of European civilization and in many ways making her far-flung empire possible. When Prince Albert died, she went into a mourning that in effect lasted the entire forty years she had left to live and rule.

Victoria hated the liberal Prime Minister William Gladstone because he wanted to give the Irish home rule. On the other hand, she loved the seductive and flattering but lazy Prime Minister Benjamin Disraeli because he made her daily life easy and wanted to help her conquer the world. From the late 1860s onward, Disraeli cobbled together new pieces of empire (handing Victoria the title of Empress of India in 1876 to add to her Queen of the United Kingdom of Great Britain and Ireland) while Victoria herself became the paragon of the stuffy decorum and the figurehead for the ardent imperialism that together defined the Victorian Age. While she may well have saved the Crown from abolition, her actual influence on government was slight.

Few of Europe's politicians, and even fewer of its soldiers, understood how the British Empire, administered by Disraeli and Salisbury, worked. They were confused over how one small island of constantly bickering people ruled over by a dowdy old widow with a ridiculously small army could control a quarter of the globe. It flabbergasted them that in India alone 70,000 British troops somehow held on to a subcontinent of 300 million people. And it irritated them that the obviously small and apparently fragile England should have so wide a range of action, even more so that the bloody British just stood there, unchallenged and unflappable, aloof and patronizing, refusing to become embroiled in the petty passions and squabbles that consumed the political life of a Europe scarcely twenty miles away across the English Channel.

At least one of Europe's statesmen took advantage of Britain's aloofness: Otto von Bismarck, the man who had expelled Austria from Germany, humiliated France and toppled Napoleon III, and unified Germany to create the modern German Empire. For three decades—from 1862 to 1890—he would loom over the European continent and determine the course of its history.

During his nineteen years as Germany's Imperial Chancellor, Bismarck used ruthless diplomacy, rather than the short brutal wars he had previously waged against Denmark, Austria, and France, to install a network of interlocking alliances aimed at isolating Russia and keeping a defeated France weak and demoralized. In effect, the Iron Chancellor moved the capital of continental Europe from Paris to Berlin, where it was more comfortable for the old diplomat to maintain single-handedly Europe's balance of power. Bismarck's entire system was premised on Britain's not becoming embroiled, that she would continue to keep her distance from her historical enemies, Russia and France. It was not that Britain ignored Europe; indeed, she meddled in the political affairs of other powers all the time all over the world. Instead, it was that she chose to stand outside the Bismarckian system of alliances, depending on her naval supremacy and the industrial might of her seaborne empire instead of formal, even secret alliances, to give her a free hand in international affairs. In fact, Lord Salisbury regarded such formal commitments as not only unnecessary, but dangerous, believing that when the time came for a fight, a democratic electorate might well decide to bring down a government rather than go to war. As the principal Great Powers other than England—Germany, Austria, France, and Russia— grouped into alliances during the last decade of the nineteenth century, Salisbury maintained what the British came to call their "Splendid Isolation." The result was that by the beginning of the twentieth century Germany had became England's principal competitor in world affairs.

When Victoria died, the poet Robert Bridges observed, "It seemed as though the keystone had fallen out of the arch of heaven." The grief was ubiquitous—even London's prostitutes walked the streets wearing black. Coming to the throne was the former Prince of Wales, now Edward VII. The stuffy old Victorian Age was over and the liberated twentieth century had ar-

rived. Edward, fifty-nine, portly, balding, his triangle of moustache and beard turning to gray, was a thoroughly modern man, a natty dresser, a roué and rake, a man with a long history of gambling, wenching, and general high living, all conducted squarely in the public eye. Content with the basically ceremonial role his mother had come to play in the latter years of her reign, he would at least preside over the empire with a sense of style and much good cheer, laying the final groundwork in the process for the modern constitutional monarchy. As Henry James, the American expatriate novelist turned British citizen, who was as fastidious as Queen Victoria had ever been, wrote about Edward's coming coronation: "We all feel a bit motherless today. Mysterious little Victoria is dead and fat vulgar Edward is King."

Edwardian England would last a decade, and in retrospect it would seem a golden age of prosperity and cultural awakening. Passion and a certain haughty abandonment were the hallmarks of a vital new England where fashion would be king and it was occasionally difficult to distinguish the enjoyment of the trivial from the embracing of the profound. When Edward, for example, got too fat to button the last button of his vest, the rest of the well-dressed males in Europe and America would follow suit, leaving their vests dangling open over their belts.

But at the turn of the century even a ceremonial king of England still had an affect on the politics of a dangerous world. A man perhaps more at home in Paris than London, Edward quickly warmed up to the French, much to the chagrin of his nephew,

Kaiser William II, a bloody-minded little martinet in charge of post-Bismarck Germany, who was determined to conquer, at the very least, all of Europe. Lord Salisbury, old, weary, and sick, had given up the foreign office the year Victoria died. He stayed on as prime minister only long enough to see his replacement abandon his principles of diplomacy and conclude an alliance with Japan in January 1902. He retired in July. By 1904, Edward had, by his geniality and his lovely speeches during a state visit to Paris the year before, paved the way with millions of French citizens of all ranks for an official Anglo-French Entente Cordiale. When an emboldened Japan the next year soundly defeated Russia in a war that set the tsar's empire tottering on the edge of collapse, the unthinkable happened: Bismarck's European system became seriously destabilized. Suddenly, Germany and England found themselves on the brink of a massive naval arms race. By 1910, the year Edward himself died, the modern world seemed to be spinning out of control.

J. P. Morgan Founds U.S. Steel (1901)

The Event: In 1901, financier J. P. Morgan engineered the sale of the massive Carnegie Steel Corporation to a team of industrialists he was backing. This company became the centerpiece of the latest of Morgan's "trusts"—U.S. Steel, the world's first billion-dollar corporation.

IF THE NINETEENTH CENTURY had been characterized by the arrogant rise of the industrial capitalist on the one hand and the development of a militant industrial proletariat on the other, the first half of the twentieth century would be marked by the tremendous growth of financial trusts and attempts at social revolutions by workers, peasants, and soldiers suffering from the economic dislocations created by the triumphant ascendancy of giant corporations. The amalgamations and combinations that made monopoly capitalism possible had actually begun in the late nineteenth century. In the United States those trusts had largely been created by the banking House of Morgan. J. P. Morgan had merged many of the country's failing railroads into gigantic trusts and helped put "the octopus" of Standard Oil together. He was the man America's working-class radicals and farm-bred and small-business minded populists most loved to vilify. The mild reforms enacted in the first decade of the new century by those middle- and upper-class do-gooders who called themselves Progressives hardly gave Morgan pause as he went about, perhaps a bit more circumspect than before, creating the kind of huge corporate institutions that would come to dominate the world in order to produce massive profits for a lucky few.

By 1901, Andrew Carnegie had worked his way up from humble Scottish origins to become one of the most powerful industrialists in the world. The asking price for the company he had skillfully and ruthlessly built was $492 million. When Morgan wrote him the check, he said, "Mr. Carnegie, I want to congratulate you on becoming the richest man in the world." After the sale, the world's richest man retired from business at age sixty-six and spent the rest of his life creating charities to spend his wealth and ease his conscience. Morgan put Judge Elbert Gary in charge of the new trust, and the corporation laid out a city in Indiana on the outskirts of Chicago, one of those twentieth-century industrial hellholes that today still bears the judge's name. Capitalized at $1.4 billion, U.S. Steel cleared $90 million in its first year of operation—hardly surprising since the mines, mills, and plants owned by the trust could produce eight million tons of steel annually, better than half the U.S. total and more than most countries in the world. For twenty-six years Gary would preside over the rapid expansion of the American steel industry, beating antitrust prosecution from the U.S. government even as he continued negotiating with more hapless barons to eliminate "unreasonable"—read "effective"—competition.

Steel would plate the culture of the twentieth century the way iron had that of the nineteenth century, at least until plastic replaced the steel-derived chrome on the bumpers of automobiles. And, while before we had Iron Horses and Iron Chancellors and even a revolutionary who called himself a "Man of Iron" (English for Lenin), now we "steeled" ourselves for bad news, gave our enemies "steely" stares, and read comic books about a "Man of Steel," (English for Stalin). The early twentieth century was the Age of Steel, which made ever bigger battleships more invincible, bullets more deadly,

horseless carriages into sleek and elegant personal statements, and canvas flying contraptions into gigantic weapons of mass destruction and effective conveyances for long-range transit.

But it was not merely the steel industry that was transformed by the kind of financial wizardry practiced by men like J. P. Morgan. The same year that U.S. Steel was formed, the Guggenheims took over the ASARCO copper trust and extended their interests into Chile, Alaska, and the Belgian Congo. Also that year, the United States surpassed Great Britain in its exports of steel, iron, and coal. Such trusts were of course not limited to the United States either, though in Europe they were more often called cartels. And as I. G. Farben and the great Krupps ironworks grew, they armed a Germany that was now third in industrial production. The monopoly capitalists and financial houses hired law firms to protect their interests, mostly from common folk and weaker competitors. Those firms, along with the great banks and the giant companies, began to send men into government service—not especially into elected office, but into the diplomatic corps and their secret agencies. Companies, the great national trusts, competed with companies in other nations for raw materials and markets at home and abroad, and when the politicians of the world went to war, it would not be at the behest of the masses they sent to do the dying, but to feed the industrial giants that ran their nations' engines, made their nation's weapons, and lined their official pockets. Even such financial disasters as the great Wall Street crash of 1929 or the industrial destructiveness of two world wars and the social revolutions they engendered would only prove at worst temporary setbacks as the giant corporations merged with, plundered, and plotted against each other. By mid-twentieth century the corporate ethos—greedy, conformist, secretive, mercilessly competitive, chronically paranoid—would dominate western culture, even the culture of those democracies that prided themselves in their love of freedom, respect for rugged individuality, and promotion of independence.

Willis Carrier Invents the Air Conditioner (1902)

The Event: In 1902, engineer Willis Carrier built a humidity-controlling and cooling system for Brooklyn's Sackett-Wilhelms Lithography and Publishing Company, which was plagued by quality-control problems due to excessive heat and humidity. This, the first truly practical air conditioner, radically altered civilized life, providing unheard-of levels of comfort and productivity in public buildings, hospitals, and homes.

A TWENTY-FIVE-YEAR-OLD engineer named Willis Haviland Carrier was given the assignment of helping the publishers of the popular humor magazine *Judge,* Sackett-Wilhelms Lithography and Publishing Company of Brooklyn, New York, solve a vexing problem with excess moisture in the air. *Judge* was printed in color, and on humid summer days the paper absorbed moisture from the air, expanded, and, since color printing requires several runs through the press, the resulting printed impressions were misregistered and blurry. Carrier combined two relatively new technologies, electricity and refrigeration, to produce a crude but effective device that used electric fans to pass air over chilled coils, which condensed excess moisture, reducing the relative humidity to 55 percent while also substantially cooling the air. The device provided the equivalent cooling effect of melting more than 100,000 pounds of ice per day. Four years after the Sackett-Wilhelms installation, Carrier patented the basis of all modern air conditioning: "Apparatus for Treating Air," a device that sprayed a fine mist of water into a box, saturating the air inside. Using refrigeration technology, Carrier cooled the spray and, since cold air holds less moisture than warm, he was not only able to blow cool air into a room, but blow cool, *dry* air. Paradoxically, by saturating the air inside the box, he made each droplet of mist function as a condensing surface, thereby drawing moisture *out* of the air.

Carrier continued to perfect his invention, but its principal applications were in industry (where cool, dry air facilitated the operation of machinery and increased worker productivity), public buildings, and theaters. In 1914, he air conditioned a facility for premature babies at Pittsburgh's Allegheny General Hospital, dramatically reducing the ward's mortality rate. He also installed the first domestic air-conditioning system in the mansion of a Minneapolis millionaire. But it wasn't until 1922, when Carrier developed the centrifugal refrigerating machine, that air conditioning became more affordable, dependable, and safer, because the toxic ammonia refrigerant was replaced by nontoxic dielene. Soon, department stores, restaurants, and especially movie theaters were buying air conditioners in quantity.

Though Carrier's air-conditioning systems increased productivity and profits— businesses, movie houses, and even entire cities like Washington, D.C., did not have to shut down for the summer, for example— the systems were relatively expensive and the profit needed to be clear to justify the cost. And while Adolph Zukor, whose Rivoli Theater on Broadway was the first movie house Carrier air conditioned, realized an increase in ticket sales of $100,000 the first summer, the average American could not afford the $30,000 or so Carrier charged to keep people cool. Despite his efforts to produce a cheaper machine—the Model T of air conditioners—he never succeeded in developing a truly economical, practical air-conditioning system for domestic use. Not until the 1950s, when consumer-oriented appliance manufacturers like Westinghouse and General Electric developed compact window-mounted units, and, perhaps more important, began marketing them as household appliances with a "pitch" aimed mainly at women, did air conditioners began to appear in many homes. It became another of the new mid-dle-class consumer society's necessities, along with the washing machine and the two-car garage.

By the end of the century, air conditioning was one convenience most people in "developed" countries took for granted. Many people, no doubt, found it relatively easy to imagine life without air conditioning; it simply meant making a few sacrifices in comfort, or so they might think. Actually, many cities in the Southwest, which boomed in the sixties, seventies, eighties, and nineties, would have remained sleepy backwaters without air conditioning. A wide range of manufacturing processes would be impossible without air conditioning, including the production of most drugs, precision instruments, and personal computers, which require silicon chips that must be manufactured in a strictly controlled atmosphere. Livable skyscrapers and jet travel would also be impossible dreams.

Air conditioning, for example, liberated architecture from the open window and allowed Le Corbusier's vision of a Cartesian gigantic glass prism to be realized in the International style of design. The 1931 Philadelphia Savings Fund Society Building, the first in America to make use of the International style, was also the country's second fully air-conditioned office tower. As architectural historian Reyner Banham said of the 1951 United Nations Secretariat Building, the apotheosis of the style, when "Carrier's practical technology for solving any environmental problem that offered an honest dollar" met the new architecture "the face of the urban world [was] altered." Beyond that one could, by tracing the development of air-conditioning technology, outline social and economic growth in the twentieth century, from the modernizing and rationalizing of industry to the rise of a consumer society, to the spread of urban business skyward, to the growth of the Sun Belt, to the mushrooming of the suburbs.

There were costs, too, of course. Ever-rising energy bills and an addiction to politically volatile and environmentally dangerous sources, such as foreign oil and leaky nuclear power plants, resulted in the release of vast amounts of freon refrigerant—chlorofluorocarbons (CFCs)—into the atmosphere. Many scientists believe that these CFCs have irreversibly damaged the ozone layer, our protection against harmful cosmic rays and ultraviolet radiation, caused a slew of physical ailments affecting those who work in hermetically sealed environments (known as "tight-building syndrome"), released bacteria lurking about air ducts causing Legionnaire's Disease, and trapped dangerous gasses—radon, for one—in air-tight homes. The emergence of air conditioning has also seen the disappearance of the front porch, and with it, neighborliness. Some people may resent air conditioning for making artificial wombs of our buildings, severing us from the natural outside. Others, like author Henry Miller who wrote the book *The Air-Conditioned Nightmare* (1940), raised moral and aesthetic objections to what he saw as the anesthetized, bland existence promoted by the century's technological wonders.

Yet, like it or not, it is our world, and air conditioning made it.

The Boer War Ends (1902)

The Event: In 1902, after three years of fighting and the deployment of nearly half a million troops, as well as the creation of the twentieth century's first concentration camps, the mighty British Empire finally managed to bring the Boers of the Transvaal and the Orange Free State to the peace table.

L ISTENING TO BRITISH empire builders like Cecil Rhodes one might have been scarcely aware that the English were hardly the first Europeans to settle on the southern tip of the huge African continent. In 1650 the Dutch East India Company had begun a colony at the Cape of Good Hope. Over the course of two and a half centuries, the Dutch settlers came to consider themselves natives of Africa, calling themselves Afrikaners and speaking a variation of the Dutch language they dubbed Afrikaans. As ideologically dedicated to black slavery as the scions of Britain born in the American South, the Afrikaners remained the majority among whites even after the British Navy gobbled up the colony during the Napoleonic Wars, and they greatly resented the English Parliament for banning slavery throughout the British Empire in 1834. Afrikaner slaveowners gathered up their belongings, including their human chattel, and set out from the Cape heading north to escape the reach of British law. During the Great Trek of 1836 and 1837, five thousand Boers rumbled across the veldt for a thousand miles, stopping only when they reached a stretch of rolling hills beyond the Vaal and Orange Rivers. Here, the Boers set up two small independent states—the Transvaal Republic and the Orange Free State—both recognized by the British government in 1854. In 1877, Disraeli changed Britain's mind and annexed the Transvaal, sending troops off to Pretoria to hoist the Union Jack. Three years later, the Boers revolted. When they defeated a detachment of British troops at Majuba Hill, a weary William Gladstone offered them autonomy within the Empire but kept British say over the republics' foreign policy. The Boers signed Gladstone's proposed constitution with much ill temper in 1881.

Five years later huge reefs of gold ore were discovered a few miles south of Johannesburg, and overnight a city of tents sprang up, housing the largest concentration of white men in Africa—some five thousand Britons, Americans, Germans, and Scandinavians, whom the Boers called derisively Uitlanders, Afrikaans for "outsiders." The area was called the Witwatersrand, "the Rand" for short, and it was fast becoming the greatest source of gold in the world, exceeding the combined production of the United States, Russia, and Australia. The Transvaal Republic's president, Paul Kruger, a neat and precise man, like his fellow Afrikaners, viewed the Uitlanders askance from his clean and manicured capital in Pretoria. They seemed to him a god-

less lot—lawless, violent, *dirty*. To make sure the Boers remained in control of these men, whom he publicly referred to as "thieves and murderers," Kruger set up a five-year residency requirement for citizenship and then stretched it to fourteen years. The Boers discriminated against the miners, taxing them liberally, insisting their children learn to speak Afrikaans in Afrikaner schools.

Not surprisingly, talk of an armed uprising against the Boers began to spread, and in such talk, Cecil Rhodes' name always seemed to come up. Rhodes, the sixth of nine children, was the son of a stern vicar and a doting mother. He had come to Africa in 1873 at age twenty to help his brother grow cotton. Rhodes fell in love with the country when diamonds were discovered in the northern reaches of the Cape Colony, and he was lucky enough to stake a claim that made him rich beyond his imagination. After buying himself an Oxford education, he had returned to fulfill his dream of establishing a federation of South African states within the empire. He was reported to have exclaimed one night as he stared up at the African heavens, "I would annex the planets if I could!" Now he was willing to settle for the Transvaal and the Orange Free State. He persuaded his best friend and factotum, Leander Starr Jameson—known thereabouts as "Doctor Jim"—to stage a raid in 1896 on the arrogant and stuffy Boers. It was a fiasco. It took Jameson four days to reach Johannesburg with his force of five hundred, after waiting months for word to start from the locally stationed British colonels, who had conveniently taken leave. In any event, the Boers made short work of Jameson's invasion force, and he ran up the white flag immediately. The Boers turned him over to the Cape government, which shipped him back to England for trial. Kruger and his minions no longer trusted her majesty's government in the slightest.

Tensions ran high, and when Britain increased troop strength in the Cape colony in 1899, the Boers attacked. On paper, the Transvaal and its ally, the Orange Free State, were not much of an enemy. With no navy, no real army, no massive industrial base, no far-flung empire, they were hardly worthy to take on the mighty British. After a few quick defeats, the Boer army disintegrated, and—back in London—Britain's ruling Union Party, admitting there were still a few marauders left to be rounded up, claimed victory. But the claim was hollow, a home-front delusion. The Union Jack may have waved in Johannesburg and Pretoria, but there were Boers still in the field fighting. No longer organized into regiments, they assembled in secret as guerrilla commandos and planned their constant and quick raids. Small bands of horsemen would suddenly strike the slow-moving British infantry and its supply columns, then vanish into the veldt. By the time a force of British or Imperial cavalry arrived to take up the chase, there were no guerrillas to be found—only peaceful, godfearing Afrikaner farmers happily plowing away in the same baggy work clothes they had been wearing a few days before when they slaughtered themselves an Englishman or two. Their weapons were hidden away, and the swift work ponies grazing in their fields looked more suspicious than they did.

Then Lord Kitchener took Lord Roberts' place as commander in chief in December 1900. Horatio Kitchener addressed the guerrilla problem with a brutal and bloodless logic. If he was unable to run to ground twenty thousand Boer horsemen with the 250,000 British troops he had on hand, he could at least use those troops to reduce their ability to maneuver, then perhaps eliminate the commandos themselves. He built some eight thousand corrugated iron and stone blockhouses, stretching them first along the railway lines, then across the veldt itself. In time, the entire Afrikaner countryside was littered with blockhouse forts, linked by barbed wire, within rifle shot of one another. Kitchener swept through the now compartmentalized Afrikaner nations as if he were on a lion hunt, and the language he used reflected his actions: he and his intelligence officers talked of so many "drives" and "bags" and "kills." As the army potted its game, it also "sanitized" its rear, burning all crops and every farm the enemy might use for food or shelter. Kitchener considered every Boer an enemy; there were no civilians in his war. Every rural inhabitant he caught in his net—mostly women and children—he uprooted and carted off to one of his newly constructed "concentration camps," twenty-four of them built and administered by the army. Hastily constructed, the camps lay exposed to Africa's scorching sun and torrential rains in the summer and—come winter—to icy winds. The sanitation was atrocious, the water filthy, the food reduced to army rations. Typhoid became endemic, and devastated camp populations suffered from hunger and malnutrition. For a year, then two months more, the camps bulged with women and children and a few Boer warriors. Some 117,000 were marched off to the concentration camps. Perhaps as many as 28,000 died before Britain learned about these horrors from the testimony of an impassioned middle-aged woman named Emily Hobhouse.

Hobhouse toured the camps and returned to England to tell somebody, anybody. First she tried St. John Broderick, the Unionist Party's Secretary of State for War. He listened politely, then sent her on her way. Next she collared Liberal Party leader Campbell-Bannerman, who sat quietly as she poured out her heart, describing the wholesale burning of farms, the deportations, the scorched earth, the convoys of prisoners deprived of clothes, the semi-starvation in the camps, the fever-ridden children lying on the bare earth, the appalling numbers of dead. When Campbell-Bannerman spoke out a week later about the nature of the war, calling Kitchener's tactics the "methods of barbarism," he found himself in the midst of a hurricane of abuse. He was denounced in the popular press, excoriated in private clubs, and excluded from polite society for defaming the British Army. Soon anyone taking up the cause of the Boers was being accused of treason.

Meanwhile the Boer commandos continued their raids, many of them deep into the Crown's Cape Colony. General Jan Smuts got within fifty miles of Cape Town. Slowly, Kitchener's drastic and brutal "methods of barbarism" paid off. The Boers had first sued for peace in March of 1901, but Kitchener ignored them. In May of 1902, the Afrikaners grudgingly surrendered. Few could have guessed at the time that the Boer War would mark the beginning of the end of the empire. The war had cost too much for too little gain; the fighting was too ugly. As if operating from a guilty conscience, the British government treated the Boers quite well at the peace conference in Vereeniging, stipulating that in return for laying down their arms, giving up their independence, and recognizing King Edward VII as their sovereign, the Afrikaners would retain their property, not have to pay special taxes to compensate for the war, and could teach both English and Dutch in their schools. Moreover, Britain would contribute £3 million toward reconstruction. And, bowing to the Afrikaners' peculiar social order, England postponed settling "the issue of nonwhite suffrage."

The Afrikaners had kept their language and their culture, and within a few short years they would gain politically most of what they had failed to win militarily. In 1909, Great Britain would pass the South Africa Act, unifying the "British" colonies of the Cape, Natal, Transvaal, and Orange River, establishing the nation of South Africa and enfranchising only the small white minority. South Africa's constitution, based on the Australian constitution of 1900, was mostly the work of Jan Smuts. The union was inaugurated on May 31, 1910 with Louis Botha, an Afrikaner, as the first prime minister.

As for Great Britain itself, after the Boer

War, which the British had nominally "won," the bloom seemed to have gone off the kind of imperial adventures that had all but defined the Victorian Age. Perhaps it was that, and the eerie familiarity of Kitch-ener's search-and-destroy tactics, which has led some recent historians to compare Britain's experience in South Africa at the turn of the century with America's during Vietnam.

Joseph Conrad Publishes *Heart of Darkness* (1902)

The Event: In 1902 the Polish-born Joseph Conrad published *Heart of Darkness*, a gripping story and a penetrating philosophical and psychological work of art, as well as a stylistic tour de force made all the more remarkable by the fact that Conrad was writing in English, a language he taught himself. A major indictment of colonial imperialism, the novella would do much to establish Conrad's reputation as one of the most powerful and important writers of the twentieth century.

AT THE TURN OF THE CENTURY, when the Great Powers had entered the final stages of their last major scramble for colonial territory, exotic tales of adventure in far away places were immensely popular. Conrad's genius was to turn the popular form on its head, to make of the adventure story a profound meditation about the self-deception and destructiveness of the colonial enterprise. And who better than this introspective expatriate from one of the most frequently conquered countries in the world to paint the best, the most definitive portrait of the innate evil of empire?

Józef Teodor Konrad Korzeniowski was born in 1857 to a poet father prominent in Poland's independence movement and a mother who died in exile when he was eight. He spent his childhood banished with his father to a frigid Russian backwater, and at seventeen he took to the sea. For two decades he worked as a sailor aboard French and British merchant ships, perfecting the English he had first begun to teach himself

at home into a dense, poetic, well-honed instrument for capturing in language the stories, the insights, and the truths he learned wandering the shadowy worlds owned by the Great Powers. The first of the twentieth century's great artists in exile, he had felt the grip of imperial hands at his throat. At a time when Europeans were wont to boast about their empires and justify their colonialism with tales of bringing civilization to savage lands, Conrad used his personal adventures and his feverish and intellectually abstract prose to show how power exercised in isolation—the experience of empire on the ground, so to speak—brought out the darkness that lurks in the human heart and made not the colonial native but the colonizing imperialist the true "savage."

Heart of Darkness was told by an Englishman named Marlow to a couple of company employees during a long afternoon spent on the Thames. The tale is about a perilous trip he took by riverboat into the remote interior of the Belgian Congo in

search of one of the company's white trad-
ers, Mr. Kurtz, a brilliant idealist who had
set off into the jungle to "educate" the natives while seeing to the shipment of ivory.
When Marlow at length reaches Kurtz's
distant outpost, he finds an ailing and insane
man, driven to despair by his own corruption. He had become a tyrannical chieftain
who decorated his hut with the skulls of his
victims and punctuated his diary with the
command, "Exterminate the brutes!" In the
grip of a fever, Kurtz dies on the way back
downriver, gasping the words, "The horror!
The horror!" When Marlow returns to London and visits Kurtz's proper Victorian
sweetheart, the fiancé in whose name he had
entered the jungle on his mission of enlight-
enment, she asks for Kurtz's dying word,
and Marlow tells her what she wants to hear:
"Your name."

Scarcely two years later Conrad produced another colonial tale, this time a full-
length novel set in a South American
country dominated by the silver mines of a
foreign company, a richly textured and
compelling masterpiece called *Nostromo*
(1904). But Conrad also had his fingers on
the pulse of other aspects of the early twentieth century, and in such novels as *Secret
Agent* and *Under Western Eyes* he did with
the espionage novel something quite similar to what he had done with the adventure
story. He made his "spy" stories gritty and
realistic portraits of the claustrophobic,
paranoid, and futile world of petty terrorists
and senseless ideologues, wrenching from
the hot-house émigré world narratives that
caught perfectly the insecure and alienated,
the lack of control and blighted vision of
daily life as it was lived by the common run
of men in Europe's great urban centers. One
of the century's culturally homeless artists,
a man who came late to his craft and wrote
in a language not his own, Conrad used his
unique perspective to create a style admired
by authors ranging from Thomas Mann to F.
Scott Fitzgerald and William Faulkner and
to capture the reality of his times more vividly and honestly than all but a handful of
others writing in their native tongues.

The Wright Brothers Fly the First Airplane (1903)

The Event: On December 17, 1903, Orville Wright—one of two brothers, both bicycle mechanics who had created a practical heavier-than-air flying machine—made the first piloted,
powered, sustained, and controlled flight in the history of mankind.

ORVILLE (1871–1948) and Wilbur Wright
(1867–1912), sons of Bishop Milton
Wright of the United Brethren in Christ, had
little formal schooling, but they were hard
workers with boundless curiosity. In 1892,
they opened a bicycle shop in their hometown of Dayton, Ohio, from which they
made enough money to finance a unique
hobby, which had mounted to a passion:
aeronautics.

Their interest in the subject began in
1896, when they read a newspaper story
about the death of Otto Lillienthal, a great
German aeronautical experimenter who

had been killed in a glider crash. The brothers bought every book and periodical they could find on the subject of aeronautics and designed and built a biplane kite in 1899. During the next three years, they built three man-carrying gliders, which they tested at Kitty Hawk, North Carolina. When the first two gliders failed to perform well, the brothers invented the world's first wind tunnel in the fall of 1901, which made it practical to test a wide variety of designs safely.

The Wright brothers were hardly content with building kites. Their goal was nothing less than powered flight, and, armed with the results of the Kitty Hawk glider flights and the wind tunnel tests, the brothers built the 750-pound fabric-and-wood plane, named *Flyer I*, fitted with a 170-pound, twelve-horsepower gasoline engine.

On December 17, 1903, on the beach at Kitty Hawk, the brothers flipped a coin, and winning the toss, Orville made the first piloted, powered, sustained, and controlled flight, remaining aloft for twelve seconds over a distance of about 120 feet. The pair made three more flights that day—Wilbur remaining aloft just shy of a full minute over a distance of 852 feet.

The modest, unassuming brothers did not immediately publicize their achievement, but returned to Dayton, where they continued their experiments in a local cow pasture. By 1905, they had achieved a flight of thirty-eight minutes' duration over a distance of twenty-four miles. With their invention now largely perfected, they received a patent on May 22, 1906, and during 1908–1909 toured with the plane throughout England, France, and Italy. Fascinated by the potential of the new invention, especially in warfare, Europeans rapidly adopted the principles of flight developed by the Wright Brothers and not only purchased planes from the Americans but improved on them and built their own. And even though the Wright brothers, after demonstrating the aircraft for the U.S. Army in 1909 (which accepted their design on August 2 of that year), organized the Wright Company and began large-scale manufacture, the United States for a time fell behind the rest of the world in developing aircraft technology.

By the time the Great War began in Europe in 1911, aircraft were considered an essential element of a nation's arsenal. Though widespread strategic bombing did not become part of the conflict, what Americans came to call World War I did in fact see the birth of all the basic tenets of aerial combat. It would be the flying "aces" of that war who—in demonstrating their skills (after the war ended in 1917) with the thrilling and daredevil stunts of traveling air shows—would introduce the mass of humanity to the new "Age of Flight" launched by the two feckless former bicycle makers scarcely a decade earlier.

The Russo-Japanese War Begins (1904)

The Event: On February 8, 1904, the Japanese fleet laid siege to a Russian naval squadron anchored at Russian-controlled Port Arthur on the coast of the Liao-tung Peninsula in southern Manchuria. Japan's surprise attack on Russia launched one of the largest armed conflicts the world had ever witnessed, a war that saw the first large-scale use of automatic weapons, one in which for the first time in modern history an Asian country defeated a European power.

FOR HALF A CENTURY Japan had watched with apprehension as the Russian Empire expanded into eastern Asia, threatening Japan's own imperial designs. Since Russia had first begun the construction of the Trans-Siberian Railroad in 1891, it had looked longingly toward China's huge Manchurian province. After the decadent Manchu dynasty lost a war with Japan in 1894, China had entered into an anti-Japanese alliance with Russia, granting the tsar rights to extend the railroad across Manchuria to Vladivostok and in the process giving Russia control over an important strip of Chinese territory. In 1898, Russia pressured the Chinese into leasing the strategically important Port Arthur (today called Lu-shun), and in 1903 the tsar reneged on his agreement to withdraw his troops from Manchuria, making the military occupation of the Liao-tung Peninsula permanent. With Russia's imperial navy stationed at Port Arthur and its imperial army occupying the peninsula, it seemed to the Japanese only a matter of time before the tsar would stake a claim to Korea, which lay just to the east of Manchuria like a dagger pointed at the heart of Japan.

Since defeating China, Japan had been building up its army, and by the turn of the century it enjoyed a marked superiority over Russia in the number of ground troops in the Far East. All that held the Japanese in check locally was Great Britain, which ruled the sea with its all-powerful navy. Then, in 1902, England abandoned her policy of "Splendid Isolation"—that is, its refusal to enter into official alliances with any national power—and signed a treaty with Japan to stop the headlong expansionism of Tsar Nicholas II. Confident of England's neutrality, Japanese military leaders began planning for the war that world leaders, certainly not unaware of the constantly escalating hostility between Russia and Japan, had long expected.

When the attack came, Japan was a small country little known in the West and Russia was one of Europe's five Great Powers. Most of the world expected Russia to make short work of the island kingdom. No country, certainly not Japan's newfound ally England, much less Russia herself, imagined the Japanese could so easily debilitate the tsar's Pacific Fleet; to replace it, Nicholas promptly dispatched his Baltic Fleet, which suffered equally disastrous treatment from the Japanese navy. Yet more shocking was the speed with which Japan's army overran Korea and crossed the Yalu River into Manchuria. Nicholas, his tsarina, and imperial court under the dolorous influence of the half-crazed monk Rasputin, was slow to react to Japanese advances. Yet, overmatched and outgunned, he refused to back down, vaguely trusting in God rather than sound military action to defend the honor and glory of Russia. "A soft haze of mysticism refracts everything he beholds and magnifies his own functions and person," a Russian minister complained to a colleague puzzled by the tsar's lassitude. Within a year, Japan had brought the mighty Russian empire to its knees.

The consequences of Japan's great victory were swift to come and far-reaching. Theodore Roosevelt, a U.S. president with his own scarcely concealed imperial ambitions, mediated the peace conference held at Portsmouth, New Hampshire, between August 9 and September 5, 1905. Japan's conquest of Korea was recognized. Japan gained control of the Liao-tung Peninsula and Port Arthur—and the South Manchurian Railroad that led to Port Arthur. A humiliated Russia meekly agreed to evacuate southern Manchuria. Within two months of signing the treaty, Nicholas II was faced with a social revolution. Ragged Russian workers, starving serfs, and dispirited soldiers rose up en masse to plead for succor from their "Little Father," only to have their pleas drowned and their bodies crushed under the hooves of Cossack horses. Though Nicholas, one of the more limited autocrats in European history, had "crushed" the 1905 Revolution, he did so only after buying off middle- and upper-class reformers by issuing the October Manifesto, the equivalent of a constitutional charter. Needing years to recover from war and revolution, Russia could no longer hold its own in the tricky system of alliances aimed at maintaining peace, however fragile, in Europe through a precarious balance of power. Forced to turn to its age-old enemy England, it seduced the British Empire further down the slippery slope of entangling alliances and destroyed the assumptions upon which Queen Victoria's ministers and Germany's Otto von Bismarck had built a world. Furthermore, British leaders, bedazzled by what they had seen as observers aboard Japanese ships attacking Port Arthur, had begun to build a new kind of battleship, the "Dreadnoughts," kicking off a dangerous naval arm's race between Great Britain and Germany.

The whiff of gunpowder swept from the harbors and battlefields of Manchuria across Europe, intoxicating leaders already slouching toward a general conflagration.

Freud Publishes His Theories on Sexuality (1905)

The Event: In a 1905 book entitled *Three Essays on the Theory of Sexuality*, the Vienna neurologist Sigmund Freud laid the cornerstone of his theories of infantile sexuality, the unconscious, and psychoanalysis—the twentieth century's most influential and pervasive hypothesis about the nature of the human mind and motivation.

B ORN IN FREIBURG, Moravia, to middle-class Jewish parents, Freud was raised in Vienna, where he proved himself to be a brilliant student of English, French, and the classics. Although he was deeply interested in literature—especially Shakespeare, Goethe, and Dostoyevsky—he embarked on medical studies, taking his M.D. at the University of Vienna in 1881. He specialized in neurology and, from this, his fascination with the mind developed. With the eminent Viennese physician Josef Breuer, Freud studied hysteria and experimented with the use of hypnosis in treating it. The two doctors published *Studies in Hysteria* (1895), and Freud began to develop the technique of free association, an attempt to probe the unconscious mind by catching the conscious "censor" off guard. From such work grew what Freud came to call psychoanalysis: the systematic analysis of the nonrational, normally submerged wellsprings of human behavior and emotional disease.

Freud's first groundbreaking work was *The Interpretation of Dreams* (1900), which was followed by the monumental *Psychopathology of Everyday Life* (1904). Both books mapped the geography of the unconscious mind, roughly dividing that territory into three parts: the ego, the part of the self we generally show to the world and think of as our personality; the id, literally, the "it," the unconscious self, a powerful motivator that is usually beyond conscious control and outside of free will; and the superego, that part of the self that seeks to control and regulate both the ego and the id, analogous to the traditional concept of the conscience.

Freud's most disturbing early work was *Three Essays on the Theory of Sexuality* (1905), which brought his major ideas into their clearest, most concise expression up to

that point. It proposed that the sexual instinct is present in human beings from birth and throughout infancy, childhood, and adulthood, ultimately motivating all behavior, relationships, and actions.

Three Essays unleashed an avalanche of hostile reaction from physicians as well as laypersons outraged by the notion that children and babies could be sexual beings. Freud nevertheless persisted in developing his controversial theories and won many adherents among medical professionals, philosophers, and grateful patients—for whom traditional methods of psychiatric treatment had proven of no avail. By the 1920s, Freud had become something of a cult hero to the intelligentsia and the sophisticates of Europe, and a fad among writers in America who were then celebrating the sexual liberation of the thrill-seeking "Jazz Age."

In 1930, Freud received the prestigious Goethe Prize, and most of the world had accepted at least one important aspect of his thought as commonplace: the existence of the unconscious. By then Freud had turned his attention toward broader cultural questions, and just as the rise of the Nazi Party allowed Hitler to cast his shadow over Europe, Freud produced what many believe to be his masterpiece, *Civilization and Its Discontents*. In the richly textured, if deeply pessimistic work, Freud speculated that civilization itself was a manifestation of the need to repress unconscious desires, a repression that doomed humans to perpetual unhappiness. Despised by the Nazis, Freud's works were among the first books to be banned and burned during the Third Reich.

Freud had not only forever changed the

treatment of mental illness, his theories had drastically altered cherished Judeo-Christian concepts of free will, morality, and accountability for actions. His formulation of the unconscious mind dealt as great a blow to humanity's sense of self-importance as Copernicus's model of the heliocentric universe had some four hundred years earlier. And—like the thinking of Charles Darwin and Karl Marx—Freud's ideas had a liberating effect, especially on art and culture, that has yet to run its course.

Einstein Proposes the Theory of Relativity (1905)

The Event: In 1905, Albert Einstein, an obscure German-born mathematician working as a clerk in the Swiss patent office, developed a theory that demolished the commonsense Newtonian concepts of the universe and that, ultimately, provided the basis for atomic energy and the atomic bomb.

ALBERT EINSTEIN WAS BORN in Ulm, Germany, on March 14, 1879, and was raised in Munich. Slow to speak, the boy worried his parents, who thought he was backward. He excelled in school, but soon proved rebellious and was expelled from his *gymnasium* (school). Hating the autocracy of his native Germany, Einstein became a Swiss citizen in 1901 and took a job as a patent clerk while he pursued mathematical studies.

In 1881, the German-born American physicist Albert Abraham Michelson secured the financial backing of telephone inventor Alexander Graham Bell to develop the interferometer, a device that split a light beam in two, then brought the two paths back together. With this device, Michelson sought to measure the earth's absolute motion. It was assumed that the earth (and everything else in the universe) moved against a "luminiferous ether," the "substance" of space itself, which was postulated to be in a state of absolute rest. Michelson split a light beam, sending its two halves at right angles to one another. The half sent in the direction of the earth's motion ought to have completed its trip a little sooner than the light traveling at a right angle to that motion. By measuring the width of the difference between the two halves of the beam, the speed of the earth relative to the ether could be determined and, therefore, the absolute motion of all other bodies could likewise be measured.

The experiment failed: there was no difference between the two beams, and no one could explain why.

Enter Einstein. He concluded in 1905 that the single constant in the universe was the speed of light in a vacuum. From this assumption, it was possible to deduce length contraction and mass increase with velocity, as well as to deduce a decrease in the rate of time-flow with velocity. Einstein called this the special theory of relativity because velocity has meaning only as relative to an observer. There is no absolute in the universe other than the speed of light itself: no absolute rest and, therefore, no absolute motion.

In the absence of such absolutes, there could also be no absolute time or space—only various "frames of reference" within these. The theory is "special" because it confines itself to the special case of objects that are moving at constant velocity. Einstein would subsequently develop a "general" theory of relativity as well.

Following his 1905 theory, Einstein wrote a paper in 1907 in which he created the single most famous mathematical expression of the century and, perhaps, of any century:

$$e = mc^2$$

According to special relativity, matter and energy are not separate entities, but, rather, mass must be viewed as a highly concentrated form of energy. Expressed in the equation, the meaning was this: An amount of energy (e), measured in joules, is equal to an amount of mass (m), measured in kilograms, multiplied by the square of the speed of light—an enormous number, which suggested the staggering amount of energy potential in even a small amount of mass. Einstein wrote: "It is possible that ra-dioactive processes may become known in which a considerably larger percentage of the mass of the initial atom is converted into radiations of various kinds than is the case for radium."

Special relativity provided the first truly cogent theory of the structure of the universe. The theory, however, seemed to go completely counter to all common sense—as Isaac Newton had so comfortably encapsulated it—and, for those who could grasp the theory at all, rendered the universe a strange and alien place. The energy-mass equivalency that followed closely upon the special theory of relativity likewise revolutionized thinking about the very nature of reality, but also pointed to a potential source of virtually limitless energy in radioactive processes. Before it had run the course of its first half, the twentieth century was destined to realize this potential in an unimaginably horrific way, as American scientists fashioned a weapon system the American military would deploy, ultimately capable of destroying cities, nations, and all life on the planet.

"Big Bill" Haywood Founds the International Workers of the World (1905)

The Event: In 1905, "Big Bill" Haywood, a radical labor organizer, presided at the founding of the Industrial Workers of the World (IWW), or Wobblies, an attempt to organize the laborers of capitalist America into "one big union," one which proved to be the most radical in American history.

WILLIAM HAYWOOD, born in Salt Lake City, Utah, lost his father at age three, and, at fifteen, went to work in the mines.

He became a passionately dedicated member of the Western Federation of Miners, the most radical labor union at the turn of the century. Haywood had worked his way up through the ranks of the union by 1903, when its long struggle with mining and smelting interests erupted into bloody and bitter class warfare in which miners fought—and lost—pitched battles with state militiamen. The experience led Haywood to conclude that, unless they organized into "one big union," American workers would lose again and again. With Socialist Party leader Eugene V. Debs, Daniel de Leon, and the seventy-five-year-old United Mine Workers organizer Mary Harris "Mother" Jones, "Big Bill" Haywood founded the IWW.

The IWW first sought to unionize those workers other unions neglected: women, blacks, certain immigrants, the unskilled, the semiskilled, and migrant laborers. The IWW struck mines in the Rocky Mountain states, lumber camps in the Pacific Northwest and in the South, and textile mills in the Northeast. They quickly earned a reputation for revolutionary rhetoric and violence, but while the rhetoric may have been revolutionary, the violence was not usually of their making. The Wobblies were jailed and beaten. Self-appointed vigilantes as well as federal agents rounded them up and prosecuted them under whatever charge presented itself—espionage, sedition, criminal conspiracy. At least one Wobbly, Joe Hill, was the victim of judicial murder, when he was framed, tried, and executed, entering into the realm of martyrdom, legend, and folk song.

As for Haywood, the state of Idaho imprisoned him on charges of conspiracy in the murder of former governor Frank Ste-

unenberg. A sensational nationally publicized trial resulted in his acquittal, after which Haywood became a leader in the Socialist Party. Recognizing that the socialists were losing ground to more radical elements, Haywood openly advocated revolution, urging workers to practice sabotage and commit whatever acts were necessary to hasten the coming of that revolution. This was too much for the socialist hierarchy, which recalled him from the party's executive committee in 1912.

From 1912 to 1917, Haywood led IWW strikes throughout the country. His activities during World War I resulted in his arrest, along with the arrest of other IWW leaders, on charges of violating espionage and sedition acts by interfering with the production of war resources. In 1918, Haywood and a hundred others went on trial in Chicago. Found guilty, all were sentenced to long prison terms. Haywood was released on bail while his case was on appeal. But it was all finally too much for him. He retreated into the bottle, and he fell ill with diabetes. In 1921, after the Supreme Court rejected his final appeal, Haywood jumped bail, fled to the Soviet Union, and died in a Moscow hospital on May 18, 1928, broken, lonely, and more alienated than he had ever been in America.

The IWW fell victim both to the Red Scare campaign of U.S. Attorney General A. Mitchell Palmer and to the displacement, in American radical politics, of the socialists by the communists. A socialist organization, it was too radical for mainstream America and not radical enough for the new leftist fringe.

Congress Passes the Pure Food and Drug Act (1906)

The Event: Working in an atmosphere of public outrage over unsanitary and adulterated food and unsafe patent medicines flooding American markets and responding to middle-class resentment of the greedy excesses of big business, the U.S. Congress enacted the Pure Food and Drug Act on June 30, 1906.

B Y 1900, MOST INDIVIDUAL states had some form of food safety laws on the books, but these went generally unenforced. Harvey W. Wiley, head of the U.S. Department of Agriculture's Bureau of Chemistry, had been agitating for federal legislation for some time, and his cause gained great momentum when an "embalmed beef" scandal rocked the nation during the Spanish-American War. American soldiers (including the father of New York City's future reform-minded mayor Fiorello LaGuardia) succumbed to food poisoning from eating tainted rations supplied by a corrupt army contractor. Muckraking journalists, in particular Charles Edward Russell, produced exposés revealing the greed and corruption rampant among the so-called Beef Trust, and the chemist Samuel Hopkins Adams showed that the majority of patent medicines were principally alcohol compounded with a variety of other substances ranging from ineffective to downright harmful.

The culminating literary work of the muckrakers was Upton Sinclair's 1906 novel *The Jungle*, a harrowing story of Jurgis Rudkis, a Lithuanian immigrant who finds work in a Chicago meat-packing plant. Not only did Sinclair's novel dramatically portray the plight of millions of ex-

ploited immigrants, it described in sensationally nauseating detail the charnel-house atmosphere and unsanitary practices of the meat-packing business, including the use of rotten meat and tubercular beef, as well as the inclusion of such foreign matter as rats and even an unfortunate human being or two in sausage. Although Sinclair's novel was no work of legitimate reportage—he had not even seen Chicago at the time he wrote the book—*The Jungle* was so vividly and convincingly imagined that Congress, responding to a great public outcry, moved quickly to pass the Pure Food and Drug Act and a Meat Inspection Act.

This legislation was one of the first triumphs of Progressive reform and a manifestation of the growing popularity of Prohibition, which was itself one of the central causes in the Progressive movement. The act not only outlawed some of the more noxious patent medicines, it also led to prohibitions against the use of such drugs as heroin (an opium derivative developed by the Bayer company and marketed originally as a sedative for children), laudanum (another opiate available over the counter for a variety of ailments), cocaine (used originally as an anaesthetic, before 1905 it was a basic ingredient in all sorts of "pick-me-up" drinks from bottled soft drinks to corked wines), and marijuana. Long after the social experiment introduced by the Eighteenth Amendment and the Volstead Act had utterly failed, the 1905 act would continue to provide the basis for prosecuting those who trafficked in or used addictive drugs. It was a "prohibition" that would remain popular throughout the century, though, by making addictive and harmful drugs scarce commodities in an eager market, it, too, would have consequences similar to those created by the ban on liquor in the 1920s—massive civic corruption, violent but wealthy and powerful gangsters, burgeoning prison populations processed through a justice system so congested it threatened to collapse, and young urban victims abandoned by society as hopeless.

The Movies Move to Hollywood (1907)

The Event: In 1907, a few streetwise Jewish entrepreneurs—attracted to a little backwater suburb of Los Angeles called Hollywood by its cheap real estate and cloud-free sky—opened up shop making dreams to sell to the poor and the lonely. They called those dreams "the movies" and made a mint off of them. In the process, they also created a system of employment that produced a peculiarly American version of aristocracy—the contract celebrity, or studio "star."

AT FIRST EAST COAST producers merely made infrequent forays into Hollywood. But in 1908, Thomas Edison and others who had been engaged in extended litigation over patent rights to produce the "flickers" of the rapidly growing film industry, buried the hatchet and formed the New York-based Motion Picture Patents Company, which independent film producers called through clenched teeth, "the Trust." Through the Trust, which controlled most of the major patents related to the making of motion pictures, Edison—who had built the first film studio back in 1893—attempted to monopolize the infant industry through vigorous lawsuits, questionable business practices, and, when all else failed, strong-arm tactics. Anyone wishing to produce, distribute, or exhibit a film in the United States had to pay a licensing fee to Edison's company or suffer the consequences. This attempt to escape the Trust's enforcers, more than Hollywood's sunny weather and varied terrain, led independent producers to begin settling permanently in what soon was called California's "movie colony."

Carl Laemmle, founder of Universal Pictures, took on Edison directly, publicly protesting the Trust's way of doing business, making films in secret far from its thugs and spies in New York, and creating what became the Hollywood studio star system. One of the more odious of the Trust's prohibitions was its ban on giving credit to those playing in its nickelodeon melodramas. Prior to 1910, the movie-going public had no idea who they were watching on the screen, and as audiences developed favorites, they began to refer to them by the names they used in the pictures. Petite, golden-haired Gladys Smith was called "Little Mary" long before she adopted the stage name Mary Pickford, while cowboy star G. M. Anderson was known simply as "Bronco Billy." Fans knew some actors only by their studios— "The Biograph Girl," "The Vitagraph Girl," "The Imp Girl." To break the hold the Trust exercised over film players, Laemmle seduced Florence Lawrence, the popular "Biograph Girl," away from the studio that along with Edison held the vast majority of shares in the Trust. He promised her more money and—for the first time in motion picture history—her name up in lights, the old Broadway dream translated into a new medium. Laemmle quickly discovered that Lawrence's devoted fans could be counted on to show up in sufficient numbers at the box office to justify increased rental fees for his pictures. He had spawned a star, and the lust for such stars would dominate Hollywood ever afterward.

Vitagraph became the first patent company to follow suit and break the Trust ban, making stars of the good-looking Maurice Costello and "The Vitagraph Girl" herself, Florence Turner. The studio's globular John Bunny became the first movie comedian known by name to the public, and its Arthur Johnson the first "matinee idol." But for sheer popular appeal, none of these could hold a candle to Mary Pickford, whom Laemmle made a star when he swooped down on Biograph again to carry off both her and her hard-drinking husband, Owen Moore. Nor could they hope to match the public's adoration of the Little Tramp, Charlie Chaplin, who worked his way to stardom from the ranks of vaudeville slapstick through Mack Sennett's Keystone

comedies. In 1917, at age twenty-seven, Chaplin signed a contract with the First National Film company to deliver eight films in eighteen months, joining Pickford— "America's Sweetheart"—as a world-famous celebrity millionaire.

Underwritten by the growing popularity of its contract celebrities and the wealth they had begun to generate, Hollywood was quick to strike back at Edison and the Trust. As early as 1912, William Fox—as in 20th Century Fox—had sued the Trust for restraint of trade, settling out of court. And by 1915, the year the federal government invoked the Sherman Antitrust Act to dissolve the company altogether, it was already falling apart because not only was it unable to enforce its edicts and collect its fees, Trust studios had stuck with the short one-reel flickers as the more innovative independent Hollywood studios captured the market with "feature-length" films, many showcasing the stars a movie-going public now demanded.

As individual players grew obscenely rich, the conspicuous consumption and loose living that typically attends fast-made fortunes began to be reported in the press to fans hungry for a glimpse at the private lives of their idols. Gossip became a prime Hollywood commodity, just as it had in New York's vaudeville days when Walter Winchell had invented the Broadway gossip column. Local columnists grew quite powerful within the "colony" as they honed the art of innuendo, and hired studio publicists fed rumors and lies to an audience fascinated by romanticized rags-to-riches stories like that of Mary Pickford, in which a girl from humble origins comes to live like royalty. Shorn of the tawdry demands for casting-couch sex and the desperate pandering of the "talent" or, in some cases, their mothers, such stories offered a glamorous alternative to dull and oppressive Main-Street respectability. They prompted young women to leave home and head for Hollywood, where their dreams often collapsed into unfulfilled longing, all of which helped to explain the licentiousness for which the suburb and its colony became infamous. Some 200,000 of them between the ages of nineteen and twenty-five came to Tinsel Town during the decade from 1919 to 1929, and a frantic Hollywood chamber of commerce, worried about the image of its municipality, posted notices in railway stations as far away as Calcutta, India, warning young women that there was no work in the movies.

Warnings had little effect, however, since stars like Pickford and Swanson were so obviously successful. They had "star quality"—an odd ability to project on film (or on stage) not just the character being played at the moment, but some ineffable essence made up of looks, manner, presence, and style that strikes a chord for a time with a broad public—and they had it at the right point in history. The attention paid Pickford and Chaplin fit neatly into a general cult of celebrity that arose from the new consumer-driven society of the 1920s based on the mass market stitched together by revolutions in transportation and by commercialized communications. Based on charisma rather than accomplishment, modern celebrity was a slave to image, and a star's success was totally dependent on the studio's ability to sell that image to an audience that was tyrannical in its demands, fickle in its loyalties, and subject to abrupt changes in its tastes—as not just Swanson, Pickford, or Chaplin were to learn, but also in the future many leaders of the free world. Three-quarters of a century later, Hollywood and its modern-style celebrity so dominated contemporary culture, and the commercial electronic media had grown so ubiquitous in our daily lives, that an ability to convey a salable image to public audiences had itself become a qualification for high political office.

Ezra Pound Moves to London (1908)

The Event: In 1908, the young American poet moved to London, where he would set up shop as a critic and editor and begin to exercise his influence over the literary world. More than any other figure in the twentieth century, Pound would shape the course of modern literature.

ONE CAN HARDLY overstate the literary importance of Ezra Pound. Not just through his own writing, but through the work of writers and poets he discovered, nurtured, and championed, he would help to define literary modernism and virtually dictate its development. He shepherded James Joyce, T. S. Eliot, William Carlos Williams, Wyndham Lewis, Marianne Moore, and Ernest Hemingway into print. He unearthed

Robert Frost and D. H. Lawrence. He badgered W. B. Yeats into writing with a leaner style. Pound's own dauntingly obtuse poems, with their obscure references and perversely complex structures, influenced poets around the globe, and continued to do so even after his intemperate, obsessive, and ultimately treasonous politics led to his virtual banishment from public life.

In London in 1912, before the Great War, he founded a literary movement called "imagism," advocating a poetry of new structures and strong images, stripped of all conventionality and sentiment. After World War I his work began to assail the "botched civilization" that could have caused the kind of destruction the war engendered, and in bitter poems of graceful construction and expression he denounced not only the war but also the commercialism of modern times, poems that included diatribes against money-lending and usurious Jews. In 1921, at age thirty-six, Pound moved to Paris, where he became the patriarchal darling of the expatriates. In 1924, he moved again, this time to Rapallo, Italy. By then he had already been working for a decade on the cycle of poems he would call *The Cantos*—a monumental 23,000-line epic gathering of his thoughts on the social order. Stuffed with cryptic historical allusions, bizarre lectures on economics, and ugly anti-Semitic ravings, the poem was a jumble of ideas, whole and half-baked, whose aesthetic

unity can only be seen by those willing to take considerable effort (and even leaps of faith) to penetrate a style that jumps wildly from colloquial to biblical to Homeric language. There are moments of great beauty and others of surpassing horror, as Pound meditates on the ideal society, ranging freely from thoughts about Confucian China to notions on Jeffersonian America. After 1920, Pound wrote almost no other poetry but *The Cantos*. He published the first volume in 1925 and the last in 1968, but he never finished the poem for which he would become best known.

As Mussolini's Italy marched steadily toward a second Armageddon, Pound's poetry increasingly reflected his fascist sympathies. During World War II, Pound expressed his opinions in a series of infamous, rambling, and incoherent propaganda broadcasts over Italian radio, which landed him in a U.S. prison camp after the allies "liberated" Italy. There, he wrote what many consider his most brilliant work, *The Pisan Cantos* (1948). Rather than condemn one of the most famous men of letters, the United States judged Pound mentally unfit to stand trial for treason and clapped him for twelve years in the mental ward at St. Elizabeth's Hospital in Washington, D.C. Released in 1958, Pound returned to Italy and wrote two more volumes of *The Cantos* before he died in 1972.

Jack Johnson Wins the World Heavyweight Championship (1908)

The Event: In 1908 in Sydney, Australia, Jack Johnson became the first African-American boxer to win the world heavyweight title when he defeated Tommy Burns in fourteen rounds that would rock the sport and scandalize the American public, even as they opened up the ring—and the road to wealth and fame—for other young black men.

IN THE DECADES AFTER "Gentleman Jim" Corbett's legendary defeat of John L. Sullivan in 1892, boxing in America increasingly became a shortcut to wealth. In the early twentieth century, it became the province of impoverished Irish immigrants driven from their country by famine and persecution. By about 1915, other immigrant groups staked their claim to the ring, and it was common to speak of Irish, German, Swedish, Jewish, and Italian fighters. Another economically oppressed American minority was also boxing at this time: A number of foreign-born black boxers, including Peter Jackson, Sam Langford, Joe Walcott, and George Dixon, came to the United States to seek their fortunes in the ring. American-born Joe Gans won the world lightweight championship in 1902, and, six years later, an African-American captured the world heavyweight title.

John Arthur Johnson was born in Galveston, Texas, on March 31, 1878. He did not behave in the docile, happy-go-lucky, submissive fashion most white Americans expected from blacks. Instead, he was flamboyant and outspoken, with a taste for high living, flashy clothes, and beautiful women—regardless of race. Many prominent white boxers refused to

fight blacks, including Louis Sullivan, who would not fight Peter Jackson, and Jack Dempsey, who would not fight Harry Wills. White audiences were drawn to the spectacle of black men beating one another and would have relished seeing a white boxer beat a black fighter into insensibility. But Johnson's victory over Tommy Burns in a fourteen-round 1908 bout in Sydney, Australia, provoked great outrage worldwide, and a search was launched for the "Great White Hope" who could defeat Johnson. The likely candidate was a former champ, Jim Jeffries, whom Johnson defeated after fifteen brutal rounds on July 4, 1910. "He said he'd bring home the bacon," Johnson's mother beamed, "and the honey boy has gone and done it."

Johnson was an affront and a challenge to cherished racial stereotypes. He had twice married white women in an era when interracial marriage was not only frowned upon, but actually illegal in some states. In 1912, Johnson was convicted of violating the Mann Act by transporting a woman across state lines for "immoral purposes"; he had driven his bride-to-be from one state to another. Convicted, he was sentenced to one year in prison, but jumped bail, and, disguising himself as a member of an African-

American baseball team, made his way to Canada, and thence to Europe, where he lived as a fugitive for seven years. During this period, Johnson successfully defended his title three times in Paris.

In 1915, Johnson traveled to Havana, Cuba, to fight Jess Willard. In the mistaken belief (he later said) that authorities would drop the charges outstanding against him if the white man won, Johnson feigned a knockout in the twenty-sixth round. The charges, however, stood, and in 1920, a homesick Johnson surrendered to U.S. marshals and served his original sentence in the federal penitentiary at Leavenworth, fighting numerous exhibition bouts within the federal prison system. After his release, Johnson appeared in vaudeville and carnivals, and at one point even shared the stage with a trained flea act. The author of two memoirs, his boxing career counted 80 victories, 7 losses, 14 draws, and 13 no-decisions in 114 bouts.

The Young Turks Revolt (1908)

The Event: On July 3, 1908, the Ottoman Empire's 3rd Army Corps in Macedonia launched a revolt against the provincial authorities in Resna that quickly led to rebellion throughout the empire and brought into positions of power and authority the Young Turks, European-influenced revolutionaries intent upon modernizing Turkey. Though they succeeded internally in reforming the government and fostering Turkish nationalism, their revolt seriously destabilized the Balkans and led to World War I, during which their ham-handed handling of foreign affairs resulted in the dissolution of the Ottoman state.

ESTABLISHED SIX CENTURIES earlier, the Ottoman Empire had at its height controlled most of central and eastern Europe, western Asia, and North Africa. For the last three hundred years, the Ottomans had steadily been losing ground, a process so rapidly accelerated in the last quarter century that by 1908 the empire had long been called "the Sick Man of Europe." All but bankrupted by constant warfare and corrupt rulers, the Turks had watched their provinces slip away "like pieces falling off an old house," losing Cyprus in 1878, Tunisia in 1881, and Egypt in 1882. However decadent, the empire yet encompassed a vast territory—including Macedonia, Albania, Palestine, Libya, Syria, Mesopotamia, Crete, Bulgaria, and lands along the Red Sea and Persian Gulf—and still played a key political role in the European balance of power established by Bismarck's system of interlocking alliances. The three Great Powers of central and eastern Europe—Germany, Austria, and Russia—all cast greedy eyes on certain Ottoman holdings, especially in the Balkans, but since no one in Europe could agree on how to carve them up, it became essential to European peace that no single major player stake a claim. The nations of Europe—including England and France—saw to it that the tottering giant did not fall in order to check any growth of their competitors.

Late in the last century, the empire's ruler, Sultan Abdülhamid II, had revoked the constitution governing its polyglot of provinces and unleashed a vicious secret police force. The sultan's state-sponsored terror horrified the empire's intelligentsia, but it was his massacre of tens of thousands of Armenians in the 1890s that made him an international pariah. Beset by a tide of rising nationalism among its subject peoples and Balkan neighbors, twisted hither and yon by the ambitions and demands of the Great Powers, Ottoman rule verged ever closer toward collapse. The Young Turks staged their revolt in 1908 to save the ailing empire, not destroy it.

By 1908, the Young Turk movement itself was some fifty years old, having begun back in the 1860s among writers inspired by European culture and philosophy. It was kept alive by exiled intellectuals, most of whom had fled to Paris in 1889 when a student-spawned plot against the sultan had been uncovered by his secret police. One faction, which included the most notable of the liberal emigrés, Ahmid Riza, advocated orderly reform under a strong central government and the exclusion of all foreign influence; another called for administrative decentralization and European assistance in creating the reforms. Both called for reinstating constitutional government and both prepared the groundwork for the future revolution against the sultan. When young officers from the 3rd Army Corps stationed in Macedonia's Salonika (now Thessaloníki, Greece), frustrated by irregular pay

and faulty equipment, formed the Ottoman Liberty Society and began conspiring with the exiled intellectuals, the stage for revolt was set.

First came a series of mutinies, then the uprising in Macedonia. The rebels did not demand that the sultan step down—however corrupt and tyrannical, he was the caliph (or spiritual leader) of many of the world's Muslims. What the rebels wanted was a restoration of the constitution and a recall of parliament. On July 23, amid the spreading revolt, Abdülhamid surprised everybody by giving the rebels what they wanted, in theory reducing his status to that of a constitutional monarch. But the deep-seated ideological differences among the Young Turks resurfaced, preventing them from taking effective control of the government, and over the next two years, the sultan staged a destabilizing counterrevolution. Not until 1913, when new leaders took over Riza's faction—the triumvirate of Talat Pasha, Ahmed Cemal Pasha, and Enver Pasha—did the Young Turks set themselves up as the arbiters of Ottoman politics.

Meanwhile, the old empire had been falling apart. Bulgaria promptly took advantage of the chaos to declare its independence in 1908, and that same year Austria annexed Bosnia and Herzegovina, which it had ruled jointly and uneasily with Turkey. Turkish Crete proclaimed its union with Greece, though threats from Istanbul kept Greece from immediately acting on the declaration. In 1911, Italy invaded and overran Tripoli (today's Libya). The Italian conquest spurred the ambition of the Balkan's small Christian states, and Serbia,

Montenegro, Greece, and Bulgaria—all once provinces of the Ottoman Empire—suddenly attacked European Turkey in October 1912. The Turkish Army collapsed. By November 3, the Bulgarians had reached Istanbul, and five days later the Greeks entered Salonika. On November 28 the Serbs took Durazzo on the Adriatic and thus provided themselves with a seaport and on December 5 the Turkish government begged the Balkan belligerents for an armistice.

Europe was shocked by the Ottoman defeat. England immediately called for a Conference of the Great Powers, which began a week later in London, on December 10, 1912. The Turks agreed to give up all they had lost to Serbia and Greece, but they drew the line at turning over to Bulgaria the city of Adrianople (today Turkish Edirne), which their troops still occupied. The Bulgars stamped their feet, the Turks stuck their noses in the air, and the armistice collapsed. As the Great Powers continued to confer, the Balkans went back to war with the Ottomans for a second time in February 1913. Adrianople promptly fell to a combined army of Bulgars and Serbs, and the Turks again sued for peace. Back in London, Austria simply insisted that either Durazzo had to be given back to the Turks or made independent; the Serbs couldn't have it. Russia put pressure on the Serbs to bite their tongues and give up the seaport, and on May 30, 1913, everybody signed the Treaty of London. Adrianople went to Bulgaria, Salonika to Greece, and an entirely new state—Albania—was carved out of Durazzo and the surrounding area.

Everything was fine for about a month.

Then on June 29, Bulgaria attacked her former Balkan allies—Serbia and Greece—grabbing up Salonika for herself and stomping all over the surprised Serbian Army. Now Romania, neutral in the first two Balkan wars, got into the act, attacking Bulgaria from the rear, crossing the Danube and marching up to the outskirts of the Bulgarian capital, Sofia. Seeing that Bulgaria was for the moment distracted, the Turks took back Adrianople. Germany's Kaiser announced that he would support his cousin, King Carol of Romania, but the Russian tsar refused to help out the tsar of Bulgaria, Ferdinand, whom he considered a maverick. So, in the Treaty of Bucharest—signed on August 6—Bulgaria lost everything she had won in the two previous wars, the Greeks took back Salonika, and a shank of Bulgarian territory was sliced off and handed to Romania.

By this time, of course, nobody was foolish enough to think matters in the Balkans had been settled. Already, the term "Balkanized" had been coined for any collapse into petty factions, and everyone "balked" at anything that did not precisely meet their fancy. For the Great Powers, still meeting in London, it didn't matter so much who was stabbing whom in the back, or which little no-account country got which piece of godforsaken real estate. What mattered was that they keep talking until they worked it out and were sure that little wars would not spread naturally through entangling alliances into general war. But, as they had always feared, without the "Sick Man of Europe" to kick around, they could not agree on what to do about his former property. Ten months after the end of the Third Balkan War, the London Conference dissolved without settling anything, even the details of the new Albania's boundaries. That year, a Serb—angry at the raw deal Serbia had gotten—would shoot the heir to the Austrian throne, and the old Europe Bismarck put together would vanish in the trenches and mustard gas clouds of the Great War that inevitably followed.

Back in what was left of the Ottoman Empire, the Young Turks in power were busy passing a whole slew of administrative reforms that would centralize their government, promote the industrialization of their economy, and secularize their legal system, none of which would prevent them from making the fatal mistake of overestimating German might and hastily entering the Great War on the side of the Central Powers. Dismembered by the Balkan Wars, the empire would be beheaded after its defeat in World War I.

British Oil Booms in the Middle East (1909)

The Event: In 1909, William Knox D'Arcy—an English soldier of fortune who had made his money at the turn of the century in an Australian gold rush—created the Anglo-Persian Oil Company, which would ultimately become known as British Petroleum, and launched the political and social transformation of the ancient Middle East by the industrialized West.

IN 1859, DRILLERS had struck oil in western Pennsylvania, kicking off an American boom that persuaded twenty-year-old John D. Rockefeller to enter the business of refining the crude stuff that came out of the earth into the kerosene that replaced whale oil as a fuel for the clean-burning new Austrian lamps. The Standard Oil Company he founded in his home town of Cleveland, Ohio, became the instrument by which Rockefeller made himself incredibly rich, becoming the first of the great American robber barons of the nineteenth century and corrupting most of the United States' municipal, state, and federal governments along the way.

In early 1901, Standard Oil rejected as pointless drilling a hill called Spindletop just outside Beaumont, Texas. This hill soon became the most desirable piece of real estate in the world. When independent drillers stuck oil underneath Spindletop Hill, it gushed two hundred feet into the air and blew out 110,000 barrels of Texas crude a day for nine days before the oilmen could cap it, touching off a new boom that—fed by other discoveries outside Tulsa, Oklahoma, and in Louisiana—made some American Indians rich before glutting the limited market. There were only so many kerosene lamps in the world, and the wildcatters, roughnecks, roustabouts, and fortune-seekers who had swelled Beaumont's population almost overnight (from ten thousand to fifty thousand) lost their shirts as speculators went bust when the price of crude fell from $1.30 to three cents a barrel. For every barrel shipped ten more oozed into the Texas dirt. A few of the sharper capitalists—men like Frank Phillips and Harry Sinclair—began to explore the use of oil as a heating fuel and something that could power ships and locomotives. One of its distillations, gasoline, could be used in the engines that propelled the strange-looking, new horseless carriages, some 8,000 of which pinged and banged their away along America's dusty roads the year Spindletop began to spew its black gold toward heaven. Suddenly the boom was back on. Not only would the companies the Texas oilmen formed—Gulf, Sunoco, Texaco—make them at least as rich as Standard Oil had made Rockefeller, but also the oil business itself would become in the twentieth century as powerful a force in shaping the world as it had been in shaping America during the nineteenth century.

It was in 1901 that William D'Arcy first heard about a French report claiming vast oil deposits might be found in Persia, known today as Iran. Two of D'Arcy's emissaries, dispatched to meet the grand vizier in Tehran, purchased from him for £40,000 in cash and stock, plus 16 percent of the profits, a concession of nearly half a million square miles, or an area almost twice the size of Texas. D'Arcy put together a crew of Canadians, Poles, and Persians who spent three years drilling dry wells in the desert and draining the Briton's capital. Forced to turn to a Scottish firm called Burmah Oil for the money to keep his team exploring, D'Arcy's gamble finally paid off. In 1908, for the first time in history, something valuable was discovered in the deserts of the Middle East, something spouting some fifty feet into the air, something gushing quite high enough to attract the interest of the British authorities, who from the start kept their eyes on this fresh new source of imperial wealth.

Persia was then a semicolonial possession of both Russia and Britain, who controlled all aspects of its economy. So it was not so odd that Great Britain should send soldiers from India to guard those drilling for the new Anglo-Persian Oil Company, which had gone public the year after the first gush of oil appeared in the desert. Nor was it so odd that the British should bring in Indian laborers to build the first great Middle East pipeline in 1910. And it was only natural that the acting British consul in the region would become the new company's informal advisor, that he should—as he put it—be "mediating between Englishmen who cannot say what they mean and Persians who do not always mean what they say." And when the Middle East collapsed in the rush to glory called the Great War, Britain in effect nationalized its Persian oil interests by buying a majority share in the company in 1914 in order to assure cheap and ample oil for its Royal Navy during the war. Forty years later the British admiral, Winston Churchill, who had overseen that purchase would be prime minister, and he would be working feverishly to prevent an independent and hostile Iran from itself nationalizing foreign oil companies.

By then, of course, oil had seeped into the political thinking of all the West's foreign office diplomats and most of its politicians. Such thinking had led the Great Powers to break up the Middle East after

World War I into essentially artificial client nations run by whichever Arab leader best understood their peculiar thirst for the black stuff. Such thinking had encouraged Hitler to gamble on invading Czechoslovakia in 1938 and put Europe on a course toward a second world war; it also led him in part to make the fatal error of invading his then-ally Russia, which opened up a second front and cost Germany the war. Such thinking would soon lead Egypt's Gamal Abdel Nasser to grab the West's main transportation pipeline for shipping oil out of the Middle East, the Suez Canal, and such thinking would lead Britain and Israel to invade Egypt to get it back. In fact, thinking about oil had by the late twentieth century become so ubiquitous in the West that when President George Bush—a nominal Texan, after all—spoke about the United States' "vital interests" in the Middle East as he launched massive preparations for invading Iraq, everyone knew he really meant that his country had to keep the oil flowing as cheaply as possible for as long as it could.

The NAACP Is Founded (1909)

The Event: In 1909, W. E. B. Du Bois—one of the foremost African-American intellectuals of the twentieth century—and a group of intellectuals, both black and white, founded the National Association for the Advancement of Colored People in New York City. Created to champion the rights of African-Americans, the NAACP became the single most influential black organization in American history.

W. E. B. DU BOIS, born in Great Barrington, Massachusetts, in 1868, lost his father shortly after birth, but he was raised in a close-knit family that supported his intellectual ambitions. The nation's first African-American to receive a Ph.D., Du Bois was educated at Fisk University, Harvard, and the University of Berlin, studying with the central social thinkers of the time. In 1909, he joined a group of socially progressive intellectuals, both black and white, who rejected the social policy of gradualism long advocated by the best-known of African-American activists, Booker T. Washington, who had founded the Tuskegee Institute, a college for black people, in 1881. Gradualism held that the achievement of economic self-determination was far more important to African-Americans than political or civil rights. "In all things that are purely social," Washington said, "we can be as separate as the fingers, yet one as the hand in all things essential to mutual progress."

Du Bois and the NAACP were not content to wait, like Booker T. Washington, for economic self-determination to bring racial equality. Instead, they instituted a vigorous program of speaking engagements, lobbying, and journalism. Du Bois himself edited the highly influential NAACP magazine, tellingly titled *The Crisis*, and the organization mounted educational as well as legal campaigns aimed at undercutting the institutions of racism and inequality.

In 1920, the NAACP successfully attacked the "grandfather clause," long used in Southern states to keep blacks from the polls, and that year the organization's ranks swelled to ninety thousand. The NAACP was always in the forefront of the early civil rights movement in America.

Relations between the organization and Du Bois were not always smooth. During the early years of the Depression, Du Bois argued that the NAACP should shift from what he saw as its narrow focus on legal rights and integration to concentrate on black economic advancement. The Depression had brought such critical hardship to blacks, Du Bois argued, that it might even be necessary to compromise—temporarily, at least—on such issues as segregation. Accused of turning back toward gradualism when he felt he was advocating even more radical change than mere legal "separatism," Du Bois resigned from the NAACP in June 1934. After teaching for a decade, Du Bois returned to the NAACP to direct research, only to be dismissed following yet another dispute in 1948.

After this final break, Du Bois turned away from primarily black issues to leftist causes, becoming chairman of the Peace Information Center. When the center declined to register in accordance with the Foreign Agents Registration Act, Du Bois and others were indicted and tried in 1951. All were acquitted, but in the red-baiting atmosphere of McCarthyism that was sweeping over the country, Du Bois was continually harassed by the government and ostentatiously shunned by colleagues. He immigrated to Ghana in 1961, began work on a massive *Encyclopedia Africana*, joined the American Communist Party, and died in 1963.

The NAACP, of course, continued to play a leading role in the civil rights movement, most momentously litigating *Brown v. Board of Education of Topeka*, in which young Thurgood Marshall successfully argued before the Supreme Court (on which, one day, he would sit as America's first black justice) that the doctrine of "separate but equal" public facilities was inherently discriminatory and unconstitutional.

Following the heyday of the civil rights activity in the 1960s, the NAACP turned its attention beyond the borders of the United States to address the problem of attaining equal rights in countries around the world, especially in South Africa, where a system called "apartheid" had been introduced that quite closely resembled—and in time would outstrip—the inequalities and racial degradations of the Jim Crow American South.

Modern Plastic Is Invented (1909)

The Event: In 1909, while trying to clean tarry residues from his chemical equipment, a Belgian-born American chemist named Leo Hendrik Baekeland stumbled upon the single most important manufacturing material of our time, which he would call "Bakelite," but which the world would come to know as "plastic."

BY THE MID-NINETEENTH CENTURY, America's billiard ball industry was in a panic. Business was great, with the demand for billiard balls at an unprecedented high. But that was the problem. The ivory for manufacturing the balls was in short supply and extremely expensive. In response, the industry collectively offered a reward of ten thousand dollars to anyone who could supply an effective substitute for ivory. An American inventor, John Wesley Hyatt, knew about a substance called pyroxylin, which had been developed in 1855 by a British chemist, Alexander Parkes. A profitable commercial use for this, in effect the first synthetic plastic, eluded Parkes, but, seventeen years later, in 1869, Hyatt improved on Parkes's original process, patented a method for manufacturing billiard balls out of the new material he called celluloid, and collected the prize money.

Celluloid found various uses over the following decades, not the least of which was as a material for stiff shirt collars and cuffs and as a medium for photographic film. Yet the industry remained limited and failed to develop any plastic substance beyond celluloid.

Leo Baekeland was an organic chemist faced with the kind of laboratory housekeeping chores that plagued all organic chemists: how to remove masses of tarry organic gunk that accumulated on expensive experimental apparatuses. Baekeland concocted solvent after solvent to clean his equipment, but to no avail. The problem became so stubborn that he combined phenol with formaldehyde to produce the residue deliberately in order to have a controlled amount of the substance on which to experiment. That is when the idea occurred to him: If this stuff was so resistant to solvents, it might actually be useful in its own right.

Baekeland refined the process of creating the resin, making it tougher and harder, and more readily controllable. He finally came up with a liquid that could be hardened into the shape of whatever vessel, or mold, contained it. Once it had solidified, it was hard, strong, water-resistant, and an electrical insulator. Not only could it be molded, it could also be cut and machined.

He named it after himself, and Bakelite became an important material in its own right for household and other goods including, for many years, the telephone, as well as items ranging from dishware to costume jewelry. The invention of Bakelite sparked the development of a staggering variety of plastics, which became the single most important manufacturing material of the century, making possible a range of products in nature, shape, and affordability previously undreamed of.

A Fire Breaks Out at the Triangle Shirtwaist Company (1911)

The Event: As she was preparing to leave at the end of the work day on March 25, 1911, one of the five hundred employees of Manhattan's Triangle Shirtwaist factory discovered that a rag bin near her eighth-floor work area was on fire. Minutes later, the sweatshop firetrap was engulfed, killing 146 workers and shocking the nation into outrage over the working conditions in American factories.

DESPITE THE EFFORTS of the workers, the fabric-laden old building burned quickly and fiercely. Factory manager Samuel Bernstein directed his employees to break out the fire hose, only to find it rotted through and completely useless. Having lost precious minutes in fruitless attempts to control the blaze, the workers looked for the means of escape. But there were only three ways out of the top three floors of the ten-story Asch Building: freight elevator, fire escape, or stairways.

Some rushed to the solitary, poorly constructed, and inadequately maintained fire escape, which descended from the tenth floor to the second, stopping above a small courtyard. Some of the young women who used it fell from one landing to the next; one of the male employees fell from the eighth floor all the way to the courtyard. Other workers chose the stairways, but, on one side of the building's eighth floor, the stairway doors had been locked, and when the panic-stricken workers rushed to the other stairway, they found it jammed with workers fleeing from the ninth and tenth floors. For workers trapped on the eighth floor, then, all that remained was the freight elevator, and several of the cutters risked their lives by taking turns operating the elevator to carry their coworkers to safety.

All seventy workers on the tenth floor managed to escape, either by way of the staircases or by ascending to the roof. Students from New York University, located across the street, stretched ladders across to the Asch Building, and the workers inched their way to safety.

Of all the Triangle employees, the 260 who worked on the ninth floor suffered the worst fate. To begin with, the fire warning from the eighth floor never reached them. By the time they detected the fire, all available avenues of escape were blocked. Some clambered down the greasy cables of the freight elevator, the elevator car itself jammed with tenth-floor employees. Others wedged their way into the narrow staircase, while others ran to the fire escape, which proved incapable of supporting the weight of so many. With a blood-curdling rip, it separated from the wall, disintegrating in a mass of twisted iron and falling bodies.

In complete desperation, some ninth-floor workers fled to the window ledges. The firemen's ladders would not reach beyond the sixth floor, so the firefighters deployed a safety net about a hundred feet below, and they exhorted the victims to jump. Some of the young women, in terror, held hands and jumped in pairs. The weight of so many jumpers split the net, and young men and women tore through it to their deaths.

There was nothing left to do but deal with the dead—146 broken bodies—and over the next few days streams of survivors filed through a temporary morgue on 26th Street to identify their coworkers.

The horrible images of the Triangle Shirtwaist fire brought an anguished outcry for laws to compel heedless, greedy, cost-cutting manufacturers to provide for the safety of employees, and the New York Factory Investigating Commission was formed to inspect factories throughout the state. The commission's report, compiled during two and a half years of research, opened many eyes, brought dramatic changes to existing laws, and introduced many new ones. The fire had struck early in an era of reform and gave that movement great momentum. Americans decided that government, even in a capitalistic democracy, had the responsibility of seeing to it that private industry protected the welfare of its employees.

Sun Yat-sen Stages a Chinese Revolution (1911)

The Event: In 1911, Dr. Sun Yat-sen, who would become known as the father of modern China, returned from a sixteen-year exile to take charge of a growing mutiny in the imperial army of the last Manchu ruler in the Qing Dynasty and turn it into a full-fledged revolution. The first Chinese Republic in history closed the book on two thousand years of imperial rule, but it proved to be short-lived, disintegrating into a chaos from which China would not truly emerge until the Communists took charge of the mainland in 1949.

IN 1907, FOUR YEARS before the Chinese Revolution, Dr. Sun Yat-sen, Revolutionary Alliance leader-in-exile, outlined his democratic program with typical Chinese precision to a meeting of 5,000 revolution-minded students in Tokyo. Dr. Sun wanted a nationalist China, in which all citizens enjoyed freedom and equality; he called for a popular sovereignty under which the Chinese would have the right of self-government; and he introduced what he called the doctrine of livelihood, a call for land and capital to be equitably distributed among China's masses. China's revolutionary elite greeted Sun Yat-sen's plans with limited enthusiasm, but students by the thousands rushed to join his Revolutionary Alliance.

The corrupt and tottering Qing Dynasty, following the Dowager Empress's recent death, was now headed by a defenseless boy emperor named Pu-Yi. His advisors made a last-ditch effort to save the dynasty by introducing constitutional reforms, but with Sun Yat-sen and other Chinese radicals determined to bring down the government, the move was too little, too late. On October 10, 1911, dissident army soldiers stationed in the Central China city of Wuhan seized the arsenal there and persuaded a brigade commander, Li Yuanhong, to lead a rebellion.

Li's sudden shift of allegiance from the Manchus to the rebels fed the mutiny, which became widespread. Given the alienation of the Qing royal court from much of Chinese society, it was very difficult for the Manchus to raise an army to put down the mutineers. By the time the dynasty had enlisted the support of the retired general Yuan Shikai, Sun Yat-sen had returned to China from his sixteen-year exile to take command of what he now called a revolution.

In December, 1911, the revolutionaries convened a congress at Nanking and elected Sun president of a new republic in South China. Sun recognized that Yuan, who retained the loyalty of most of the army's officers in North China, was a powerful force, and casting a cold eye on the frailty of his divided nation, the good doctor offered the presidency to the general on the condition that he force the boy emperor to abdicate and dissolve the dynasty. Yuan immediately agreed, marched into the Forbidden City, rattled his saber in the face of the inexperienced Pu-Yi, and demanded that the last emperor step down. On February 12, 1912, Pu-Yi formally resigned; the next day, Sun Yat-sen stepped aside; Yuan Shikai was now president of the whole of China.

Almost instantly, the general betrayed Sun Yat-sen. When Sun's Nationalist Party, the Kuomintang (KMT), won a breathtaking majority in China's first parliamentary elections, Yuan balked. Attempting to seize unilateral control of the government, the general outlawed the KMT, forcing Sun yet again into Japanese exile, and dissolved the parliament. But Yuan had a fight on his hands against the nationalists. By early 1916, Sun Yat-sen had mounted an armed revolt, backed by the Japanese government, against the self-declared dictator. Sun encouraged restive warlords to declare the provinces under their control independent of Yuan's republic, and many did. In March 1916, two of Yuan's own sons refused to support him, and the aging general, exhausted and disenchanted, succumbed to illness two months later.

Sun Yat-sen found it more difficult to control the warlords he had unleashed than he planned. In the absence of a strong constitutional tradition, Sun could not regain the presidency. Instead, the warlords declared that they would decide the succession. But Yuan's death had left China without a clear political leader even among its powerful military men, and the fledgling republic plunged into a chaos of feuding warlords fighting for control of a China that would spend the next thirty-three years searching for true political stability.

Robert M. La Follette Founds the Progressive Party (1912)

The Event: In 1912, Robert M. La Follette, a senator from Wisconsin, led a group of Republican insurgents calling themselves Progressives to break away from the Republican Party and found the most important third party in American history.

THE PROGRESSIVES ROSE to prominence at the turn of the century in a movement that grew out of the decay of Populism and a farm-fed revival of Puritanism that had first manifested itself in a series of "temperance" campaigns. Fueled by the sensational writings of muckraking journalists and supported by the involvement of America's churches in social issues, Progressives reacted to the growing power of organized labor, the revolutionary demands of America's new intellectual radicals, and the changing racial and ethnic composition of America's cities with a moral "uplift" program of reform intended to check the excesses of capitalism while essentially preserving it. As such, the Progressives spoke for upper- and middle-class reformers and developers, business and religious leaders, and the more successful newspapers. Appalled by corruption, they wanted a clean government as well as economic growth, and they spoke of "progress," "civic reform," and "modernization." They attacked patronage politicians and crusaded for "good government," calling for the public control of the all-powerful railroads and public utilities. They supported, to a carefully pitched degree, trust-busting and such Populist causes as primary elections, the popular election of senators, women's suffrage, and Prohibition.

Progressives did not count among their numbers the urban poor, racial, and ethnic minorities, or labor radicals, all of whom they viewed with distrust and distaste as morally decadent at best, and viciously criminal at worst. Progressives tended to be xenophobic nativists, who were quite willing to crusade against saloons and brothels—the gathering places of radical workingmen—as long as they could conduct the crusades from the comfort of their country clubs, spacious homes, and Protestant churches. It was a Progressive administration's attorney general who launched the great "Red Scare" that followed World War I; for radical workingmen, and the intellectuals who took up their cause, appeared to the "decent folk" Progressives claimed to represent as much a threat to good government and safe communities as did greedy, dishonest, and corrupting monopolists. World War I itself provided the Progressives with an opportunity to attack ethnic cultures and homogenize America's white population. The merit system they introduced into state and federal government to replace the spoils system proved just as impervious to the inclusion of blacks and other ethic minorities in local, state, and federal government as had its predecessor.

The genesis of Progressivism may be traced to the autumn of 1889 and the founding of Hull House by Jane Addams and Ellen Gates Starr. These dedicated social workers inspired the likes of John Dewey and George Herbert Mead to develop a pragmatic philosophy aimed at addressing the problems of democracy. The early years of the movement also produced a new breed of journalists—whom Theodore Roosevelt later derisively labeled "muckrakers"—dedicated to exposing social problems. The movement captured the imagination of two charismatic young men, New York's Theodore Roosevelt and Wisconsin's Robert La Follette.

With Roosevelt, the Progressives' political fortunes were made. He had helped define the very nature of Progressivism in his political speeches of the 1880s and 1890s, when he argued basically for the same kind of managerial approach to government that made large businesses function efficiently. Not boodling and cronyism, but rationalized organization would make for good civic policy. Roosevelt's domination of the early Progressive movement ensured that the once-radical demands of the Populists—the initiative and referendum, public control of the railroads and utilities, breaking up of the big trusts, primary elections, secret ballots, popular election of senators, women's suffrage, and a graduated income tax—would be met by reform measures drawn and administered by those at whom they had been aimed; he did not want to kick the rich out, most of whom he knew personally, but merely to make them behave and work strenuously for the good of the governed as well as for themselves. At any rate, when Roosevelt became president in 1901, the movement had in the nation's "bully pulpit" a national hero capable of reforming the entire country—on those days when he was willing.

On the other hand, in La Follette the Progressives had a true reformer, dedicated to real change and never much trusting Teddy Roosevelt's progressive credentials. When La Follette became governor of Wisconsin, he instituted the full range of Progressive reforms, including public administration by nonpartisan civil servants mostly drawn from the University of Wisconsin faculty. With the progressive press touting his "Wisconsin Idea," La Follette

was elected to the U.S. Senate in 1905, where he would remain until his death in 1925. In 1912, La Follette led the insurgent Progressives out of the Republican Party when it renominated the incumbent William Howard Taft, himself a mild Progressive in the Roosevelt mold who had been coddling up to conservative party regulars in order to win the nod. The newly founded third party, however, immediately abandoned La Follette to back a very willing Teddy Roosevelt. Roosevelt would win a quarter of the popular vote and eighty-eight electoral votes, far outstripping Taft (with only eight electoral votes) and helping ensure Democrat Woodrow Wilson's landslide victory.

In that election, in fact, ran all three of the presidents who could be said to have come out of the Progressive movement. As president, Roosevelt, however truculently, had moved against the trusts and backed government regulation of the railroads, got a pure food and drug law enacted, and championed the conservation of natural resources. The more conservative President Taft, virtually hand-picked by Roosevelt to follow him into office, had continued the trust-busting, had strengthened both the Interstate Commerce Commission, and had put bigger teeth in the federal court system. Now Wilson—in whom perhaps the absolutist Puritan strain in Progressivism was most evident—would lower tariffs, introduce the graduated income tax and the Federal Reserve, and enter into World War I on a Progressive footing, seeking to make the entire world safe for democracy *and then* impose on it "good government."

La Follette broke with Wilson, whose domestic policies he supported, over entry into the war and became leader of the isolationist opposition. He ran as a third-party candidate against Calvin Coolidge in 1924, carried only Wisconsin, and demonstrated that the Progressive era had disappeared into the rubble left by Wilson's high-faluting postwar foreign policy. Indeed, with its agenda tainted from the start by a reluctance to abandon the status quo, Progressive reform was ultimately inadequate to the challenges of the new century. Prohibition spawned organized crime, creating a nation of lawbreakers rather than sober, civic-minded do-gooders. Women gained the vote—a positive good to be sure, but, nonetheless the electorate voted Warren G.

Harding into the White House, whose administration was as corrupt as any that had disgraced the late nineteenth century. With Progressivism's promises little more than a bitter memory, Harding's successor, Calvin Coolidge, gave big business a free hand to create the climate that helped propel the nation and the world into crippling depression.

Franklin Delano Roosevelt would revive some of the spirit of the best Progressive reform, his New Deal serving as an extension of the kind of social work that gave birth to Progressivism in Chicago. But the Progressive party was a shell by 1948, when it fielded its last presidential candidate, Henry A. Wallace, who captured a meager 2 percent of the popular vote and no electoral votes.

The *Titanic* Sinks (1912)

The Event: The *Titanic*, a British passenger liner and the largest passenger ship of its time, sunk after striking an iceberg off southern Newfoundland on the night of April 14–15, 1912, becoming one of the most celebrated disasters of the twentieth century.

THE TITANIC WAS not only the summation of the art and science of shipbuilding, it was a monument to technology and a veritable floating cathedral dedicated to the worship of mechanical as well as financial power. It embodied the most advanced naval architecture and engines, and it was also the most luxurious passenger ship built up to that time. Its builders and owners, the White Star Line, confidently claimed that its advanced double-hull construction with multiple watertight compartments made the vessel "unsinkable."

The *Titanic* was on its maiden voyage from Southampton, England, to New York, carrying more than 2,200 people. The captain, eager to make the maiden crossing in record time, sailed at 22 knots in iceberg-strewn seas off the Newfoundland coast. The night of April 14–15, 1912, was cold and clear, but by the time the lookout saw the looming berg, it was too late for the enormous and fast-moving vessel to avoid a collision.

The impact, under the vessel's waterline, tore a gaping hole long enough to quickly flood five of the much-touted watertight compartments, and the ship took on too much water to prevent it from sinking.

Worse, the *Titanic* carried enough lifeboats for only less than half its passengers and crew. The ship *was* equipped with Guglielmo Marconi's recent invention, the wireless telegraph, or radio, and the operator sent out the newly agreed-upon universal Morse code distress signal—S.O.S.—marking the first time in history that signal was broadcast.

The steamship *Carpathia*, positioned some hours distant, received the distress call and steamed to the rescue. Tragically, the lone radio operator on the *Californian*, which was close enough to the *Titanic* to see its lights, had gone to sleep for the night. When *Titanic* crew members fired signal rockets, the *Californian's* skipper mistook the frantic call for help as an exhibition of recreational fireworks. As a result, the *Californian*, which could have reached the stricken vessel before it sank, did not come to the aid of the *Titanic*.

By the time the *Carpathia* arrived on the scene, the unsinkable *Titanic* had disappeared below the waves of the frigid North Atlantic. Some 1,500 passengers and crew members drowned.

The shipwreck, considered the worst in history, prompted the implementation of many national and international safety measures and demonstrated the enormous potential of the radio as a vital instrument for communication. But the disaster shook the world for reasons far beyond the immediate and terrible loss of life: Many saw an immense cautionary tale in the loss of this proud ship—on its maiden voyage, no less—as if the impersonal forces of nature had conspired to deflate the technological arrogance of modern civilization, declaring that the struggle between humankind and the elements had hardly been resolved.

United Fruit Sets Up a Banana Republic (1913)

The Event: In 1913, the American-owned United Fruit Company established the Tropical Radio and Telegraph Company in the impoverished Central American country of Guatemala, creating a monopoly of the little nation's communications system and placing a stranglehold on its infrastructure—a shining example of what the twentieth century would come to call "dollar diplomacy" in a "banana republic."

IN THE NINETEENTH CENTURY, muckraking progressive American journalists had dubbed the Standard Oil Company—the country's first great financial trust—"the octopus." And that is precisely what the hapless Guatemalans called the hated American-owned United Fruit Company, formed in 1899 by the merger of the Boston Fruit Company and the Tropical Trading and Transport Company, that dominated the economy and politics of their nation.

Folks called Guatemala a banana republic (despite the fact that its major export was coffee) precisely because it was so thoroughly under the control of United Fruit, the leading ambassador of America's dollar diplomacy—good old-fashioned imperialism with a perverse new twist. In the name of free trade and capitalism, the United States could promote its interests—and be spared the inconvenience, not to mention the political headaches for a country proud of its freedom at home, of setting up a colonial government—through the auspices of huge export firms doing business in Central America and the Caribbean.

In Guatemala it worked like this: Guatemala's ruling elite were persuaded to grant United Fruit tax exemptions, vast acreages for its plantations, and the ownership of Guatemala's main port exchange in exchange for help building a railroad, since Queen Victoria's heyday the *sine qua non* for any nation that mattered. Seduced by promises of further American investment, Guatemalan leaders turned over control of all the nation's railways to the company, whose merchant navy already dominated local shipping. Here, and in other Latin American countries, United Fruit functioned as a shadow government.

Like the other big fruit companies—Standard Fruit and Steamship in Honduras, for example—United Fruit ruled its vast plantations with an iron fist. Company commissaries drove peasants into unredeemable debt, and thus peonage. When malaria weakened its much-exploited workers, United Fruit imported black workers from Jamaica and the West Indies—whose immune systems were supposedly resistant to the disease—to pick the crop, imposing a U.S.-style racial segregation on those it forced to work together. True, it built a number of hospitals, but that made economic sense if it wanted to keep its workers healthy enough to harvest its products. On the other hand, the company did not bother much with schools, building only a few, which were mostly for show; it did not need many workers who could read, and consequently Guatemalan literacy rates remained shamefully low. Peasants owned only tiny plots of land, while United Fruit kept hundreds of thousands of acres in reserve and uncultivated. By 1930, the company had made so much money that it easily absorbed twenty of its closest rivals, becoming Central America's biggest employer. And because so much land was dedicated to agriculture, Guatemala could hardly industrialize, and it thus remained hostage to the constantly shifting world demand for its two cash crops, coffee and bananas—a predicament that continues to plague both Central and much of South America today.

When America began to develop its secret intelligence organizations after World War I, their personnel, like many in its foreign service, tended to be agents of the dollar diplomats as well. It was the managing partner of the Wall Street law firm Sullivan and Cromwell who in 1936 put together the deal that gave its client, United Fruit, control of the International Railways of Central America (IRCA) and drew up the papers for a new ninety-nine-year lease in Guatemala signed by Jorge Ubico Castenada, the Guatemalan Caudillo ("leader"). Ubico so despised the Mayan rabble that constituted a majority of his subjects and United Fruit's workers that he had his initials stamped in every bullet fired by his soldiers to ensure that malcontents "would carry his personal emblem into eternity." Then a 1944 revolution led by reform-minded army officers ousted Ubico and set up national elections, the second of which six years later brought to power Jacobo Arbenz Guzman. Pledging "to convert Guatemala from a backwater country with a predominately feudal economy into a modern capitalist state," President Arbenz planned to open a second port on the Gulf of Mexico, build a national highway to break IRCA's monopoly on transport, and generally compete with the foreign United Fruit. In 1952, he squeezed through a legislature corrupted by foreign bribes an agricultural reform bill and began expropriating uncultivated land leased by United Fruit, which amounted to some 400,000 acres (a seventh of the arable acreage in Guatemala) by 1954, when United Fruit struck back with a vengeance. Meanwhile, in the U.S. Senate, Massachusetts's Henry Cabot Lodge ("the Senator from United Fruit") and Speaker of the House John McCormack, also from Massachusetts, set off a drum roll in Congress demanding action to clean up the mess in Guatemala.

In 1952 John Foster Dulles became the U.S. Secretary of State, and his brother, Allen, head of the CIA. Suddenly Arbenz found himself accused of consorting with communists and subverting the free world, and a CIA-backed coup was underway. Kermit Roosevelt, the United States' man in Teheran who had helped engineer the Iran prime minister's fall from power and the return of the Shah earlier in the year, declined the Dulles brothers' invitation to participate, believing the plan reeked of Nazi methodology. It did, but in any case Arbenz was forced out within the year, replaced by the "rebel" leader Castillo Armas. Armas brought back Ubico's head of security, a man adept at terror and torture. Suspected "communists" were treated as common criminals, and the hunt was on. Armas just missed capturing a young, contemplative left-winger named Che Guevara, who left the country for glory elsewhere. If the Dulles brothers, enforcers for United Fruit, had qualms about overthrowing the democratically elected president of a sovereign power and replacing him with a brutal dictator, they never mentioned it. Their clients—in government, on Wall Street, around the board room table—were pleased, and they felt "covert action" had been vindicated. They would use it again.

The Rite of Spring Premieres in Paris (1913)

The Event: The May 29 premiere performance of Igor Stravinsky's ballet *Le Sacre du Printemps* (*The Rite of Spring*) sparked a riot. The music that so offended the Parisians would shock the entire musical world as well and, in the long run, would radically change the nature of music—and of culture—in the twentieth century.

B ORN ON JUNE 17, 1882, in Oranienbaum, near Saint Petersburg, Russia, Igor Stravinsky was the son of a famous bass singer at the Imperial Opera. Surprisingly, young Stravinsky showed little interest in music until, while a law student, he began to study composition with the eminent Nikolai Rimsky-Korsakov. His earliest compositions were in the lush romantic Russian nationalist vein Rimsky-Korsakov and his contemporaries had first mined, but Stravinsky soon broke with his teacher and created the musical score for three stunning ballets for Serge Diaghilev's Ballets Russes in Paris: the *Firebird* in 1910; *Petrushka*, in 1911; and *The Rite of Spring* in 1913.

Each of these musical works was increasingly daring and discordant, and as the riot triggered by *The Rite of Spring*'s use of the wild, exuberant, sexually charged rhythms of primal ritual grew into an international scandal, some protested that Stravinsky, Diaghilev, and choreographer/starring dancer Vaslav Nijinsky were bringing about the downfall of everything decent and valuable in Western art and culture. Others argued just as vociferously that artists such as these were in the process of liberating an artistic and cultural tradition that had become stagnant, even moribund.

Stravinsky had obviously tapped into something essential in Western society in the second decade of the century, something that the eminent Swiss psychologist Carl Gustav Jung would capture in the title of his 1933 book, *Modern Man in Search of a Soul*. The title might well be applied to the whole of art and philosophy in the twentieth century. Stravinsky, in the manner of such radical emerging visual artists of the period as Henri Matisse and Georges Braque, plumbed the soul-satisfying depths of primitive urges and primal rituals to create a modern, highly complex work of art featuring orchestrations, harmonies, and rapidly shifting, ever-driving rhythmic patterns never before heard, yet seemingly rooted in some distant, shared, but forgotten primordial past.

To many, the artistic vision of Stravinsky and other so-called primitivists seemed threatening and anarchistic, uncomfortably expressive of the volatile political climate of an Old World precariously balanced on the brink of war and revolution. To others, works such as *The Rite of Spring* pointed the way to an aesthetic and spiritual rebirth, an exciting new way of connecting with a challenging, discordant, and alienating world.

The United States Imposes a Tax on Personal Income (1913)

The Event: In 1913, the states ratified the Sixteenth Amendment to the U.S. Constitution granting the federal government the legal right to impose taxes on personal income, which in the long run would virtually ensure the growth of a stronger central government as well as help to underwrite the social services that came to typify Western industrial nations in the twentieth century.

THE IDEA OF AN income tax is hardly a twentieth-century innovation. The U.S. Treasury considered levying an income tax to help finance the War of 1812, but it was the Civil War, some fifty years later, that actually brought about the first such tax in this country, with rates ranging from 3 to 5 percent.

The original U.S. income tax ended in 1865 with the end of the Civil War, but the Bureau of Internal Revenue it had spawned in 1862 lived on, the foundation of what would become a mighty new bureaucracy. It was the common folk who agitated for an income tax, which they saw as a way of evening out the lopsided distribution of wealth in America by taxing those who earned the most money. Congress acted to bring income taxes back in 1894, but the act was declared unconstitutional by a staunchly conservative Supreme Court, which denounced the notion as a "communistic threat."

Undaunted, Progressive reformers kept alive support for a graduated income tax, and in 1909 President William Howard Taft suggested putting the proposal in the form of a constitutional amendment in order to get around the high court.

The first rates imposed by the new law collected 1 percent of taxable income above $3,000 for individuals or $4,000 for married couples and rose to a maximum of 7 percent on incomes over $500,000. However, during World War I, rates reached a high of 77 percent. Scaled back during the prosperous twenties, they rose again to finance the New Deal during the Great Depression. World War II made even greater demands than World War I, and the top tax rate reached a staggering 91 percent. Moreover, to improve cash flow and "taxpayer compliance," Congress imposed an automatic withholding system in 1943, doubling the funds collected in its first year. Congress also lowered the exemptions that

had placed most of the burden on the wealthy, thereby turning a class tax into a mass levy.

With war's end, the tax rates were somewhat reduced, but had to be hiked again to finance the Korean War. With the introduction of Lyndon Johnson's Great Society in the 1960, more of the tax burden was again shifted to the wealthiest taxpayers. Indeed, even more than the rate, it has been the degree of progression of the income tax that has been subject to sharpest debate. The result of debate, argument, and compromise was a bewildering thicket of rules, logic-defying deductions, credits, subsidies, and exemptions, all patchworked into what became a voluminous tax code.

Charged with collecting the income tax since 1953, when it was created in a sweeping reorganization of the scandal-ridden old Bureau of Internal Revenue, the Internal Revenue Service exploited the code's complexity to confound the machinations of clever accountants and tax lawyers, many of them former IRS agents. The IRS became an extraordinarily powerful—and much-feared and resented—bureaucracy, against whom some 40 percent of all those filing taxes employed professional accountants and lawyers in a battle to pay as little as possible without getting fined or going to jail.

The reality is that all Americans, regardless of economic status, pay less income tax than the citizens of almost all other industrial nations. In fact, income taxes have become the chief source of revenue for every major industrialized nation in the world. They are a fixture of life in this century and are almost certainly destined to remain a fixture for centuries to come.

Henry Ford Introduces the Modern Factory (1913)

The Event: Ten years after starting the Ford Motor Company, Henry Ford retooled his plant to incorporate the assembly line method of mass production, introducing into the United States the modern factory and making it possible for most Americans to afford a private automobile.

BORN ON A DEARBORN, MICHIGAN, farm on July 30, 1863, young Henry Ford soon discovered an aptitude for machinery, apprenticed himself to a machinist, and worked as a traveling repairman for a farm machinery company. After a stint as a sawmill operator, he became chief engineer for the new Edison Illuminating Company in Detroit and then turned to another emerging technology, the automobile, then better known as the horseless carriage. Ford built his first car in 1896, completing it in his shed at two A.M. on June 4. He found employment with a manufacturer of custom-made automobiles for whom he designed and built an early racing car christened the "999."

In 1903, he organized the Ford Motor Company. Ford built good, dependable vehicles from the start, and the company was immediately profitable. However, Ford recognized that he was only one among a growing number of makers of automobiles, which were turned out, one at a time, as essentially custom-crafted items for the well-to-do. Ford determined to create an automobile that could be sold at a price within the reach of the masses. To do this, he redesigned not only the car, but the process by which it was manufactured.

In 1908, Ford introduced the Model T, which was produced not as the individual work of a team of craftsmen, but as the collective product of a larger group of semi-skilled workers. This was the origin of the assembly line, and in 1908, Ford was able to sell his Model T for $850—pricey enough, but still cheaper than any other vehicle available at the time. By 1913, however, Ford's employee William Knudson had thoroughly developed the assembly line throughout his plant. He paid his workers well, attracting better-than-average labor, but they were still less costly to employ than highly skilled craftsmen. Each worker was trained to perform a specific task—no more and no less—and then the assembly was passed down to the next worker, who performed his assigned task, and so on down the line. The pace was set not by the individual worker, but by the mechanical motion of the line. As a result, whereas Ford had turned out 10,607 cars in 1908, by 1916, he manufactured 730,041, priced not at $850, but at $360 each—well within the reach of most Americans. By 1927, the last year the model was made, Ford had produced fifteen million Model Ts.

That car became a ubiquitous feature of America's roads. A sturdy, reliable, and generic product of the early perfection of mass production, it transformed not only the American scene, but civilization itself. It fostered a consumer-driven society; it bestowed upon virtually all economic classes equal and unprecedented mobility; it began the unification of the American nation—and other nations—through vast networks of roads; it promoted travel and tourism, helping make possible not only the "family" vacation, but all that such vacations imply—designated leisure time, tourist traps, inexpensive accommodations, gas stations, and carefully planned sites and amusements.

Ford's assembly line also dramatically changed the relationship between labor and management and forever changed the nature of labor itself. At first, the paternalistic Ford rewarded his workers with wages and working conditions far superior to those ac-corded most factory or mill workers. But soon the assembly line proved to be a mechanized tyrant, chaining laborers to an inhuman pace of production and robbing them of creative freedom or human expression. Ironically, in producing an automobile that promised the fulfillment of American democracy and unprecedented freedom of movement, Henry Ford had wrought upon the world a factory system in which both human beings and parts were interchangeable, and therefore expendable, recalling vividly the world of slave labor that propelled the ancient Roman galleys and built the ancient Egyptian pyramids.

Cubism Comes to the Armory Show in New York (1913)

The Event: In New York City in 1913, works by the Paris-based avant-garde artists called collectively the "Cubists" were displayed at America's most influential art show, the International Exhibition of Modern Art. Shocking to some, exciting to others, the works introduced America to nothing less than a new way of interpreting reality.

HOUSED IN THE Sixty-ninth Regiment Armory in New York City in 1913, the International Exhibition of Modern Art was better known as the Armory Show. It drew more than 300,000 visitors in New York and even more as it traveled to Chicago and Boston. Its purpose was to introduce Americans to "antiacademic" artists, whose work was generally neglected by the mainstream. Two-thirds of the sixteen hundred artworks exhibited were by Americans and were, for the most part, competent but unexceptional. However, a significant percentage of the five hundred-plus European works were aggressively avant-garde, attracting most of the attention paid the show and causing a sensation.

Among the European artists exhibiting at the armory were Paul Cézanne, Henri Matisse, and Pablo Picasso, but the artist whose work caused the biggest stir was Marcel Duchamp. The painting in question was called *Nude Descending a Staircase*, and it had already made a sensation at the Salon des Indépendants in Paris in 1911. Now receiving a much wider viewing, it would soon become the most famous of the cubist works, perhaps because it was such an extreme example of the new style, making no attempt whatsoever to reproduce the conventional reality of representational art that—despite the slight exaggerations of Impressionism—most art patrons then still considered "true" painting. Instead, Duchamp attempted to portray relative time and motion itself, distorting his "nude" by painting a series of figures "disfigured" by the geometric forms the Cubists used to create simultaneous multiple perspectives.

Duchamp had not invented the style; Pablo Picasso and Georges Braque had. In 1907, the young Picasso, just coming out of his famous "blue period" and determined to make his mark in the art world, abandoned the styles, subjects, and colors that were beginning to bring him recognition and painted a group of prostitutes from a brothel on Barcelona's Avignon Street in a new style that would revolutionize painting. So different was the new concept of art, in fact, that, as art historian Hershel Chipp described it, "the means by which images could be formalized in a painting changed more in the years 1907 to 1914 than they had since the Renaissance." The painting was, of course, Picasso's masterful *Les Demoiselles d'Avignon*, which many argue is the most important work of art thus far in the twentieth century.

Picasso sought his inspiration almost equally in the early works of Cézanne and in the African sculpture that was enjoying a vogue in the Parisian salons of the day. He used violently fragmented forms to create images as they would appear if they could be seen from all perspectives at once. Despite their unsettling power, for an audience of art patrons used to seeing female figures treated with something approaching awe, the breakdown of bodies into sharp fragments seemed inhuman, even an outrage. The following year, Picasso's friend Geor-

ges Braque took the fragmentation of conventional imagery a step further, reducing his figures to geometric forms in a series of paintings that, as Henri Matisse observed, seemed to be made up of images that resembled "little cubes."

Exactly, Picasso and Braque might have responded. As they saw it, they were trying to find the "truth" of an object, its authentic reality, through its decomposition. They disdained such traditional techniques as light and shadow, perspective, and realistic representations of three-dimensional objects on two-dimensional canvases, perceiving these methods as somehow dishonest, a hoax perpetrated on the viewer. They wanted to analyze their subjects by ripping them apart, then represent each angle and detail of the object so destroyed with geometric shapes. By 1911, they were being called derisively "Cubists," after Matisse's *bon mot*, and by 1912, they had reversed their original artistic process, building images by starting with geometric shapes.

The movement spread rapidly through the streets of Paris. Artists all over town, attracted by the promise of freedom from the bonds of a phony reality, embraced the new and liberating aesthetic, among them Juan Gris, Marie Laurençin, Fernand Léger—and Marcel Duchamp. At the 1911 Salon des Indépendents, Guillaume Apollinaire—Paris's reigning cultural guru—enthusiastically welcomed the controversial new style under the formerly disapprobative label, Cubism, which had the effect of placing an all-but-official seal of approval on such shocking aesthetic innovations as two eyes appearing on the same side of a head or a stack of cones being called a "nude."

By the time the Armory Show opened in New York, few Americans had ever heard of Apollinaire, and many who later came to the show were simply bewildered. Some grew angry, like the critic who dismissed Duchamp's masterpiece by saying it looked like "an explosion in a shingle factory." Others, however, began to see in the tower of sharp-edged geometric crystals a series of images of a lean female figure sweeping down a spiral staircase, as Duchamp had intended, and for them the new painting was a revelation, an embodiment not only of the latest conceptions in art, but also of physics and psychology—both of which stressed the perspective and relativist nature of reality. This, though, did not stop a public outcry against Duchamp and the other "modern" artists. In Chicago, for example, two other Armory Show artists, Henri Matisse and Constantin Brancusi, were hanged in effigy.

The assault of the avant-garde on bourgeois sensibility, which would come to characterize modern art in the twentieth century, was underway. Duchamp himself would stop painting at the age of twenty-

five and spend his final years studying chess, but his *Nude Descending a Staircase* virtually defined the term "avant-garde," and before he had finished his short career as a painter he was considered the most revolutionary artist in a century of revolutionary artists. After the Armory Show, Duchamp began producing what he called "ready-mades," and in 1917 he signed a common urinal "R. Mutt," entitled it *Fountain*, and included it in another exhibition in New York City. By placing his ready-mades in museum and gallery settings, Duchamp erased the distinction between high and low art, opening the door for great art to treat the casual, the common, the disgusting, the ugly, even the trivial, as subject matter, another hallmark of twentieth-century art.

Like so much of the aesthetic production of the early 1920s, Duchamp's *Fountain* was a gesture, one he used to decree, in effect, that art was no longer a matter (or merely a matter) of technique and training; art was whatever the artist said it was. That assertion, today commonplace, came to define art and literature of the twentieth century, from Dada to Post-Modernism, from Joyce to Borges.

The United States Builds the Panama Canal (1914)

The Event: In 1914, after spending eight years and over $300 million moving 240 million cubic yards of earth to overcome enormous obstacles of geography and climate, the United States opened the Panama Canal to shipping, symbolizing the new world power's technological and financial might.

IN THE FLUSH OF imperialist fervor brought by victory in the Spanish-American War (1898) and encouraged after 1900

by the expansionist president Theodore Roosevelt, the United States persuaded Great Britain to relinquish its claims to share control of a Central American canal under a fifty-year-old treaty giving both nations rights of passage across the Isthmus of Panama. Then, in 1901, an American commission recommended building the canal not in Panama, but in Nicaragua; however, the New Panama Canal Company persuaded Roosevelt to build the canal through Panama and offered its rights to the Canal route not for its original asking price of $109 million, but for $40 million. Early in 1902, the Congress authorized construction and the next year ratified the Hay-Herrán Treaty, granting the United States a ten-mile-wide strip of land across the isthmus in return for a $10 million-dollar cash payment and an annuity. At the time Colombia had jurisdiction over Panama City (then called New Granada) and when the Colombian senate held out for a higher price, the United States helped engineer an uprising, by means of which Panama became an independent republic. A fresh treaty was concluded with the new government on the same terms that had been offered to New Granada. It was ratified in 1904.

Construction through the Panamanian jungle was a logistical nightmare. Climate and terrain presented tremendous difficulties, but disease—chiefly yellow fever and malaria—threatened to undermine the project from the start. U.S. Army Colonel William Gorgas waged an all-out war against mosquito-breeding swamps, and he improved sanitation practices. By 1906, his efforts had largely eradicated the two jungle plagues, and it was now up to Colonel George Washington Goethals of the U.S. Army Corps of Engineers to build the forty-mile-long channel, which had a complex system of locks. Though opened for commercial use in 1914, the Panama Canal was not formally dedicated until July 12, 1920, by which time the United States, flexing its imperial muscle and showing off its know-how with the planning and construction of the canal, had succeeded in changing the political and the physical geography of the planet.

A Balkan Terrorist Assassinates Austria's Archduke Ferdinand (1914)

The Event: In 1914, in the obscure Balkan capital of Sarajevo, Bosnian nationalist Gavarilo Princeps gunned down Austria's heir apparent Archduke Francis Ferdinand and his wife, setting into motion a complex series of alliances and enmities that resulted in what was then called the Great War, the costliest conflict a bellicose humanity had ever fought.

A T THE BEGINNING of the twentieth century, the nations of Europe were both bound together and torn apart by a ragged web of alliances and counter alliances. The act of a suicidally desperate assassin, the Bosnian nationalist Gavarilo Princeps, did far more than end the lives of the Austro-Hungarian Archduke Francis Ferdinand

and his wife Sophie in Sarajevo on June 28, 1914. It set into motion a lumbering juggernaut of alliance and enmity as, one by one, the nations of Europe declared war on one another and committed their unsuspecting populations to a course of mindless self-destruction unparalleled in the experience of the world.

The war commenced with a sweeping German drive deep into France, which boded a German victory as devastating as that of the Franco-Prussian War of 1870–1871. But, some thirty miles outside of Paris, German forces, fearful of overextending their supply lines, wheeled about and dug in. It was as fateful a maneuver as any in the history of war: the deadly stalemate of trench warfare followed for more than four years, resulting in a brutal contest of mutual death and destruction without significant gain in territory.

If none of the combatant nations gained significant real estate, all concentrated their resources on developing and employing new instruments of murder. First the French, then the Germans, developed an arsenal of poisonous gases that dissolved the lungs and asphyxiated men on their own blood and tissue. The British fielded the tank, an armored, mechanized mobile artillery piece. The French and Germans invented successively more destructive fixed artillery. The Germans made extensive use of deadly submarines. And all sides turned out airplanes, capable of raining death from the skies.

Although the European combatants hammered one another for almost three years before the United States, responding to German depredations on the high seas

and an anti-American overture to the government of Mexico, entered the war on the side of Allies, it was the American troops who would turn the tide against the Central Powers. Allied shipping losses were at an unprecedented high; major French land offensives had failed, leading to low morale and mass mutinies throughout the French army; and the British offensive in Flanders had been inconclusive and very costly. Worse, the Eastern Front was in collapse as a vast but ill-equipped and poorly led Russian army suffered one terrible defeat after another, and the nation was propelled inevitably toward revolution and a humiliating "separate peace" with Germany. With the withdrawal of Russia, vast numbers of German troops were sent to the Western Front.

The isolationist United States was poorly prepared for war, and, although General John J. ("Black Jack") Pershing arrived in Paris on June 14, 1917 and his first troops followed at the end of the month, it was not until the spring and summer of 1918 that significant numbers of American forces were fielded. The Americans suffered heavy losses, but, during July and August, they were instrumental in crushing the last major German offensives and turning the tide of the long war. From the end of September through the day of the Armistice, November 11, 1918, all available U.S. forces were concentrated along a sector between the Meuse River and the Argonne Forest. The campaign, aimed at cutting the Germans' principal line of supply, involved 1,200,000 American troops, who suffered a heavy 10 percent casualty rate. But the success of this offensive brought Germany to its knees, an armistice was declared on November 11, 1918, and the Treaty of Versailles concluded on June 28, 1919.

The Great War ended America's isolationist innocence forever, and it visited unprecedented death and devastation on Europe. The war left the participants economically, intellectually, and morally drained, determined never to fight another war, yet (as would become tragically apparent) they were economically, intellectually, and morally incapable of avoiding a second, even more destructive world war later in the century.

Margaret Sanger Publishes *Family Limitations* (1914)

The Event: In 1914, pioneer birth control advocate Margaret Sanger, a nurse and radical feminist, published a pamphlet for mass distribution that contained explicit instructions for contraception, which led federal authorities to issue a warrant for her arrest for using the U.S. mail to disseminate "obscene" materials.

MARGARET SANGER was born Margaret Higgins in Corning, New York, on September 14, 1883. In 1910, she began working as a nurse in the slums of Manhattan and became active in radical politics, joining the Socialist Party and the Industrial Workers of the World (IWW). Her nursing experience acquainted her firsthand with the desperation that drove impoverished women to self-induced—and often fatal—abortions. In 1912, sponsored by the Socialists, Sanger began to write and speak on sexual and health-related issues to an enthusiastic audience, and it was she who coined the term "birth control." Censorship of one of her columns by U.S. postal authorities in 1913 served only to bring her more attention, and in 1914 she published a radical feminist newspaper called *Woman Rebel*, which was followed by *Family Limitations*, a how-to manual on contraception.

When the publication of *Family Limitations* led to an arrest warrant, Sanger fled to Europe to evade prosecution. There she studied with pioneering sexologist Havelock Ellis and the Dutch feminist physician Aletta Jacobs. When she returned to the United States in 1915, a national birth-control movement was already under way, and charges against her were dropped. However, the next year, Sanger and her sister, Evelyn Byrne, opened a birth-control clinic in Brooklyn—a deliberate act of civil disobedience that resulted in Sanger's arrest. Her highly publicized battle with the law, and the fact that birth-control clinics, legal or not, were opening all across the country, resulted in winning the right of the medical profession to dispense birth-control information to patients.

Sanger was instrumental not only in promoting the cause of birth control, but also in raising the consciousness of women all over the world. By the 1920s, she had distanced herself from left-wing politics and focused on birth control, sometimes even using a eugenic argument in its support, suggesting that it was a way of reducing the birthrate of "inferiors."

Sanger founded the American Birth Control League in 1921, which evolved into Planned Parenthood in 1942.

Her advocacy of eugenics, which betrayed a strain of racism, has made Sanger a highly controversial figure. Planned Parenthood regards Sanger as a modern hero, even as it downplays the history of birth control as a women's rights issue dating from the last century. However, antiabortionists in the 1980s have often used Sanger's racist and eugenic arguments to discredit the very idea of birth control. Sanger's radical feminism and her assertion of a woman's right to regulate reproduction opened possibilities for women that have yet to be fully realized, posing moral challenges that have yet to be resolved.

Germany Turns to Chemical Warfare (1915)

The Event: On April 22, at the Second Battle of Ypres in Belgium, German combat engineers released chlorine gas in the first major poison gas attack of World War I, introducing not only the British soldiers but the world to the horrifying spectacle of chemical warfare.

THE NATIONS OF Europe agreed under the *Hague Declaration of 1899 Concerning Asphyxiating Gases* "to abstain from the use of projectiles the sole object of which is the diffusion of asphyxiating or deleterious gases." Despite this agreement, the French had used tear gas rifle grenades during the first month of the war, and the Germans had used tear gas in artillery shells against the Russians at the end of January 1915. The attack at Ypres was different. It was the first major, deliberate use of deadly poison gas in the war.

Chlorine does its damage by burning tissue. Five thousand troops died that day, clawing at their throats, writhing in pain, and another ten thousand were seriously injured. Large numbers of troops, panic-stricken, deserted the line.

The German triumph did not last long. Chlorine is deadly, but it is easily counteracted, and within days of the attack, the women of London had turned out 300,000 pads of muslin-wrapped cotton to be soaked in hyposulfite, a substance that would neutralize the chlorine. These were the first gas masks—the first defensive measures against chemical warfare.

Three of Germany's most honored scientists, Otto Hahn, Fritz Haber, and James Franck, all of whom would eventually go on to win Nobel prizes, were among the many scientists and technicians who created Germany's gas warfare program. With the Western Front at a standstill, all of the combatants were eager to find a "secret weapon" that would allow a breakthrough. Some of the scientists rationalized their work by reasoning that, if gas would shorten the war, lives would be saved.

Certainly, the French and the British did not delay in creating poison gas weapons of their own, so that by the end of the war some 200,000 tons of chemical warfare substances had been produced—half by the Germans, half by the Allies. The most abundantly produced agent was phosgene, ten times more toxic than chlorine, which was fatal in ten minutes at a concentration of half a milligram per liter of air. Most cruel, perhaps, was the fact that, unlike the foul-smelling chlorine, phosgene had the odor of new-mown hay, which the soldiers, many of whom were raised on farms, instinctively inhaled in deep drafts. Phosgene was carbonyl chloride, which became hydrochloric acid on contact with water. When a soldier breathed it in, the water-saturated tissue of his lungs turned the gas to acid, which dissolved the lining of the lungs. More than 80 percent of the war's deaths from gas were caused by phosgene.

But there were others, too. Chloropicrin, what the British called vomiting gas and the Germans called *klop*, was compounded of picric acid and bleaching powder. It had the advantage of not reacting to many neutralizing agents, which meant that most gas masks were useless against it. Although not lethal in itself, it could be mixed with phosgene. When soldiers would lift their gas masks to vomit, they would breath in the phosgene and die.

Then there was mustard gas, dichlorethyl sulfide, which smelled like horseradish or strong mustard and was first used by Germany on July 17, 1917, again at Ypres. It was the deadliest of the war's gases. The first effects were subtle, nothing more than a sneezing attack. Then came the vomiting, followed by the burning and blistering—inside and out—so intense that the eyelids blistered shut, temporarily blinding the troops. Those who remained in the field soon died. Worst of all, the gas persisted for weeks, and even in low concentrations— when there was no telltale mustard odor—it remained lethal. It ate not only flesh, but leather, cloth, and rubber, so gas masks were of little use. Trace amounts of it, brought in, for example, on the sole of a boot, could diffuse throughout a closed dugout and temporarily blind and disable a platoon. In the spring of 1918, the Germans blended mustard gas with xylol bromide, a form of tear gas that smelled like lilacs. So, for some on the Western Front that year, the first breath of spring was deadly.

Many other gases were developed during the war, including forms of cyanide, potentially the most lethal of all. But, in a century scarred with warfare, World War I was the only major conflict in which poison gas would be used. Mussolini employed it briefly against Ethiopia in the 1930s, and Saddam Hussein used poison gas in his war against rebellious Kurds in Iraq during the 1980s. But none was used in World War II, Korea, or Vietnam, although all nations developed and maintained stockpiles of chemical and biological weapons. Perhaps more significant than the particular weapons produced and used (or not used) was the precedent set by scientists in 1915—Nobel-caliber scientists—working together not to further knowledge, but to end lives in greater numbers and with greater efficiency. Thus in the 1930s and 1940s, Germany's top scientists fashioned the deadly rockets that would rain terror on London, and America's best minds collaborated with even more brilliance to produce a weapon capable of destroying civilization itself.

A German U-boat Sinks the *Lusitania* (1915)

The Event: The *Lusitania*, a British passenger ship, was sunk by a German submarine in the Atlantic on May 7, 1915, with the loss of 1,198 lives, among them 128 Americans, bringing the United States one important step closer to entering World War I on the side of the Allies.

WHEN THE 1914 assassination of Archduke Francis Ferdinand and his wife Sophie plunged Europe into the manifest mass insanity of the Great War, the majority of Americans observed the horror with a thankfulness that a vast ocean separated their nation from the warring parties of the Old World. Some Americans tended to be pro-Allies—especially favoring the British—while others supported the Central Powers, particularly the Germans. Relatively few, however, advocated aid of any kind to either side, and even fewer spoke of active American participation in the "European War."

Yet, even early in the war, stories reached American shores about German atrocities against civilians, particularly in Belgium. Then, in 1915, the Germans warned the international community that they intended to employ their most effective naval weapon, the U-boat, or submarine, against all Allied shipping, including civilian vessels that were often used to carry war materiel in addition to noncombatant passengers. On May 7, 1915, a U-boat, without warning, torpedoed the British liner *Lusitania*, sinking it with massive loss of lives, including 128 Americans.

To the Allies and the United States, the attack was an outrage and a monstrous display of underhanded brutality. The sinking provoked a massive outcry in the United States, and President Woodrow Wilson protested strongly to Germany, demanding reparations and the cessation of unrestricted submarine warfare. The German government justified the action on the grounds that the *Lusitania* carried munitions, which the British denied, but years after the war, the accusation was proven to be true. This was the reason why a single torpedo impact caused a massive explosion that resulted in the vessel's sinking as rapidly as it did. Privately, the German government, fearful that the United States would renounce its neutrality and enter the war on the side of the Allies, ordered German submarines not to sink passenger ships without warning. Despite this measure, relations between the United States and Germany deteriorated. In February 1917, a hard-pressed Germany resumed unrestricted submarine warfare, and, on February 3, the *U.S.S. Housatonic* was torpedoed and sunk without warning. One month later, on March 1, 1917, the American public learned of the so-called Zimmerman Telegram, through which Alfred Zimmerman, Germany's ambassador to Mexico, proposed to the Mexican government a Mexican-German alliance against the United States. On April 2, 1917, President Woodrow Wilson asked Congress for a declaration of war against Germany and the

Central Powers. After eighteen hours of acrimonious debate, the measure passed on April 6, and the United States entered the "War to End All Wars."

For its role in propelling the United States into the "European War," the sinking of the *Lusitania* is momentous enough. However, it was also a horrific demonstration of what warfare had evolved into by the second decade of the twentieth century. The submarine, which had its origin in the ineffectual "Bushnell's Turtle" built by the American inventor David Bushnell early in the American Revolution, had evolved into an example of a new kind of terror weapon, which, unseen and undetectable, could deal instant and massive destruction—impersonally, from a great distance, and seemingly at will.

D. W. Griffith Directs *The Birth of a Nation* (1915)

The Event: Twenty-five years after Thomas Alva Edison invented the first crude motion picture process, American director D. W. Griffith created what many believe to be the single most important and influential film in the development of cinema as an art, *The Birth of a Nation*.

THE FIRST SIGNIFICANT commercial film, directed by Edwin S. Porter for the Edison Company, was *The Great Train Robbery* of 1903. Although extraordinarily crude by today's standards, the film introduced such cinematic conventions as cuts to show parallel and overlapping action and thereby transformed a technological curiosity and vaudeville diversion into a popular art form capable of a tremendous range of expression.

Among the greatest of the pioneering exponents of the new medium was David Wark Griffith, a onetime stock actor, traveling salesman, laborer, and perennially unsuccessful writer until he managed to sell a few scripts to the fledgling Biograph Film Company of New York. By 1908, he was directing several Biograph releases, and by 1913 he virtually ran the company, having directed an amazing total of some 450 films. Not only did this output contribute to the making of Biograph, it was instrumental in the making of Biograph, it was instrumental in creating the American film industry by developing audience demand for relatively high-quality cinematic productions.

Parting company with Biograph in 1913, Griffith joined Reliance-Majestic, where he directed a number of feature-length but perfunctory films as he increasingly devoted himself to the most ambitious motion picture project of the time, the Civil War epic *The Birth of a Nation*.

Originally three hours in length, *The Birth of a Nation* summarized all that was known about filmmaking and added Griffith's own innovations. It was a stunning success, not only drawing international critical praise as a significant work of art, but commanding from audiences the unprecedented admission price of two dollars a ticket in an era when most films could be seen for a nickel or a dime.

If *The Birth of a Nation* demonstrated the emotional power and artistic possibilities of film, it also suggested the medium's potential for political manipulation and abuse. Its vision embodied a racist bias against African-Americans and, in some respects, was an apologia for the Ku Klux Klan. The film was, after all, based upon the novel, *The Clansman*, by Thomas Dixon. Throughout the century, film would reflect even as it helped shape the collective values of various peoples at various times, and nowhere was this more true than in the United States. In the hands of the most unscrupu-

lous political leaders, the medium became a powerful and deliberate instrument for the dissemination of propaganda. Adolf Hitler's propaganda chief Josef Goebbels was a master of the politically manipulative film, and Leni Riefenstahl used her considerable talents as a filmmaker to promote the ideals of Nazism in the 1935 film *Triumph of the Will*, undoubtedly the most powerful propaganda film ever made.

Irish Nationalists Stage an Uprising (1916)

The Event: On Easter Sunday, 1916, a handful of Irish Nationalists staged a not-very-popular revolt in Dublin that the British commander-in-chief, by summarily executing the participants, would make into a rallying point for Ireland's resistance to England's three-hundred-year-old colonial occupation and provoke a crisis that would last nearly the entire twentieth century.

THE "IRISH QUESTION" began to simmer to a boil when England's Liberal Party seemed as if it might finally pass a Home Rule bill for Ireland in 1911. The Irish Protestants reacted by insisting that the Ulster provinces be excluded. Hot-blooded Irish Unionists formed the Ulster Volunteer Force to ensure the Protestant north remained in the union by any means necessary.

The bill failed and back in Ireland, nationalist revolutionaries gained sympathy and support from those alienated by the pro-British Unionists' attitude. By the end of 1914, the Irish Republican Brotherhood had completed its plans for revolution. Sir Roger Casement went to Germany seeking aid, but he managed to obtain only a few obsolete arms, and he was arrested on his return to Ireland on April 21, 1916, pretty much scuttling the nationwide uprising the IRB

had scheduled. Regardless, a handful of the faithful went ahead with the plan to siege Dublin three days after Casement's arrest.

That Easter Sunday was quiet in Dublin. Because it was a holiday, many Dubliners were at the races. Only a few curious passersby looked on with amazement as the rebels stormed the largely deserted General Post Office and rebel leader, Patrick Pearse, declaimed from the front steps: "Irishmen and Irishwomen: In the name God and the dead generations from which she receives her old tradition of nationhood, Ireland, through us, summons her children to her flag and strikes for her freedom." In short, Ireland had just declared its independence from Great Britain.

The Easter Uprising lasted scarcely a week. By Thursday, the British Army had captured strong positions in the city and was shelling the post office. On Saturday, with more than 450 dead and 2,614 wounded, Pearse surrendered. What little initial support there had been for the doomed revolt had by then evaporated, and Dubliners jeered as the rebels were led off in chains. That was when, having quashed the rebellion, General Sir John Maxwell, commander of the British troops, made his big mistake. He summarily ordered the execution of fifteen insurrectionists and ran to ground members of the tiny Sinn Fein, the nationalist organization he presumed was behind the uprising. It mattered less that he was wrong than that he was harsh. His brutality inspired a new patriotism, and Irish citizens joined the Sinn Fein in droves, transforming it into Ireland's most powerful organization, as the slain rebels became martyrs to the cause.

In the wake of the uprising, a surviving leader, Eamon de Valera, came to prominence and demanded a Republican government. A provisional government was set up, elected by Irish members of the British Parliament, and the Irish Republican Army (IRA) was organized to resist British administration and secure official recognition for the Republic. Soon the IRA was engaged in widespread ambushes and attacks on local barracks, and the British retaliated with ruthless reprisals. Most of the Irish police force resigned. The British replaced it with a group of English recruits, known from their temporary uniforms as the Black and Tans. As Ireland descended into something very much resembling civil war, Britain bit by bit alienated Irish public opinion. Soon forced, partly by American pressure,

to pass a Government of Ireland Act of 1920, it continued its bungling by partitioning the island into two administrative regions, each with limited autonomy, which pleased none of various factions and thus merely laid the groundwork for future sectarian violence.

Outraged by the way the north had been divided to create a Protestant majority, the IRA stepped up its guerrilla war against the British. Britain retaliated by imposing martial law and setting loose the Black and Tans. The violence peaked on Bloody Sunday, November 21, 1920. In Dublin that morning, the IRA assassinated eleven men it suspected of being British intelligence agents. The Black and Tans struck back that afternoon, opening fire on a crowd watching a football match in a Dublin park. When the smoke cleared, twelve lay dead, and sixty others were wounded. Across Ireland, hostility toward the British boiled over, and as the terror continued, British Prime Minister David Lloyd George found it was time to revisit the Irish Question. In 1922, Britain granted the twenty-six counties of southern Ireland dominion within the commonwealth, but the partition between those and the six Protestant counties in the north remained.

The 1922 proposal to establish an Irish Free State, ending the Anglo-Irish guerrilla war for the time being, wreaked havoc on Ireland's sense of identity. Free Staters accepted dominion as a step toward true independence. Radical Republicans considered it an insult. Then IRA mastermind Michael Collins signed Lloyd George's treaty and helped set up the new provisional government. Collins, a larger-than-life figure who would inspire the likes of Mao Tse-tung and Yitzhak Shamir, had just signed his own death warrant. IRA diehards, vowing never to accept a separate Northern Ireland, ambushed and killed its former leader in his native Cork County before the year was out. The IRA, born from the ashes of the Easter Uprising, would fight on—said its members—until the whole island was both free and united.

The U.S. Congress Creates the National Park Service (1916)

The Event: On August 25, 1916, the U.S. Congress created the National Park Service, which grew to manage eighty million acres of federal lands earmarked for natural preservation and public enjoyment.

THE ROOTS OF THE National Park Service can be traced to 1864, when the federal government turned over to the state of California land in the Yosemite region to be held "inalienable," as a park for future generations to enjoy. On March 1, 1872, President Ulysses S. Grant created the first truly national park, setting aside some 3,300 square miles of wilderness as Yellowstone Park. In 1890, the federal government added Yosemite, Sequoia, and General Grant national parks, all in California, and in the years leading up to 1916, Mount Rainier (Washington), Crater Lake (Oregon), Mesa Verde (Colorado), Glacier (Montana), Rocky Mountain (Colorado), and Mount Lassen (California) national parks were added to the federal park lands.

At the outset of an industrial century hungry for the raw materials of industry—minerals, water resources, timber, fossil fuels—the national parks movement competed fiercely with mighty commercial interests for control of vast tracts of wilderness. In 1915, conservationists looked to Stephen Tyng Mather, assistant secretary to the secretary of the interior, to direct efforts toward the formal creation of a separate agency to manage what was then 4.75 million acres of national parks—and to acquire more. The nation's railroads, always a powerful lobbying group, allied themselves with the conservationists to create a massive "See America First" campaign, which promoted tourism and, in consequence, the establishment of a National Park Service. When the agency was created, Mather was named director and the important naturalist Horace M. Albright was tapped as his second-in-command. Together, Mather and Albright created the great eastern parks—Acadia, Shenandoah, Great Smoky Mountains, and Everglades—and more western parks, Zion, Bryce, and Grand Teton.

In the course of its seventy-five-year stewardship of the national park lands, the service has enjoyed stretches of autonomy and endured periods of congressional and commercial pressure. It has drawn praise and weathered criticism from all quarters, and must tread the fine line between fulfillment of its mission of recreation and providing for the needs of wilderness and wildlife. Yet, in a century of unprecedented industrial and technological growth, no nation has placed greater value on preserving areas of natural wilderness than the United States, and the National Park Service is both evidence and instrument of a collective resolve to preserve some portion of the earth from the transformations wrought by civilization.

Lenin Leads an "October" Revolution in Russia (1917)

The Event: The first Bolshevik government was officially formed on November 7, 1917, after the overthrow of the provisional government that had replaced the government of the tsars. Vladimir Illyich Lenin was named its chairman. The specter of Communism that had haunted Europe for half a century had at last arrived, spooking the capitalist countries of the industrial west more than perhaps any other event of the century.

LENIN WAS BORN Vladimir Ilyich Ulyanov on April 22, 1870, in Simbirsk (later renamed Ulyanovsk after him) to prosperous middle-class parents (both were teachers by profession), from whom he learned to care about the plight of the impoverished Russian masses. Lenin's older brother Aleksandr became an active revolutionary and, in 1887, was hanged for plotting against the tsar. A profoundly shaken Lenin immersed himself in the works of Karl Marx and other radical political philosophers, but he did not turn immediately to revolutionary activity. After graduating from secondary school, he enrolled at the University of Kazan, from which he was expelled for his growing radicalism. Despite his expulsion, Lenin earned a law degree from the University of St. Petersburg in 1891 and started a law practice in Samara (present-day Kuibyshev).

By 1893, Lenin abandoned his law practice for full-time pursuit of revolutionary activity. Intensely intellectual, he methodically reshaped Marxist theory to fit the conditions he perceived in czarist Russia. Marx had theorized that the seeds of the radical transformation of government lay in emerging industrial capitalism, that industrial workers—unlike agricultural peasants—would spontaneously and inevitably develop a radical group consciousness that would energize a popular political movement. Lenin agreed with Marx that the key to revolution was the radical consciousness of the industrial proletariat, but he observed that the requisite radical consciousness was failing to develop in Russian workers, who still perceived themselves as peasants. The essence of what came to be called Leninism—Lenin's reformulation of Marxist theory—was the creation of political programs through which radical consciousness might be deliberately cultivated among workers. This required the creation of a thoroughly organized revolutionary party, which would inform, persuade, generally agitate, and then direct the proletariat.

At this time, the revolutionary thinker adopted the pseudonym "Lenin," which did not, however, save him from arrest and Siberian exile in 1895. Five years later, he left Russia and published, with Georgy Valentinovich Plekhanov, an underground newspaper called *Iskra* ("The Spark"). In its pages, Lenin argued for an extreme radicalism that spurned common cause with moderates, liberals, or other members of what he identified as the bourgeoisie, who (Lenin argued) would ultimately attempt to assert dominance over workers and peasants. He also developed and promulgated the conviction that the basis for individual liberty would be found not in mere political democracy, but in a social democracy that rendered society entirely classless. In 1902, he expressed these ideas in their final form in his seminal pamphlet *What Is to be Done?* and created within the Russian Social Democratic Labor Party the radical Bolshevik wing during 1903.

From the Bolsheviks Lenin sought to create a revolutionary vanguard, which he forged over the long period from 1903 to the revolutionary year of 1917. He returned to Russia during 1905–1907, but his most intense revolutionary activity was conducted in exile, in London, Paris, Geneva, and other European cities as he ruthlessly condemned the Social Democratic revolutionaries who did not share his radicalism. He called them the minority (Mensheviks) in contrast to his own majority (Bolshevik) faction, even though the Mensheviks actually outnumbered the Bolsheviks.

As the disastrous Russo-Japanese War of 1905 had precipitated an abortive revolution in that year, so the even greater disasters of World War I sparked the revolutions of 1917. The tsar personally led his armies to defeat, humiliation, and massive loss. At home, the government was allowed to drift. Severe food shortages provoked street demonstrations in Petrograd on March 8, 1917. Ordered to suppress the demonstrations, the garrison soldiers mutinied. Leaders of the Duma (the parliament established after the 1905 revolution) demanded that Nicholas II transfer power to a parliamentary government. With the Petrograd Soviet of Workers' and Soldiers' Deputies, a special Duma committee on March 15 established a provisional government headed by the liberal Prince Georgi Lvov. On the same day, Nicholas abdicated and attempted to give the crown to his brother Michael, who, exercising the better part of valor, refused it. With that, the three hundred-year-old Romanov dynasty came to an end.

The March Revolution brought a provisional government. But despite mild reforms, the liberals were out of touch with the war-weary population, who turned to the powerful Soviets when they promised to end the war with Germany immediately. In October 1917, Lenin's party came to power in a virtually bloodless coup, and signed a separate peace with Berlin.

Lenin soon had to cope with splinter groups and outright civil war, which raged from the Black Sea to the Caspian Sea, with the Whites (monarchists), who opposed the Reds (Communists), gaining support from the nations allied against Germany. The bitter and destructive war lasted until 1921, when the Whites were finally defeated, leaving the Russian economy in shambles and prompting Lenin to retreat from Marxist absolutism by granting economic concessions to foreign capitalists and reinstituting some private enterprise.

Lenin's invitation would have been welcomed by the capitalist countries had he not set to work to extend the Communist revolution to the rest of the world. This agenda turned much of the world against Soviet Russia and established the battle lines of one of the basic ideological struggles that would dominate the century at least through the 1980s.

By the end of the Russian Civil War, Lenin was installed as absolute dictator of the Soviet Union, but his control of the Communist Party was torn by rivalries and disputes. Wounded by an assassin's bullet in 1918, Lenin's health deteriorated, and he suffered a severe stroke on May 25, 1922. Weakened and partially paralyzed, he never fully recovered, and he died on January 21, 1924, at which time control of the party passed to Josef Stalin, who brutally crushed dissent, even within the Bolshevik party, turning the revolution—for a time—inward.

An International Flu Epidemic Breaks Out (1918)

The Event: The worst pandemic of modern times originated, probably, with soldiers returning to Europe from Indo-China in March 1918 near the end of World War I. Infected with the influenza virus, they helped the disease to spread throughout the world, turning it into a modern plague that killed some 20 million people—about the same number as the casualties of the war itself—before it had run its course.

THE WORD INFLUENZA is Italian, derived from the medieval Latin *influentia*, meaning "influence" and reflecting an astrological belief that the disease was the result of the influence of the stars. Like the word, the disease was hardly new to the twentieth century, even in epidemic form. As recently as 1889–1890, a pandemic—that is, an epidemic of worldwide proportions—originated in China and swept through Europe. The outbreak that began in Europe in March 1918, also believed to have originated in China, developed into a pandemic of devastating proportions.

The vehicle that carried flu in 1918 was war. Those who witnessed the horrors of the

Great War saw the sum total of early twentieth-century industry, science, and technology directed against the very civilization that had brought industry, science, and technology to an advanced state of development. The new means of mass destruction—the machine gun, poison gas, the tank, the airplane—made World War I the first truly modern war. But, since the days of Alexander the Great and before, war had often brought in its wake a killer more deadly than any man-made weapon: disease. And, in this respect, World War I proved to be a very ancient war indeed.

At first, the disease was called the "three-day fever" among armies on the

Western Front. By the autumn of 1918, American soldiers were dying from it at the rate of 250 *per day*—far more than the number who fell victim to German bullets. The outbreak on the battlefield was the second wave of the pandemic, which followed a summer lull after the initial onslaught of early spring. It was carried back to the United States by soldiers returning from Europe, and it hit, first in Boston, with a terrible rate of mortality. In October and November 1918, 20 percent of those infected died of pulmonary complications within a few hours of falling ill. In the dozen large American cities for which the U.S. Public Health Service kept records, 22 percent of the population caught the flu. By the time a

third and final wave swept the world and America, between January and March 1919, twenty million Americans had contracted the disease, of whom more than half a million died, *not* including the fifty thousand soldiers who also succumbed—a figure that represents more than half of all American military casualties in the war (the battle deaths totaled 48,909).

War and disease visited the second decade of the century with apocalyptic fury, and the flu pandemic may well have left a more lasting legacy of misery by causing a pandemic of encephalitis in the 1920s that led, decades later, to unusually high incidences of Parkinson's and Alzheimer's disease.

Rosa Luxemburg Is Murdered (1919)

The Event: In 1918, on the heels of Kaiser Wilhelm's hasty departure from Germany, young leftist revolutionaries formed the Spartacus League and moved to take over the tottering government, only to find their leaders—Rosa Luxemburg and Karl Liebknecht—murdered and their rebellion crushed by the gangsterish German Freikorps in January 1919. Instead of the workers' democracy imagined by those participating in the Spartacus Revolt, postwar Germany would be governed by the weak and decadent Weimar Republic, installed with the aid of men who despised it, the same men who within a decade would help boost Adolf Hitler to dictatorial power.

IT WAS NOT A proletarian vanguard nor the natural collapse of capitalism under the weight of its own social contradictions, but years of senseless slaughter at the behest of arrogant leaders indifferent to the effect of their decisions on the lives of those they ruled that galvanized the masses of workers, peasants, and soldiers of the world into a series of spontaneous uprisings throughout Europe as World War I drew to a close. In Russia, the

relatively tiny Bolshevik Party ultimately took control of the inchoate mass revolt in 1917, calling for the end of the war and turning chaotic protest into social revolution. But in Germany, the leading party on the left was the Social Democrats, who had supported the nation's war effort and who could not tolerate the kind of radical changes being attempted by the Bolsheviks and being proposed by some German communists.

The situation in Germany was desperate enough. The Kaiser had fled and the Junker leaders of a defeated German army were keeping a low profile. Workers and common soldiers organized into councils called *Rates*, Germany's version of Russia's "soviets," and took control of the factories and the streets. Gangs of petty thugs and mercenaries ranged about at night, preying where and when they could on defenseless citizens and the propagandizing revolutionaries. The government was being run, more or less, by a six-man Council of Peoples' Deputies. Though revolution was in the air, the council seized no property and conducted no purges of the old regime's once-powerful bureaucracy or the military caste that had led the country into war. The moderate head of the cautious Social Democrats, Friedrich Ebert, dominated the council, which set January 19, 1919, for election to a new National Assembly and looked to the old regime's military officers—unscathed by the carnage they had created on the road to an inglorious defeat that should have discredited them—to provide security.

Ebert was the kind of reformist who feared social revolution more than right-wing reaction, and when the People's Marine Division—a thousand sailors strong, joined by a equal number of supporters—showed up in Berlin in December of 1918 to back the more radical three Independent Socialists on the council against Ebert and his Social Democrats, Ebert feared a Bolshevik-style coup was in the making. He turned to the Junkers, creating a fatal alliance that would cause blood to run in the streets of Berlin and pave the way for the rise of the Nazi Party. Ebert asked the sailors to leave Berlin; they mutinied instead. He ordered loyal troops to remove them. Thousands of demonstrators filled the streets, forcing Ebert's troops to withdraw, and the outraged Independents on the ruling Council of Peoples' Deputies resigned in protest. With them gone, the council fired Berlin's police chief, an Independent Socialist, and once again radicals took to the streets, this time led by the week-old Communist Party. Ebert had conjured the very coup he feared. The Communist Party was headed by the far-left faction of Germany's Marxist revolutionaries, the once-tiny Spartacus League, and when party leaders declared that the council was deposed and they would assume power in its stead, the putsch became known as the Spartacus Revolt.

The Communists themselves were divided on the question of whether Germany was ripe for a complete revolution. Even if it was, Rosa Luxemburg—founder of the Spartacus League, one of Europe's most eloquent leftist leaders, and Lenin's only true theoretical rival in the international communist movement—opposed on principle the Bolshevik's dictatorial and terrorist tactics. She was overruled by Karl Liebknecht, a former Social Democrat legislator and cofounder of the Spartacus League, who was for a Bolshevik-inspired takeover. Ebert panicked in any case. For some time, the German Minister of Defense Gustav Noske had been organizing Germany's street gangs into a mercenary force he called the Freikorps. Mostly made up of disgruntled former imperial troops thrown out in the cold without pay when the war abruptly ended, the gangs had from the beginning been under the clandestine control of members of the former Kaiser's officer caste. Ebert authorized Noske to call in the Freikorps. "I guess somebody has to play the pig," responded Noske.

And play the pig he did. Freikorps troops murdered both Luxemburg and Liebknecht on January 19, 1919, the day of the national elections. They attacked the mobs in the streets with a vengeance, busting heads and breaking bones, looting, and raping. Over the next two months, they killed some twelve hundred Berliners before viciously crushing a rebellion in Bavaria. During the elections, Ebert was swept into office on the tide of reaction, becoming president of a new republican government temporarily housed in Weimar, hometown of Germany's great Romantic poet Goethe, while Berlin was being cleaned up for Ebert's return. The Weimar Republic's constitution was the most liberal in the world, but it was written in the blood spilled by the very thugs who would become Adolf Hitler's brown-shirt stormtroopers, and the entire German military establishment was in the hands of men who not only despised liberalism, socialism, and Communism, but also hated the very concept of democracy.

The Eighteenth Amendment Brings Prohibition (1919)

The Event: In 1919, the Eighteenth Amendment was ratified by a sufficient number of state legislatures to become the law of the land, plunging the country into what U.S. President Herbert Hoover would call a "noble experiment," but that American citizens described more soberly as "Prohibition."

IT LASTED FROM January 1920 to April 1933: a constitutional ban on the manufacture, sale, distribution, and consumption of alcoholic beverages anywhere in the United States. It had been years in the making. Prohibition was the crowning triumph of a fundamentalist movement, which, since the middle of the nineteenth century, had been slowly and certainly winning the hearts and minds of the nation's rural population, which considered the confusing welter of urban life to be a cauldron of sin in which the primary ingredient was alcohol. Throughout the nineteenth century, the Temperance Movement was its chief beneficiary.

By 1855, the manufacture and sale of alcoholic beverages had been outlawed in thirteen of the thirty-one states. During the Civil War and Reconstruction period, however, the dominant Republican Party refrained from taking a stance favoring prohibition, fearing that doing so would weaken its control of government at both the state and federal levels. Yet, in the 1870s, various women's groups banded together as the Woman's Christian Temperance Union, and began a concerted crusade against liquor. In 1895, members of the newly created Anti-Saloon League succeeded in influencing state and local elections in favor of "dry" candidates, and by 1916, twenty-one state legislatures had outlawed saloons. That year, too, voters sent a "dry" majority to Congress. These Congressmen secured the passage of the Eighteenth Amendment, which was submitted to the states for ratification in December 1917.

Once the states ratified the amendment, the Volstead Act gave it the legal teeth necessary for enforcement, and the Prohibition Bureau went into operation, fielding 1,500 to 3,000 agents instructed to find and bring to justice all those engaged in the illegal liquor trade.

The Eighteenth Amendment was a "noble experiment," intended to create a nation of hard-working, sober, responsible citizens. In reality, what it did, with remarkable speed, was to transform a nation of basically law-abiding citizens into a nation of lawbreakers. In the big cities, Prohibition had been consistently voted down, and in urban America the new law was consistently violated. Neighborhood folk set up stills in their basements, brewing bathtub gin and other alcoholic concoctions. Within the neighborhoods, informal networks quickly developed: Grocers stocked the raw materials necessary to brew moonshine. Former saloon keepers, restaurant owners, and ice cream and soft drink parlor operators helped local bootleggers distribute their wares. And that wasn't all. The friendly cop on the beat usually didn't like the law any more than the citizens, so, routinely, he looked the other way. When higher authorities periodically moved in to conduct surprise raids, usually the neighborhood was informed well in advance.

But the liquor business was not all a mom-and-pop affair. Even before the Eighteenth Amendment went into effect, the urban underworld geared up to supply what they knew would be a tremendously lucrative demand for an illegal medium of indulgence. And certain elements among the underworld realized that meeting the demand effectively would require a degree of organization hitherto unheard of in criminal activity. Thus began the amendment's most enduring legacy to twentieth-century America: organized crime.

The mobsters began by moving in on the mom-and-pop operations. The gangsters, like those they preyed on, were immigrants, but they were ruthless and brutal, and convinced that crime was the quickest way of "making it" in America. They began by extorting protection money from the illegal traffickers and brutalizing the uncooperative. Within a short time, though, the gangs scrapped their protection schemes in favor of outright control of all liquor production and smuggling as well as distribution, including illicit bars, saloons, and nightclubs through a network of "speakeasies." Rival gangs, their members often no more than teenagers, battled each other for territorial control, making liberal use of sawed-off shotguns and Thompson submachine guns ("Tommy guns"), which were cheap and available in quantity as U.S. government surplus.

The mainstream press, pandering to its nativist, middle-class audience, tried to make a racial issue out of the crime wave that Prohibition created in the major American cities, and their headlines announced almost weekly yet another Sicilian gang war or the discovery of one more illegal warehouse in this or that town's Little Italy. But the first well-known mobster in New York was an Englishman, Owney Madden, and the second a Jew, Arnold Rothstein. The Irish and Germans, too, had their own highly formidable gangs in most every major city. The mobsters worked hand in glove with local political machines, securing votes and furnishing graft in return for protection from police interference. They poured their profits into clubs to play jazz over the machine-gun rat-tat-tat in the background, and the Jazz Age was born in the speakeasies of Prohibition. The deals struck in the mean streets of the Jazz Age steadily percolated up the power structure, until much of the country's political administration and law enforcement had been corrupted and co-opted. Thus Prohibition not only organized crime, it forged links between it and other American institutions that have yet to be broken.

George Herman "Babe" Ruth Becomes a Star after the "Black Sox" Scandal Rocks Baseball (1919)

The Event: New York and Boston gangsters bribed eight members of the Chicago White Sox to throw the World Series of 1919. The public scandal that resulted threatened the integrity of the game Americans had come to regard as their national pastime, which prepared the way for the almost mindless adulation baseball fans would heap on the young Babe Ruth when he batted his way into the league the following year.

B Y THE FIRST DECADE of the twentieth century, Americans had long looked to baseball, played on the freshly groomed grass of stadiums often built in the midst of urban squalor, as an oasis of pastoral innocence in a world of speed, pressure, frustration, and corruption. The game had developed in the heart of the city, where gangs of urban youths had since the early decades of the nineteenth century played "rounder" or "one o' cat." They began to call the games generically "baseball" sometime before one of the youth gangs organized as the Knickerbocker Base Ball Club and wrote the first rule book in 1845.

Metropolitan New York became the baseball capital of the world, boasting dozens of Manhattan and Brooklyn clubs who were followed by a strange breed of promoters called "sportswriters" and by a growing number of fans. With the help of an adoring press, the club games—at first local entertainments and occasions for civic pride—would become the self-proclaimed "national pastime." The need of these small businesses to attract paying crowds led them to look far and wide for first-rate players, and the remarkable success of the undefeated Cincinnati Red Stockings' national tour during the 1869 season widened the growing economic gap between club owners and the game's players.

By 1876, club owners had formed the National League of Professional Base Ball Clubs, which was nothing less than a Gilded Age monopoly or "trust." Through the league, owners controlled the market by granting franchises, and they ruthlessly exploited the players using the infamous "reserve rule," a system of fines, blacklisting, salary limits, pay reductions, and even the use of antilabor Pinkerton agents. A Players League, formed in 1890 by unionized players, failed to break the monopoly because their own financial backers sold them out to the National League, which ruled baseball virtually unchallenged for decades. Only the American League, formed in 1901, managed to compete effectively with the National League by appealing to immigrant and working-class fans, charging less for tickets (a quarter versus fifty cents), selling beer in the ball park, and instituting Sunday afternoon games.

Unquestionably a big business, baseball was frequently plagued by scandal, being charged with game "fixing" as early as 1865. In 1877, the St. Louis Browns were ejected from the National League for throwing games. But the biggest blow came in 1919, with the revelation that eight members of the Chicago White Sox had taken bribes from New York and Boston gangsters to take a dive in the 1919 World Series, throwing it to Cincinnati, the team on which the gangsters had laid their wagers. The connection between the national pastime and organized crime threatened to end professional baseball forever, but the timely appointment of the prominent Judge Kenesaw Mountain Landis as commissioner of base-

ball brought a reprieve. Landis worked vigorously to restore the integrity of the game by enforcing strict regulations on player integrity. At this time, too, the commissioner approved the use of a livelier baseball with a new cork and rubber core, which dramatically increased the frequency of crowd-thrilling home runs.

But what really brought baseball back into the hearts and minds of American fans was the appearance on the scene of a genuine sports hero the year after the scandal, one George Herman Ruth, whom everyone called "Babe."

When the New York Yankees paid Babe Ruth $125,000 for his contract in 1920, they launched a golden age in baseball that has rarely, if ever, been equaled in sports history before or since.

Ruth's accomplishments in the 1920s were the stuff of legend. In 1921 he hit an amazing fifty-nine home runs, and in 1923, 1927, and 1928, he led his team to world championships. When Yankee Stadium opened in New York City in 1923, the city's sportswriters dubbed it "The House That Ruth Built." In short, the Yankees were the marvel of the decade, and Ruth was the marvel of the Yankees. Even today many consider the 1927 Yankees the greatest baseball team of all time—small wonder, since that was the year the Babe hit sixty home runs (still the record for a 154-game season). And perhaps because it was the 1920s, even Ruth's less heroic qualities— his womanizing, carousing, and profligate spending of what, by the standards of the time, was an enormous salary—only fed the public's apparently insatiable appetite for more news, however outrageous, about the already legendary figure.

In time, of course, Babe Ruth's, exuberant habits and the stiff-necked public piety of baseball's new commissioner were bound to come into conflict, and the Babe's later career was marred by numerous brawls with the institution of baseball and even touchy spats with baseball's always demanding fans, a syndrome that would become more familiar as sports figures routinely became celebrities, from Pete Rose to Michael Jordan. But no one (except the thoroughly unlikable Ty Cobb) ever played the game of baseball better than Babe Ruth played it in the 1920s, and fans never appreciated a player more than baseball fans appreciated the Babe in the wake of the Black Sox scandal.

H. L. Mencken Publishes *The American Language* (1919)

The Event: Journalist, writer, and acidic social critic H. L. Mencken published the first of four editions (and two supplements) of his monumental study of American idioms and expressions, providing America with a crucial, if acerbic, new sense of its own identity.

THE UNITED STATES declared its political independence in 1776, yet, despite generations of highly significant writers, philosophers, and artists, the nation remained in many respects an *intellectual* colony of Europe well into the twentieth century, habitually deferring to the Old World in most matters of culture. In 1919, the iconoclastic essayist and journalist H. L. Mencken published the first edition of *The American Language*, the greatest single-author work on the English language since Dr. Samuel Johnson wrote his famed *Dictionary* in 1755.

If Ralph Waldo Emerson, Nathaniel Hawthorne, Herman Melville, and Walt Whitman gave America its own truly independent literature in the nineteenth century, Mencken bestowed upon the nation its own language in the twentieth. His book is a witty, scholarly compendium and study of the richness of American speech at its most common and most eloquent. Mencken, in effect, probed and preserved the very fabric of the national culture, adding a significant dimension to American identity.

The Treaty of Versailles Ends the Great War (1919)

The Event: Concluded on June 28, 1919, the Treaty of Versailles ended the Great War, but imposed punitive and crippling conditions on Germany, which paved the way to another worldwide conflict. Shortly afterward, U.S. President Woodrow Wilson's cherished League of Nations, given birth by the treaty, was rejected by the U.S. Senate, ensuring that it, too, would fail as a forum designed to avert future war.

THE UNITED STATES entered World War I late but effectively broke the stalemate of the Western Front and brought defeat to Germany.

U.S. President Wilson was determined that the war not be fought in vain. On January 8, 1918, before American troops were even actively engaged in combat, he described to Congress his Fourteen Points for peace, as far as the interests of the United States were concerned. Announced in the tones of a higher moralism typical of the reform-minded American Progressive movement that had initially swept Wilson into office, the points included the elimination of secret treaties (the kind of interlocking secret alliances that many—blaming a symptom for the cause—thought led to war in the first place), freedom of the seas, withdrawal of invading armies and restoration of occupied territories, adjustment of borders, and the establishment of a general association of the world's nations to ensure the political independence and territorial integrity of all states, regardless of size.

When, following the Armistice of November 11, 1918, it came time to hammer out a formal treaty, President Wilson wanted to base it on the idealism of his Fourteen Points. Put off by the sanctimonious demands of the American president, French Prime Minister Georges Clemenceau remarked scornfully that "ten commandments were enough for God Almighty." To European eyes jaded by centuries of internecine warfare, the American moralizing seemed hypocritical, and the United States's assertions about the purity of its motives, based on an almost ingrained belief in its own innocence, seemed at best naive, at worst a mere pose. France was not interested in the American crusade for "good government," nor did it want to extend a helping hand to the vanquished out of the goodness of its heart. What France wanted was a treaty that would punish, cripple, and weaken its traditional Great Power rival, Germany, forever. Clemenceau saw Germany as the sole instigator of the war, and also saw that much of France, nominally among the victors, lay in ruin. He demanded gargantuan financial reparations from Germany, complete disarmament, abrogation of the Treaty of Brest Litovsk (in which Soviet Russia had ceded large tracts of Eastern Europe to Germany), and the installation of French garrisons in the Rhineland. His was a draconian peace in the tradition of European wars fought among the continent's ruling classes. Clemenceau underestimated the damage the war had done to Europe's ability to form legitimate governments. Not only had the Great War destroyed for good the political claims of the old European aristocracy, but it had also laid bare the destructive potential of a world dominated by unchecked capitalism. Clemenceau sought to treat Germany as if it were a matter yet again of limiting the territorial ambitions of its Hapsburg royalty, and in doing so he missed the point that Wilson's protocols—stripped of their American moral baggage—were a way of establishing liberal democracies that could function in the place of the discredited ancient regimes.

British Prime Minister David Lloyd George attempted to navigate a conciliatory course between Wilson and Clemenceau.

The Germans and Austro-Hungarians could only wait to see what terms the victors would dictate.

Although the final treaty was less punitive than Clemenceau had proposed, Germany lost all of its colonial possessions. It lost much that it had held or gained in the east. It restored Alsace and Lorraine to France in the west. The Austro-Hungarian Empire was dismantled, and heavy reparations were levied. Disarmament was extensive, and Clemenceau did get his garrisons in the Rhineland. As for Wilson, he managed to salvage the most important of his Fourteen Points: written into the Treaty of Versailles was the intent to create a League of Nations.

The treaty was concluded on June 28, 1919. But just as Wilson had not consulted the other Allies before promulgating his Fourteen Points back in January of 1918, neither had he conferred with the U.S. Senate before creating the League of Nations. Wilson needed a two-thirds majority to ratify the treaty—and the League—in the Senate. Most Democrats were on his side, but Henry Cabot Lodge of Massachusetts, playing to the traditionally strong isolationist sentiment among the American people and insisting that the treaty was a threat to American sovereignty, led the Republican opposition to the treaty. In a set of proposals called the Lodge Reservations, he declared that Congress, based on its constitutional treaty-making authority, should have the right to decide when to abide and when not

to abide by any decision made by the League. In addition, he held that Congress could vote to ignore the League's commitment to the political independence and territorial integrity of the signatories.

Wilson, for his part, having given way so often at Versailles, stubbornly refused to make any compromise with Lodge. Instead, he took his case to the American people by making a 9,500-mile speaking tour of the nation, beginning on September 4, 1919. On September 25, he collapsed in Pueblo, Colorado, was rushed back to Washington, and there suffered a crippling stroke on October 2. Incapacitated, he nevertheless insisted that his followers brook no compromise, and the debate dragged on until July 2, 1921, when Congress resolved that war with Germany and the other Central Powers was indeed concluded, but that the United States would not participate in the League of Nations. Doomed from the start without America, the League was little more than a Franco-British committee.

The mistakes of Versailles would prove costly, creating a world in which international corporations flourished while national governments were racked by revolutions both from the extreme right and the extreme left. It especially fed a virulent and clandestine nationalism in Germany that was particularly dangerous to international stability. Twenty years later, when Nazi troops captured the French archives, they seized the master copy of the Treaty of Versailles and publicly burned it.

America Becomes an Urban Society (1920)

The Event: The U.S. Census of 1920 revealed that for the first time more people lived in cities than on farms, documenting a historical phenomenon that had begun with the birth of the Industrial Age (in America during the nineteenth century and in Europe a century earlier) but reached its apotheosis after 1900. By the 1920s, the "metropolis" fired the imagination and dominated the cultures and the societies of the twentieth century.

AT LEAST SINCE Thomas Jefferson, Americans had taken pride in the notion that they were a nation of farmers, and nineteenth-century American ideologues had invented a myth based on that pride to explain the growth and development of the country. According to the myth of the frontier, American pioneers marched into a great wilderness and secured it for civilization from nature and the native savages. They were followed by settlers—farmers—who actually built the civilization that then produced a few great cities to serve as their entrepôts. In reality, urban centers usually came first, radiating farmers outward just as far as the lines of supply and communication they could provide would stretch. Most of America's great cities grew out of these urban centers in the rapidly industrializing nineteenth century. Ringed by small towns and agricultural communities, American cities were what they had always been: seats of government, financial centers, industrial complexes, cultural meccas, business headquarters, and home to a great mass of workers and the impoverished.

In the early decades of the twentieth century three inventions greatly accelerated the urbanization that in the late nineteenth century already had begun to pull people from their farms toward the big city. The widespread production of cheap automobiles first introduced by Henry Ford vastly improved the mobility of people previously dependent on urban mass transportation; the commercial development of radio greatly increased the power of mass communication, once limited to urban newspapers; and the moving picture camera spawned a huge industry that immensely influenced the mass culture that had first developed in the previous century. Through the radio the siren call of the saxophone beckoned the young in the back parlors and the small-town cafes to jump in their roadsters and head for a speakeasy or a blind pig in the city. On the silver screen, Gloria Swanson, Clara Bow, Rudolph Valentino, and Douglas Fairbanks showed them how to act once they got there. The car, the radio, and the picture show broke down the isolation of rural life and dispelled the claustrophobic atmosphere of Main Street culture, precipitating the decline of small towns and the depopulation of the rural countryside. When the bank foreclosed on the mortgage or the local dry goods merchant cut back on staff, one could go to where the jobs were—in the big city. When the young and the poor left, they never came back. Books like Sherwood Anderson's *Winesburg, Ohio*, dissected the small-town life now in decline, while F. Scott Fitzgerald's *The Beautiful and the Damned*, *The Great Gatsby*, and *Tender Is the Night* extolled the high life and traced the costs of urban life during what he called the Jazz Age. A vogue for Freud and a new faith in everything scientific and new marked such an age, when the old sexual mores of the Victorian Age were being overturned and the young were revolting against family life. In the city, the young could sleep with whom they wanted, drink, spend all night listening to music, or join the Communist Party.

Others reacted with fear to this modern world. To the folks back home, the music and glamour, the excitement and danger that attracted the young to the city seemed based entirely on demon alcohol served by loose-living men and women in sleazy bars and glitzy nightclubs belonging to violence-prone gangsters hosting the rich and the reckless who cared more for gossip than they did for the gospel—and, of course,

they were dead right. The reaction to urbanization helped spawn Nazism in Germany, fascism in Italy and France, and nativism in America. And by the time those immensely destructive anti-urban movements had run their course, the very things that had made metropolis the center of twentieth-century life had begun to undo their work. After the war, cheap housing in the suburbs became viable in part because of the mobility provided by the automobile and the widespread means of mass communication and mass culture, such as television and telephones. White America moved halfway back to the small town, and the big city became a burned-out shell where the violent preyed on the poor. For those of us raised on the late twentieth-century demonizing of the American downtown, we should remember that the city once promised for almost everyone what it still promises to the youthful and the adventuresome: not only alienation and fear but also sophistication and individual freedom.

The Great Black Migration to the Cities Begins (1920)

The Event: Around 1920, African-Americans living in the American South, dislocated by the Great War in Europe, chased from their work as sharecroppers and tenant farmers by International Harvestor's introduction of the row tractor, and seeking the low-paying jobs that opened up when Henry Ford hooked industry on the assembly line, began migrating to the nation's city's en masse, changing utterly the demography, culture, and political landscape of America.

A FRICAN-AMERICANS had been leaving the hardscrabble life to which they were condemned in the Jim Crow South since the end of the Civil War, heading for cities filled with a growing number of East-

ern European and Irish immigrants. By the end of the second decade of the twentieth century, more people lived in those cities than in America's rural communities. Yet the majority of the country's black population still lived in the agrarian South, until a series of conditions turned the trickle of blacks northward into a great flood comprising one of the most remarkable internal migrations in history.

World War I accelerated the assembly-line production techniques introduced by Henry Ford when he first started turning out Model Ts by the hundreds. Factories in the North's industrial regions could offer low-paying semiskilled or unskilled jobs to the country's poorest, and they could travel to those jobs easily in increasingly abundant cheap transportation, on the newly built good roads that accommodated the growing number of internal-combustion engine vehicles.

Henry Ford had not only transformed American industry and small-town life with his assembly-line cars, he had also changed American agriculture with the world's first mass-produced tractors. In 1915 gasoline-powered tractors had been so expensive and unwieldy that less than 1 percent of U.S. farms used them. By March of 1918, the Ford Motor Company was producing eighty cheap Fordson tractors a day, scarcely a year after their invention. The new tractors allowed American farmers to meet the soaring demands of a war-torn Europe as former draught horses and farm boys were shipped off to fight. By the early 1920s, International Harvestor was in a heated competition with Ford, essentially running the automobile maker out of the market with its introduction of a gasoline-powered row tractor in 1922.

At first, Americans praised the technological changes, which had after all helped

them win World War I. Land formerly reserved for feed could now grow crops, and for the first time crop surpluses became normal. But as the changes accelerated throughout the 1920s, their downside became more apparent. Surpluses brought low prices, but farmers could not cut production since they needed to sell everything they could to pay for the new equipment. As they expanded, they specialized, growing dependent on chemical fertilizers and pesticides. Family farms went bankrupt, and corporate agribusinesses bought up the bank-foreclosed farms. As tenant farming and sharecropping spread among whites, black tenant farmers and sharecroppers were forced out of fields that required ever-fewer hands to bring in a crop. Almost a third (32.5 percent) of American workers were engaged in agriculture in 1910; a decade later barely a fourth (25.6 percent) were. Displaced farmers swelled the cities, and so did farmhands rendered obsolete by mechanization.

A good many of the latter were African-Americans. They poured into the segregated neighborhoods of the North's urban centers—New York's Harlem, Chicago's South Side—by the millions. It was no accident that the Harlem Renaissance occurred in the 1920s, nor that Chicago and Kansas City became centers for blues and jazz, as New York and New Orleans already had.

The Great Depression fed the migration. Even after the federal government began granting subsidies to farmers, the biggest beneficiaries were large landowners, driven by the logic of economics to increase mechanization. And World War II, which brought the Depression to an end, also stimulated further migration because it spawned a growing number of industrial jobs at the same time that it created a labor shortage.

Some African-Americans, of course, prospered in the cities. And even those who did not reported the relative openness of northern society to their families back home, and praised the greater opportunities and the increased—if still quite limited—freedom of the cities. Recent studies have showed that even as the black urban ghettos of postwar America swelled into urban hells of neglect and poverty, the highways be-tween the rural South and the country's tarnished cities continued to draw new recruits for what many feared was becoming a permanent urban underclass. For the jobs in the city, too, had vanished, just as they once had long ago on the farms. By 1990 fewer than 3 percent of Americans of any color worked on farms, the black middle class had deserted the inner cities, and wealthy whites were busy barricading themselves in a world of private communities, private schools, private police, private health care, and even private roads, all walled off from the spreading squalor beyond.

Gandhi Launches a Nonviolent Protest (1920)

The Event: After assuming leadership of the Indian National Congress, Mohandas Karamchand Gandhi developed a doctrine of "Progressive Nonviolent Noncooperation," which he put into practice in 1920 against the British as a tactic for achieving independence from the Empire, profoundly affecting the nature of antigovernment protests around the world throughout the twentieth century.

GANDHI WAS BORN in Porbandar, India, on October 2, 1869, the son of the chief minister for the maharajah of Porbandar. From his mother, a devout Jainist, he first imbibed ideas of nonviolence and vegetarianism. Gandhi went to London to study law when he was eighteen and was admitted to the bar in 1891, practicing in Bombay before moving to South Africa, where he worked for an Indian firm from 1893 to 1914. The racism of South Africa propelled Gandhi into activism on behalf of the country's Indian community, and in South Africa he first experimented with the tactics and principles of nonviolent resistance. Gandhi called the kind of personal resistance he promoted *satyagraha* ("steadfastness in truth"). It involved a moral stance much like that described by Henry David Thoreau in the essay "On Civil Disobedience," which discusses Thoreau's nonviolent protest against the United States' war with Mexico in the 1840s.

Returning to India in January 1915, Gandhi became a labor organizer. The April 13, 1919, Amritsar Massacre, in which troops commanded by British general Reginald Dyer fired on Indians peacefully demonstrating against the repressive Rowlatt Acts, resulted in 379 deaths and some 1,200 injuries. The event turned Gandhi from labor issues to direct political protest, and within a year he was the leading figure in the most important Indian independence party, the Indian National Congress. Gandhi led the Congress to demand *purna swaraj* ("complete independence") and developed his South African tactics of nonviolent civil disobedience and noncooperation to gain this end. Gandhi and others, who led strikes, boycotts, and other dramatic demonstrations, were frequently imprisoned. Gandhi even turned imprisonment into an instrument of protest, resorting to widely publicized hunger strikes as part of his program of civil disobedience. By the 1930s, Britain had made some concessions. Gandhi was imprisoned a final time from 1942 to 1944, when he demanded the complete withdrawal of the British in the "Quit India" movement of World War II.

Unlike many leaders of mass movements during the century, Gandhi refused to let political ends obscure the human needs of those for whom he struggled. In addition to working for political independence, he campaigned to improve the lot of the lowest of India's low, the casteless Untouchables, whom he called *harijans* ("children of God"). He also set an example of humility that was foreign to virtually all of the era's political leaders. A fragile-looking ascetic, he believed in the virtues of manual labor and simple living (again, like Thoreau of *Walden Pond*), devoting much time to spinning the thread and weaving the cloth for his own garments. He persistently argued with those leaders who wanted India to industrialize.

Gandhi and the movement he fostered

and led ultimately prevailed, because Great Britain, subtly but persistently pressed by the United States after World War II to give up much of its empire, granted India's independence in 1947. Yet this victory was tempered by what Gandhi took as his personal failure to unite India's Hindu majority with the nation's many minorities, especially the Muslims. Gandhi could not dissuade Muslim leader Muhammad Ali Jinnah from persuading Britain to sanction the partition of a separate Muslim state of Pakistan from India. Gandhi launched a new mass movement against the partition, and while he was leading a march in Delhi on January 30, 1948, he was assassinated—not by a Muslim, but by a deluded Hindu, who thought his protest of partition was both pro-Muslim and pro-Pakistan.

Gandhi's legacy lived on, not only in India, but as an inspiration to other of the century's grassroots political leaders. As the political theorizing behind nonviolent resistance was developed by the diverse likes of Ho Chi Minh, Dr. Martin Luther King, Jr., and Nelson Mandela, acts of nonviolent protest were increasingly employed in mass movements for civil rights in the American South, against American involvement in Vietnam, and to end apartheid in South Africa. With the growth of television as a medium for disseminating news, nonviolent resistance become an effective political tool for powerless individuals to turn their very powerlessness against the repressive potential of the national states' security apparatus.

Pittsburgh's KDKA Offers the First Commercial Radio Broadcast (1920)

The Event: On November 2, 1920, radio station KDKA in Pittsburgh broadcast the results of the presidential election, inaugurating a new industry and a new system of entertainment and mass communication that remolded the century's politics, its economies, and its cultures.

ON CHRISTMAS EVE, 1906, Reginald Fessenden, inventor of the high-frequency alternator (basis of the first practical radio voice transmitter), sent out a program that included music and voice. Lee de Forest—who had greatly improved John Ambrose Fleming's rectifying diode or "valve" by introducing a third element in 1906 to create the triode, the modern radio tube—broadcast opera in New York between 1907 and 1909. Within a decade, a host of amateur radio enthusiasts in a dozen American cities were regularly transmitting music and speech, as well as coded communications, before security restrictions during World War I put an end to their activities. But following the war, they picked up where they had left off, and radio hurtled into commercial development.

Within three years of the KDKA broadcast there were 556 commercial radio stations in the United States, bringing unbridled chaos to the airwaves, which, despite a precocious 1912 federal licensing act, lacked precisely assigned frequencies. The first attempt at imposing order came from the station owners themselves, who banded together into networks to broadcast the same show at the same time. Broadcasters also experimented with on-air advertising, which was greeted with widespread objections to what was perceived as an invasion of privacy, nothing better than admitting a traveling salesman into one's home. Station owners temporized with "indirect" advertising in which singing groups, comedians, and bands adopted a company's name without ever mentioning a product's merit, price, or point of purchase. Despite the obstacles, advertisers were quickly drawn to the new networks—the National Broadcasting Company (NBC), the Columbia Broadcasting System (CBS), and the Mutual Broadcasting System (MBS)—which had forged a national audience.

The 1912 federal legislation licensing radio stations had introduced a crude and inadequate wavelength allocation system. Congress expanded the Radio Act of 1912 in 1927 and again in 1934, strictly assigning frequencies and setting up the Federal Communications Commission (FCC) to consider license applications and renewals. The airwaves were deemed a public resource, and the FCC mandated that stations demonstrate every three years their responsible commitment and service to the public interest. The FCC's mandate went far beyond questions of technology, issuing guidelines to check obscenity and fraudulent advertising. With the avowed object of providing the public with best possible broadcast quality, the FCC allocated most of the broadcast spectrum and all of the best wavelengths to those operators who owned the most powerful transmitters. This gave well-financed big-business interests a wide edge over more independent, more modestly financed groups, many of which sought to establish noncommercial educational stations.

By the late 1930s, radio—decidedly commercial radio—was woven into the fabric of American life, broadcasting everything from heavyweight championships to hoary vaudeville. More than that, radio had become a worldwide enterprise, offering new opportunities not only to educate and to entertain, but also to spread political messages to audiences on a scale previously unimagined. Adolph Hitler effectively used radio in his rise to power in Germany, and many observers at the time credited the almost hypnotic power of his radio voice for the hold he and his message had on Germans. During the dark days of the Great Depression, with the United States seemingly on the brink of dissolution or revolution, President Franklin Delano Roosevelt also made masterful use of the medium to unite Americans around their receivers for his soothing "fireside chats." The coming of World War II made broadcast journalism a serious competitor for newspapers, as Edward R. Murrow, Eric Sevareid, Howard K. Smith, Charles Collingwood, and other distinguished correspondents brought the conflict into America's living rooms with an immediate eloquence and urgent sense of courage more powerful than anything print news could convey.

From the beginning, radio—with its mass audience—had played a key role in the growth of the cult of celebrity that would shape not only twentieth-century culture but its politics as well. After the war, many radio "stars" went on to greater wealth and fame in the new medium of television, even as the less photogenic lost their access to wider audiences. Facing stiff competition from television for audiences and sponsors, radio lost some of its "national" voice but pioneered the kind of "narrowcasting" television would be unable to achieve until the development of fiber optic cables would allow it, too, to tailor programs for almost every taste imaginable. Though postwar radio surrendered to television almost entirely the production and broadcast of original dramas and comedy programs, Elvis Presley and the Beatles owed their phenomenal popularity and wealth to the power of radio to reach a broad public, as did Frank Sinatra and Bing Crosby. In fact, radio both served as a historical model for setting up network television in the 1950s and evolved as a unique venue for the introduction of popular music that allowed it to continue as a major force in American and world culture. Radio helped shape the "rock and roll" generation, with its superstars and anti-heroes, as surely as it had played a major role in shaping the World War II generation.

The Nineteenth Amendment Grants Women the Right to Vote (1920)

The event: By 1920 the Nineteenth Amendment had been ratified by enough state legislatures to become the law of the land, culminating a struggle that had begun in the previous century to give women in the United States the right to vote.

THE LONG STRUGGLE for women's suffrage in the United States did not commence until 1848, when 240 women met at the Seneca Falls Convention to draw up a list of grievances and a set of resolutions for action. Organized by Elizabeth Cady Stanton and Lucretia Mott, both active in the abolition movement, the meeting became an annual event in this upstate New York town. Following the Civil War, suffragists split over whether to tie the campaign for women's rights to the campaign to enfranchise former slaves. Stanton and Susan B. Anthony fought strenuously for constitutional amendments that would enfranchise both blacks and women, and Mott was elected chair of the Equal Rights Association. When the Fourteenth and Fifteenth Amendments, extending the vote to black men, failed to address women's rights, Stanton and Anthony broke with Mott's group to form the National Woman Suffrage Association, which accepted only women as members and opposed the Fifteenth Amendment on the grounds that it did not include women. Another splinter group, the American Woman Suffrage Association, supported the Fifteenth Amendment as a necessary first step in the broadening of voting rights.

Later in the nineteenth century, these groups were joined by federations of women's clubs, as well as the Woman's Christian Temperance Union, all of which pressed for the vote. In 1890, the two rival women's rights organizations, the National Woman Suffrage Association and the American Woman Suffrage Association, merged under the leadership of Anna Howard Shaw and Carrie Chapman Catt to become the National American Woman Suffrage Association, and from 1900 to 1920, this new organization led a massive propaganda campaign for suffrage. Despite the existence of the independent Congressional Union's National Woman's Party, the new century brought new unity to the suffrage movement. The Congressional Union, organized by Alice Paul, differed from the Suffrage Association in its adherence to militancy, staging a series of pickets, hunger strikes, and other forms of civil disobedience aimed at both obtaining the vote and securing a constitutional amendment guaranteeing women equal rights with men.

At last, in 1919 Congress and President Woodrow Wilson approved the tersely worded Nineteenth Amendment, giving women the vote, and it was ratified by the states in August 1920.

Following this hard-won victory, the Congressional Union suffragettes formed the National Woman's Party to push for more laws to secure equality for women, and in 1923 it began a campaign for an Equal Rights Amendment. The National American Woman Suffrage Association was reconstituted as the League of Women Voters, a nonpartisan organization that works to educate voters on political issues.

Perhaps surprisingly, women's suffrage did not have a radical impact on the American political scene. Warren G. Harding and Calvin Coolidge, the two presidents who succeeded Wilson, were not merely conservatives, but virtual throwbacks.

Women did not vote as a bloc, nor did they support female political candidates. The exigencies of World War II gained women a measure of employment equality, but that was greatly diminished when the soldiers returned to their jobs after the war. Indeed, in a kind of postwar backlash, women not only rushed to return to their domestic lives, but feminism was regarded as deviant and, worse, even laughable. This changed in the 1960s, a decade of heightened activism, when the cause of women's social and economic equality became part of the ongoing struggle for civil rights.

The U.S. Courts Declare James Joyce's *Ulysses* Obscene (1921)

The event: In 1921 a U.S. court upheld the post office's right to seize issues of an avant-garde American journal called *The Little Review*, which since 1918 had been serializing a work in progress by Irish writer James Joyce. The court ruled that the material—which would become *Ulysses* and would be universally acknowledged as the most important twentieth century novel in the English language—was obscene and should not be read by the American public.

B Y 1918, James Joyce, an impoverished Irish expatriate living in Europe, was already recognized by the cultural avant-garde as a major writer for a collection of short stories called *Dubliners* (1914) and his autobiographical first novel *Portrait of the Artist as a Young Man* (1916). Though hardly familiar to the general reading public, his work helped to define literary modernism, with its emphasis on mundane subject matter, its reliance on irony, and its stylistic eclecticism.

Dubliners is a survey of the city and its inhabitants' everyday lives drawn from

autobiographical experiences. It struck many of the Irish not as a series of tales about the soullessness of modern times or about the vast wasteland of urban-industrial society and how it blunted and blighted individual existence, which it was; rather, it was perceived as an arrogant attack on Irish life and culture. Like all of Joyce's work, *Dubliners* relied on a kind of all-pervasive, structural irony, based largely on the "epiphany"—a word the Jesuit-educated Joyce borrowed from Catholicism, which he had long rejected—meaning the manifestation, by God, of his divinity to mortal eyes. Young Joyce, exploring the possibilities of prose in short narrative passages, used the word to describe his accounts of moments when the real truth about some object or person is revealed. Striving for the epiphany, Joyce developed a concise language of incredibly accurate observation that infused "small" events with tremendous significance. It took Joyce many years to find a publisher for the work, and the book's *succes d'estime* belied its meager sales. Its inhospitable reception by the reading public, and particularly by the Irish, served to support his decision to lead a life of intellectual exile and to strengthen his disdain for a popular audience; he became the premier of the century's many culturally homeless geniuses.

Portrait of the Artist as a Young Man was published by the English Press, a small press owned by Harriet Shaw Weaver, editor of the influential literary magazine, *The Egoist*, from pages printed in America after a series of British printers refused to typeset the manuscript. In that work, much more obviously experimental than *Dubliners*, Joyce honed his skills as a stylist, developing the "stream of consciousness" narrative for which he would become famous. Encouraged by the acclaim afforded the novel, *The Little Review*, a small literary magazine in the United States, began publishing episodes from a work in progress by the young author, living then in Zurich off the proceeds he made from giving English lessons and on grants from wealthy patrons like Edith Rockefeller McCormick and Harriet Shaw Weaver.

When *Ulysses* appeared in installments in *The Little Review* it immediately generated controversy as well as excitement among the literati. Its exuberant narrative spun around an average day—June 16, 1904 (the day Joyce had fallen in love with his common-law wife, Nora)—in the life of its protagonist Leopold Bloom, a Jewish-Irish antihero and newspaper advertising agent, his wife Molly, and the young Stephen Dedalus, who had been the central figure of *A Portrait of the Artist as a Young Man*. Bloom's wanderings, mental and physical, about Dublin symbolically paralleled the nineteen years of adventure-filled travel undertaken by the Greek warrior-king Ulysses following the Trojan War as recounted in the Homeric classic, the *Odyssey*. Once again, the overarching structure of the work was ironic, counterpointing Bloom's mundane adventures during a single day—which literary historians would come to call "Bloomsday"—with the legendary exploits of the West's original culture hero. Greek myth was hardly the only literary reference Joyce used, however. A host of other, often quite obscure, allusions echoed throughout the book's tour de force of styles, covering everything from the Bible to Einstein's theory of relativity ("Whorled without end," as Joyce put it), all served up in language that here employed the sonorous tones of religious liturgy and there engaged Gypsy slang. Bloom's interior journey as he trundled about the city included meditations on sex, masturbation, defecation, urination, flatulence—in short, all the earthly matters so often ignored in polite fiction. In Joyce they were elevated to the status of monster slaying and military triumph by an idiom awash in detail, thickly textured, vital, and immediate. *Ulysses*, with its stylistic virtuosity, its ambitious and daunting structure, its richly human story, and its boisterously frank narrative was quickly recognized as a celebration of language as well as a work of art.

But none of this impressed the U.S. Post Office. Commissioner Anthony Comstock, the self-appointed censor of American morality, may not have understood the obscure literary allusions in *Ulysses*, but he knew dirty words when he saw them in *The Little Review*. In 1919, the post office seized an entire issue of the magazine, the first of four such seizures leading up to the 1921 court ruling that the work was obscene. Though two of the three ruling judges admitted they could not understand Joyce's abstruse style (and the third no doubt lied), they fined *The Little Review* for printing pornography. In Paris, Joyce's sense of exile increased, bordering on despair, since the court's finding meant that publication of the completed work as a book in America was impossible—and consequently was unlikely in Britain. But Sylvia Beach, the American owner of a Paris bookshop called Shakespeare and Company that served as the hub of the city's expatriate art and smart set, offered to publish *Ulysses* under the bookstore's imprint. Joyce accepted, and he and his secretary, Samuel Beckett—another son of Ireland, albeit a Protestant one, who would become world famous as a master of modernist plays and fiction—worked diligently to prepare the manuscript for print. On Joyce's fortieth birthday, February 2, 1922, *Ulysses* was launched on its faithful journey to the forefront of contemporary literature.

From the moment "[s]tately, plump Buck Mulligan came from the stairhead, bearing a bowl of lather on which a mirror and a razor lay crossed" to the instant Molly Bloom closed her famous punctuation-free soliloquy, the apotheosis of stream-of-consciousness narrative, with the words "And yes I said yes I will Yes," the universe of reading had changed utterly. Immediately acclaimed as a work of genius, *Ulysses* partook of and influenced every aspect of the "modern" cultural temper. Its reliance on ancient myth to shore up a debased "reality" was reminiscent of the direction taken by modern classical music. Its range of style, its love of parody, its difficulty, obscurity, and abstraction married it to much of modern art. Its stream-of-consciousness narration and its focus on the ordinariness of everyday life marked its affinity with psychoanalysis. Its attempt to be all-inclusive, its tying all of reality to observation and reflection, and even its rigorous demands on the reader made common cause with contemporary science. Its irony allowed Joyce to create a synthesis of two rival literary movements, the haughty and obscure Symbolists and the more worldly Realists, while its somewhat madcap adherence to point-of-view narration put the book in the tradition of the modern novel created by another genius who had lived in self-imposed exile, Henry James, though Joyce exploded the Jamesian novel inward. No major work of fiction in the twentieth century outside Soviet Russia and its cultural satellites would be written after 1922 that failed to reflect the existence of *Ulysses*, and even those works penned by authors who resolutely ignored

Joyce's masterpiece were often written in conscious "opposition" to the "modernism" the novel defined.

Even as Joyce began to change the face of American fiction, especially in his influence on the young William Faulkner, *Ulysses* remained banned to the reading public. This did not mean that no one read Joyce in the United States, because "pirated" copies of the book appeared almost immediately; it simply meant that Joyce, always in need of money, never got paid for his work. While England's snobbish Edwardian-spawned cultural critics attacked Joyce's work as vulgar and in poor taste, America's guardians of public morality not only labeled the book obscene but lashed out at Joyce himself as a pervert. *Ulysses* happened to appear when America was going through a Puritan phase, so Joyce's work became truly subversive in a way, perhaps, it never would have if the post office had allowed it to drift obscurely through American bookstores. Bennet Cerf at Random House led an army of the aesthetically correct against the rigid government bluenoses and in 1934 the case came before the United States District Court in New York. Here lawyers for Random House quoted educators, writers, clergymen, businessmen, librarians, and such literary lights as Stuart Gilbert, Rebecca West, Arnold Bennett, and Edmund Wilson to prove that *Ulysses* was a classic of modern fiction, far too complex to appeal to the lascivious, and written for "edification and delight." Judge John M. Woolsey—observing ironically that, while the book might be too strong a draught for a sensitive, normal reader, its effect was more likely to be emetic than aphrodisiacal—handed down a landmark decision overturning the lower court's ruling and striking a deadly blow against censorship of literature of any kind in the United States. Two years later, England followed suit.

Free to buy *Ulysses*, few purchasers understood the book any better than the original three justices who had declared it obscene. For Joyce's work was "modern," too, in its refusal to compromise with the desires and demands of a general commercial audience. Joyce had begun his literary career with an attack on the Dublin Abbey Theater (then called the Irish Literary Theater) for catering to the popular taste of what he called the "rabblement," and he would end it by producing a work more difficult than *Ulysses*, more highly praised by Joyce acolytes than *Ulysses*, and less read by anyone than *Ulysses*. In *Finnegans Wake*, as in *Ulysses*, Joyce proved himself the quintessential twentieth-century artist, a man of immense talent and undisputed genius producing masterpieces of wide and lasting influence based on the experiences and alienations of everyday life that the average reader living such a life could not, or would not, read; and *that* is the irony of art in our times.

Benito Mussolini Comes to Power in Italy (1922)

The event: On October 28, 1922, Mussolini led a Fascist march on Rome, obtaining a mandate from King Victor Emmanuel III to form a coalition government with his Fascist Party and obtaining "temporary" dictatorial powers, becoming the first Fascist leader in a Europe destined to see more of them.

BENITO MUSSOLINI was born on July 29, 1883, the son of a blacksmith with strong socialist and anti-church beliefs. His mystical-minded mother convinced the boy that he was destined for greatness. A voracious reader, Mussolini devoured the works of such political philosophers as Louis Auguste Blanqui, Friedrich Wilhelm Nietzsche, Georges Sorel, and Machiavelli. He trained as a schoolteacher, traveled widely, then turned to a career as a socialist journalist, arguing strongly against Italy's entry into World War I. But, in the single most momentous decision of his life, he suddenly broke with the socialists and urged Italy's entry into the war on the side of the Allies. Expelled by his party for his reversal, Mussolini started his own newspaper in Milan, *Il popolo d'Italia*, and in its pages propounded the message of what became the Fascist movement.

After service as a private in the Italian army during World War I (he was wounded in the buttocks by trench mortar fragments), he resumed publication of his newspaper, and on March 23, 1919, with poet, novelist, romantic patriot, and glamorous adventurer Gabriele d'Annunzio, he and other war veterans founded the Fasci di Combattimento. The Italian word *fascio*, "bundle" or "bunch," suggested union, and the *fasces*, a

bundle of rods bound together around an ax with the blade protruding, was the ancient Roman symbol of power.

Fascism may have originated with the socialist left, but it was almost immediately transformed into radical right-wing nationalism—a vision of re-creating in modern Italy the imperial grandeur of ancient Rome. Intoxicated by this vision, powerful landowners in the lower Po valley, important industrialists, and senior army officers joined Mussolini, who formed squads of thugs—the Blackshirts—whom he deployed in a street-level civil war against Socialists, Communists, Catholics, and Liberals. By October 28, 1922, the Fascists were powerful enough to march on Rome. There Mussolini demanded that King Victor Emmanuel III form a coalition government with his party, granting Mussolini himself dictatorial powers for one year.

During that year, Mussolini radically reshaped Italy's economy, slashed government expenses for public services, reduced taxes on industry to encourage production, and streamlined the rickety government bureaucracy. For many observers, the single most symbolic evidence of Mussolini's reforms was his introduction of a new discipline into the notoriously undependable Italian railroad system, and "Mussolini made the trains run on time" became a cliché that characterized the early years of his regime.

Mussolini replaced the king's guard with his own Fascist *squadisti* and a secret police force, the Ovra. He made bellicose moves against Greece and Yugoslavia and brutally suppressed the strikes that, in the past, had continually crippled industry. In 1924, Mussolini publicly relinquished his dictatorial powers and called for new elections—but rigged the outcome by obtaining legislation that guaranteed a two-thirds parliamentary majority for his party regardless of the popular vote. When the popular Socialist leader Giacomo Matteotti dared to voice opposition, exposing Fascist criminality, he was murdered, and the opposition press attacked Fascism.

Mussolini responded by summarily establishing single-party rule, imposing strict censorship, and dispatching thugs to silence all opponents by whatever means were necessary. To consolidate his power base among Italian capitalists, he abolished free trade unions and secured the support of the Catholic church by the Lateran Treaty of 1929, which established the Vatican under the absolute temporal sovereignty of the pope.

Now called *Il Duce* ("the leader"), Mussolini flexed his foreign policy muscle by turning a clash over a disputed zone on the Italian Somaliland border into an excuse to invade, bomb, and gas Ethiopia during 1935–1936. Italy annexed the African nation, and Mussolini turned to forging alliances with Generalissimo Francisco Franco to establish a Fascist government in civil war–torn Spain and, most important, with Adolf Hitler, who saw Mussolini as a precedent-setting political role model and proposed, in effect, dividing the world between Germany and Italy.

In April 1939, Italian armies were dispatched to occupy Albania, but Mussolini stayed out of World War II until June 1940, when the fall of France was imminent and Germany was poised to conquer Europe. Hitler warmly greeted his partner in fascism, but his new ally soon proved a liability rather than an asset, as Italian military forces suffered disaster after disaster from Greece to North Africa.

Italy suffered greatly in World War II, and popular feeling turned against Il Duce. King Victor Emmanuel dismissed Mussolini as premier on July 25, 1943, and ordered his arrest. Hitler sent a rescue party and installed the tottering dictator as a puppet in northern Italy, which had yet to be taken by the Allies. By the spring of 1945, with Allied forces closing in, Mussolini and his mistress, Clara Petacci, fled, but were captured by Italian partisans. They were executed by a firing squad on April 28, and their bodies hung by the heels in a Milan public square.

Archaeologists Uncover "King Tut's" Tomb (1922)

The event: On November 7, 1922, British archeologist Howard Carter and his patron, George Edward Stanhope Molyneux, Earl of Carnarvon, opened the sealed burial chamber of Tutankhamen, a pharaoh who had reigned over ancient Egypt from 1361 to 1352 B.C. Their discovery of the tomb's fabulous wealth captured the interest of the world and the imagination of generations to come.

T HE GREAT ARCHAEOLOGICAL event of the nineteenth century was Heinrich Schliemann's 1870 discovery of the site of ancient Troy, the first physical confirmation that the fantastic world evoked by Homer in the *Iliad* was based on historical fact. Many people had likewise long been aware of the equally fantastic realm of the ancient pharaohs of Egypt, but, up through the early twentieth century, surprisingly little of that magnificent civilization had ever been discovered. It was known that the pharaohs had elaborate burials, their tombs heaped with treasures magnificently wrought in gold and other precious materials. The pharaohs' tombs were designed with secret chambers and heavy stone partitions to foil grave robbers, but, over the ages, such measures proved futile. By 1000 B.C., the greatest days of the pharaohs had come to an end, and every tomb had been emptied of its contents.

Except for one.

Indeed, robbers had attempted to loot Tutankhamen's tomb, but they were caught in the act, and the treasure was restored. Tutankhamen and his artifacts remained unmolested for another two centuries until an excavation for another pharaoh's burial place in the late nineteenth century sent earth and stone crashing down over the entrance to Tutankhamen's tomb. As a result of this accident, the site was preserved into the twentieth century.

After World War I, the Earl of Carnar-von, an English Egyptologist and collector of antiquities, backed an expedition led by archaeologist Howard Carter to discover the entrance to the tomb and to gain access to it. Widely publicized local legend spoke of a "pharaoh's curse" that would strike down anyone who violated the tomb, but Carter and Carnarvon pressed on to discover the entrance, and on November 4, 1922, they found the first sign of it. Three days later, they had penetrated into the burial chamber and recovered a staggering hoard of rich artifacts.

The find not only gave great impetus to ancient Egyptian studies, but it captivated the collective imagination of the entire world by giving solid substance to an ancient civilization. Lord Carnarvon's death, from an infected mosquito bite and pneumonia five months after the discovery gave the popular press a sensational news bonanza as manifest proof of the pharaoh's curse, giving birth to a subgenre of horror movies. Carter, however, lived in good health and prosperity for seventeen years after opening the tomb of "King Tut," and the talks he gave in his widespread travels further enhanced the appeal of both the discovery and of the archeological profession. On display in Cairo, the treasures of Tutankhamen attracted innumerable tourists, and in the 1970s an international traveling exhibition of those treasures proved immensely popular, bringing record crowds to museums around the world.

African-American Poet Claude McKay Publishes *Harlem Shadows* (1922)

The event: The publication of a slim volume of lyrically militant verse about African-American urban life marked the beginning of the Harlem Renaissance, the most important movement in African-American literary and visual art.

THE SO-CALLED Harlem Renaissance, which spanned the 1920s to the mid-1930s, is usually associated with writer, teacher, and sociologist Alain Locke, who compiled an influential anthology of African-American urban writing in 1926 and declared that "Negro life is seizing its first chances for group expression and self determination." The movement, which commanded the attention of prominent white critics and social commentators, included such distinguished figures as Jean Toomer, Langston Hughes, Rudolph Fisher, Wallace Thurman, Jessie Redmon Fauset, Nella Larsen, Arna Bontemps, Countee Cullen, and Zora Neale Hurston. It also attracted such older, already established African-American writers as James Weldon Johnson and Charles S. Johnson. However, it was the remarkable poet Claude McKay, whose 1922 Harlem Shadows first crystallized the movement in skillful verse combining lyrical, evocative beauty with unflinching, hard-edged, even militant realism.

McKay was born in the Clarendon Hills of Jamaica on September 15, 1890. He was well educated there, and, assisted by the patronage of a wealthy Englishman living in Jamaica, he published his first book of poems, *Song from Jamaica*, in 1912. It so beautifully embodied the Jamaican dialects

that McKay was hailed as "a kind of Robert Burns among his own people."

The year *Song from Jamaica* was published, McKay came to the United States and studied agricultural science at Tuskegee Institute and Kansas State University, but soon he abandoned notions of scientific farming for a career as a poet in what was evolving into the urban cultural center of African-American life: the uptown Manhattan neighborhood of Harlem. Supporting himself with menial jobs as a porter, houseman, longshoreman, barman, and waiter, McKay published poetry and gained a reputation among African-American writers as well as among white intellectuals as an important cultural figure. He became an associate editor of *The Liberator* and *The Masses*, joined the Communist Party, traveled in Russia as a representative of the American Worker's Party. He published poetry and prose that expressed the admixture of hope, beauty, energy, potential, despair, oppression, and degradation of African-American life. His first novel, *Home to Harlem* (1928), was a best seller, and his last novel, *Banana Bottom* (1933), was his best work.

The writers and artists of the Harlem Renaissance brought African-American expression into the white American cultural mainstream. This amazed and delighted progressive white intellectuals, but upset more conservative whites as well as blacks, who were more comfortable with familiar cultural stereotypes and were fearful of disturbing the status quo. The movement pe-

tered out by the mid-1930s, and Harlem, which had flowered for a time into a kind of magnificent cultural incandescence, receded into the "shadows" of poverty, violence, and despair.

Time Magazine Hits the Newsstands (1923)

The event: In 1923, two young Yale graduates published a new magazine called *Time*, which hit the newsstands dated March 3. Priced at fifteen cents, it was the first periodical of a publishing empire that would come to include *Life*, *Fortune*, and *Sports Illustrated*—and would change the very nature of the journalistic enterprise.

IN THE PROSPECTUS they put together, Henry Luce and Briton Hadden explained their new brainstorm for a weekly magazine digest of news obtained from a wide range of daily papers that emphasized world events and cultural matters: "People in America are, for the most part, poorly informed, because no publication has adapted to the time which busy men are able to spend on simply keeping informed." *Time* was conceived precisely to fill the needs of the busy twentieth-century reader. Its stories were studiedly concise, its tone was cockily omniscient, and its style was decidedly odd ("Backward ran sentences until the mind reeled" went a famous parody), and within a decade the magazine had spawned its own far-flung news-gathering organization. *Time*'s resounding success inspired a host of others to launch news magazines over the course of the first half of the century. American imitations appeared immediately, *Business Week* in 1929 and both *Newsweek* and *U.S. News and World Report* in 1933. *Der Spiegel* was first published in Germany in

1947, followed by France's *L'Express* in 1953, and Italy's *Panorama* in 1962.

Hadden, a native of Brooklyn, died young and suddenly in 1929 from what had begun as a strep infection. Luce—the son of a Presbyterian missionary stationed in China and an ardent anti-Communist—soldiered on to make millions as his political feelings invariably seeped into the warp and woof of their creation, lacing its purportedly objective news coverage, especially its highly touted cover stories. A supporter of Chiang Kai-shek in China, Mussolini in Italy, Franco in Spain, and Ngo Dinh Diem in Vietnam, Luce was no stranger to the attractions of autocracy, and he did not suffer lightly those foolish enough to disagree with him to his face. The enfant terrible of American cinema, Orson Welles, in *Citizen Kane* poked fun at the corporate blandness and soulless anonymity of the new style of journalism introduced by Luce, but Theodore H. White, who went on to became a distinguished American journalist after Luce bounced him from the magazine when they disagreed over China, regarded Luce himself as anything but bland. He wrote of *Time* and of Luce, who died in 1967, that "it was exhilarating to be working for a man who could discuss, all at the same time, the Bible, Confucius, and the itchy gossip and color which sells readers on a magazine."

Thomas Mann Publishes *The Magic Mountain* (1924)

The event: In 1924, Thomas Mann published *The Magic Mountain*, a novel almost universally regarded as his masterpiece, garnering for him a Nobel Prize in 1929 and establishing his reputation as one of the twentieth century's foremost authors, a writer who chronicled throughout his career the increasingly precarious position of the artist—and art itself—in a modern world by definition antagonistic to the very individuality on which true art depends.

THOMAS MANN burst on the German literary scene in 1901 at age twenty-six with his first novel, *Buddenbrooks*. In a highly descriptive prose style, dependent on the leitmotif (a recurring set of words, images, phrases in different contexts meant to mimic the musical leitmotifs of Wagnerian opera), which would become his trademark, Mann traced the decline of the Buddenbrook family over four generations. The story was based loosely on his own family, gradually declining from social and financial prominence into decadence and ultimately oblivion. The book turns on the clash between life and art, a theme Mann would take up time and again throughout his long career. Immediately acclaimed in Germany, the novel was more coolly received by critics elsewhere. For the literary modernists who had already begun to define the century's literary avant-garde, Mann's first work seemed too naturalistic, almost old-fashioned and out-of-step with a changing social and political landscape.

It became clear that they had misjudged the young artist by the time Mann returned to his theme with the powerful and widely acclaimed 1912 novella, *Death in Venice*. Mann's account of an aging and famous German writer's growing obsession with a beautiful young Polish boy was drenched in the distinctively modern irony he used as a bridge between the realistic traditions of the nineteenth century and the experimentations of the early twentieth century to explore his great themes of decline and alienation. Already recognized as a leading German writer by the First World War, he became one of the world's preeminent authors between the world wars.

In *The Magic Mountain*, a vast allegory of European civilization's headlong march into the Great War, Mann explored not only his familiar themes of artistic decadence and intellectual alienation, but also the cultural and political fragmentation of Western Europe and its affect on the average bourgeois citizen. Numerous influences clearly shaped Mann's work as he tried to put the world he knew "on ice" and look at the maelstrom of European culture and politics with Olympian detachment: the freewheeling ethos and the ideological tensions of the Weimar Republic; Mann's own attempts to remain both apolitical in the strictest sense and what Friedrich Nietzsche, whose writings tremendously influenced him, would have called "a good European;" and the intellectual challenges thrown his way by George Luckacs, the leading Communist literary critic in middle Europe. The result was a novel that perhaps better than any other captures the social texture of a modern bourgeois Europe that would disappear within the next few years into the cauldron of Nazism.

And so, almost, would Mann himself. His books burned by Hitler's minions, his work denounced by Germany's racist professorate, Mann—the quintessential good German and a scion of Christianized Jews—barely escaped his homeland with his life and the thousands of pages he had written that would become the his four-volume work on the biblical Joseph, a remarkable meditation on myth and the origins of Judeo-Christian culture. In exile for the remainder of World War II in England (briefly) and the United States, where he spent time with other German intellectual and artistic refugees in southern California, Mann wrote and broadcast propaganda for the Allies. After this time he returned with a passion to those themes surrounding the decline of art in a world damned by cultural decadence and political corruption in his novel *Doctor Faustus*. He reworked the Faust myth around a Nietzschean composer trapped in Nazi Germany and doomed by his acquiescence in the nihilism inherent in the very notion of a "modern Europe." Mann's darkest novel was—as he said—an attempt to take back Beethoven's Ninth Symphony, to unmask the promise of the *Ode to Joy* and reveal the horror that it had made possible by "tricking" us into believing in the redemptive power of art. A blend of twentieth-century history and fiction, *Doctor Faustus* was more unremitting in its irony than anything the young *fin de siècle* disciple of a pessimistic Schopenhauer and an iconoclastic Nietzsche could ever have imagined.

Settling after the war in Switzerland, Mann—seemingly purged by the writing of *Doctor Faustus*—continued to produce delightful, even beautiful, works of fiction until his death in 1954.

J. Edgar Hoover Is Appointed Director of the Bureau of Investigation (1924)

The event: Harlan Fiske Stone, reform-minded attorney general, appointed "Red-hunter" J. Edgar Hoover to head the inept and scandal-plagued Bureau of Investigation on May 10, 1924, launching a controversial career that would make Hoover the most powerful, unelected official in American history.

B ORN IN WASHINGTON, D.C., J. Edgar Hoover took as his first job out of law school a position with the Justice Department in 1917, a division of the government he would not leave until his death fifty-five years later.

At the end of World War I, Attorney General A. Mitchell Palmer undertook a sweeping campaign to identify and prosecute "foreigners" with communist ties or who had openly opposed the American war effort. Palmer chose Hoover to head the Justice Department's General Intelligence Division, which conducted raids, illegal searches and seizures, and generally harried thousands of immigrants, most of whom were ultimately acquitted. While carrying out Palmer's infamous "Red scare" Hoover began his lifelong practice of keeping detailed files on people under investigation or, for that matter, on whomever he wished.

Officially transferred to the Bureau of Investigation—forerunner of the FBI—in August 1922, Hoover was appalled by its disorganization and corruption. When the scandals of the Harding administration broke, both the attorney general and the director of the Bureau were forced out, and J. Edgar Hoover was named to head the Bureau on May 10, 1924. He spent the next seven years radically reorganizing the newly renamed Federal Bureau of Investigation, firing most of the old regime and mandating rigid rules of conduct and ethics.

In the 1930s, Hoover concentrated the Bureau's efforts on the rash of highly publicized Depression-era bank robberies perpetrated by such notorious figures as the Barker clan, Pretty Boy Floyd, Baby Face Nelson, and the figure who became for Hoover a personal enemy, John Dillinger. By solving them, Hoover hoped to enhance the public prestige of his agency. With a genius for public relations equal to his talent for administration, the director enlisted the help of Hollywood to propagandize the FBI, fashioning the invincible, all-seeing, and utterly incorruptible image that Hoover came to glory in. Any time the FBI was mentioned, Hoover wanted his name to be associated with it. He forced out several agents popular with the media when he feared that their renown would eclipse his. He forbade anyone other than himself to issue statements to the press, and he would often invite reporters to his house for dinner, which was frequently interrupted by prearranged phone calls in which the director would make dramatic, split-second decisions designed to make him appear every bit the "G-Man" he wanted the press to think he was. Hoover deliberately cultivated a cadre of journalists who cast the FBI in a positive light, and he even employed some to ghostwrite publications issued under his own name.

In time, Hoover came to loom larger than the FBI itself, a figure of frightening personal power, whom many presidents would have liked to force out. Hoover wielded his clout with high-handed arrogance, habitually bypassing the attorney general (by law his superior) and reporting directly to the president. It was not until 1961 that Hoover was challenged by an attorney general, Robert Kennedy, and the two men quickly became bitter personal enemies. Hoover was particularly resistant to Kennedy's demand that the FBI investigate civil rights violations and organized crime. He began compiling files on the Kennedy brothers, carefully charting extramarital affairs and financial histories.

Hoover had files of this sort on most politicians in Washington—and everyone knew it. It was his way of maintaining power through silent, unspoken blackmail. Some administration insiders have suggested that John Kennedy would have removed Hoover from office had he been elected to a second term, but it was Hoover who took sadistic pleasure in informing Robert Kennedy and the rest of the family that the president had been assassinated in Dallas.

As Hoover grew older, his eccentricities became increasingly bizarre and his personal tyranny more open. He amassed his files with increasing zeal and wielded a whimsical dictatorial authority throughout the Bureau. He summarily dismissed an agent for being ugly. He fired another for wearing a tie he did not like. And he drummed out another for marrying a foreign woman.

Part genius, part demagogue, and part monster, J. Edgar Hoover almost single-handedly created one of the most powerful, most respected, and most sophisticated investigative bodies in the world. His FBI defined the standard of criminal investigation for the twentieth century. At the same time, he personally used the bureau to undermine many of the rights and liberties it had been formed to preserve and protect. Hoover's FBI was virtually an autonomous agency operating independently of executive, congressional, and judicial oversight until his death of a massive heart attack in 1972.

Raymond Arthur Dart Discovers the Fossil Remains of *Australopithecus* (1924)

The event: In 1924, the Australian-born South African anthropologist Raymond Arthur Dart examined a fossil skull discovered in a South African stone quarry and determined it to be the earliest ancestor of modern humankind.

THE SEVENTEENTH-CENTURY Irish prelate James Ussher devised a scheme of biblical chronology that dated the creation of the universe to the year 4004 B.C., but fundamentalist defenders of the biblical account of Creation had been having a tough time of it at least since 1856, when the French anthropologist Pierre-Paul Broca identified bones that had been found in a limestone cave in Germany's Neander River Valley as the remains of humanoid beings who had lived some eleven thousand years in the past. Then, in 1890, a Dutch paleontologist, Marie Eugène François Thomas Dubois, discovered part of a skull, a thigh bone, and two teeth of an even more primitive humanlike (or hominid) being, which he called *Pithecanthropus erectus*, meaning "erect ape-man." Since Dubois had found these remains in Java, this evolutionary ancestor of humanity was popularly called Java Man and is now more generally known as *Homo erectus*.

The evolutionary origins of modern humankind were pushed back even further by Raymond Dart's discovery of an unusual skull in a South African quarry site. At the age of thirty-six, Dart was an accomplished paleontologist and physical anthropologist leading digs in his adopted home of South Africa. In 1924, near the great Kalahari Desert, he unearthed the skull of what appeared to be a child, complete with face, mandible (jawbone), skull base with brain cast, and a full set of "baby teeth" with the youth's first permanent molars. He made the skull the type-specimen of a new genus he labeled *Australopithecus africanus*. Dart concluded that he had found a previously unknown species, an evolutionary link between the ape and the human and that his specimen dated from the Pleistocene Epoch, some one to two million years ago.

Most scientists at that time believed Asia, not Africa, to be the cradle of human-

kind. They initially received Dart's interpretation of his find with hostile skepticism, owing in part to the youthfulness of the specimen and to the fact that his was the only known example of its kind. In the following thirty years, additional examples of Dart's *Australopithecus africanus* found in African and discoveries of other evolutionarily linked species proved the validity of his findings: Robert Brown's 1936 and 1938 discoveries of *Australopithecus robustus*, the *Australopithecus boisei* unearthed by Louis and Mary Leakey in 1959, the 40 percent complete skeleton of "Lucy," *Australopithecus afarensis*, found in 1979 by Donald Johanson and Timothy White, and White's subsequent discovery in 1995 of *Australopithecus anamensis*. Dart's discovery strengthened evolutionary theory and facilitated, eventually, its broad popular acceptance.

The U.S. Congress Restricts Immigration (1924)

The event: In 1924, The U.S. Congress passed the Johnson-Reed Act, placing strict limits on immigration and fixing quotas based on national origin, favoring northern Europeans and limiting Slavs, southern Europeans, and Asians, a new turn for a country whose very motto *e pluribus unum* echoed the pride it once took in being a haven for the disenfranchised.

IT IS A COMMONPLACE observation that the United States is indeed a nation of immigrants. Its most visible national symbol, the Statue of Liberty in New York Harbor, bears a poetic inscription welcoming the world's "huddled masses" and "wretched refuse" to these shores. In practice, however, Americans have periodically sought to curb immigration through restrictive, often racist, legislation and quotas. In the seventeenth

century, the vast majority of colonial Americans spoke English, became farmers, and espoused the Protestant religions. The nation was uncrowded and largely homogeneous. The next century saw waves of German immigration, which made many native-born Americans nervous about the capacity of American society to absorb foreign-speaking newcomers. The next "assault" on the nation's perceived cultural identity came in the nineteenth century as large numbers of Irish Catholics fled to these shores to escape life-threatening famine and political oppression. Consequently, entrenched citizens fretted about the impending disintegration of their Anglo-Protestant culture. The Irish newcomers were openly persecuted and discriminated against, often with full sanction of the law.

Despite this widespread fear and distaste for the new immigrants, nineteenth-century America needed cheap labor for its burgeoning industries. By the 1880s, spurred by such demand, the nation admitted vast numbers of Italians, Greeks, Turks, Russians, Slavs, and Jews, rekindling fears about the dissolution of the American identity. A Chinese Exclusion Act was passed in 1882, halting Chinese immigration into the United States for a period of ten years. Throughout the 1920s, the act was regularly renewed. In 1917, legislation was enacted requiring immigrants to pass a literacy test, and then, in 1924, Congress passed the highly restrictive Johnson-Reed Act, which limited immigration to 154,000 persons annually, in addition to the wives and minor children of U.S. citizens. Moreover, the act established quotas based on national origin and favored northern European "stock" over that of southern Europe, the Slavic countries, and non-European nations. The justification for these quotas was the assertion and belief that northern Europeans would naturally make "better Americans" than those from other regions.

The Great Depression and World War II kept immigration rates low, but, in the wake of the war's devastation, much of the restrictive legislation was lifted to allow the admission of large numbers of refugees. It was not until 1965, however, amid a growing consciousness of equality and civil rights issues, that amendments to the Immigration and Nationality Act formally repealed quotas based on national origin and generally increased the number of immigrants allowed into the country.

More recently, the United States has been confronted with the challenges of illegal aliens from Mexico and South America, Asian refugees from the Vietnam War, and Haitians fleeing poverty and political terror. Congress passed the Immigration Reform and Control Act of 1986, aimed at expediting the entry of temporary workers into the United States under the full protection of U.S. laws and establishing programs for special agricultural ("migrant") workers, making them eligible for permanent resident alien status and eventual citizenship. The Reform Act seemed to signal a shift from punitive exclusion to humane acceptance of often oppressed immigrants, but in the mid-1990s, a more severe, and locally based reaction set in, recalling once again the nativist fears of the 1920s.

Franz Kafka's *The Trial* Is Published (1925)

The event: In 1925, Franz Kafka's friend and literary executor Max Brod published Kafka's novel *The Trial*, the tale of a man called simply "K" who finds himself charged with a crime he is helpless to defend himself against in a world run by a nightmarish and inhuman bureaucracy. *The Trial* came out a year after Kafka's death; a second novel, *The Castle*, was also published posthumously the following year. Together, these novels would secure Kafka's reputation as the premier author who portrayed the anxiety and alienation prevalent in twentieth-century totalitarian societies.

IN PUBLISHING KAFKA'S masterpieces, Max Brod, who had met Kafka in 1902 when the latter was a desultory law student at the University of Prague, acted against the express wishes of the author, who had asked his friend on his deathbed in 1924 to burn his manuscripts. Though the leading avant-garde publishers had sought out Kafka during his lifetime, he reluctantly published few of his writings. Born in 1883 in Bohemia (now the Czech Republic), the troubled scion of middle-class Jewish merchants, Kafka did not get along with his father and was indifferent to his mother. Rebelling early against parents who could not comprehend his unprofitable and probably unhealthy dedication to the literary recording of his "dreamlike inner life," in his teens Kafka declared himself a socialist and an atheist, though even then he was essentially passive and politically unengaged. And though he sympathized with the socialist cause throughout his life, and in later life with Zionism, even attending meetings of the Czech anarchists before World War I, he always considered himself an outcast, not a revolutionary: a Jew in a Christian society; a cultural German trapped in Slovene Prague. Throughout his adult life he led a dual existence, working miserably at a job he hated with an accident insurance company during the day and writing eerie tales of alienation and despair at night, which he refused to publish.

Only a small literary coterie appreciated Kafka at the time of his death, but Brod's decision to ignore his friend's dying request would ultimately bestow upon Kafka an international literary fame of such magnitude that his very name became synonymous with paradox and absurdity. The first sentence of Kafka's short story, "The Metamorphosis," would become one of the best known in twentieth-century literature: "As Gregor Samsa awoke one morning from uneasy dreams he found himself transformed in his bed into a huge dung beetle"—or "cockroach" or "insect," depending on the translation. Regardless of the translation, however, the sentence caught the essence of what the world would call the "Kafkaesque," a state of being spawned by the hopeless search for meaning in a world where nothing made sense, a world where one found oneself trapped in a nightmare, suffering constantly from an inexplicable anxiety and an ineffable dread. Kafka's fame grew swiftly through the late 1920s, but his writings were suppressed by the Nazis as the work of a "decadent" Jew. Just as he was gaining worldwide posthumous fame, Adolf Hitler's Germany deported his three sisters to Kafkaesque concentration camps and killed them—along with six million others—with the horrible casualness he captured so well in his portraits of bureaucratic officialdom.

After the war, Kafka was rediscovered in Germany and Austria, where his work began to greatly influence German literature. It had already cast its shadow over writers in Britain and France, where it became particularly popular with the French surrealists, who especially appreciated Kafka's nose for the absurd. By the 1960s, Kafka even began to hold sway over the intellectual, literary, and even political life of communist Czechoslovakia. Only in Kafka's works—whether one considers his works to be profound existential allegories or simple direct stories—can one find so powerful an evocation of the essence of the administered world in which we live.

The First Art Deco Exposition Opens in Paris (1925)

The event: In 1925 the French Ministère des Beaux-Arts, the Association des Arts Decorateurs, and the City of Paris opened *L'Exposition Internationale des Arts Decoratifs et Industriels Modernes*, a show that displayed a new style in art that would define the very notion of modernity and shape the look of the twentieth century.

ORIGINALLY KNOWN AS Art Moderne, the name Art Deco caught on when critics and writers began to shorten the title of that first "international" display of objects in the style. The origin of the style, however, lay in Léon Bakst's exotic colors and striking Oriental designs for the 1909 Ballets Russes in Paris. The Ballets Russes's influence on decorative arts was interrupted by the Great War, but from 1917 onward company director Sergei Pavlovich Diaghilev commissioned French painters of the first rank to create his sets, including Georges Braque, André Derain, Juan Gris, Marie Laurencin, Henri Matisse, and Pablo Picasso. Through their work for the theater, the European public was introduced to a popularized version of the more arcane "high" art of futurism, expressionism, and cubism.

With roots in Art Nouveau, much influenced by the great prewar high-art movements, Art Deco mixed traditional subjects with modern techniques and concentrated on the surface of things. Smart rather than pretty (indeed, it consciously avoided the pretty), Art Deco exuded the toughness and the coolness that the term *smart* implies, as illustrated in that quintessential magazine of the 1920s, *Smart Set*. Art Deco's practitioners agreed with F. T. Marinetti, who had declared in the Futurist "manifesto" published in the Paris newspaper, *Le Figaro*, that "the splendor of the world has become enriched with a new beauty: the beauty of speed," and with Andre Lhôte, who argued that cubism needed to be humanized. Art Deco sported cold, hard textures and colors on the one hand, and luxurious, decadent, sensual imagery and detail on the other, drawn at once to metal and flesh, to the automobile and the naked body. Primarily a French movement, the Art Deco style developed in France and in response to the demands of mostly French patrons, and like the French between the wars, it dallied with both fascism and hedonism but succumbed to neither.

Art Deco was the style of the decade known as the *Années Follies*, the Jazz Age, and the Roaring Twenties—between the last machine gun bursts in the trenches on the Marne and the first cries of panic on the sidewalks of Wall Street. It was a decade dominated by rich, ruthless, merger-mad businessmen, who set the tone of the times. To survive, art had to come to terms with them. Since fame and enjoyment were the businessman's only aesthetic values, the artists of the "mad years"—unlike the pre-war avant-garde years—did not reject the ethos of capitalism altogether by creating difficult, obscure, or even revolutionary works, but instead tried to compromise with that ethos by enshrining success as the great god of their work, and by defining the modern not as an experiment with form, but as the creation of a new elegance and grace.

It was precisely Art Deco's concentration on stylishness, on the surface of things—its studied shallowness—that made it attractive to the rich, especially to the decadent aristocracy of *Mittel Europa*. The old-line "nobles" were on the defensive: they had led the world to war and in the process nearly destroyed themselves as a class, along with millions of common people. They were left with very few countries in Europe to rule and even their money wasn't safe in a France gone mad with speculation. Lacking real power, the best they could imagine was pleasure (which they called beauty), lots of it; they chased it with real abandon, concentrating on clothing, on bearing, on style. Politically, they followed *Action Française*, a right-wing, purportedly royalist group led by Charles Maurras, who said he wanted to restore the pretender, the Comte de Paris, to the throne. Instead, after the war, he actually led the world-weary aristocrats—as well as aesthetes and artists on the Left Bank—into the arms of Il Duce. Fascism, in the words of Janet Flanner, who covered high culture in Paris for *The New Yorker* (essentially a literary clone of *Smart Set*) under the pen name Genet, seemed to them an exciting political innovation. Perhaps fearing subconsciously that they counted for much less than they once had, they hid their self-doubt behind the rigid posture, the arrogance, and the personal irresponsibility they had learned from birth, and followed the strong man who promised to give the world back to them. In short, they admired Mussolini and lived for new sensations. They responded to the rapid rise of monopoly capital, the jolting displacements of social revolution, and the unimaginable destruction of world war by retiring to their estates. Art Deco expressed the alienation of the rich.

An essentially urban phenomenon, like socialism, Art Deco came to define the look of the modern city, and it is no accident that Fritz Lang's cinematic masterpiece on the soullessness of the modern city, *Metropolis*, is one of the essential artifacts of the Art Deco style. Art Deco's influence on early Hollywood was obvious and ubiquitous, and through all those upper-class drawing-room comedies the movie industry produced in response to the Depression, the style came to dominate the look of daily life in the twentieth century, influencing the shapes of everything from alarm clocks to automobiles.

Gertrude Stein Defines the "Lost Generation" (circa 1925)

The event: An American expatriate author as well known for the literary-artistic salon she maintained in her Paris apartment as for her own books, Stein told Ernest Hemingway that he belonged to a "lost generation."

Born on February 3, 1874, in Allegheny, Pennsylvania, Gertrude Stein attended Radcliffe College and studied with the great American psychologist and philosopher William James before moving in 1903 to live with her brother, Leo, at 27 Rue de Fleuris, Paris. Destined to become perhaps the most famous literary and artistic address of the century, Stein's home served as control center for the American avant-garde. Stein amassed a large, advanced, and highly discriminating collection of modern paintings and developed enduring friendships with Picasso and Matisse. She wrote two groundbreaking avant-garde works of literature before World War I, *Three Lives* (1909) and *Tender Buttons* (1914). With her lifelong companion Alice B. Toklas, Stein was active in relief work during the dark days of the war, but Stein is best remembered for her postwar role as the nucleus around which America's rising literary generation gathered.

Paris in the 1920s attracted young American writers like a magnet, and many of them inevitably found their way to 27 Rue de Fleuris, most notably Ernest Hemingway, F. Scott Fitzgerald, William Faulkner, and Sherwood Anderson. Stein not only encouraged, nurtured, and generally mothered such young expatriate geniuses, she also inspired them with her literary radicalism. Stein had an uncanny sense of the tenor and significance of the period between the two world wars—a time of great creative ferment, but also frenzy, despair, moral decay, and a struggle to bring to birth a new creativity and a new order of civilization. About 1925, in conversation with Hemingway and other expatriates, she told the young writers that theirs was a "lost generation." In those two words, Stein captured the mood of an era.

Hemingway's novel, *The Sun Also Rises*, became the bible of America's lost generation almost immediately upon its publication in 1926. The twenty-seven-year old author quoted Stein's use of the phrase in the novel's preface to describe those coming of age in a moral world shattered by World War I. The book centers on a group of Paris-based expatriates, modeled on the less-eminent members of the circle Hemingway encountered at Stein's salon. The

American narrator, like Hemingway, is a journalist, named Jake Barnes, who is in love with the reckless Lady Brett Ashley, also loved by a young, idealistic novelist named Mike Campbell. Suffering from a war wound and from impotence, Barnes, along with his unhappy soulmates, haunts the cafes and nightclubs of Paris, unable to connect to any great cause, looking for meaning in brave, exquisite, even cruel gestures, much like those of the bullfighters Barnes admires. Hemingway's famous lean prose style guides the narrative to reveal the equally famous tough-guy code, based primarily on the aristocratic, public-school mores of the Englishmen Hemingway had met in the war and had admired. The book was scarcely in the stores before undergraduates began to adopt the terse, world-weary cadences of Hemingway's dialogue, and other writers began aping his tough-but-sensitive narrative persona—not least of whom was the hard-boiled American detective writer, Dashiell Hammett (though Hammett consistently denied he took inspiration from Hemingway). By year's end, Hemingway was an international literary personality, playing young genius and Everyman's man with equal aplomb.

Another of Stein's lost American expatriates, F. Scott Fitzgerald, had published arguably an even greater masterpiece than *The Sun Also Rises* the year before. *The Great Gatsby* was not set in Paris, nor did it center on the literary avant-garde. Instead, it concerned itself with the glamorous creatures of the Jazz Age (Fitzgerald was the first to use this term), and the rich, brash, cynical young people who moved between parties and love affairs with heedless savoir-faire were modeled, like Hemingway's characters, from life. Fitzgerald's subtle, haunting prose was not as flashy as the rhythmically tense writing of Hemingway, but it was more flexible and, ultimately, more profound. Almost everyone now knows the story of Jay Gatsby, the lowborn millionaire hopelessly in love with the wild, gorgeous, and carelessly married Daisy Buchanan. Perhaps only Huck Finn, the rascally boy hero of the novel that Hemingway claimed to be the source and inspiration of all American fiction, is better known than the damned, and yet somehow glorious, Great Gatsby.

Hemingway and Fitzgerald were two of the more famous members of the Lost Generation, itself created by the rapid rise of monopoly capital, the jolting displacements of social revolution, and the unimaginable destruction of world war. They fled from the past, embraced the present, and refused to think about the future. For them significance and meaning existed, if at all, in the here and now, and the here and now was the Roaring Twenties. Their goal was to make something new, something for their times, something modern. And yet they wanted to be more than simple celebrities providing mere entertainment. So they based their aesthetics instead of their lives on the code of behavior of the prewar social elites they admired. However, the conflict between their aesthetic code and their mode of living was bound to cause trouble.

For all Fitzgerald's famous carousing, he maintained steadfastly that "character was the only thing that did not wear out." On the other hand, Hemingway's insistence on grace under pressure never stopped him from being a drunken boor and a bully. They both tried to resolve the tensions between their work and their lives by creating works of art about the way they lived, running on sheer energy and defying time and history, by trying to use their art to make their experiences so much an expression of their times that they transcended them.

Sooner or later the energy had to give out. When it did, Hemingway shot himself. Long before, Fitzgerald had drank himself to death in that new home to the life of gesture, Hollywood.

Robert Goddard Launches the First Liquid-Fuel Rocket (1926)

The event: On March 16, 1926, the American physicist Robert Hutchings Goddard fired his first liquid-fuel rocket, which was the first modern rocket and the direct ancestor of rockets, guided missiles, space probes, lunar vehicles, and space shuttles of the later twentieth century.

FASCINATED BY ROCKETS since his teen years, physicist Robert Goddard used his own time and money to conduct research in improving solid-propellant rockets, developing a rocket technology that had been in existence since the days of the ancient Chinese. He secured funding from the Smithsonian Institution, and in 1919 the Smithsonian published the results of his experimentation under the title of *A Method of Reaching Extreme Altitudes*.

In the succeeding years, Goddard worked on designs for liquid-fuel rockets, reasoning that a rocket fueled by a liquid propellant and carrying its own oxidizing agent—in the form of liquid oxygen—would be far more powerful and more controllable than a solid-fuel rocket. On March 16, 1926, Goddard fired the world's first successful liquid-propellant rocket. Standing a mere four feet high and measuring six inches in diameter, it was a simple pressure-fed projectile, that burned gasoline and liq-uid oxygen. The first flight attained an altitude of 184 feet—hardly spectacular, but it proved Goddard's principle.

After the 1926 launch, Goddard continued to develop increasingly powerful rockets. With the outbreak of World War II, the War Department had no interest in developing the rocket as a weapon, but it did ask Goddard to develop rocket-assisted-takeoff systems for aircraft. In the meantime, during the war years, German scientists under the technical guidance of the young Werner von Braun developed very powerful and highly sophisticated rocket weapons, most notably the V-2, which rained terror upon London. After the war, American and Russian scientists scrambled to obtain the German technology, and both nations used it as the basis for an extremely competitive "space race." This was marked by the Soviet launch of *Sputnik* in 1957, the first artificial orbiting satellite, the flight of the Soviet cosmonaut Yuri Gagarin in 1961, the lunar expedition of the American space vehicle *Apollo 11* in 1969, and the various flights of the American space shuttles beginning in 1981.

If Goddard and von Braun's Germans had laid the foundation for space exploration, they also made possible the development of terrifying weapons systems, long-range intercontinental ballistic missiles (ICBMs), capable of delivering apocalyptic nuclear warheads to any target, anywhere in the world.

The American government was slow to recognize the scope and value of Goddard's contribution to the science of rocketry. In 1951, his widow and the Guggenheim Foundation filed a joint patent infringement suit against the U.S. government, and in 1960 a $1 million settlement granted the government the rights to more than 200 patents covering—in the words of the settlement—"basic inventions in the field of rockets, guided missiles and space exploration."

Years after Goddard's death in 1945, the National Aeronautics and Space Administration (NASA) named its Goddard Space Flight Center just outside Washington, D.C., in the pioneer's honor.

Nicola Sacco and Bartolomeo Vanzetti Are Executed (1927)

The event: In 1927, two self-proclaimed anarchists were executed, both Italian immigrants arrested in 1920 for murdering the paymaster and guard of a shoe company in South Braintree, Massachusetts. Their trial set off the political cause célèbre of the decade.

DESPITE THE TESTIMONY of Nicola Sacco and that of corroborating witnesses placing him at the Italian consulate in Boston on the day that two employees of a shoe company were murdered, the two hapless Italian immigrants were arrested and convicted by a justice system laced with xenophobic prejudice and a rabid fear of Communists and anarchists. The verdict, based on questionable witness identification, "consciousness of guilt," and (most significant) the radical affiliation of the defendants, raised an outcry from intellectuals and writers not only in the United States, but across the globe, and funds were raised to appeal the decision.

For seven years appeal after appeal was denied—the final appeal denied by the Massachusetts Supreme Court—and Nicola Sacco and Bartolomeo Vanzetti were condemned to die. In response to mass demonstrations, Massachusetts governor Alvin T. Fuller convened a special fact-finding committee to investigate the case, and when it failed to find legal grounds for a retrial, the governor permitted the executions, by electric chair, to be carried out on August 23, 1927.

The Sacco and Vanzetti case became the most blatant example of the rampant xenophobia sweeping the United States during the 1920s, a period of worldwide political ferment and the spread of Communism. The trial was seen as a case study of what happens to the lower class in a country whose courts cater to the monied elite and whose middle class had been conditioned to react to radical politics with unthinking fear.

The Sacco and Vanzetti case received renewed attention in the 1970s when an underworld informant revealed that the robbery and murders in Braintree had actually been committed by the notorious Morelli gang, five Mafioso brothers who had moved to New England from Brooklyn during World War I. After a review of the case in 1977, Massachusetts governor Michael Dukakis declared that any "disgrace should be forever removed from their names."

Charles A. Lindbergh Solos over the Atlantic (1927)

The event: On the rain-soaked, muddy morning of May 20, 1927, at 7:52 aviator Charles Augustus Lindbergh set off from Long Island, New York, for Paris, France—alone, except for the fascination, enthusiasm, and prayers, it seemed, of the entire world.

IN 1922, WHEN Charles Augustus Lindbergh made his first flight, aviation was neither a profitable nor respectable occupation, and Lindbergh eked out a living as a "barnstormer," an itinerant stunt flier who also gave passengers thrill rides at five dollars a pop—hard to come by in the backwater rural districts that were the barnstormer's province. After two years of this life, Lindbergh was even more committed to flying and realized that the best place to learn the most about it was in the U.S. Army. After graduating from flight school, Lindbergh was commissioned as a second lieutenant in the Army Air Service Reserve in March 1925. Without a war to fight, Lieutenant Lindbergh was never called to active service, becoming instead an air mail pilot, undoubtedly the most demanding and hazardous type of flying done at the time. In antiquated, unreliable aircraft, air mail pilots flew in all kinds of weather, day and night, in a valiant effort to prove the value of aviation for the fast, dependable delivery of mail. During this period Lindbergh conceived of another method of proving aviation's worth: He would fly solo across the Atlantic, from New York to Paris.

Lindbergh approached the task with a deliberation previously foreign to him. The deed would require courage in abundance, but it was no mere stunt. Lindbergh secured the backing of a group of St. Louis businessmen and worked closely with the Ryan Aviation Corporation to custom-build a plane, *The Spirit of St. Louis*, designed expressly for the task at hand. The flight would not only advance aeronautical technology, it would win public acceptance of aviation and, therefore, stimulate investment in the emerging industry. If a Lone Eagle—as the newspapers christened Lindbergh—could make it across the ocean safely, the future seemed bright for commercial aviation.

Others who had recently attempted the crossing had died in the attempt. Even Lindbergh's ascent from Roosevelt Field, an unpaved dirt airstrip (reduced to a muddy soup by days of rain) in Long Island's Nassau County, was perilous as the single-engine craft, heavily laden with fuel, barely cleared a stand of trees at the end of the field. For the thirty-three and a half hours of the passage, Lindbergh fought sleep and the elements to guide his plane to Le Bourget Field, just outside of Paris. When he touched down at 10:22 P.M. (local time) on May 21, he was greeted by a tumultuous sea of well-wishers, who had followed his progress through radio reports relayed worldwide from observers scanning the skies for the *Spirit of St. Louis*.

On his return to the United States, Lindbergh was riotously hailed as a hero. His feat had put him in a position from which he could encourage the development of aeronautical technology and commercial aviation, and he became a key adviser to aircraft manufacturers, airlines, and the government.

Lindbergh married Anne Spencer Morrow in 1929. Their marriage faced tragedy in 1932 when their infant son was kidnapped and murdered, after being taken from their home in New Jersey. Soon after, the "Lindbergh law" was passed by the U.S. Congress, making kidnapping a federal crime.

An outspoken pacifist and isolationist, whose heroic image in the 1930s was tainted by the stain of anti-Semitism and an avowed admiration for Adolf Hitler, Lindbergh nevertheless served as a private consultant to the military when World War II erupted, even flying fifty secret and unofficial combat missions in the Far East. During the last four years of his life, Lindbergh became a vigorous environmentalist, opposing, on environmental grounds, the development of the most advanced commercial aircraft of the 1970s, the supersonic transport (SST).

The *Threepenny Opera* Opens in Berlin (1928)

The event: On August 31, 1928, Bertolt Brecht's *Threepenny Opera* opened to rousing acclaim in Berlin. Perfectly capturing the spirit of the wide-open capital city of Germany between the two world wars, Brecht's Marxist masterpiece quickly became the most popular stage play of the Weimar Republic.

PERHAPS ONLY UNDER a government like that of the Weimar Republic, which the German right wing did not want and the German left wing did not respect, could a talent like Bertolt Brecht's flourish. Brecht's theater of alienation, the product of theoretical debate and dramatic collaboration, was meant of course to function as propaganda—the spread of politically informed ideas through ideologically committed stagecraft—but it also led to radical innovations in modern dramaturgy. Brecht's work had an immense influence on the subsequent twentieth-century theater throughout the world, which was evident especially in the 1960s as young dramatists tried to break down the aesthetically imposed barriers (the so-called "fourth" or "invisible" wall) between audiences and actors that had once ruled supreme.

The Threepenny Opera marked the birth of Brechtian drama. The play was the result of the brief collaboration between the leather-jacket-wearing, guitar-slinging playwright-poet Brecht and a diffident, bespectacled composer of atonal orchestral music named Kurt Weill. Like Brecht, Weill was a Marxist who aspired to a new kind of opera, one stripped of sentiment, eschewing naturalism, and open to politically didactic works aimed at the working class. Their joint effort, *The Threepenny Opera*—part revolutionary sloganeering, part barroom musical, part gangster melodrama—perfectly captured the mood of postwar Germany, with its inflation-driven crime and corruption, its freedom and cynicism, its loose-living gaiety, and its debilitating despair, all the turmoil of a decadent and worldly Berlin ripe for the rise to power of Adolf Hitler. *The Threepenny Opera* transformed the London underworld of John Gay's 1728 satire, *The Beggar's Opera* (from which it was adapted), into the Berlin underworld of 1928. The play centered around the attempt of a gangster named Macheath to wed the daughter of the city's beggar chief, and his betrayal by a whore played in the Berlin production by Weill's wife and Brecht's sometime lover, Lotte Lenya. Macheath represented the decadent bourgeoisie, not dampening in the least the raucous enthusiasm of Germany's theater-going bourgeois audiences.

The opening of *The Threepenny Opera* did not go smoothly. The rehearsals were nothing short of disastrous. Peter Lorre, who left the country after the Nazis took over Germany for a career in American-

made movies, was then a promising young German stage actor. He was supposed to play the Beggar King but instead fell ill and had to be replaced. The actress cast as Lorre's wife turned up her nose at the lyrics to the "Ballad of Sexual Slavery," and refused to sing it. She, too, was replaced. The dress rehearsal ended in a shouting match, not an uncommon occurrence in Brecht's theater. But on opening night, sometime during the rabidly antimilitarist "Cannon Song," the play connected with its audience and the Berliners in attendance began to stomp in rhythm with the music. From that moment on *The Threepenny Opera* was a hit, unquestionably the biggest stage success of the theater-mad Weimar years. Brecht's illustrious career as the industrial democracies' favorite Marxist playwright was launched.

Recent biographies have attacked Brecht for the tyranny with which he treated his dramatic collaborators and coauthors (and for the aplomb with which he appropriated their work as his own). And, at the time, he was attacked for plagiarizing John Gay's work as well as for his radical innovations. Nevertheless, *The Threepenny Opera* is still one of the world's most popular productions, and its earthy, in-your-face, jazz-laced songs—from "Pirate Jenny" to "Mack the Knife"—have been recorded by torch singers, folksingers, and rock stars. Even tonight, one of them is probably being "covered" by a mike-wielding crooner in a hotel lounge somewhere in America as Brecht rolls over in his East German grave.

Louis "Satchmo" Armstrong Records "West End Blues" (1928)

The event: New Orleans–born Chicago cornet virtuoso Louis "Satchmo" Armstrong recorded what many musicologists consider the first fully realized specimen of classic American jazz—perhaps the century's most significant form of popular musical expression—with his 1928 version of the "West End Blues."

THE AMERICAN MUSICOLOGIST Gunther Schuller wrote of Armstrong's 1928 recording of "West End Blues" with the Hot Five that it presents "in capsule form all the essential characteristics of jazz inflection."

The origins of jazz are complex and richly textured. They can be traced at least as far back as the late nineteenth century, when African-Americans began performing the music that would became known as the blues. This musical form harked back to the work songs and "hollers" of slavery days, but by the beginning of the twentieth century, the blues had evolved into popular commercial music confined mainly to an African-American audience. Then, in 1911, black orchestra leader W. C. Handy wrote a campaign song for Memphis mayor Edward H. "Boss" Crump. Adapting the homegrown African-American idiom to "sophisticated" European conventions of orchestration and harmony, Handy produced in "The Memphis Blues" far more than a winning campaign tune. Three years later, his "St. Louis Blues" became a smash hit, a tremendously influential and enduring standard to this day. The song also created the first major demand, among both African-Americans and a vast white audience,

for a kind of music that would soon be called "jazz."

Early exponents of jazz were active in many cities and towns throughout the southern United States, but it was New Orleans that spawned most of the acknowledged pioneers of jazz, including Jelly Roll Morton, King Oliver, Alphonse Picou, Sidney Bechet, Kid Ory, and, paramount, Louis Armstrong.

Armstrong was born on July 4th, 1900, in a section of New Orleans known as The Battleground, a neighborhood famed and feared for its endemic violence, casual shootings, frequent knife fights, general whoring, and widespread disorder. His parents separated while he was still an infant, and young Louis was taken in by his grandmother. Later, he found his mother living in the most squalid of the city's red light districts, and on New Year's Eve of 1913 Louis "borrowed" a .38 caliber pistol from one of his "stepfathers," discharged it into the air, was arrested, and remanded to the Colored Waifs' Home for Boys. There he learned to play the cornet, became a member of the Home's marching band, and subsequently found work as a cornetist with a series of Mississippi riverboat bands.

Armstrong found his first major audience in Chicago, when he joined King Oliver's Creole Jazz Band in 1922. His recordings with Oliver the following year were among the first in the United States to feature African-American performers. In 1925, after playing a stint in the New York band of Fletcher Henderson, Armstrong returned to Chicago to start his own group, Louis Armstrong's Hot Five (sometimes expanded to the Hot Seven).

In 1932, Armstrong made the first of what would be many triumphal European tours, and from that period until his death in 1971, he enjoyed tremendous popularity with audiences of many tastes and a wide range of sophistication. He was not the first to play jazz, nor the first to record it. No one really knows to whom the former honor belongs, but it was the Original Dixieland Jazz Band, a rhythmically stilted and improvisationally mediocre group of white musicians led by Canadian-born Nick LaRocca, who cut the first jazz recording— "The Darktown Strutters' Ball"—in New York City in 1917. But Satchmo was the first true revolutionary of jazz.

And what a revolution he started. Primarily a twentieth century phenomenon, jazz's creative energy and influence have extended to every corner of the globe. Often considered to be America's foremost cultural gift to the world, jazz is both a serious art form and a popular music, capable of being entertaining *and* profound. Jazz terminology and slang have enriched our language, many of its key figures have become household names, and its influence and sensibility can be found in every aspect of our culture. Jazz is performed today in nightclubs and concert halls; musicians learn their lessons in basement jam sessions and universities; jazz CDs flood the record stores; and jazz festivals draw audiences from around the world. Moreover, jazz is all around us, on radio and television, where it provides the soundtrack to scenes of urban life on cop shows and sitcoms, and more insidiously, it is used to sell everything from cars to computers—with the underlying message suggesting that the product is hip, popular, soulful, and sophisticated. Louis Armstrong made sure it was all that and more.

Penicillin Is Discovered (1928)

The event: In 1928, after accidentally leaving a culture of staphylococcus uncovered for a few days, bacteriologist Sir Alexander Fleming was about to discard the contents of the petri dish when he noticed that a mold had grown in it and destroyed some of the bacteria. When he investigated further, he realized he had discovered something that would change human life on earth, a new "wonder" drug he called penicillin.

SINCE 1862, when Louis Pasteur proposed the germ theory of disease, doctors understood that a host of deadly or debilitating ailments were caused by microorganisms, but there was little that physicians could do to combat these tiny adversaries.

During World War I, Scottish-born Alexander Fleming began a research effort to identify antibacterial substances. In 1921 he discovered an lysozyme, an enzyme present in human tears and mucus that attacks many types of bacteria. But the far more significant breakthrough came in 1928, when he found that a *Penicillium notatum* mold had accidentally contaminated one of his experimental staphylococcus cultures and halted the bacteria's growth. Fleming succeeded in isolating the mold's antibacterial substance, which he named penicillin, and tested it to confirm that it was not only nontoxic, but remarkably effective against a wide spectrum of disease-causing bacteria.

Fleming shared the 1945 Nobel Prize for physiology of medicine with British scientists Ernst Boris Chain and Sir Howard Walter Florey, who had arrived at a process

for purifying sufficient quantities of penicillin to conduct definitive human trials.

Fleming's accidental discovery gave medical science its first dramatically effective weapon against disease. True, penicillin did not destroy all bacteria, but, in the coming decades, other researchers would develop an entire arsenal of antibiotics to combat most bacterial disorders. For most of the century these "wonder drugs," as they came to be called, held out the promise of a disease-free world. But now, as the twentieth century draws to a close, it has become apparent that antibiotics have been overused, and, over the years, new bacterial strains have developed that are resistant to antibiotics, posing a formidable challenge for medical science.

The New York Stock Market Crashes (1929)

The event: October 29, 1929, became "Black Tuesday" when the stock market in New York collapsed and securities lost an average of forty points, sending the country and the world into the worst financial panic in history—the Great Depression.

THE YEAR 1929 promised to be another boom year for the soaring New York Stock Exchange. But, come September, the first signs of trouble surfaced as the market fluctuated wildly, the average prices nevertheless trending downward. On October 24, a spasm of selling put almost 13 million shares up for sale, and, five days later, the market crashed, burned, and died—with stocks losing an average of forty points.

Tens of thousands of Americans lost everything they owned on Black Tuesday. Companies and entire industries fell to their knees. Some investors, mortgaged to the

hilt after buying on margin and now unable to cover their debt, saw only one way out: through the open window of a Wall Street skyscraper. Yet the stock market crash was not the cause of the Great Depression so much as its harbinger. At the root of the depression lay the headlong industrialization of the nation, and much of the world, that had concentrated a preponderance of wealth in the hands of a very few. Production soared, but the markets shrank. Few consumers had enough money to buy all the products industry made. Thus began a vicious cycle: workers lost their jobs because of industry cutbacks; industries could not hire workers because there was no market for their goods; there was no market for their goods because the workers had no money; the workers had no money because industries could not hire them.

Once the industries shut their doors, banks across the country failed, and the jobless found themselves with neither income nor savings. Even the flow of capital dried up as the banks collapsed and disappeared. There was no escape, as every sector of the economy was hard hit, virtually grinding to a halt.

President Herbert Hoover saw that his task was to restore public confidence. He issued pronouncements that prosperity was "just around the corner." He called on businessmen to maintain prices and wages, proposed a cut in federal taxes and in interest rates, designed public works programs and cooperative farming plans, asked states and localities to institute relief programs for the unemployed, and proposed a plan of federal aid to homeowners who could not meet their mortgage payments.

The problem with Hoover's programs was their reliance on state and local governments, which were already effectively bankrupt. The president balked at committing the federal government to shoulder the burden during what amounted to a national emergency. He blocked the use of federal funds to be spent directly on relief for individuals, believing that individual relief was the responsibility of private charities and city agencies. But neither cities nor charities had any money, and Americans queued wretchedly in bread lines for what little public and private relief was available. After losing their homes, they moved to miserable slums or into what they called Hoovervilles—squatter collections of dwellings constructed of packing crates and sheet metal. And when even the bread lines ran out of food, the hungry lived on scraps foraged from garbage cans.

In the summer of 1932, twenty thousand out-of-work World War I veterans marched on Washington to demand the bonuses that had been promised to them. Nearly two thousand of this "Bonus Army" remained in the capital even after Congress refused to issue the funds. Living in shacks and tents along Anacostia Flats, they settled in with their families, having nothing to do but outwait Congress. Hoover, a decent man now driven by desperation, declared that the majority of the "Bonus Army" were criminals, and he dispatched federal troops under Douglas MacArthur to clear out Anacostia Flats with bayonets, clouds of tear gas, and even the menacing advance of armored tanks.

This spectacle of the army running down unarmed Americans—even veterans—desperate for nothing more than to feed their families doomed the Republicans at the polls in 1932 as the nation looked to an ebullient, eloquent, hard-driving Franklin Delano Roosevelt, who promised his fellow citizens a "New Deal."

Ludwig Mies van der Rohe Introduces the International Style of Architecture (1929)

The event: Architect Mies van der Rohe designed the German Pavilion for the 1929 International Exposition in Barcelona, introducing the world to the so-called International Style, the building style that would become *the* look of the modern world.

IF ARCHITECTURE EMBODIES, reflects, and, in turn, shapes the "feeling" of an era, no building style has been more pervasive and more powerful than the International Style created by Ludwig Mies van der Rohe. It became the functionalist aesthetic and dominant look of the century's modernity.

Van der Rohe, like two other European giants of twentieth-century architecture, Le Corbusier (Charles Édouard Jeanneret) and Walter Gropius, was a disciple of Peter Behrens in Berlin. He worked with the remarkably innovative architectural master from 1908 to 1911. His career was interrupted by World War I, but after he left the German army in 1919, he embarked on a vigorous career at the forefront of German avant-garde architecture, building a series of all-glass skyscrapers, which precociously announced the airy and sleekly elegant look that became identified with the twentieth-century modern city. In domestic architecture, van der Rohe created several country houses, which owe much to the great American architect Frank Lloyd Wright.

In the mid-1920s, the German Werkbund, an association of industrialists and artists, decided to build a vast architectural exhibition in Stuttgart called the *Weissenhofsiedlung* and tapped van der Rohe to prepare the master plan, to choose the architects for the more than thirty buildings, and to design a major housing block for the project. The *Weissenhofsiedlung* created a sensation that established the principal forms of modern architecture for the next forty years.

Yet even more than *Weissenhofsiedlung*, van der Rohe's design for the German Pavilion for the 1929 International Exposition in Barcelona marked the true beginning of the new style. Smooth, hyperfunctional surfaces, expanses of glass, a feeling of purity, elegance of materials, absence of ornament, and careful proportioning of masses became the pervasive elements of world architecture at least until the early 1980s, when the so-called Postmodern Movement rebelled against what many had begun to perceive as a look of sterility and monotony. Nor was the International Style confined to architecture; by the early 1930s, it was also evident in furniture made of chromium-plated steel, leather, glass, and marble, perfectly echoing the design elements of the buildings themselves.

In 1930, van der Rohe became director of the Bauhaus, the tremendously influential center of design located in Dessau, Germany. The intense intellectualism and airy elegance of Bauhaus design ran counter to the bombastic monumentality of Nazi architecture, and Hitler's party forced the

Bauhaus to close in 1933. Like many German thinkers, writers, scientists, and artists, van der Rohe left Germany for the United States and became director of the School of Architecture at Chicago's Armour Institute, now the Illinois Institute of Technology (I.I.T.) in 1938. For the new I.I.T. campus, Mies designed an entirely new architectural idiom that grew out of the functionalism of the International Style. An aesthetic of exposed steel columns and beams filled in with brick or glass, it expressed the height of rationalism and embodied the values of what is undoubtedly Mies's most-often quoted pronouncement on design: "Less is more."

The style of Mies van der Rohe has had many critics who find it overly rationalistic, creating an urban landscape of uniform glass-and-steel boxes. But even those who hanker after looser, more ornamental architectural styles acknowledge that such structures as the thirty-eight-story Seagram Building, built in New York City in 1958, is a serene masterpiece, clad in bronze and bronze-tinted glass. "God," the architect once said, "is in the details," and, at its most successful, the modern design he created and inspired incorporates a perfection and refinement of proportion, materials, and surfaces that lend spiritual meaning and permanence to the often frenetic and ephemeral activity of the century's enterprises.

Jean Piaget Creates Developmental Psychology (1929)

The event: In 1929, having founded the science of child development, Swiss scientist Jean Piaget was appointed professor of psychology at the University of Geneva, where he began to explore the nature of knowing and knowledge, developing a comprehensive theory of epistemology.

JEAN PIAGET, born in Neuchâtel, Switzerland, on August 9, 1896, revealed his talent for science at the age of ten, when he produced his first scientific paper about his remarkable observations of an albino sparrow he had discovered near his home. Later, he took an after-school job at the local natural history museum, which inspired him to produce a series of articles on mollusks and earned him an invitation to become a curator at a museum in Geneva. Piaget, who had yet to graduate from high school, politely turned down the invitation.

While the teenaged Piaget continued to pursue zoology, his godfather, the Swiss scholar Samuel Cornut, introduced him to philosophy, in particularly epistemology— the study of knowing, of the process of acquiring knowledge of the world beyond the self. Piaget received his Ph.D. in zoology in 1918, when he was twenty-two. His writing credits already included his doctoral dissertation on mollusks, some twenty scientific articles, and a philosophical novel revolving around questions of epistemology.

Piaget next studied experimental psychology in Zurich and worked in Eugen Bleuler's psychiatric clinic. He took logic courses at the Sorbonne and studied psychopathology at the Salpetriére Hospital in

Paris. In 1920, he began working with Theodore Simon, who had developed the famed IQ test with Alfred Binet. With Simon, Piaget set about developing a standard French version of the English-language intelligence test.

Piaget soon became bored with the test itself and far more fascinated by a remarkable observation he had made: Children of the same age very often gave the same *incorrect* answers to questions. As anyone who has endured the modern educational system well knows, testers are concerned only with the "right" answers. But Piaget reasoned that the consistency of incorrect answers suggested the existence not just of *quantitative* differences in raw knowledge, but consistent, *qualitative* differences in the nature of reasoning at different ages. The observation was the start of Piaget's painstaking study of how children think—how they perceive their world at different points in their development.

By 1929, when he received his appointment as professor of psychology at the University of Geneva, Piaget had formulated the basics of his theory, which distinguishes four major phases of epistemological devel-opment in children (done, in part by observing the growth and development of his own children). In so doing, he not only made an important contribution to psychology and philosophy—virtually inventing the discipline of developmental psychology—but he also created the first cogent, systematic picture of the intellectual development of human beings. His contribution is even more momentous when we recognize that, prior to Piaget, thousands of years of philosophy and science and tens of thousands of years of childhood had passed, yet no one had ever thought to determine in any systematic way how children think and, therefore, how human beings come to know the world around them.

From roughly 1940 until his death in 1980, Piaget devoted much of his work to a theme suggested to him by Albert Einstein: the study of how children comprehend such basic concepts as space and time. In recent years, many have questioned Piaget's theoretical work on epistemology, but his contributions to psychology and to the concepts of childhood and what it means to be members of a feeling, thinking species are ambitious, enduring, and profound.

The Empire State Building Is Completed (1931)

The event: The Empire State Building, a monument to commerce, enterprise, and the capitalist system, was opened to the public on May 1, 1931, in the depths of the Great Depression.

IT WAS CONCEIVED and ballyhooed as the world's greatest building in the world's greatest city of the world's greatest nation: the Eighth Wonder of the World. That was in the Roaring Twenties. By the time construction began, the stock market had fallen and the Great Depression had set in. When New York's lame-duck governor cut the ceremonial ribbon to dedicate the building one local wag christened the Art

Deco-style colossus on Fifth Avenue "Al Smith's Last Erection."

As an achievement in design and technology, the building was an unqualified success. The architectural firm of Shreve, Lamb, and Harmon had built it in under two years at a cost of $41 million—a remarkably brief time span and, considering its size and its limestone and steel construction, a remarkably modest cost. Time and money were saved chiefly through the use of advanced building techniques, including the extensive use of prefabricated building elements—especially the ornamental metalwork—industrially manufactured off-site. In effect, then, the building was in large part a monument to the technology of the American factory system. Less advanced was the architectural style, which was not innovative, yet, for its conservatism, was more representative of the vigorous commercial energies that had financed it. Critics then and now have pointed out that its most distinctive architectural characteristics are superficial—its shimmering facade, partially composed of a chrome-nickel-steel alloy, and its monumental foyer—suggesting that these were all too apt symbols of the nation's economy as it swayed at the brink: all shimmering facade and no firm foundation.

But what most interested the general public, however, was that it was the tallest building in the world. Its backers had all along been well aware of the importance of making it the tallest. As the Empire State was under construction, another skyscraper, the Chrysler Building, was going up, slated to rise to 1,048 feet, becoming, by far, the tallest building in the world. Indeed,

it was—for a few months after its completion in 1930—until the builders of the Empire State added an elaborate mast intended as a mooring for dirigibles. That brought the building to a record-breaking height of 1,250 feet.

It was never really clear how passengers were to be transferred from a mooring more than a hundred stories in the air, and the mast was never used for its intended purpose. It might, therefore, have been written off as nothing more than an empty gesture just to gain a height advantage over its uptown rival. A far more serious issue, though, was the emptiness of the building's 2,158,000 square feet of rentable space. For months that stretched into Depression-dogged years, much of the building remained a shell, graffiti-scarred and deteriorating. Soon, the owners of the Empire State Building were scrambling for funds just to pay the enormous real estate taxes of the structure. They turned to sightseers—more than four million people by April 1940—who were willing to pay to visit the top-story observation decks.

Despite the long delay in its commercial viability, the Empire State Building survived the Depression, becoming not only a symbol of New York City, but an affectionate icon of American popular culture. It seemed only natural, for example, that the makers of *King Kong*, the 1933 film version of *Beauty and the Beast*, would have a gargantuan embodiment of sheer animal passion scale the World's Greatest Building while clutching the personification of all-American womanhood, Fay Wray.

The height of the Empire State Building was increased in 1950 by the addition of television broadcasting antennas, but although it ceased to be the tallest building in the world in 1971, it remained the icon of the American skyscraper, an image of power and pride that virtually defined the popular notion of modernity.

Adolf Hitler Becomes Chancellor of Germany (1933)

The event: Nazis polled 37 percent of the German vote in 1932, compelling President Hindenburg to appoint Adolf Hitler *Reichskanzler* (Reich Chancellor, or prime minister) on January 30, 1933, from which position Hitler would become the nation's absolute dictator and one of the most destructive political leaders to which the world has ever fallen victim.

THE MAN WHO would hold terrible sway over Germany and much of Europe for more than a decade was born into squalid circumstances on April 20, 1889, in the Austrian town of Braunau am Inn. Raised mainly in Linz, he left secondary school in 1905 with failing grades and, encouraged by his doting mother, he set out to become an artist, but failed to gain admission to the Academy of Fine Arts in Vienna. However, from 1907 to 1913, he eked out a meager living in Vienna by painting advertisements, postcards, and the like. The only direction in his otherwise aimless existence was the crystallization of racial hatred focused primarily on the Jews, whom Hitler began to see as polluters of the Germanic (Aryan) race.

In 1913, Hitler moved to Munich to evade conscription into the Austrian army. But, in August 1914, with the outbreak of World War I, Hitler rushed to enlist in the 16th Bavarian Reserve Infantry (List) Regiment. He seemed to thrive on the war, serving in the front lines as a runner, and rising to the rank of corporal. He was decorated four times for bravery and seriously wounded twice. Hitler remained with his regiment until April 1920, serving as an army political agent and joining the German Worker's Party in Munich in September 1919. When he left the army in April 1920, he worked full time for the party during an era of ferment and crisis in Germany.

The Treaty of Versailles ended World War I and forced Germany to pay overburdening reparations. Germany at the time struggled against economic disaster, the threat of Communist revolution, and widespread humiliation and demoralization. Inspired by the climate of his time and place, by August 1920 Hitler was instrumental in transforming the German Worker's Party into the *Nazionalsozialistische Deutsche Arbeiterpartei*, commonly shortened to NSDAP or the Nazi Party. After associating with Ernst Roehm, an army staff officer, Hitler rose to become president of the party in July 1921 and became an increasingly effective and popular street-corner orator, lashing his audiences into frenzies of nationalist fervor laced with vitriolic anti-Communism and anti-Semitism.

During November 8–9, 1923, Hitler led

the Munich Beer Hall Putsch, a bold, if premature, attempt to seize control of the Bavarian government. For inciting this abortive rebellion, Hitler was sentenced to five years in prison. While incarcerated, he wrote his political autobiography, *Mein Kampf* ("My Struggle"), the distillation of his political philosophy and the most concentrated expression of his hatred for Jews, Communists, effete liberals, and exploitive capitalists. He offered a vision of Germany reborn in racial purity and achieving world domination.

Released after having served only nine months of his sentence, Hitler established his party in the industrial German north, recruiting the men who would lead the nation into mass atrocity and all-consuming war: Hermann Göring, popular World War I air ace; Josef Goebbels, master propagandist; Heinrich Himmler, skilled in strong-arm, terror, and police tactics; and Julius Streicher, a popular anti-Semitic journalist. When worldwide economic collapse came in 1929, the Nazis gained the backing of industrialist Alfred Hugenberg and increased the number of Reichstag seats they held from 12 to 107, becoming the second-largest party in Germany. But, like his role model in Italy, Benito Mussolini, Hitler did not confine his party's activities to politics. He formed the SA—*Sturmabteilung*, called Brownshirts, after their uniforms—paramilitary thugs who beat up those who opposed the party.

Hitler ran for election as president of the German republic in 1932, narrowly losing to Paul von Hindenburg, the aged but popular hero of World War I. The Nazis won 230 Reichstag seats, 37 percent of the vote, making it the largest party represented, and Hindenburg was compelled to appoint Hitler *Reichskanzler* (Reich Chancellor, or prime minister) on January 30, 1933. Hitler used this position to build his dictatorial power. When a fire destroyed the Reichstag on February 27, 1933, Hitler blamed the Communists, summarily abolished the Communist Party, and cast its leaders into prison. On March 23, 1933, he gained passage of the Enabling Act, which granted him four years of unalloyed dictatorial powers. Immediately, he disbanded all German parties except for the Nazis, purged Jews from all government institutions, and brought all aspects of government under the direct control of the party. Next, he cleaned his own house during the Night of the Long Knives, June 30, 1934, which saw the murder of Ernst Röhm and hundreds of other party members whose radicalism posed a threat to Hitler's absolute domination. Next, on August 2, 1934, Hindenberg died and Hitler, assuming the full function of the presidency, christened himself *Führer*—supreme leader—of the Third Reich.

The Führer replaced the SA (Brownshirts) with the SS—*Schutzstaffel*, or Blackshirts—under Himmler. Together with a secret police organization called the Gestapo, the SS established a network of concentration camps to which political enemies, Jews, and other "undesirables" were "deported." In 1935, Hitler enacted the Nuremberg Racial Laws, which deprived Jews of citizenship. Propaganda minister Goebbels carefully combined such policies of terror with programs of economic recovery as, in defiance of the Versailles treaty, Hitler put his nation on an industrial war footing by creating the *Luftwaffe* (air force) under Göring, remilitarizing the Rhineland (in 1936), and generally rearming as a timid and war-weary world passively watched.

In October 1936, Hitler made an alliance with Mussolini, and in March 1938, Hitler invaded and annexed Austria in the *Anschluss*. This was followed by his usurpation of the Czech Sudetenland. No world power acted against Germany. Rather, as a result of the Munich Conference of September 29–30, 1938, France and England acquiesced in the dismemberment of Czechoslovakia, hoping this would "appease" the Führer.

In fact, it only whetted his appetite for world domination. Hitler annexed not only the Sudetenland, but the remainder of western Czechoslovakia, then gobbled up the Memel strip from Lithuania in March 1939. Clearly, Hitler had no intention of stopping there. It became clear that it would take more than appeasement to contain the Nazi juggernaut.

Franklin Delano Roosevelt Launches the New Deal (1933)

The event: Within the first hundred days of taking office as the nation's thirty-second president, Franklin Roosevelt announced and enacted with great vigor the social programs of a "New Deal" he had promised voters during the 1932 campaign.

REPUBLICAN PRESIDENT Herbert Hoover responded to the onset of the Great Depression with an extensive menu of programs for economic recovery, but he steadfastly refused even to consider direct relief to desperate individuals. Hungry and homeless, Americans voted into office the Democratic governor of New York who had already pioneered a model relief program in his state as well as other social programs, including old-age pensions, unemployment insurance, and public utility programs.

Crippled with polio in 1921, Roosevelt was paralyzed from the waist down, but nevertheless conducted a nationwide campaign of unparalleled dynamism. In November 1932, Roosevelt polled 22.8 million votes to Hoover's 15.8 million, carrying the Electoral College 472 to 59. As if driven by this whirlwind, Roosevelt used the opening months of his administration—called "The Hundred Days"—to push sweeping legislation through Congress in order to deal with the national emergency. In its first session of the Roosevelt administration, Congress established the Federal Deposit Insurance Corporation to guarantee bank deposits, expanded the powers of the Federal Reserve Board, established the Home Owners Loan Corporation, and enacted a Federal Securities Act requiring companies to disclose full financial information on new stock issues. To combat unemployment, Roosevelt called on Congress to appropriate $500 million in relief programs and to create job programs, including the Civilian Conservation Corps (CCC).

In addition to these direct-relief programs—the kind of measures Hoover would not consider—to stimulate industry Roosevelt also picked up where his predecessor had left off. Over private sector objections, he achieved passage of the National Industrial Recovery Act, which established the Public Works Administration (PWA) and compelled industrial leaders to enact codes of fair practices, allowing them in turn to set prices without fear of antitrust prosecution. Wage minimums and work-hour limits were established by the law, which also guaranteed the workers' right to collective bargaining. The omnibus legislation also created the National Recovery Administration, led by General Hugh Johnson. The new agency drafted business codes, enabling the federal government to institute such progressive reforms as the regulation of child labor in the textile and other industries.

Roosevelt was also greatly concerned about the desperate plight of American farmers, and, with Congress, he established the Agricultural Adjustment Administration in May 1933. This program set production limits and established federal subsidies, all aimed at elevating agricultural prices to "parity" with the prices farmers had enjoyed when agriculture was in its best years.

The Tennessee Valley Authority was also formed within the fateful Hundred Days. This agency was responsible for broad social and utility programs within the chronically impoverished Tennessee River Valley region. Hydroelectric plants, nitrate manufacturing for fertilizers, soil conservation, flood control, and reforestation were all part of the program, headed by a three-man board and covering parts of seven states.

In the prosperous 1920s, the New Deal would have been regarded as unthinkable socialism, and FDR would have been treated as little better than a traitor. In the desperate 1930s, however, the American people adored their leader. The New Deal proved to be no panacea—nine million people were still out of work by the 1934 congressional elections—but it was effective, and, perhaps most important of all, it gave people hope. The Democrats succeeded in gaining even larger majorities in both houses of Congress. In 1936, Roosevelt secured re-election by a landslide and thus began the so-called Second Hundred Days.

The president persuaded Congress to establish the National Labor Relations Act, known as the Wagner Act, to increase labor union power; the Social Security Act, to create old-age pensions through payroll and wage taxes; the Public Utility Holding Company Act, which restricted the control of electric and gas companies; the Rural Electrification Administration, which brought electricity to nine out of ten farms in America by 1950; and the Wealth Tax Act, which increased the rate of taxes on incomes over $50,000 to 75 percent.

By the middle of 1937, with social disaster at bay but the economy still lagging, Roosevelt asked Congress to pass a $3.75 billion public works bill. It was, perhaps, his most momentous decision. As much as the New Deal programs had cost, the federal budget had been maintained close to a balanced state. Now Roosevelt proposed to put the budget on a deficit footing, raising a conservative outcry that nevertheless failed to keep FDR from capturing an unprecedented third term.

The New Deal had not only fulfilled much of the progressive agenda of reform that had been developing support for over a century, but it also reshaped the America of the twentieth century.

America's Great Plains Become a Massive Dust Bowl (1934)

The event: 1934 was the first of three years of widespread and devastating drought that triggered environmental, social, and economic disaster as well as giant dust storms that swept across the American West, initiating a massive federal response from FDR's New Deal government.

EVEN BEFORE THE Great Depression swept the country—and the world—in 1929, farmers and ranchers of the Great Plains were having a difficult time. The 150,000-square-mile area encompassing the Oklahoma and Texas panhandles as well as portions of Kansas, Colorado, and New Mexico offered poor, light soil, scant rainfall, and high prevailing winds that regularly took off vast quantities of precious topsoil. The farmers themselves had greatly compounded the problems of natural topography and climate by heedless agricultural practices. The boom years of World War I and a lucrative market for grain and cattle prompted farmers to plow up thousands of acres of natural grass cover in order to plant wheat. Elsewhere, land was overgrazed by cattle. The result was a widespread disruption of the root systems that held the arid soil together.

In 1934, just when the Depression was making life that much tougher, a massive drought struck and did not let up until 1937. It was accompanied by vicious, raking wind storms that created "black blizzards," literally carrying away tons of topsoil, even as it

choked starving livestock to death. Fully 60 percent of the Great Plains population left in a massive, desperate, impoverished exodus west, mostly toward California, where (they were told) the soil was still lush. Many others sought work in cities and towns, which soon posted billboards along the highways warning the itinerants that their community had no jobs to offer.

Franklin Delano Roosevelt's New Deal government responded to the crisis with an array of aid agencies and programs, the most prominent of which was the Soil Conservation Service, founded in 1935. Not only were farmers given direct monetary aid, but they were instructed on conservation practices such as planting trees and grass to anchor the soil, contouring their plow rows in terrace fashion in order to hold the precious rainwater and prevent erosion, and rotating crops to allow the soil to regenerate. In a massive subsidy program, the government purchased 11.3 million acres of land with the express purpose of keeping it out of production.

During this period, the federal government's Farm Security Agency also subsidized a group of extraordinarily talented photographers, including Dorothea Lange and Walker Evans, to record conditions in the Dust Bowl—as the Great Plains were now called. These photographers and others produced a series of moving photographs that did much to raise the consciousness of the nation, making it aware of the plight of so many farm families. Perhaps the best-known expressive work to come out of the era was John Steinbeck's novel *The Grapes of Wrath*, which narrated the saga of one desperate family of "Okies." The story reached an even wider audience in the film version he scripted in 1940.

The programs of the New Deal ultimately prevailed against the Dust Bowl, and most of the devastated land was reclaimed by the beginning of World War II. It was a dramatic demonstration of the destructive power of nature and the heedlessness of human action on the one hand, and the effectiveness of centrally coordinated and rationalized government action on the other. However, it soon became apparent that America had not learned its ecological lesson. As soon as the Dust Bowl was reclaimed and was again the Great Plains, World War II sent the price of wheat soaring and prompted farmers to plow up the grasslands, just as they had during the first world war. When drought struck again in the early 1950s, Congress acted quickly to avert a new Dust Bowl by granting large-scale (and highly controversial) subsidies to farmers, paying them *not* to produce in order to return millions of acres back to grassland.

Stalin Launches a Purge of the Communist Party (1934)

The event: When the 17th Communist Party Congress in 1934 showed support for Sergei Kirov, a moderate and a potential rival of its chairman Josef Stalin, the Soviet leader not only engineered Kirov's assassination in December 1934, but used the murder as a pretext for arresting most of the party's highest-ranking officials as counterrevolutionary conspirators, launching the first of a series of sweeping and deadly purges of the Soviet government that would last until 1938 and destroy even the hope of a challenge to Stalin's already all-but-absolute control of Russia.

STALIN WAS BORN Josef Vissarionovich Djugashvili on December 21, 1879, in Gori, a rural town in the tsarist state of Georgia. His brutal father, an impoverished and alcoholic shoemaker, was killed in a brawl when Josef was eleven, whereupon the boy's indulgent mother groomed him for the Orthodox priesthood. By the time he entered the Tiflis Theological Seminary at age fourteen, the youth's rebelliousness had earned him the nickname "Koba," after a legendary Georgian bandit and rebel. Koba became involved in radical anti-tsarist political activity in 1898, and a year later left the seminary to become a full-time revolutionary. Soon, he was touring the Caucasus, stirring up laborers and organizing strikes on behalf of the Social Democrats.

In 1903, the party split into two groups, V. I. Lenin's radical Bolshevik faction and the more moderate Mensheviks. Stalin fell in with the radicals and grew close to Lenin. For the next decade, from 1903 until he was exiled to Siberia in 1913, Stalin worked to expand the Bolsheviks' power, organizing cell after cell across the nation, and financing the party's work through a series of daring robberies. Repeatedly arrested, he always managed to escape, which has led some to speculate that he was in the pay of the tsarist secret police. Regardless of such rumors, Lenin in 1912 elevated Stalin to the Bolshevik Central Committee, the party's inner circle. Reticent, even inarticulate, Stalin nevertheless became the first editor of *Pravda* ("Truth"), the Bolsheviks' official newspaper, and adopted the name Stalin, meaning "Man of Steel."

In 1913, the wily Stalin was at last exiled to Siberia, returning to Russia only after the overthrow of Nicholas II in March 1917. When the first Bolshevik attempt to seize power during the summer of 1917 failed, resulting in the arrest of Leon Trotsky and the self-imposed exile of Lenin, Stalin worked to reorganize the party and played a central role in the successful October Revolution.

Stalin served in a succession of commissar posts in the Bolshevik government while working quietly to consolidate greater power. By 1922, he was named general secretary of the party's Central Committee, a position from which he could control most of the party. By the time Lenin fell victim to the stroke that would kill him, he had grown disenchanted with Stalin and was taking steps to prevent him from assuming a leadership role after his death. But when Lenin died in 1924, despite a letter to the party he left behind warning against Stalin, the latter promoted himself as the Communist leader's handpicked successor and ruthlessly exploited his position as general secretary to eliminate all who opposed him.

Once his position was secure, Stalin announced a retreat from Lenin's ideal of world communist revolution by advocating "socialism in one country." He also proposed an economic program far more moderate than the one Lenin had envisioned. Opposed by party leftists, Stalin eliminated much of the left. Having accomplished this by about 1928, he instantly shifted ground and adopted radical leftist economic programs, including the forced collectivization of agriculture and a hyper-accelerated program of industrialization. With his original left-wing opponents neutralized, Stalin attacked the party's right wing. By 1930, opposition on the left *and* the right had been quashed. Stalin had become the undisputed dictator of the Soviet Union.

In order to transform the Soviet Union from an agricultural nation into a modern industrial power, Stalin expropriated the lands of the middle-class farmers, or *kulaks*, "deporting" or killing those who offered resistance. His regime decreed a series of five-year plans to enforce collectivization and industrialization, financing the plans by exporting grain and other produce despite a devastating famine that swept the Soviet Union in 1932. Millions who resisted were executed, and millions more starved to death. A 1988 estimate put the number of deaths that directly resulted from the forced collectivization of 1928–1933 at 25 million.

During the first five-year plan, opposition to Stalin mounted, and there was a short-lived peasant revolt, which the dictator easily crushed. More challenging was the 17th Party Congress and its mild support for Sergei Kirov, a moderate rival to Stalin. With Kirov's murder as an excuse for arresting most of the party's highest-ranking officials as counterrevolutionary conspirators, beginning in 1936 Stalin conducted a series of public trials of party officials and senior military officers. As a result of the massive purges, by 1939, 98 of the 139 central committee members elected in 1934 had been executed, and 1,108 of the 1,966 delegates to the 17th Congress had been arrested. Moreover, Stalin's KGB (secret police) chief Lavrenti Beria directed the arrest, execution, exile, and imprisonment of millions of ordinary Soviet citizens.

The deaths caused by forced collectivization—through execution as well as starvation—would have been more than enough to make Josef Stalin the most prolific mass murderer in a century that offered tough competition for that dubious title. And to these must be added the devastation of the purges, which went well beyond the hundreds of party officials neutralized and the millions of citizens persecuted or executed. For, in eliminating so many of his top military officers, Stalin badly crippled the Red Army, making Russia ripe for Hitler's invasion of 1941. The purges, coupled with the short-lived Hitler–Stalin Pact of 1939, not only shocked the citizens of Western nations but also disillusioned many Communists and would-be Communists worldwide, including a number in the United States. To them, as to the recently purged old party faithful, Stalin had betrayed the Revolution.

John Maynard Keynes Suggests a New Economic Theory (1935)

The event: In 1935, John Maynard Keynes, the darling of London's Bloomsbury literary set, published *The General Theory of Employment, Interest and Money*, a work whose notions of deficit spending would set economic theory on its head and change the way national governments the world over did business.

B ORN A GIFTED CHILD in 1883 to an esteemed economics scholar and the first female graduate of Cambridge University, John Maynard Keynes traveled the educational path customary to Britain's professional elite, from prep school to Eton to King's College, Cambridge, and he excelled

socially and academically at all of them. By the time he had graduated Cambridge to join the British civil service and move to the India Office at Whitehall, Keynes was already the dominant figure—along with essayist Lytton Strachey—of the Bloomsbury crowd, an exclusive circle of aesthetic highbrows, writers, and artists. They included historian Leonard and novelist Virginia Woolf, painter Duncan Grant, art critic Clive Bell, and writer E. M. Forester.

Keynes's experience at the India Office formed the basis for his first major work, still today the definitive examination of pre-World War I India's finance and currency. For a while Keynes left government service to return to Cambridge, where he taught economics as had his father before him. But the onset of the Great War led His Majesty to draft Keynes yet again, this time to Treasury, an agency many times more powerful than its American counterpart. There he looked after Britain's relations with her allies and conserved the country's scant supply of foreign currency. He was lauded for his success which is no doubt why he was able to attend the Versailles Peace Conference, accompanying Prime Minister David Lloyd George as an economic adviser.

Distressed by the political chicanery and the vindictive demands for insanely high reparations to be imposed on the defeated Germany, Keynes—his health rapidly deteriorating—resigned his post, retired for the summer, and wrote a book about the whole mess called *The Economic Consequences of the Peace*. Polemical and trenchant, the essay correctly analyzed the effect of the reparations on the German economy and predicted they would never be paid, but what created the book's scandalous success were its blistering sketches of Woodrow Wilson, France's George Clemenceau, and Keynes's old boss, Lloyd George. What his friend Lytton Strachey had done to the icons of Victoria's England

in *Eminent Victorians*, Keynes did to the world leaders of his own day, and he was never trusted in Whitehall circles ever again. In fact, he was considered by career government men to be that most dangerous of public servants, one willing to rock the boat. And of course they were right.

For Keynes was a die-hard iconoclast, a genius who knew his own measure, lived life to the fullest, and slept every day till noon. After Versailles, he returned to Cambridge by day, Bloomsbury by night, and became esteemed as the most brilliant student of Alfred Marshall and A. C. Pigou, two eminent Cambridge economists who between them had produced the authoritative account of how competitive markets worked, business firms functioned, and consumers spent their money. For a decade, Keynes managed to keep his mouth shut, writing only an occasional essay mildly skeptical of his mentors' complacent views about laissez-faire capitalism—tempered slightly, perhaps, by public policy—as the wellspring of all happiness. Then came the worldwide Great Depression of the 1930s.

When the world caved in on Wall Street's Black Tuesday, bewildered politicians and economists, with a few exceptions, had little to say, and as banks and businesses folded across the globe and workers and farmers went grumbling onto the public dole, the pundits sputtered with an ever growing lack of confidence that time and, well, nature would restore prosperity if government would just, for a little while longer now, resist trying to manipulate the economy. After all, the unemployed could always get jobs if they were willing to work for less, and businessmen could always restore their sales by slashing their prices. Sure some people would get hurt, and yes, some—the weaker ones—would be wiped out permanently, but if everybody stuck together and accepted the discipline of competitive adjustment, soon recovery, prosperity, higher profits, and better wages would gloriously return.

The trouble was, the years went by, and it did not happen. In America, a blithe aristocrat named Franklin Delano Roosevelt promised the poor and the out-of-work a new deal, swept aside President Herbert Hoover and his hollow-sounding promises that prosperity was just around the corner, and took the White House in a landslide. In Britain, in Germany, across Europe and much of the world, membership in Communist parties began to swell. Laissez-faire capitalism had suddenly gone politically bankrupt. New explanations and new policies were desperately needed.

About that time Keynes began writing a *Treatise on Money* in 1930, and then *The General Theory of Employment, Interest and Money*. The most influential essay composed by an economist in the twentieth century, *The General Theory* was comparable in stature to the great economic and public policy works of the eighteenth century, Adam Smith's *Wealth of Nations* and Robert Malthus's *Essay on Population*, and to another great iconoclastic economic work of the nineteenth century, Karl Marx's *Das Kapital*. In essence, Keynes's message came down to two powerful propositions, the first declaring the existing theory of unemployment utter nonsense, the second

offering a different explanation of the origins of unemployment and depressions.

First, said Keynes, in an economic depression there was no wage so low that it could eliminate unemployment, and hence it was simply wicked to blame those out of work for their predicament. Second, prosperity depended upon aggregate demand, that is, upon the total spending of consumers, business investors, and public agencies. When the aggregate demand was high, times were prosperous. When aggregate demand was low, sales dropped off and jobs disappeared. From these two general propositions flowed a beautifully comprehensive view of economic behavior. Because consumers, obviously, could not spend any more than they made (Keynes wrote in the days before the credit card), they were not the source of the ups and downs of the business cycle; instead, those fluctuations could be laid at the feet of business investors and governments. During depressions, the thing to do was to beef up private investment, or if investors proved frightened—which they often did; it was one of the causes of depressions in the first place—the government needed to create public substitutes for the missing money of the hoarding rich. In times of milder economic distress (we now call them recessions) a change in monetary policy to make credit easier to come by and lower interest rates might be enough to stimulate business investment and, hence, restore the high aggregate demand caused by full employment. The very worst of times, such as the Great Depression, called for sterner measures—deliberate public deficits, either in the shape of public works or subsidies to afflicted groups, or both.

Thus was born the modern economy of the twentieth century, with its goal of full employment and its panacea of deficit spending. Keynes's words were sweet music for a desperate world, and he had, in a very short span of time, converted most of his colleagues to his economic theory. By World War II, politicians were listening intently, and during the war and later, one after another of the Western democracies proclaimed their new commitment to maintaining high employment. In 1946, the United States passed the Full Employment Act, formally imposing upon all future presidents and congresses the *duty* of maintaining prosperity, and Americans fell into the habit of forever afterward holding the federal government to its word. And, ah, how Keynsian economics seemed to work. Regardless of whether his policies were the reason, which many economists now grumble was not the case, the United States and the world began to enjoy the longest sustained period of growth and prosperity in history. Without Keynes, there would have been no Marshall Plan, no European Economic Miracle, no postwar consumer boom. Without government investment, especially in defense spending, many of the technological innovations and economic benefits we now take for granted, from commercial airline travel to widespread private home ownership to quality public universities to excellent interstate highways to home computers, would never had developed so rapidly, if they had developed at all.

Nowadays, economists and politicians are apt to point out that all that public spending came at a cost, and, indeed, the problem with public works and subsidies, i.e., welfare, is that the government has to have money to spend it. And the government gets its money from only two places—taxes from businesses and individuals or loans from banks and financial institutions. For fifty years conservative economists harped about wrong-headed Keynesian assumptions, and when interest rates shot sky high in the 1970s following the Arab oil embargo, folks began to get worried. The middle-class tax revolt of the 1980s in the United States posed a serious threat to an economy based on Keynes's theories, but the answers President Ronald Reagan proposed when he was swept into office by that revolt were not so much anti-Keynes as they were crypto-Keynesian. The Reaganites simply swept worries about taxes and public investment under the rug for a while, and kept on borrowing and spending, running up huge deficits and calling their policies "supply side" rather than "demand side" (i.e., Keynesian) economics. And Reagan most assuredly did not cut military spending; in fact, he increased it. Reagan carefully never answered questions about what such huge federal deficits meant for the country in the long run, being in this—as in everything—much less candid than Keynes himself would have been. For, when asked similar questions about his theories during his lifetime, Keynes responded, "In the long run, we are all dead."

By the end of the century, more traditional economists were responding to that statement with words to the effect of, "Yes, but our children are not." In the United States and around the world, free market economists were gaining control, again talking about balanced budgets, lower taxes to stimulate private investment, and doing away with public spending, if not entirely, then certainly substantially. And again, politicians and economists were blaming the unemployed for being jobless and the poor for being poor. For them Keynes had become demonized, and the kind of entitlement programs his theories had engendered

were being held responsible for all current economic woes. Lest we forget, though, there were economic downturns—and severe depressions—long before there were entitlements, and so far the only thing the dismantling of the Keynesian-inspired U.S. economy had produced was a growing gap between the very rich and the very poor and a disappearing middle class. Once, Keynes's works were credited with saving the world; we shall see how well his detractors do at securing the future.

The Hoover Dam Is Completed (1936)

The event: When Franklin Delano Roosevelt's New Deal government completed Boulder Dam—renamed Hoover Dam in 1947 for the former president—in 1936, it was the biggest structure of its kind in the world. At 726 feet high, it spawned a new era of building high-rise dams in nation after nation, remaking "the face of the earth and altering the distribution of social and economic power" around the globe, as historian Donald Worster recently noted.

A FAMOUS 1936 New Deal government report, *The Future of the Great Plains*, blamed more than nature for drying up the farmlands of the American Midwest during the Dust Bowl. According to the reports' authors, farmers during the 1920s—not understanding plains agriculture and driven by destructive acquisitive values in American culture—had so recklessly plowed under the prairie that the great dust storms sweeping the lands in the West were inevitable. It did seem at the time though as if nature was taking her revenge for American greed and hubris. Not only did years of drought plague western agriculture in the 1930s, but also swarms of locusts and mercilessly cold winters frightened farmers yet again of an angry God.

Today much of the New Deal era's grand planning seems like a massive counterattack. It was as if those who could engineer and perfect the most powerful capitalist nation on earth were determined not to be undone by the whims of a fickle environment. In the America of the 1930s nothing so stirred the contemporary imagination and renewed the American people's faith in their ability to conquer nature than the building of Boulder Dam. Gleaming white in the blazing desert sun, Boulder Dam was a modern engineering marvel, America's answer to the pyramids of Egypt and the ancient Colossus of Rhodes. It was also an direct assault on one of the mightiest streams on earth, the Colorado River.

In the late 1920s the demand to bring

the Colorado River under human domination first produced a scheme to build a gargantuan storage dam and reservoir. Among those clamoring for water from the Colorado was a group of real estate promoters who had turned Los Angeles from a backwater adobe outpost of ten thousand people into a big city with a starry-eyed population of two hundred thousand. Already William Mulholland and his fellow civic salesmen had drained the Owens Valley dry, and now they turned to the Colorado River where, in the 1920s, only seven thousand or so people lived in clusters along the river basin or up in sleepy, dusty Las Vegas.

L.A. boosters fanned out over the country, promoting to Iowa farmers and New Jersey factory workers—those the Hollywood movie colony would come to call "the folks"—a new life in the sun along the dry, warm California coast. If the folks came, L.A. was certainly going to need water, though the "need" was originally hatched in the minds of the West Coast promo men. "If we don't get the water," said Mulholland, "we won't need it. We have to get the water or quit growing." L.A.'s demand for the sparkling Colorado water was part of the classic Western real estate baron's dream: Build it, and they will come. Big capitalists who had bought huge stretches of farmland down in the Imperial Valley just north of Mexico wanted that water even more badly, if possible, than the L.A. land hucksters. They had their 3,000-acre "agribusinesses," an army of Chicano workers to exploit for planting and harvesting, and railway links to urban entrepôts for shipping whatever

they decided to grow. But they did not have control over the Colorado River, their only source of irrigation that sometimes raged into their valley and flooded everything, sometimes refusing to give their ditches and canals even the smallest wet kiss. Last there were the U.S. government's Bureau of Reclamation professionals, whose very job description required that they undo nature. These bureaucrats were Pharaonic administrators who had grown drunk on New Deal power; all they wanted was to build "the biggest dam ever built by anyone anywhere."

All of them—the bureaucrats, the imperial farmers, the L.A. promoters—were filled with dreams and desires beyond imagination: All wanted to dominate nature. All wanted to conquer the Colorado, as if only a river so wild, so full of life, could satisfy their lusts. George Santayana would have called them fanatics, men who redoubled their efforts as they lost sight of their aims, and their efforts were aimed at taking the river apart from headwater to mouth, to kill it as surely as their fathers had killed the Indians. The Boulder Dam, then, was only the beginning. It was followed by more than twenty-five additional dams. Blocked, caught, becalmed, bled on every side, the mighty Colorado would finally cease to flow to the sea, but instead die with a whimper in a wasteland of salt somewhere in Baja California.

In the twentieth century, it seemed, for the first time, men had the ability not merely to bend nature to their own whims, but if they wanted, to destroy her altogether.

The Spanish Civil War Begins (1936)

The event: On July 18, 1936, Fascist General Francisco Franco entered into a conspiracy of military men and right-wing political conservatives to overthrow the ruling left-wing Popular Front, leading a mutiny against the government and touching off the Spanish Civil War.

FRANCISCO PAULINO HERMENEGILDO Teodulo Franco-Bahamonde was, at thirty-four, Spain's youngest brigadier general. Two years later, he took over as director of the *Academia General Militar* at Saragossa during the dictatorship of General Primo de Rivera. However, in 1931, after Republican forces overthrew the Spanish monarchy, Franco was accused of monarchist sympathies and was transferred to duty in the Balearic Islands. His reassignment effectively removed him until 1934 from participation in the military's many conspiracies against the new republic. That year, the government summoned him back to Spain to suppress a miners' revolt in Asturias, a mission that earned Franco the respect of the conservative right wing and the hatred of the left. With the conservative faction now on the rise, he was named chief of the general staff in 1935. But the following year (typical of the Spanish politics of a turbulent period), the left-wing Popular Front gained a majority in the elections, and Franco was once again "exiled," this time to a command post in the Canary Islands. Nevertheless, Franco was able to play a leading role in the military and conservative conspiracy that erupted into the Spanish Civil War on July 18, 1936.

Franco flew to Morocco, took over the Spanish Foreign Legion garrison, and airlifted a large contingent of it to Spain later in the month. During July and August, he led a motorized advance on Madrid, but was repulsed by government forces during September and October. By then, the country was divided into government and Nationalist territories, and on September 29, 1936, the Nationalists established their own government with Franco as head of state. In April 1937, Franco became head of the fascist Falangist party.

The bitter and virulent Spanish Civil War drew interested outside parties into a struggle between the political right and the political left, between fascism on the one hand and a range of left-wing political ideologies (from anarchy to democracy to Communism) on the other. The Falange gained support from Fascist Italy and Nazi Germany, while the government (or Loyalists, as they were often called) found support in thousands of volunteers from all over the world, including those from the United States who joined the famous so-called Lincoln Brigades. They came to fight in a just war against the seemingly inexorable forces of fascism. Among the volunteers was Ernest Hemingway, whose novel *For Whom the Bell Tolls*—centered around a Lincoln-Brigade protagonist and published in 1940—portrayed the bitter ironies and high idealism of the war.

Stalin, his eyes steadily fixed on Russia and its place in a dangerous world, refused any real aid to the Communists fighting in Spain, and in fact encouraged those under the influence of Moscow to betray their United Front comrades in any number of ways. Without support from the Soviets, leftist idealism proved no match against military aid to the right from Italy and Germany. With the fall of Madrid on March 28, 1939, the Spanish Civil War ended, the Falangists were established in power, and Franco became de facto dictator of Spain. He did not formally ally himself with his benefactors, Mussolini and Hitler, during World War II, maintaining instead an offi-

cial policy of neutrality. It was always clear where Franco's allegiance lay, and he not only sent workers to Germany, but created a volunteer Blue Division to fight for the Germans on the Russian front. Not until the tide of the war manifestly turned against Germany did the ever-pragmatic Franco enforce a more genuine neutrality.

For thousands of American, British, and other idealistic young men, the Spanish Civil War was the defining event of their generation. It gave them the opportunity to get into the fight against oppression and intolerance in the form of fascism. For Italy and Germany, the conflict in Spain was not only an opportunity to secure a new ally, but it was also a convenient stage on which to rehearse for the much greater world war to come.

The War of the Worlds Airs on American Radio (1938)

The event: On Halloween evening in 1938, a young dramatic genius named Orson Welles broadcast a radio adaptation of H. G. Wells's novel about an invasion from Mars that ignited a major panic among listeners.

ORSON WELLES, at the helm of a New York dramatic company called the Mercury Theatre—partially financed by federal WPA money—was in trouble. The radio spinoff of the Mercury group, "Mercury Theatre on the Air," suddenly found itself airing opposite the "Chase and Sanborn Hour," the nation's most popular show, starring ventriloquist Edgar Bergen and his dummy Charlie McCarthy. "Mercury Theatre" was losing listeners, so Welles decided to try something different—a radio adaptation of an old H. G. Wells novel about Martians invading from outer space. The

twists Welles introduced were to update the time and place and to present the story as if the listener had just tuned in to a program of live dance music that gets interrupted by a series of flash bulletins, in effect narrating the story of the Martian invasion as it unfolds.

As scheduled, at eight o'clock on Halloween evening, 1938, the announcer began: "Orson Welles and the 'Mercury Theater on the Air' in *The War of the Worlds* by H. G. Wells," and the show began with a program of the insipid dance music of a fictive Ramon Raquello performing in the Meridien Room of the equally fictitious

Hotel Park Plaza. Suddenly, the announcer broke in with "a special bulletin from the Intercontinental Radio News": a "huge flaming object" had just descended on a farm near Grover's Mill, New Jersey.

With that, the musical broadcast was continued until newsman "Carl Phillips" again interrupted: "Ladies and gentlemen," he gasped, "this is the most terrifying thing I have ever witnessed. . . . Wait a minute, someone's crawling. Someone or . . . something. I can see peering out of that black hole two luminous disks . . . are they eyes? It might be a face. It might be . . . good heavens, something's wriggling out of the shadow like a gray snake. Now it's another one, and another one, and another one. . . ."

And then it was back to the Meridien Room for more music, punctuated by a series of bulletins culminating in the "grave announcement" that "incredible as it may seem, both the observations of science and the evidence of our eyes lead to the inescapable assumption that those strange beings who landed in the Jersey farmlands tonight are the vanguard of an invading army from the planet Mars."

As all of this was going on, Welles did not know that he had not only succeeded in outdrawing Edgar Bergen and Charlie McCarthy that evening, but he had also touched off an unprecedented panic in a significant portion of the American public. Police agencies were flooded with frantic calls. Even as the broadcast *described* the swarms of crazed humanity thronging the streets of New York City, swarms of crazed humanity *were* thronging the streets of New York City. Police fielded calls from people earnestly reporting that they had sighted the Martians. One woman was so distraught that she was about to swallow poison, when her husband stopped her just in time. People stumbled and fell, breaking arms and legs, and a rash of miscarriages was also reported.

Were Americans so gullible in 1938? Not necessarily. They were, however, scared, anxious about an alien invasion of another kind—stories about Hitler's annexation of Austria were reported in spotty and sporadic news flashes interrupting regular radio broadcasts. Welles had created a script that played on the broadcast conventions audiences had learned to accept as gospel truth. They trusted the media and were fully prepared to believe what they heard from the loudspeaker behind the cloth grille and below the gently glowing dial of the benign wooden console in their living rooms. Welles had inadvertently taught the nation a lesson about the awful power of the century's most advanced communications medium. It was, of course, a lesson that Hitler and his man Josef Goebbels, appointed to the office of propaganda minister of the Third Reich, already knew quite well.

Hitler and Stalin Sign a Non-Aggression Pact (1939)

The event: On August 23, 1939, Adolf Hitler and Josef Stalin, representatives of the century's two irreconcilably opposed totalitarian ideologies, stunned the world by signing a Non-Aggression Pact.

As ADOLF HITLER came to dominate more and more of Europe in the late 1930s, Stalin lost all desire to oppose this ideological antithesis of Communism. He approached Hitler, proposing and concluding a Nazi–Soviet non-aggression pact, guaranteeing that neither nation would act against the other. The pact stunned the world, particularly Stalin's apologists in the West, mostly intellectuals and others who forgave Stalin his excesses—the deadly consequences of forced collectivization of Soviet farmlands and the purges of 1936–1938—because he was leader of the only ideology actively and aggressively opposed to fascism. Now, it seemed, Stalin had shirked his historical duty and, indeed, had climbed into bed with the enemy.

The non-aggression pact gave Hitler license to invade Poland, actively abetted by Soviet forces attacking from the east, on September 1, 1939. Stalin also decided to increase Soviet influence in the West by invading Finland on November 30, 1939, which ignited a short but costly war that secured Finland's surrender on March 12, 1940. Then, on June 22, 1941, Hitler, without warning, violated the non-aggression pact by invading the Soviet Union.

Early resistance to the invasion was weak and poorly coordinated because Stalin was, in a word, stupefied, and be-cause the 1936–1938 purges had stripped the Red Army of most of its senior officer corps. Within a short time, however, the dictator shook off his panic and took personal command of the Red Army, mounting an increasingly effective defense. He moved with swift and strategic deliberation, evacuating vital war industries east, into Siberia and Central Asia, just ahead of the advancing German armies. As Winston Churchill had emboldened the British people, so Stalin rallied the Soviets, appealing to patriotism and, for the sake of morale, disbanding the Communist International while at the same time officially rehabilitating the Orthodox Church. Despite the severe damage he himself had inflicted on his officer corps, Stalin showed a genius for identifying capable—sometimes brilliant—commanders in Marshals Georgi Zhukov and Ivan Konev, whom he fully supported in extremely costly but ultimately successful campaigns against the invaders. Stalin, who had wantonly bled so many of his country-men, now realized that his first great asset in the struggle against Hitler was the great number of Soviet citizens who were willing to bleed in order to save their country. Stalin's second asset was the country itself, the vastness of Soviet Russia, which had defeated would-be invaders before, most notably and disastrously Napoleon in 1812.

Stalin would employ these assets with grim and unyielding genius in a scorched-earth defensive campaign that, eventually, allowed him to take the initiative, drive the Nazis out of the USSR, and push them back, ultimately all the way to Berlin.

By the middle of the war, Stalin would earn great prestige as a military leader among Soviet citizens as well as his allies, Britain and the United States, allowing him to assume a strong negotiating position at the major allied war conferences conducted in Tehran, Yalta, and Potsdam. By the end of the World War II, many Russians—and others—would be hailing the dictator as the savior of his nation.

World War II Begins (1939)

The event: Without bothering with the formality of declaring war, Adolf Hitler attacked Poland at 4:30 A.M. on September 1, 1939, commencing a second worldwide conflict.

THE PUNITIVE Treaty of Versailles, which ended World War I, "disarmed" Germany by limiting its army to 100,000 men, including 4,000 officers, depriving it of its heavy weaponry—including aircraft—and closing most of the military academies. Its navy was reduced to 15,000 men, and it was prohibited from building any new submarines. In fact, under General Hans von Seeckt, a Prussian military aristocrat, the ostensibly skeletal postwar German army was developed into a *Fuhrerheer*, an army of leaders, an all-volunteer force of the very highest caliber. It would serve as the core around which a new army would be formed—when the time came.

Germany also found ways to circumvent the armament restrictions imposed by the Versailles treaty, including an agreement with the Soviet Union—the Treaty of Rapallo of April 1922—which established a program of military cooperation between Germany and the USSR and which gave Germany facilities *in Russia* for developing the advanced ground weapons and aircraft forbidden by Versailles. In addition and apart from the treaty, both the German army and navy undertook programs of clandestine rearmament, and the London Naval Treaty of June 1935 not only allowed Germany increased tonnage in warships, but kindled Hitler's hopes that Great Britain might actually be an ally in the war he knew was coming.

For years following the Great War, German strategists were also hard at work developing a new combat doctrine. It was called *blitzkrieg*—literally, "lightning war"—a system of weapons and tactics capable of piercing an enemy's front and then encircling and destroying all or part of his forces. Its hallmarks were great speed, great violence, and the retention of the initiative at all costs. Reconnaissance identified weak points in the front, and these—called *schwerounkt* (thrust points)—were rapidly exploited by crack *kampfgruppen* (combat teams), followed swiftly by massive attacks.

The Spanish Civil War of 1936–1939 gave Germany its first opportunity to test its new army and air force as well as some of the tactics of *blitzkrieg*, but in Poland the doctrine was given its first full-scale demonstration. As devastating as the attack was, it proved no more than an overture to a darkness yet more horrible than any the first war had brought.

Without a declaration of war, Hitler's Luftwaffe (air force) raided airfields all across Poland beginning at 4:30 on the morning of September 1, 1939. Almost simultaneously, a superannuated German battleship, which had been "visiting" the port of Danzig, opened fire on Polish fortifications, and the *Wehrmacht* (army) surged across the Polish frontier. Despite the mounting tensions that had preceded the invasion, the massiveness, swiftness, and violence of blitzkrieg took Poland—and the world—by complete surprise.

The campaign lasted little more than a month. On September 27, Warsaw, plagued by typhoid and starvation, fell. The next day, the town of Modlin surrendered, and 164,000 Polish soldiers were taken prisoner. A holdout, the isolated coastal fortress

of Hel, gave up on October 1, and five days after that the German Tenth Army crushed the last organized Polish force at Kock. An entire nation had been invaded, its army defeated, its cities taken in little more than a month. Such was blitzkrieg.

Two images dominated the campaign and, to the watching world, characterized the German war machine and the European "situation": great hawklike Stuka dive bombers swooping in for the attack, their large, nonretractable landing gear resembling horrible talons; and the Polish cavalry—a spectacle of mounted warriors wielding lances against Panzer tanks. These were images of the uneven development that the Versailles peace treaty had helped foster in Europe, images of the political unpreparedness of the rest of the world in the face of the aggressive fascist nations, images of war at mid-century.

On September 27, 1939, Hitler announced his intention to launch an attack in the West at the earliest possible moment. Britain and France, bound by treaties with Poland, declared war. And so it began, again.

Richard Wright Publishes *Native Son* (1940)

The event: This angry, violent, eloquent novel about being a Negro in America caused a sensation when it was published in 1940.

ONE OF RICHARD WRIGHT'S first published works begins, "My first lesson in how to live as a Negro came when I was quite small." Born in 1908 near Natchez, Mississippi, Wright learned that the white world beat you down and, in an effort to keep you from being beaten down by the

white world, your own family beat you down "for your own good." He learned that the code was to be passive in the face of white aggression, that, in fact, the best protection in a white world was invisibility. He learned what slaves had long ago learned: that the way to live with whites was by shambling deception—"puttin' on ol' massa." Deprivation of civil rights was no abstraction to Wright, but an intimate, daily experience. His father deserted the family when Wright was very young, leaving the boy with his mother, a domestic worker. She subsequently fell ill and became a helpless invalid, casting young Wright adrift in the world of the Jim Crow South, where each oppressive, intimidating encounter left a scar. As soon as he could, Wright fled to Chicago and then New York, struggling to make a living and finding a temporary intellectual home with the Communist Party. At this time, with the Depression bearing down hardest on blacks, he published his first piece in a WPA anthology, the 1937 "Ethics of Living Jim Crow," an autobiographical catalog of the accommodations African-Americans had to make in order to survive.

Three years later, Wright exploded onto the national literary scene with *Native Son*, which tells the story of Bigger Thomas, a young black man trapped in the hell of a Chicago slum, who strikes out in his anger at the fear of and the misunderstandings about "white" America by killing, all-but-accidentally, the daughter of his employer. In the subsequent chase, trial, conviction, and execution of Thomas, Wright is able to exploit the irony that his protagonist—destroyed by the life of violence and crime he has in some sense chosen—lives an existentially more free life, a life more authentic in its "blackness," than he would have had he followed the wishes of his mother, who dreamed of an American middle-class future for him. From the grim opening scene,

when Bigger chases a rat around the family's tiny tenement apartment and brutally beats it to death, to Bigger's sexually charged murder of a young and thoughtless suburban white girl, to Bigger's manipulation at the hands of his radical Jewish ACLU lawyer (as a symbol of capitalist oppression), the novel is a bleak anatomy of the limits and options of black Americans in the United States of the twentieth century.

Although critics, then and now, have found the novel aesthetically flawed, all agree that not since *Narrative of the Life of Frederick Douglass* was published in 1845 had a work of literature communicated the African-American experience so vividly and persuasively. Four years after *Native Son* came out, Wright published his autobiography, *Black Boy*, an unalloyed artistic masterpiece that revealed through a boy's eyes, the inversion of the American dream, a world of desertion, hunger, liquor (Wright was an alcoholic by the age of six), orphanages, beatings, lynchings, and a series of smaller but no less brutal humiliations.

Native Son and *Black Boy* embody feelings as much as ideas, the root of their success as literature, but also a gauge of the depth of Wright's emotional scars, which left him hating not only white society, but his own blackness and that of everyone closest to him. Through Richard Wright, both the author and the man, readers grasp the true price of the racism that has marred some three hundred years of life on the American continent, even into the "enlightened" twentieth century.

Japan Attacks Pearl Harbor (1941)

The event: On December 7, 1941, the empire of Japan launched an air attack on the American fleet anchored at Pearl Harbor, Hawaii, killing 2,403 Americans, destroying 19 ships and 150 planes, and propelling the United States into World War II.

THE ATTACK, when it came, at 7:55 Sunday morning, took Pearl Harbor completely by surprise. It shouldn't have. Even while Japanese negotiators were conducting business in Washington, ostensibly to avert war, "PURPLE" and "MAGIC" messages (Japanese diplomatic ciphers U.S. intelligence had broken) were being decoded continually. By November 24, Admiral Harold Stark had telegraphed Admiral Husband Kimmel, commander of naval forces at Pearl Harbor that "Chances of favorable outcome of negotiations with Japan [were] very doubtful" and that "a surprise aggressive movement in any direction" was anticipated. On November 25, Stark told Kimmel that FDR and Navy secretary Cordell Hull would not be surprised if the Japanese launched a surprise attack. Before war alert messages were issued to the military on November 26, Secretary of War Henry Stimson even spoke of the strategic *desirability* of maneuvering the Japanese into war. Yet, through inertia, inaction, and just plain blundering, the Pacific fleet and an array of aircraft, including many B-17 bombers, were left as easy prey for the Japanese carrier-based dive bombers and torpedo planes.

As costly as the attack was in terms of American lives lost and materiel destroyed or damaged, it cost the Japanese and their German allies far more. Pearl Harbor in-

stantly forged an America more unified than it had ever been or, perhaps, would ever be again. Congress immediately gave President Roosevelt his declaration of war, along with unprecedented powers to mobilize a massive war machine. On the Monday following the Pearl Harbor attack, tens of thousands jammed recruiting offices, rushing to enlist, and the government conscripted millions more, rapidly building a fighting force of more than sixteen million men and women. As in World War I, these were citizen soldiers, torn suddenly from homes and families, thrust into a bureaucratic machine fighting a global conflict. Overnight, it seemed, boys hardly old enough to shave or drive a car were dropping bombs on the centers of a centuries-old civilization or slogging through dense jungles in remote parts of the world.

The war that began for America that sleepy Sunday morning changed everything. For much of the world, including the United States, it meant what war has always meant: widespread death and devastation. For many American soldiers and sailors—even the majority who escaped physically unscathed—there was boredom, isolation, loneliness, homesickness, and fear. There was often the first taste of liquor, the first game of cards, the first night spent with a woman. There were magazines, comic books, paperbacks, movies, and the tunes of Frank Sinatra and

Glenn Miller. Most and best of all, there was mail call and letters from home.

Those at home, too, were caught up in the war. Most families had a loved one serving "overseas," and as they waited and worried, they lived in a land of rationed cars, car tires, gasoline, shoes, meat, sugar, and almost everything else. The rationing system allotted fifty points per month for canned goods, and with a can of tomatoes going for twenty points, Americans planted "victory gardens" to grow their own vegetables, finding whatever corner could be cultivated, even in the city. Women did not sit at home waiting for their husbands and lovers to return, but went to work in factories and war plants, and in the process got a taste of what it meant to have a measure of economic freedom and responsibility. Boys left the farms—most to go off to war, others to find high-paying war-related work in the cities. As a result, shorthanded farmers had to learn to improve their productivity and began using commercial fertilizers, pesticides, scientific crop rotation, and hybrid seeds. With war, the last of the Great Depression melted away in a cascade of munitions, aircraft, uniforms, boots, guns, and tires.

And when they weren't tending the victory garden or operating the punch press, Americans at home followed the war, poring over newspapers and huddling near radios. At the beginning, the news was never good. A strike against Clark Field, the principal U.S. base in the Philippines, came within two hours of the attack on Pearl Harbor, trapping General Douglas MacArthur's Far East air force on the ground and destroying half of it. Soon, Japanese troops overran the islands, capturing vast numbers of American troops. Then they soundly beat the British in Singapore and seized control of the Pacific. These defeats were humiliating and demoralizing, and the American public wanted personal vengeance against the Japanese, even though Roosevelt's official war aims were directed first and foremost to the defeat of Nazi Germany and the salvation of Europe.

The first counterstrike against Japan came far sooner than the United States was properly prepared to deliver it, but Lieutenant Colonel James Doolittle, looking for *anything* to lift American morale, pushed the limit. On April 18, 1942, he led sixteen Army Air Force B-25s—launched as none had ever been launched before, from the deck of a flattop, the carrier *Hornet*—in a spectacular low-level bombing raid on Tokyo. Damage to the Japanese capital was minimal, and the trip (as all who flew the mission well knew) was one way. It was impossible for the B-25s to carry enough fuel to get them back to the *Hornet* and, in any case, while it might be possible to get a twin-engine bomber *off* a flattop, it was certainly not feasible to *land* one on the flight deck. The plan was to land in China, dodge the Japanese occupying the country, and somehow get back to U.S. military control. Astoundingly, for most of the crews, the plan worked, and the Japanese, shocked at the bombardment of their capital city, kept four fighter groups at home as they moved against the remainder of the American Pacific Fleet at Midway Island, where the Navy, under Admiral Chester Nimitz, was ready for them. This hard-fought battle was the first major defeat the Japanese suffered and was the first step in America's fight to regain control of the Pacific.

An ocean away in the war's Atlantic theaters, U.S. troops joined their British allies in North Africa, fighting the crack German Afrika Corps under the command of the "Desert Fox," Field Marshal Erwin Rommel. After suffering initial defeat, the U.S. high command brought in one of its best commanders, General George S. Patton, who, in often contentious collaboration with British commander Field Marshal Sir Bernard Law Montgomery, ultimately defeated Rommel and pushed on from North Africa to begin the invasion of Europe by way of Italy. In the meantime, the Red Army had yet to recover from the early ravages of blitzkrieg, though Hitler's advance seemed stalled for the moment by the harsh Russian winter.

Throughout 1942 and 1943, MacArthur fought the Japanese one godforsaken island at a time—slogging it out on Guadalcanal, for example, from August 7, 1942, until February 8, 1943, when the Japanese finally withdrew. At the same time, in Europe, the American Eighth Air Force was flying a strategic bombing campaign over France and Germany. Pursued by Messerschmidt and Focke-Wulf fighters and dogged by blanket barrages of antiaircraft "flak," the average life expectancy of a B-17 crew was fifteen missions, while the prescribed tour of duty was twenty-five. "Skipper," one navigator remarked to his pilot, "mathematically there just ain't any way we're gonna live through this thing."

The strategic bombing campaign was always controversial, and, though it was an example of magnificent and poignant heroism, it accomplished few of its objectives—except, perhaps, to exact vengeance on the Germans, who "blitzed" London and other English cities with bombs, V-1 ("buzz bomb") rockets, and, later, V-2 rockets. The war in Europe, everyone knew, would be won by nothing less than full-scale invasion from the west, from the coast of France, and that would not come until June 6, 1944, D day.

As to the Pacific, the Japanese had begun to lose the war from a strategic perspective following their defeat at the Battle of Midway in June 1942, but, of course, they fought on and on, exacting a terrible toll for every inch of sea or land yielded. For many, the war looked as if it might drag on forever.

The U.S. Government Interns Japanese-American Citizens (1942)

The event: On February 19, 1942, President Roosevelt signed Executive Order 9066, ordering all Japanese-Americans, citizens as well as resident aliens within two hundred miles of the Pacific coast, to evacuate their homes and submit to government authorities.

At the time of the attack on Pearl Harbor on December 7, 1941, some 127,000 Japanese were living in the United States. Of this number, about eighty thousand were "Nisei," born in the United States and, therefore, American citizens. In the wake of the "sneak attack" on Pearl Harbor came a multitude of rumors of Japanese conspiracies to sabotage war industries and soften the West Coast for imminent invasion. There arose a widespread demand that something be done about the Japanese roaming abroad in the land. The loudest, most insistent demands originated with farmers and politicians on the West Coast, particularly California, where most of the Japanese-Americans lived. Whatever their concerns about sabotage and espionage, the farm interests mostly wanted a way to eliminate competition from the intensely hard-working and efficient Japanese farmers. As for the politicians, they saw an opportunity to exploit the desires of their constituents and the fears of the general public in order to gain popularity.

The Roosevelt administration allowed itself to be persuaded that a threat did indeed exist, and on February 19, 1942, President Roosevelt signed the order requiring all Japanese-Americans, citizens as well as non-citizens living within two hundred miles of the Pacific Coast, to evacuate their homes. Some 110,000 were moved to ten "relocation" camps located in California,

Idaho, Utah, Arizona, Wyoming, Colorado, and Arkansas. About 1,200 young men among these groups won release from the camps by joining the U.S. Army, many serving with great distinction in the European theater. The remainder, however, remained in the camps until the president announced the termination of the mass exclusion of Japanese-Americans from the West Coast, effective January 2, 1945.

The Japanese-Americans, forced to leave behind their land, their homes, and most of their belongings, brought suit against the United States government, but the Supreme Court upheld the government's actions in *Hirabayashi v. United States* and *Korematsu v. United States*. In 1968, however, the government reimbursed many of those who had been relocated for lost property, and in 1988 Congress appropriated funds to pay $20,000 to each of the sixty thousand surviving internees.

The episode demonstrates the delicate nature of democracy in a complex time. A nation willing to spill its blood in defense of freedom abroad was also willing, for a time, at least, to sacrifice that freedom at home.

American Scientists Trigger an Atomic Chain Reaction (1942)

The event: At 3:45 P.M. on December 2, 1942, in a squash court at the University of Chicago's Stagg Field, scientists led by the Italian-American physicist Enrico Fermi triggered a self-sustaining atomic chain reaction, creating the world's first nuclear reactor.

IN 1939, the Hungarian-born physicist Leo Szilard had theorized that nuclear fission

could produce an atomic chain reaction capable of producing enormous amounts of energy, which might be used for any number of purposes, including an explosive device of unprecedented destructiveness. On December 6, 1941, just one day before Japan's devastating surprise attack on the American naval fleet at Pearl Harbor, Hawaii, President Franklin Delano Roosevelt signed a secret order authorizing the Manhattan Project, charged with developing a nuclear fission bomb. Under the auspices of the Manhattan Project, the Italian-born physicist Enrico Fermi was given the assignment of producing the kind of chain reaction about which Szilard had theorized.

Fermi, who was born in Rome on September 29, 1901, became interested in physics when he was fourteen years old. His brother Giulio, from whom he had been inseparable, had died suddenly during minor surgery for a throat abscess. Deep in depression, he was wandering among the secondhand book stalls of Rome's Campo de Fiori when he found two volumes of *Elementorum physicae mathematicae*, published in 1840. Fermi spent his entire allowance on the books, brought them home, and devoured them—so eagerly (he later told his sister) that he had not even noticed that they were written in Latin. Fermi graduated from the *liceo* at seventeen and was awarded a special scholarship to the University of Pisa submitting a complex essay on vibrational analysis.

Fermi quickly became the leading light of Italian physics and began to specialize in nuclear physics, particularly the effects of neutron-induced radioactivity. As was true in Hitler's Germany, Mussolini's Fascists had a policy of persecution that sent many

scientists and intellectuals packing. Fermi was married to a Jew, and when Mussolini promulgated the first of his anti-Semitic laws in 1938, Fermi secured a professorship at New York's Columbia University and immigrated to the United States.

The nuclear reactor experiments were conducted at the University of Chicago in a closely guarded squash court commandeered for the purpose of constructing an atomic pile. Uranium and uranium oxide were piled up in combination with graphite blocks. Neutrons colliding with the carbon atoms in the graphite would not affect the carbon nuclei, but would bounce off, giving up energy and moving slowly as a result, thereby increasing the chance that they would react with the uranium 235. By making the atomic pile large, the chances that neutrons would strike the uranium 235 were increased. The pile had to be just large enough—that is, it had to reach what the scientists called *critical mass*—to start and sustain the chain reaction. To control the reaction, cadmium rods were inserted into the pile. When the pile approached critical mass, the rods would be slowly withdrawn, and the number of neutrons produced would increase. At some point during the process, more neutrons would be produced than were being consumed by the cadmium. And it was at that point that the pile would "go critical," and the nuclear chain reaction would begin. Because not all of the neutrons would come out of the bombarded nuclei at once, there would be time to reinsert the cadmium rods and stop the reaction before a horrible atomic explosion took place.

At least, such was the theory. There was

a possibility that something would go wrong, and no chain reaction would take place—or that something else would go wrong and a large part of the city of Chicago would be instantly transformed into a crater. Some even theorized that an out-of-control chain reaction might set off a reaction in the atoms of the atmosphere, effectively bringing the world to an end.

But 1942 was a desperate year, and, in Europe and the Pacific, other forces were likewise working, it seemed, to bring the world to an end. Just before 3:45 in the afternoon of December 2, Fermi gave the order to withdraw the cadmium rods. The Geiger counter needles twitched, flexed, and indicated a large release of energy. A nuclear chain reaction was underway. At 3:45, it became self-sustaining, and Fermi ordered that the rods be shoved back into place. The reaction subsided.

Fermi and his team had liberated the atomic genie, then returned it safely to its bottle—for the time being.

Jean-Paul Sartre Publishes *Being and Nothingness* (1943)

The event: In 1943, Jean-Paul Sartre published *Being and Nothingness*, the seminal statement of existentialism, the philosophy perhaps most expressive of the twentieth century as a whole, providing as it does a philosophical structure for the inchoate feelings of emptiness and dissatisfaction that had plagued thinkers throughout the century and that swept even more vehemently through a Europe devastated by the horrors of the Second World War.

IT IS RARE that a work of philosophy takes a generation by storm, particularly when the work is as abstruse, knotty, and intellectually challenging as *Being and Nothingness*. Sartre's work, however, could hardly help but be all three since it was so highly influenced by the German philosopher Martin Heidegger. An erstwhile Jesuit novitiate who many believe to have been the greatest mind of the century, Heidegger, in his own seminal work, 1927's *Being and Time*, posited a new method of investigating the nature of being, which Heidegger was careful to capitalize with a big "B."

Heidegger haughtily dismissed the dichotomy traditional German philosophy posited between rational man and the universe of "things" that he inhabited. It was pretty hard for most people to tell if Heidegger was systematic in his thinking, since his opus was nigh-to-unreadable, and Heidegger himself, like Friedrich Nietzche before him, railed against systematizing. Always on his way somewhere in his thinking, but never actually arriving at anything approaching truth, Heidegger was certainly creative, reinterpreting (some might say reinventing) the original Greek terms that lay at the foundation of Western philosophy in order to crack open what he argued was the Greeks' true meaning. The result was the invention of a new philosophical language uniquely his own, written in an abstruse, if not otiose, style liberally sprinkled with Greek and German neologisms, that was less a system and more a challenge to think, *really* think about things.

Influenced by both Søren Kierkegaard and Nietzsche, Heidegger was a professor at the University of Freiberg when he wrote *Being and Time*, and after the Nazis took over Germany, he joined the party and became rector of the university during its book-burning days. By 1934, however, he had had enough of Nazism, resigning his post, semi-retiring into relative obscurity, and—after the war—repudiating Nazism. At about that time, the young Jean-Paul Sartre began to make *Being and Time*'s methodology the corner-stone of his existentialism, much to the irritation of Heidegger, who spent his later years exploring the meaning of the techno-logical world and the dehumanization of modern life while finding ever-new ways to say that he was not a proponent of existen-tialism, at least not Jean-Paul Sartre's brand of existentialism.

Sartre's *Being and Nothingness* had as its central theme the opposition of objective things and human consciousness. Conscious-ness is a non-thing because its reality comes from standing apart from things and taking a point of view on them. Because consciousness is "*neant*" ("non-thing," not literally "noth-ing," as the translation of the title would have it), it is not borne out by the causal relation-ships that all things have with other things. What this means is that consciousness—and, therefore, human beings—are at their most es-sential when free, despite hosts of individuals, authorities, churches, and schools that would have human beings believe otherwise. (And to believe otherwise is no more than self-de-ception, an act of "bad faith.")

The great irony of Sartre's philosophy, and the irony that spoke most directly to the spirit of Western civilization at mid-century, is that this freedom is perceived not as a boon, but as a burden. "Man," Sartre wrote, "is condemned to be free." The great major-ity of human activity is directed toward achieving the impossible goal of becoming a free consciousness, a conscious entity, by identifying oneself as some *thing*: an intel-lectual, a soldier, a parent. Because this task of becoming a conscious thing—what Sar-tre called a "for-itself-in-itself"—is neces-sarily impossible, yet irresistible, Sartre defined humankind as "a useless passion."

Sartre's philosophy did not attempt to provide *the* answers, but it did furnish a con-text for thought in the chaotic, smoldering ash of the world in the wake of World War II. Some interpreted the definition of humanity as "a useless passion" to mean that life was essentially futile, and this interpretation gave rise to a whole range of later twentieth-century literature filled with "antiheroes" ranging from Albert Camus's nameless Stranger to the kind of troubled teenagers played by movie actors James Dean and the young Marlon Brando. Others, however, in-terpreted existential philosophy as invigorat-ing life with a new freedom—a freedom from the ironbound orthodoxies that led, among other things, to two calamitous wars. *Being and Nothingness* suggests that humankind has the capacity for inventing itself and reinvent-ing itself, infinitely and at will.

Sartre's own active life suggests that he himself was of the second camp. Born in Paris, on June 21, 1905, Sartre graduated from the École Normal Supérieure, Paris, in

1929 and became a secondary school teacher until 1945, when he devoted himself exclusively to writing philosophy as well as fiction and drama and editing the journal *Les Temps Modernes* (Modern Times). Sartre was never an ivory-tower intellectual, but a political activist who risked great personal danger as a member of the Resistance during the Nazi occupation. He spent a year as a prisoner of war on account of his anti-Nazi activities. He was also a playwright and a novelist. Indeed, the themes worked out philosophically in *Being and Nothingness* made their first appearance in the 1938 novel *Nausea*. Sartre's best-known play, 1944's *No Exit*, was also a profound existential work of art.

In the decades after the war, Sartre became *the* grand old man of French letters, producing what he considered his philosophical masterpiece, the *Critique of Dia-*

lectical Reason, and one of the more brutally honest biographies anyone is ever likely to read, *Words*. Offered the Nobel Prize in 1964, he turned it down. Before he died on April 15, 1980, Sartre was intellectually much abused in turn by the various new schools of French critical thought, first by the structuralists, then by the post-structuralists, then by the deconstructionist followers of Jacques Derrida, whose work—also much influenced by Heidegger—formed the starting point, if not quite the basis, for the Post-Modernist thought that Americans began to hear about toward the end of the century. However, all of them—though they would despise us for saying so—owed much to the intellectual ground Sartre plowed in his quintessential philosophy of the twentieth century, existentialism.

The Allies Invade Nazi-held Europe (1944)

The event: On June 6, 1944, the United States and Britain launched an invasion of Fortress Europe, as the German Nazis had begun to call their empire of occupation. Officially code named Operation Overlord, the long-awaited Allied invasion hit the beaches of France's Normandy region on the morning of what the entire world would soon call "D day." Along with Russia's recent great defeat of Germany at Stalingrad, D day marked the turning point of World War II.

HAVING INVADED, crushed, and occupied all but Italy and the neutral nations of Western Europe, Hitler dubbed the continent Fortress Europe and, in effect, dared anyone to invade. Early in the war, the British had attempted an assault at Dunkirk, a military disaster mitigated by a brilliant evacuation that saved the invading army from total annihilation. But as the war

ground on, it became apparent that aerial bombardment was not sufficient to obtain victory. Nor would invasion solely from the Italian peninsula suffice. These operations, plus the Soviet push from the east, would have to be combined with an all-out invasion from the west if the war was to be won once and for all.

U.S. General Dwight D. Eisenhower,

as supreme Allied commander, took charge of coordinating the invasion plan, which was code named Operation Overlord. It called for an invasion of the coast of Normandy originating from England via the English Channel. Eisenhower and the other Allied commanders knew that Fortress Europe was at its most formidable along these French western coastal regions, but they also knew that, at this stage of the war, the German army was spread thinly along the coast. If the element of surprise could be maintained, it would be possible to make a beach assault where it was least anticipated and where, therefore, German defenses were at their weakest.

It is, of course, one thing to make a surprise attack with, say, a small force of guerrillas, but quite another to attempt to hide preparations involving one million troops, together with unprecedented numbers of ships, landing and assault craft, tanks, artillery, and planes. But that is precisely how preparations for Overlord were executed, through an elaborate scheme of transmitting "disinformation" through double agents and compromised spies bolstered by decoy forces (plywood planes and inflatable tanks) deployed at supposed staging areas along the British coast and even a phantom army under the command of the Allies' most visible general, George S. Patton.

The Germans, anticipating an invasion, were nevertheless unaware of the exact invasion point, and therefore broadcast fifty infantry and ten tank (panzer) divisions across France and the Low Countries under the command of Field Marshal Gerd von Rundstedt. To ensure that these dispersed forces could not readily be transported to the point of the invasion, British-based warplanes bombed rail lines, bridges, and air fields throughout France for two months preceding the assault. Then, on June 5, the night before the Normandy landings, paratroopers were dropped inland to disrupt communications. Next, naval artillery began to pound the reinforced shore batteries.

At a four A.M. meeting held on June 5, there were serious questions about the unsettled weather. If the weather was calm enough to land a few waves of troops, then suddenly kicked up waves too high to land more, those caught on the beach would be doomed. On the other hand, to wait would mean losing the element of surprise, and that, too, would spell defeat. Eisenhower pondered the dilemma, looked at his advisers, and said, "O.K. Let's go."

At low tide, in the early morning gloom of June 6, 1944, the greatest amphibious invasion in the history of the world began. Five thousand Allied ships approached the Normandy coastline, which the invaders—British, Canadian, and American—had divided into beaches code-named Gold, Juno, Sword, Utah, and Omaha. The landings on all but Omaha Beach went smoothly, and the troops encountered surprisingly light resistance. At Omaha, however, which was the key position for securing the landing, American soldiers encountered withering German fire that exacted a heavy toll even before many of the landing craft had unloaded. Some landing craft sunk, drowning the invaders before they even reached the shore. Those that did hit the beach were raked by machine gun, artillery, and mortar fire. Yet even vital Omaha Beach was eventually secured, and over the next five days sixteen Allied divisions had landed in Normandy.

Fortress Europe had been breached by a combination of advanced tactics of twentieth-century warfare: notably, the achievement of Allied air superiority over a German *Luftwaffe* badly reduced by four years of combat; a brilliant campaign of deception and decoy; and timeless courage and determination. Considering the strategic, technological, tactical, and human forces involved, the D day operation was perhaps the single greatest battle of all time. Certainly, given the stakes involved—nothing less than the fate of humankind, a very large segment of it anyway—Operation Overlord was also among the most momentous battles the world has ever seen.

For the Soviet Union, however, fighting along the eastern front of what it would come to call the Great Patriotic War, it was not the much-welcomed invasion of France by its allies that would prove crucial in halting the German juggernaut and ultimately crushing the Nazi menace in Europe; it was the Battle of Stalingrad.

In fact, the Russian dictator, Joseph Stalin, and his generals were much frustrated by the numerous delays of the invasion by their allies in the West. From the start, the Americans had been anxious to engage the enemy on its own turf, but British leaders—veterans of the bloodletting of World War I, who knew the kind of slaughter ill-laid plans could produce—had rejected a hasty, badly prepared American plan to invade the European continent early on. Instead, the Americans enlisted in

British Prime Minister Winston Churchill's beloved North Africa campaign at a point when Germany's eastern front against Russia had become stagnant.

The year before, while Hitler's brilliant Field Marshal Erwin Rommel, the Desert Fox, fought the western powers to a stand still in a daring desert offensive, the *Führer* went ahead with his plans to invade Russia, against the advice of his general staff. Having launched the invasion, Hitler was determined to crush the Soviets, and he ordered a drive into the Caucasus Mountains, only to be held back by rains until June 1943. Encouraged by his earlier successes, Hitler decided to mount a major attack on Stalingrad as well as the Caucasus when the rains let up. By fall, victory seemed certain. Then the Russians struck back. Like Napoleon before him, Hitler became mired in the frozen mud of the harsh Russian winter, and the Russians knew how to take advantage of such weather. In a tremendous counterstrike at Stalingrad, the Soviets encircled Hitler's Sixth Army, and more than two hundred thousand German troops were utterly annihilated.

In North Africa at about that time, the Desert Fox's Afrika Corps, in part as a result of massive Allied bombing raids on the German homeland, fell to the British and American armies, leaving the West in a position to launch the D day invasion. Long before D day, however, it was clear that Germany had all but lost the war in the East. Russia began its march on Berlin, fighting against desperately determined, but retreating, German forces.

The D day invasion was the realization

of every German general's worst nightmare—the culmination of a two-front war. One month after the Allies first secured a beachhead in France, U.S. General George Patton's Third Army managed to break out and begin an incredible dash across Europe. On July 20, 1944, worried German generals almost succeeded in assassinating Hitler. On August 25, the Allied forces liberated Paris. By the fall, they had driven the Germans back into the Fatherland. Faced with disaster, Hitler again ignored the advise of his general staff and attempted one last, desperate counteroffensive. At the Battle of the Bulge on December 15, 1944, U.S. troops retreated for eight days before regrouping and routing the Nazis. Two weeks later, the Red Army crossed the Vistula. As both sides advanced toward Berlin Hitler shot himself rather than surrender. The war in Europe was at an end.

The U.S. Congress Enacts the G.I. Bill (1944)

The event: The Servicemen's Readjustment Act—popularly called the G.I. Bill of Rights and usually shortened to the G.I. Bill—provided educational and economic assistance to veterans of World War II and helped kick off a postwar boom in housing and in babies.

WHEN CONGRESS PASSED the first G.I. Bill in 1944, legislation was already in place to help disabled veterans. What was revolutionary about the new bill is that it was designed to assist all military personnel reentering the civilian world by providing fifty-two weeks of unemployment compensation, vocational training and rehabilitation, low-interest mortgages, and tuition and stipends to help with higher education, including college.

Such was the official purpose of the G.I. Bill of Rights. *Unofficially,* the legislation was part of a new world in the making, a world transformed by technology, transportation, and popular entertainment. In the United States, it was a world that was riding the crest of postwar prosperity to unprecedented heights on a suburban real estate boom that had returning veterans hungering after the "good life" they had dreamed about in the dugouts and foxholes of Europe and the Pacific.

It was a challenging world, especially to those whose adolescence, not to mention education, had been interrupted for two, three, or four years. But it was a world that was willing to educate those who wanted to learn, and it was ripe with opportunities that simply hadn't existed before the war. As the soldiers donned civilian clothes once more, poured into classrooms and new tract homes, filled the ranks of the aerospace, automobile, communications, plastic, steel, and service industries, the months and years of separation, hardship, and fear yielded a new hope. Those who had lately dealt death at the behest of their nation and in defense of what they believed now produced the biggest "Baby Boom" in history.

DNA Is Discovered (1944)

The event: In 1944, a Canadian-born American bacteriologist named Oswald Avery isolated deoxyribonucleic acid, which became popularly known as DNA, and demonstrated that it was the most basic genetic material—in essence, one of the keys of life.

VERY EARLY IN THE CENTURY, scientists understood that the cellular organelles known as chromosomes carried the genetic material by which an organism's characteristics were reproduced. Somewhat later, they determined that chromosomes were nucleoprotein and contained protein molecules as well as deoxyribonucleic acid, or DNA. Because protein appeared to be the key ingredient in all living tissue, scientists readily assumed that the genetic material in chromosomes must be protein. Their assumption was bolstered by the observation that proteins were big, complex molecules, while the nucleic acid molecule was small and relatively simple. However, researchers subsequently discovered that nucleic acid proteins were not small at all. They had *seemed* small only because the methods scientists used to isolate DNA were so crude that the molecules they retrieved were fragmentary. When researchers developed new techniques for isolating molecules, they discovered that DNA, too, was actually quite large and quite complex. Moreover, in sperm cells, where chromosomes are condensed to minimum size, scientists observed that the *protein* component was quite small and simple, while it was the DNA component that proved big and complicated.

Few scientists thought much about this, and the protein theory held sway until Oswald Theodore Avery performed an elegantly simple experiment with two strains of bacteria. He cultured a form of pneumococci that had a smooth coat and another that had a rough coat. Avery reasoned that the rough-coated pneumococci, the R strain, lacked the gene necessary to create the complex carbohydrate that gave the S strain its smooth coat. Avery prepared an extract from the S strain that contained no living matter and added it to the R strain. The result was that the R strain was converted into the S strain. Avery further refined the nonliving extract to eliminate the protein but retain the DNA. Again, the extract transformed R strain pneumococci into S strain organisms. The conclusion was inescapable: DNA was the basic substance of the *gene*, the transforming principle of life.

Avery's discovery was the biggest single advance in genetics since Gregor Mendel published his first paper on genetic inheritance in 1865. It opened the door to the detailed study of genetics, preparing the way to a brave new world of gene therapy, which promised not merely to cure disease, but to eliminate it. And, for better or worse, his discovery allows scientists, should they so choose, to select certain characteristics in plants, animals, or human beings as "desirable," while suppressing others.

British Troops Liberate the Bergen-Belsen Concentration Camp (1945)

The event: Toward the end of World War II, British troops, hardened by battling their way across Europe into the heart of Nazi Germany, were horrified when they marched up to the Bergen-Belsen concentration camp in Lower Saxony and found emaciated and diseased Jewish prisoners, together with some 13,000 unburied corpses. They had just discovered the consequence of a genocidal policy the Nazis called the "final solution to the Jewish problem." A stunned world—after years of investigations into the origins, operation, and unspeakable outcome of the policy, as well as manhunts for those responsible and public trials of those who were caught—would come to call this the Holocaust.

THE TWENTIETH CENTURY has no monopoly on unbridled intolerance and irrational hatred, but what the century did have was the political and technological means to act upon such collective psychopathologies with unprecedented viciousness, thoroughness, and bureaucratic efficiency—all on an inconceivably vast scale. Jews have been persecuted for some 1,800 years, but between 1933 and 1945, Adolf Hitler directed the murder of more Jews than had been killed in eighteen centuries of pogroms and organized persecution: some six million human beings, two-thirds of Europe's Jewish population.

Early in his political development, Hitler fixated on the Jews as the cause of Germany's degradation. He did not tailor his anti-Semitism from whole cloth, but summoned up a welter of pseudoscientific theories and allegations that had been around at least since the nineteenth century in the writings of the Anglo-German political scientist H. S. Chamberlain, who developed theories of racial purity, and the

French ethnologist J. A. Gobineau, who argued the superiority of the "Aryan race." Indeed, anti-Semitism was a well-organized movement in Germany long before Hitler came to power; his Nazi party, however, made it official government policy.

Between 1933 and 1938 the Nazis instituted boycotts of Jewish businesses, established Jewish quotas in Germany's professions and schools, enacted the Nuremberg Laws of 1935 that banned intermarriage between Jews and Gentiles, and, in 1933 established the first concentration camp, at Dachau, near Munich. The camp was first intended for the detention of Communists and other political undesirables. By 1935, Theodor Eicke, acting under the direction of Hitler's Gestapo chief, Heinrich Himmler, standardized the administration of the camp, which would serve as the pattern for others, including those at Buchenwald and Sachsenhausen. In 1938, after years of persecuting them, Hitler decided to "deport" all Jews from Germany and instituted mass arrests in May. Dachau and the other camps were soon supplemented by additional forced-labor facilities, all intended to house the deported Jews.

On November 9–10, 1938, he used the assassination of Ernst von Rath, a German legation secretary in Paris, as a pretext for sending Nazi storm troopers in to burn 267 synagogues and arrest 20,000 Jews. Jewish homes and businesses were destroyed, and so much smashed glass littered the streets that the nocturnal orgy of destruction was given the ironically poetic name *Kristallnacht*—crystal night, "the night of broken glass." Following the arrests came more deportations to the camps, but not before Hitler levied an atonement fine of $400 million against the Jews to pay for the damage that had been done—to their own property.

In 1940, after Poland had been overrun, the German invaders rounded up Warsaw's more than 400,000 Jews and confined them to the ancient Jewish ghetto, which was then cut off from the rest of the city. Many died from starvation and disease, and about 300,000 more were sent to concentration camps. Then German authorities drastically contracted the size of the ghetto, and, on April 19, 1943, attacked it, with two thousand German regulars supplemented by a force of Lithuanian militiamen and Polish police and firefighters. The attackers had expected to execute a slaughter. Instead, they were confronted by some 60,000 Jews—all those who remained in the ghetto—armed with a few pistols, rifles, machine guns, and homemade weapons. They put up a heroic resistance, but it was ultimately futile. The Nazis countered by setting fire to the ghetto block by block, then flooding and smoke-bombing the sewers, through which the ghetto inhabitants attempted escape. On May 16, 1943, General Juergen Stroop reported: "The former Jewish quarter of Warsaw is no longer in existence." Stroop further reported that his men had killed about 56,000, some 20,000 in the streets of Warsaw and the remainder, presumably, in death camps.

For that is what the concentration camps had become: not places of deportation and detention, not even primary sites for the forced labor the German war machine desperately needed, but the instruments for execution of what Hitler, following a January 1942 conference at Wannasee, chaired by Himmler's aide Reinhard Heydrich, had called the "final solution."

Auschwitz, as the Germans called the southern Polish town of Oswiecim, was the site of the camp chosen as the center of annihilation. Here one to three million—no one knows just how many—human beings were herded naked into gas chambers that were disguised as delousing showers and murdered with hydrocyanic gas produced by Zyklon B crystals. (Other Nazi methods of execution included carbon monoxide asphyxiation, electrocution, phenol injections, immolation by flamethrower, death by hand grenade, gunshot, beating, torture, and "medical experimentation.") Their clothing and valuables were systematically collected, including gold dental fillings, which were melted down to finance the war machine. The bodies themselves were burned in massive crematoria constructed expressly for the purpose. The killings at Auschwitz began in March 1942 and included large numbers of Poles, Russians, and gypsies in addition to Jews. Concentration camps at Oranienburg, Buchenwald, Dachau, Bergen-Belsen, and elsewhere all became death camps as well.

There was Jewish resistance, not only in the Warsaw ghetto, but at seventeen concentration camps, most notably Sobibor and Treblinka, and in the ghettos of Vilna, Kaunas, Minsk, and Slutsk. As many as 60,000 Jews served in partisan resistance units from North Africa to Belorussia, but to

no avail. Worse, the Allies—who undoubtedly were unaware of the full extent of the execution programs—did nothing to prevent the murders and persecution of which they were aware. Only after the liberation of Europe, as British, Soviet, and American forces marched into camp after camp, did the horror of six million Jewish deaths— and those of some three million more ethnic civilians and prisoners of war the Nazis considered "subhuman"—become all too apparent.

The United Nations Is Chartered (1945)

The event: In June 1945, even before World War II had ended, delegates from fifty nations met in San Francisco to draft the charter of the United Nations, an attempt to stabilize world politics more successfully than the Versailles Treaty had done after World War I by bringing the nations of the planet into a single, cooperative, deliberative forum with sufficient authority to resolve international disputes peacefully.

A S THE END OF World War II approached, nations saw everywhere about them the ruin of large parts of the world and desired to find some means of averting future military catastrophes. The San Francisco meeting had been scheduled by the Big Three—British Prime Minister Winston Churchill, United States President Franklin D. Roosevelt, and Russian President Josef Stalin—during the 1945 Yalta Conference in the Crimea. It was called for the express purpose of discussing the final Allied assault on Germany and the postwar division of Europe.

The League of Nations, the international body formed at the end of World War I, hardly provided an encouraging model for the contemplated organization. As World War II

demonstrated, the League had failed, but the nations were prepared to try again.

In San Francisco, the delegates devised a charter that called for a General Assembly, composed of delegates from each member country, and a Security Council, made up of delegates from five permanent member nations and six other members elected for two-year terms. The permanent members of the council—the United States, the Soviet Union, Great Britain, France, and China— were given responsibility for maintaining world peace and could employ a variety of diplomatic, economic, and military measures to achieve that end. To ensure that no coalition or alliance could be formed within the Security Council, the five permanent members were bound to agree unanimously on any action. Given the disparity of ideology among the permanent members, such unanimity was sure to be rare, and the United Nations quickly became a forum for international discussion rather than an organization that exercised military or concerted diplomatic action.

The General Assembly of the new organization first met in London in 1946, but later assemblies convened at the permanent headquarters in New York City. Built by an international team of architects under the general direction of the great French modernist LeCorbusier, it was located on an $8.5 million parcel of land along the East River donated by John D. Rockefeller, Jr.

At that first London meeting, bitter debate surrounded the Soviet Union's continued occupation of the Azerbaijan region of Iran and Great Britain's continued occupation of Greece. Another early issue centered on the control of atomic energy. An Atomic Energy Commission was created by the General Assembly in 1946 to explore the area of atomic control, and in June of that year it devised a plan to outlaw all atomic weapons. The debate ended with a Soviet veto of the plan; the Soviet Union refused to allow U.N.-mandated inspectors inside its borders and likewise declined to relinquish its veto power over atomic matters in the Security Council by entrusting the regulation of such matters to the Atomic Energy Commission.

This failure to eradicate the nuclear threat was a major disappointment and, from the start, a crippling blow to the prestige of the United Nations. With the superpowers holding one another hostage to a policy of mutually assured destruction, the world was doomed to almost five decades of Cold War, and as the members of the "atomic club" played a potentially deadly game of ideological chess, so-called Third World nations found in the United Nations little more than an often hollow debating society. And warfare—hot warfare—was by no means brought to an end: not in Korea, not in Southeast Asia, not in the Middle East. Nevertheless, as the Cold War began to wind down in the 1980s, the mission of the United Nations at first seemed to become clear again, and the organization played a strategically central political role in the Gulf War, but though the effectiveness of the United Nations in this instance seemed to bode well for the future, it has remained relatively powerless in the ethnic and tribal conflicts spawned by the end of the Cold War.

America Drops Atomic Bombs on Hiroshima and Nagasaki (1945)

The event: On August 6, 1945, the United States unleashed on the Japanese city of Hiroshima the most destructive weapon ever devised. Three days later, U.S. Army Air Force B-29s dropped a second A-bomb on Nagasaki. The nuclear attacks encouraged a Japanese surrender and brought World War II to a close, even as they made possible the age of potential—and sometimes imminent—mutual destruction called the Cold War.

THE POSSIBILITY OF nuclear fission had been considered theoretically possible in Germany since 1938, but it was not until 1943 that British scientists came up with a realistic plan for building an atomic bomb. In the meantime, the Hungarian-born physicist Leo Szilard—who had first imagined that nuclear fission could produce an atomic chain reaction capable of releasing enormous amounts of energy—had prevailed upon the prominent scientist Albert Einstein to speak to U.S. President Franklin Roosevelt about the destructive possibilities of such a weapon and to warn him that German scientists were perfectly capable of producing an atomic bomb. And, on December 6, 1941, just one day before Japan's attack on Pearl Harbor, Roosevelt signed a secret order authorizing the Manhattan Project to investigate the feasibility of nuclear weapons and to create a fission bomb.

The project was headed by Brigadier General Leslie R. Groves, the army engineer who directed construction of the Pentagon. Since everyone mistakenly assumed that German scientists—under the leadership of the brilliant theoretical physicist Werner Heisenberg—had a head start in what became the first nuclear arms race, Grove's assignment was stated in starkly simple terms: develop a bomb before the Nazis do. Groves assembled a group of scientists directed by physicist Robert J. Oppenheimer, who spent months confined to a secret base at Los Alamos, New Mexico, feverishly experimenting with the "gadget," as they called it. The scientists and their gadget were backed by the costliest engineering and manufacturing program the U.S. government had ever undertaken to develop a single weapon, for extracting plutonium in sufficient quantity to make a bomb required extraordinary facilities.

As it turned out, Heisenberg never had much faith in the possibility of producing the "secret weapon" that Hitler often hinted was going to win him the war at the last minute. Though Heisenberg's immortal uncertainty principal, which lay at the heart of quantum theory, and other feats of incredible mathematical skill had made him the preeminent physicist of his day, he was something of a klutz in practical matters. And, as the German atomic program meandered off toward dead-end experiments in developing a "heavy-water" atomic bomb, the Allies marched toward the successful construction of an implosive device that would trigger a chain-reaction in "enriched" uranium. "Trinity," the first test of the bomb, took place in the Alamogordo desert at 0529:45 on July 16, 1945, well after Germany had been defeated, and shortly after the death of Franklin Roosevelt. It fell then to Harry S Truman to decide whether to use the weapon against the remaining enemy, the empire of Japan. Even with most of their cities already reduced to rubble by the massive firebombings and with their navy and air force effectively neutralized, the Japanese steadfastly refused to accept unconditional surrender. Invading the islands, it was estimated, would cost the lives of perhaps tens of thousands Allied soldiers, not to mention the toll it would take on Japanese civilians. Fearful, too, that Japan's refusal to submit would give Soviet dictator Stalin sufficient time to enter the war against the

Japanese and claim his share of the spoils of victory as he had in Europe, Truman ordered the only nuclear attacks in world history. More than two hundred thousand Japanese civilians perished, horribly, in the greatest human-made explosions ever.

During the war, a small group of scientists—including many of those who had played roles in theorizing about and building the bomb—had argued against its deployment, especially against civilians, and had proposed steps that could be taken to avoid the potential for a nuclear arms race in the future. Roosevelt, and Harry Truman after him, had already become enamored of the advantages they and Winston Churchill imagined would result from an American-British nuclear monopoly. Just how much a role such musings played in Truman's decision to drop the bombs is a matter of conjecture, but it is true that immediately after the

war the United States was content in the knowledge that it and only it possessed the atomic bomb. Unknown to Truman and the others, Klaus Fuchs, who had worked on the Manhattan project and was among those scientists who objected to the deployment of the bombs, passed atomic secrets to the Soviets. Stalin knew all about the bomb. He hadn't built one yet, but he soon would, and over the succeeding decades the USSR and the United States would create thousands upon thousands of nuclear weapons that could be launched from almost anywhere on land, at sea, or in the air. Within a few years the victors in World War II had become prisoners of their own technology, former allies turned "superpower" rivals who would spend forty years locked in a Cold War dance of death called "mutually assured destruction" that neither could really control nor bring to a good end.

Two Professors Invent the Computer (1946)

The event: In 1946, two University of Pennsylvania professors, John W. Mauchly and John P. Eckert, Jr., directed the construction of the world's first entirely electronic computer, a thirty-ton behemoth that began a revolution in the way the world counts, writes, thinks, and communicates.

THE COMPUTER HAS its historical origins in the tabulating of the U.S. census. An army of clerks failed to finish counting the 1880 census until 1888. At that rate, experts estimated that the 1890 census wouldn't be counted until 1902, two years after the 1900 census had begun, and the lag between census and tabulation would only continue to increase. John Shaw Billings, a Census Bureau official, had the idea of using punch-

hole cards to record and then process census information, and he hired Herman Hollerith to develop the cards and an electric machine to read them. The result: the census of 1890 was completed in less than three years, and Hollerith went on to join the company that, in 1924, became International Business Machines (IBM). Destined to become one of the nation's largest corporations, IBM was willing to pour untold amounts of time and money into developing calculating machines to help companies and governments conduct ever more complex tracking, accounting, and analysis.

Hollerith's device was really a tabulating machine, and not a computer in the truest sense, that is, a general-purpose device that can be programmed to solve any specific solvable problem. Actually, the first theoretical breakthroughs in computer science had come earlier, when French mathematician and philosopher Blaise Pascal developed a calculating machine in 1642, followed by a device that German philosopher Gottfried Wilhelm Leibniz produced in 1693, and culminating in the never-quite-completed "analytical engine" Englishman Charles Babbage and Lady Lovelace cobbled together in 1835. Then, in 1930, American electrical engineer Vannevar Bush produced a machine capable of solving differential equations. At about this time in England, mathematician Alan Turing presented the most fully developed theory of the modern computer with a concept that came to be called the "Turing machine." During World War II, Turing was part of a British intelligence team that designed computer devices to encrypt military messages and, even more important, to decrypt intercepted German communications.

Back in the United States, in 1939, IBM joined a development team at Harvard University to create the Mark I, an advanced electromechanical device that is generally acknowledged to be the first truly modern programmable computer. But it was electro*mechanical* and, as such, a prelude to the first fully electronic computer: the Electronic Numerical Integrator And Calculator, or "ENIAC," the product of two American engineers, John William Mauchly and John Prosper Eckert, Jr.

Like the Mark I, ENIAC was largely funded by the war effort. The military needed a device capable of calculating complex mathematical tables to determine the speed and trajectory of artillery shells directed at targets such as slow-moving warships and fast-moving aircraft. Mark I was successfully demonstrated in January 1943, but, because of its partially mechanical design, it was relatively slow in producing complex calculations. ENIAC, unveiled at the University of Pennsylvania in 1946, came too late to serve the war effort, but, as a fully electronic device, it was much faster than the Mark I and much more flexible doing the kinds of tasks it could perform.

ENIAC did share with the IBM device the quality of monstrous size: Mark I was fifty feet long and eight feet high, while ENIAC displaced three thousand cubic feet of volume, weighed thirty tons, and, in the days before the transistor, required 18,000 vacuum tubes as well as a fleet-footed technical team to locate and replace them as they burned out. A highly publicized technical wonder of its time—the public thought of it as a giant "mechanical brain"—ENIAC is outclassed and outperformed by today's most basic hand-held calculators, let alone the ubiquitous desktop or laptop personal computer.

The U.S. Congress Passes the National Security Act (1947)

The event: The National Security Act reorganized the Department of Defense and created the Central Intelligence Agency.

FACED WITH THE possibility of a communist takeover of Greece and Turkey, President Harry S Truman announced his new "doctrine" that called for combating Communism by containing its spread using all means necessary, including military force. In effect, the Truman Doctrine meant that the United States was put on a footing of perpetual preparedness, and that degree of preparedness required permanent and continual sources of information about foreign governments, both hostile and potentially hostile. It required the capability for "covert action"—foreign policy initiatives that the government must keep hidden from the American public.

In the chilly climate of the Cold War, the CIA—an outgrowth of America's World War II espionage organization, the Office of Strategic Services (OSS)—expanded rapidly in size and power, until it became a kind of shadow government, exploiting statutes that granted the agency great leeway and ensured the secrecy of its operations. The CIA was sometimes quite effective at gathering information yet sometimes grossly inaccurate, and the covert ac-

tions it staged often failed. Its operation of U-2 spy planes over Russia led to an aborted summit conference when the Soviet Union shot down a craft piloted by Francis Gary Powers in May 1960. The CIA's planned invasion of Cuba ended in disaster at the Bay of Pigs, leading President John F. Kennedy to threaten to dismantle the agency.

Despite its often questionable record, the CIA repeatedly managed to circumvent legitimate congressional oversights and even to conceal all but the most blatant of its failures and excesses from the public. That changed, however, in the wake of Watergate, when Congress was in the mood to investigate the agency. The revelations of Senator Frank Church's committee, among others, shocked Americans, who learned that the CIA had planned and helped to secretly invade and overthrow Central and Latin American countries, assassinate foreign heads of state, conduct a mass murder campaign in Vietnam (code named Phoenix), spy on American citizens, traffic drugs to support its "dummy" corporations, and constantly seek to subvert the legal oversight power of the Congress that had created it.

Chuck Yeager Breaks the Sound Barrier (1947)

The event: On October 14, 1947, American test pilot Charles Elwood Yeager flew the Bell X-1 rocket plane faster than the speed of sound.

HUMAN PROGRESS IS commonly measured by obstacles that are overcome and barriers that are broken. Such was the case with the concept of "breaking the sound barrier." Since the Wright Brothers made their first flight in 1903, aircraft had been getting faster and faster. World War II brought propeller-driven flight to its maximum development, and fighter planes such as the American P-51 Mustang could reach speeds in excess of 500 miles per hour— 240 miles per hour shy of the speed of sound, which travels at about 740 miles per hour. At the beginning of the war, a British aeronautical engineer named Frank Whittle designed and built the first aircraft propelled not by a piston engine driving a prop, but by a jet engine. As early as 1921, engineers had theorized that an engine could be designed to burn fuel and eject a "jet" of exhaust at high speed, thereby producing enormous forward thrust. This theory, of course, was the basic principle of the rocket. However, unlike the rocket engine that carried fuel plus an oxidizing agent, the jet engine carried only fuel, taking its oxygen from the surrounding air, which it "breathed" in at high speed as it flew.

Whittle proved that the principle was practical, yet, despite the impetus of combat, neither the British nor the Americans concentrated on developing jets during World War II. The German Luftwaffe did develop them and actually introduced a handful into combat late in the war. They greatly outclassed prop-driven Allied craft and would have been devastating had Hitler been able to fight the war much longer.

After the war, however, the United States, Great Britain, and the Soviet Union advanced jet development rapidly, and, as jets became capable of higher and higher speeds, the so-called sound barrier loomed closer.

What was so formidable about it? At speeds of less than 740 miles per hour, the air molecules encountering an aircraft smoothly move out of the way, up and over and around the airfoils and other surfaces. As the aircraft approaches the speed of sound, however, the molecules cannot move out of the way before being overtaken. Therefore, they pile up in front of the aircraft, which, in effect, flies into compressed air. Popularly, as well as among many scientists, engineers, and pilots, this situation was conceptualized as flying into a wall: the sound barrier. Some theorized that, in hitting this wall, an airplane might simply disintegrate, and it was true that experimental aircraft suffered tremendous vibration and turbulence as they neared 740 miles per hour.

Engineers at the Bell Aircraft Company created a special rocket plane, the X-1, with an extremely streamlined profile and short, very thin wings in order to minimize turbulence and give the aircraft and pilot the best chance of piercing the "sound barrier" in one piece.

Without fanfare of any kind, Air Force test pilot Charles "Chuck" Yeager flew the X-1 at just over the speed of sound on October 14, 1947. Observers on the ground were treated to a "sonic boom," the result of air piling up, suddenly slipping to one side of the aircraft, then re-expanding with a loud crack. It was the first such boom produced by a manned aircraft. (As an example, the crack of a whip is a miniature sonic boom produced by air compressing, passing by, and expanding at the tip of the fast-moving whip.)

Although the sound barrier proved to be more of an imaginary construct than an actual entity, Yeager's flight through it was an act of tremendous courage. This feat greatly advanced aviation and, perhaps even more important, was a singularly inspiring instance of a human being confronting the unknown and transforming it into knowledge.

President Harry S Truman Desegregates the Armed Forces (1948)

The event: In 1948, over the objections of many in the military, President Truman issued Executive Order 9981 directing an end to segregation in the Armed Forces, the first step in a brewing civil rights battle that would dominate American politics at mid-century and beyond.

DURING THE CIVIL WAR many African-Americans—runaway slaves, former slaves, and free men—were eager to serve in the Union Army. General Benjamin Butler raised a small unit of black soldiers in New Orleans, and another unit was mustered in Cincinnati, but President Lincoln personally vetoed a second and third Louisiana brigade and put an end to the recruitment of African-Americans in South Carolina. It wasn't until the signing of the Emancipation Proclamation on January 1, 1863, that Lincoln himself called for four African-American regiments, who fought bravely and well for the freedom of their own people. But, despite their heroism and sacrifice, few white Americans welcomed black soldiers.

Still, African-American men began to serve in greater numbers, especially in the West, doing the dirty, dangerous, and miserably paid jobs that, among whites, only poor immigrants would accept. The African-American troops of the nineteenth century were led by white officers, and they were strictly segregated from white soldiers. In both world wars, black soldiers often fought alongside whites, but barracks and other accommodations were kept strictly separate. Nevertheless, for many, military service was the closest and most extended contact with members of another race, and during the World War II era organizations such as the NAACP brought increased pressure to end institutionalized segregation. In 1944, all-white primary elections in the South came to an end, and 1947 saw passage of the Fair Employment Practices Act, barring discrimination in hiring on the basis of race or national origin. In 1948, President Truman brought the military into step with the changes sweeping civilian life and issued an order to desegregate the armed forces.

The executive order was met in some quarters by dire predictions of morale problems and assertions that whites would leave the service. Base commanders in southern states expressed concern over how their civilian neighbors and host communities would react to a practice to which they were bitterly opposed. But, despite the anxieties and complaints, as well as numerous racially motivated outbreaks of violence, the services were integrated, and that became one more vehicle for effecting change in society at large. For many men in the military, World War II introduced blacks to whites and vice versa, postwar desegregation provided many people with their first impression of what a racially integrated society would be like, thereby making the unthinkable a reality and accelerating social change throughout the postwar years.

Physicist George Gamow Formulates the Big Bang Theory (1948)

The event: In 1948, Russian-born American physicist George Gamow, the man who had explained the source of the sun's energy, turned his attention to furnishing a detailed account of the origin of the universe, revolutionizing the way scientists—and many others—thought about the creation of the world.

GEORGE GAMOW, who in 1929 had theorized that solar energy was the result of the conversion of hydrogen nuclei into helium nuclei, turned his attention in 1948 to the question of the origin of the universe. He examined the theories proposed by Dutch astronomer Willem de Sitter in 1917, Russian mathematician Alexander Alexandrovich Friedmann in 1922, and Belgian astrophysicist Georges Henri Lemaître in 1927, then based upon their implications the most widely accepted account of how the universe came into being.

De Sitter followed through the implications of Albert Einstein's general theory of relativity to their most extreme conclusion—that the universe was not static, but, in fact, was expanding. De Sitter's calculations applied to a theoretical universe, one devoid of mass. In 1922, Friedmann worked out calculations for a universe containing mass and, like de Sitter, demonstrated that the universe is expanding. Following this, in 1927, Lemaître reasoned that if the universe was expanding as time went forward, it would contract if time were imagined to run in reverse. That is, the implication of an expanding universe is that it had developed from what must have been a relatively small, highly compressed body, which Lemaître colorfully termed the "cosmic egg." He further speculated that, at some point in time, this cosmic egg must have exploded, broadcasting the matter that is now the universe and that, as a result of this primordial explosion, is still traveling, expanding outward from the original egg.

Gamow set about working this speculation into a fully developed theory, showing how the chemical elements were formed in the aftermath of the explosion, on which he bestowed the delightfully unscientific name "Big Bang." Gamow theorized that the Big Bang had wrought a vast surge of energy, but that the universe had necessarily cooled as it expanded, so that it was now—on average—barely above absolute zero (-217.15 degrees on the centigrade scale). Gamow reasoned that such a temperature would cause a background of microwave radiation at a certain wavelength. At the time, however, there was no practical means of measuring such radiation. In 1964, Arno Allan Penzias and Robert Woodrow Wilson, two American radioastronomers, were studying radio-wave emissions originating from the outer reaches of the galaxy. They found an excess of emissions they could not explain and called on Robert Henry Dicke, a physicist, for help. He recalled Gamow's prediction of background microwave radiation as an artifact of the Big Bang. Penzias and Wilson determined that the level of microwave radiation indicated a universe with an average temperature just three degrees above absolute zero. They therefore confirmed by practical observation Gamow's speculation and established the event—the Big Bang—by which the universe most likely had come into being. The two scientists shared the 1978 Nobel Prize for physics.

George Kennan Proposes the "Containment" of Communism (1947)

The event: Writing under the pseudonym of X, diplomat George Kennan published a highly influential article in the journal *Foreign Affairs* presenting the idea of containment of the Soviet Communism "by the adroit and vigilant application of counter-force at a series of constantly shifting geographic points."

THE AIMS AND DESTINY of great governments are often expressed in profound public documents such as the Declaration of Independence or the U.S. Constitution, but, in the twentieth century, an anonymous article placed in a small but prestigious journal played a key role in determining the shape of the postwar world. In 1947, career diplomat George Frost Kennan, head of the State Department's policy planning staff, wrote—using the pseudonym "X"—an article for the journal *Foreign Affairs*, which cogently outlined America's foreign policy assumptions at the end of World War II and developed the concept of "containment" of the spread of Soviet Communism.

In September 1947, the Soviet Union tested its first atomic bomb, a weapon the United States had felt secure in thinking it alone in the world had the capacity to develop and detonate. Though the United States and the Soviet Union had been allies against Germany two short years before, relations between them in the late 1940s had degenerated from cooperation to mistrust, and mistrust soon became hostility. As the postwar years continued, the Cold War grew frosty indeed.

The United States embarked on a series of actions influenced by George Kennan's theory. The Truman Doctrine of 1947 supplied economic aid to Greece and Turkey in a effort to keep those countries from falling under Soviet control. The Marshall Plan, also called the European Recovery Program, poured over $13 billion into Western Europe to "restore the confidence of the European people in the economic future of their own countries and of Europe as a whole." The North Atlantic Treaty Organization (NATO), formed in 1949, joined the United States to Canada and ten Western European nations in a military alliance. An attack on any one member nation was deemed an attack on all of them. NATO became the model for the military alliances the United States organized with Mediterranean nations in the Central Treaty Organization (CENTO) and with the nations of Southeast Asia in SEATO. By the 1950s, the United States had a string of allies around the world that all but enclosed the Soviet Union and its satellite nations. And the United States used its military might against attempts to expand Communism—whether the Soviet brand or the Chinese brand—in Korea and Vietnam.

Of course the Soviet Union countered U.S. efforts against Communism. In 1948, Russia attempted to cut off the city of Berlin—controlled by the World War II Allies but located deep in the center of the eastern section of Germany the USSR occupied—from the United States and Britain. Only a prolonged airlift of food, fuel, and supplies saved Berlin from falling under Soviet domination. When a rearmed West Germany joined NATO in 1955, Nikita Khrushchev, the Soviet Union's new leader, responded with the Warsaw Pact, an alliance of his East European satellites. Krushchev also formed alliances with India and other "neutral" nations. He used tanks in 1956 to ensure Soviet control over Hungary and Poland. In 1961, he built a wall—which quickly became a symbol to all the world of the harshness and hopelessness of Communist oppression—separating the Soviet sector of Berlin from the rest of the city. And when Fidel Castro gained power in Cuba, the Soviet Union placed its nuclear missiles a scant 90 miles off America's shores.

The Cuban Missile Crisis of October 1962, perhaps more than any other event in the Cold War, made the American public realize that the world, divided into two camps, both armed to the teeth with weapons of unimaginable destruction, had strayed dangerously close in the postwar years to touching off a war, not one to "end all wars," but to end the world itself. Containment, in the end, had proved almost as dangerous as the dangers it sought to avoid.

The Dead Sea Scrolls Are Discovered (1947)

The event: In 1947, shepherds tending their flocks discovered the first of several scrolls that turned out to be two-thousand-year-old holy manuscripts in caves near Wadi Qumran on the northwest bank of the Dead Sea.

IN 1947, when shepherds stumbled on the first of a large number of Hebrew, Aramaic, and Greek manuscripts preserved in dry caves near Wadi Qumran, an important archaeological site, the Judeo-Christian world was electrified. Here were documents, dating from the second century B.C. to the first century A.D., that gave unprecedented firsthand evidence for Jewish thought and religion in the New Testament period. After some two thousand years, a window had suddenly been thrust open onto the world of the Bible.

The discovery of the scrolls, which took place from 1947 to 1956, has had three principal effects on historical and religious knowledge. First, those portions of the scrolls that are copies of certain books of the Bible are older than any others in existence and, therefore, closer to the "original" version of what became the Bible. The scrolls have explicated many previously obscure passages of the standard Hebrew Bible. Second, the scrolls revealed a wide diversity of ancient Jewish literature, providing profound insight into the real-world context in which Judaism and Christianity developed. Finally, the scrolls furnished a picture of life in the ancient Qumran community, which considered itself to be the true Israel, keepers of biblical law, and the chosen of the chosen.

In recent years, the Dead Sea Scrolls have given rise to considerable controversy, since many of the manuscripts had disintegrated into scraps and fragments that had to be identified, pieced together, and interpreted. Although a small international team of scholars has been working on the fragments since the 1950s, many of the uninterpreted texts remained unpublished and virtually hidden. The Huntington Library in San Marino, California, made unauthorized photographs of the unpublished texts available to the public in September 1991, prompting Israeli authorities to remove the last restrictions on access to the scrolls, so that these core documents of Judeo-Christian culture, perhaps the most significant spiritual discovery of the century, are now universally available.

George C. Marshall Announces A Postwar Recovery Plan (1947)

The event: George C. Marshall, secretary of state under Harry S Truman and former army chief of staff during World War II, announced in his June 5, 1947, commencement address at Harvard University a bold plan of economic assistance to rebuild war-ravaged Europe.

A BRILLIANT MILITARY LEADER, whose energies had so recently been focused on destroying the might of Germany and Japan, Marshall became Harry S Truman's secretary of state and developed a sweeping plan for rebuilding what war had devastated. France, England, and other European Allies had been economically crippled by the war, and the United States feared that they would fall easy prey to Communism, which had already engulfed the nations of Eastern Europe. Marshall promulgated a policy of economic aid on an unprecedented scale to restore "normal economic health in the world, without which there can be no political stability and no assured peace."

Great Britain and France spearheaded the formation of a Committee for European Economic Cooperation, made up of delegates from sixteen nations, and the committee officially requested $22.4 billion from the United States. Congress appropriated more than $13 billion in funds to be disbursed through the Marshall Plan, and it also authorized a Displaced Persons Plan, through which nearly three hundred thousand Europeans, including many survivors of the Holocaust, became American citizens. As a direct result of the Marshall Plan, Western Europe was able to get back on its feet and form new alliances, which (in part) resulted in the formation of the West German Republic out of the western sector of divided Germany. In outraged response, the Soviets, who governed the eastern sector of Germany, blockaded the city of Berlin (squarely in the eastern sector, but divided into western and eastern zones) in June 1948. During the blockade, the United States airlifted supplies to the residents of West Berlin for nearly a year.

The aid the United States gave to the European nations paved the way for a grand military alliance, the North Atlantic Treaty, signed in April 1949 and creating the North Atlantic Treaty Organization (NATO). The Soviet Union now responded by overrunning Czechoslovakia in February 1948 and by creating a military alliance of Communist-controlled countries, the Warsaw Pact. Despite Marshall's pronouncement at Harvard that the policy of aid was not aimed "against any country or doctrine but against hunger, poverty, desperation, and chaos," the Marshall Plan occasioned the drawing of the battle lines on which a long, tense, and debilitating Cold War would be fought, dominating world politics for some four decades.

The Nation of Israel Is Carved Out of Palestine (1948)

The event: Faced with continual conflict between Arabs and Jews in Palestine, which they had occupied since 1917, the British withdrew from the country and turned it—and the Jewish-Arab conflict—over to the United Nations, which responded by partitioning Palestine into Jewish and Arab sectors. Over Arab protests, the Jews established the state of Israel in 1948.

SINCE THE DIASPORA, the Babylonian exile of the sixth century B.C., the Jews had been without a homeland. In the nineteenth century, largely in response to rising nationalist sentiment throughout Europe coupled with unrelenting persecution of European Jews, especially in Russia, early proponents of Zionism including Moses Hess, David Luzatto, Leo Pinsker, Zvi Kalischer, and Yehudah Alkalai worked to raise the national consciousness of ghetto Jewry. Financiers such as Moses Montefiore, Edmond de Rothschild, and Maurice de Hirsch backed several plans for the return of Jews to the Middle East.

But it was not until 1897, when Theodor Herzl's World Zionist Congress was held at Basel, Switzerland, that a worldwide political movement was created. After much struggle, the Zionist Congress secured the so-called Balfour Declaration. On November 2, 1917, British Foreign Secretary Lord Balfour wrote a letter to Lord Rothschild, head of the British Zionist Federation, endorsing the establishment of "a national home" for the Jewish people in Palestine. Shortly after the Balfour Declaration, British General Sir Edmund Allenby invaded Palestine, capturing Jerusalem in December. In 1922, the League of Nations approved a British "mandate" over Palestine and neighboring Transjordan, and the provisions of the Balfour Declaration were written into the mandate document.

The mandate was intended to encourage the development of self-government, and Transjordan (modern Jordan) became autonomous in 1923 and was recognized as independent in 1928. But in Palestine, independence was withheld because of conflicting Arab and Jewish claims. Throughout the 1920s and 1930s, Arab-Jewish violence became increasingly frequent, especially as more and more Jewish immigrants fled to Palestine from Nazi-dominated Europe. During the 1930s, the British proposed various solutions to the crisis, all of which were rejected, and from 1936 to 1939, Palestine erupted into civil war. Finally, in 1939, the London Round Table Conference produced a "White Paper" promising the creation of an independent Palestine within a decade and limiting Jewish immigration to 1,500 per month until 1944, when Jews would no longer be admitted to Palestine. Reeling from this blow, Zionists turned from Britain to the United States for support, demanding, in the May 1942 Biltmore Conference in New York, the formation of an independent Jewish state—a demand that attracted much U.S. support. Following World War II, large numbers of Holocaust survivors sought homes in Palestine. Met by British resistance, renewed violence erupted and, at last, a war-weary Britain caved in, turning the entire problem over to the United Nations in 1947. In November, that body voted to split Palestine into Arab and Jewish states, and, on May 14, 1948, the eve of Britain's evacuation, Palestine's Jews proclaimed the state of Israel.

The immediate result was the first of several Arab-Israeli wars, as armies from neighboring Arab states invaded Palestine. By 1949, however, the Israelis had pushed back the invaders, more Jews had immigrated into Israel, and some 700,000 Arab Palestinians had left Israeli territory, whereupon the Israelis confiscated their property. Israel's survival, however, is something of a modern miracle and a testament to the Is-

raeli resolve that what had befallen European Jewry at the hands of Adolf Hitler would "never again" happen (as the phrase of the time went). Still, the state's resources were strained by unremitting conflict with the Arabs as well as by an influx of Jewish immigrants that doubled the population from 650,000 in 1948 to 1,300,000 by 1952. However, the situation stabilized between 1953 and 1956, as immigration slowed to 30,000 a year, and funding from many Jewish organizations overseas, along with restitution money paid by West Germany for Nazi war crimes, provided finance for ambitious programs of agricultural and industrial development. After eight centuries, the Jews once again had a homeland. The challenge would be to persuade the world of that very fact.

Russia Blockades Berlin (1948)

The event: Shortly after the United States and its Western allies announced that they would create the Republic of West Germany from the portions of defeated Germany that they occupied, on June 24 the Soviet Union blockaded Berlin, the divided city squarely in the Soviet (eastern) sector of Germany. President Truman responded with a daring airlift, launching the first major confrontation of the "Cold War," which lasted for nearly the rest of the century.

TWO YEARS AFTER World War II, American columnist Walter Lippman described the deteriorating relations between Russia on the one side and the United States and Great Britain on the other—recent allies against Nazi Germany—as a "Cold War." The first true crisis of that "war" came in June 1948 when, in a provocative move, the USSR cut off all rail, barge, and highway traffic into the western section of Berlin, controlled by France, Britain, and

America, but located deep within the Russian section of eastern Germany. Though ground routes to Berlin were cut off, the Western powers retained the use of three, twenty-three-mile-wide air corridors leading directly into the city from the British and U.S. zones. Airlifting supplies to its own troops and some two million Germans in the city through those air corridors offered the West its only alternative to abandoning Berlin entirely.

U. S. President Harry S. Truman called on the newly created United States Air Force—part of the U.S. Army until 1947—to accomplish the airlift, along with Britain's air force. The Berlin Airlift was an operational, logistical, and supply nightmare, and only through the tightly coordinated, highly efficient labors of the British and U.S. military did it work at all. "God is in the details," Mies van der Rohe once said, but it was the details that made the Berlin Airlift a stunning military and political success.

Planes from seven bases in western Germany took off at three-minute intervals and flew stacked two high down the narrow corridors round the clock for months. Each aircraft flew at a specific altitude and a set air speed, specifications that required a succession of aircraft to land in Berlin every six minutes. There was no room for error: pilots flew their prescribed routes religiously regardless of weather; they got one pass at landing in Berlin; if they missed it, they headed back to West Germany. The slightest variation in these plans spelled disaster. Heavy use wore out the planes, the full loads made them less manageable, and the crowded skies, limited airspace, and shortage of terminal fields greatly increased the risk of accidents. And for a while the Russians engaged in a war of nerves, harassing incoming planes with fighter feints and antiaircraft fire carefully aimed at the edges of the corridors.

The weather constituted the greatest single threat to the airlift. Though air turbulence and icing proved much less serious a problem than the Allies anticipated, thick fogs turned out to be a major hazard. When visibility fell below one mile, weather observers stationed at the end of each runway counted the number of runway lights they could see and reported the actual runway "visibility" by field telephone to the weather office. The introduction of sophisticated radar equipment ensured the safety of the air traffic and the success of the airlift. During the Berlin crisis, military personnel perfected the air-traffic-control techniques that later dominated the busy, modern airports of America's cities.

Ground crews worked nonstop servicing and loading the planes, then dropping the goods in Berlin. The city's paramount need was for food (hence the American code name for the airlift: "Operation Vittles"), but as the harsh winter set in, coal became almost as important, making up two-thirds of the tonnage delivered. Crews loaded a block of seventy C-54s (transport planes) every six hours, day and night. To be safe, payloads had to be weighed carefully and balanced, floor stresses checked, loads distributed evenly by compartment, cargo securely tied down, and high-density commodities (like sugar) "married" to low-density ones (like macaroni) to make the most of load capacity. Speed was of the essence, and every effort was made to reduce the time spent loading and unloading. To supplement the military crews, Germany's displaced persons and, later, German laborers pitched in. On average, it took an hour and twenty minutes to load a plane on base, and forty-nine minutes to unload it in Berlin.

By September 30, 1949, when the Russians relented and reopened the roads to

Berlin, the airlift had become routine. The operation delivered nearly 2 million tons of food, fuel, and supplies. The airlift accident rate for America's aircraft was half that of the USAF; despite the heavy traffic, there was only one mid-air collision; and casualties were astonishingly low: thirty-one Americans lost their lives in twelve crashes out of a total of 272,000 flights. When it was over, the Berlin Airlift was one of the Cold War's few moments of unalloyed victory, greatly uplifting the morale of a Europe still reeling from World War II and now huddled in the long shadow of the Soviet giant. The airlift also seemed a timely vindication of the Western European and American policy of containing Communism.

Milton Berle Gives America a Reason to Buy Television Sets (1948)

The event: Former vaudeville comic Milton Berle premiered his "Texaco Star Theater" television show on September 21, 1948, catalyzing the transformation of America into a nation of televiewers.

TELEVISION IS ONE of the true technological wonders of the century, and the history of its development is complex, involving many developments over many years. It is the product of the work of many people, including numerous scientists, engineers, and inventors—and its development is not yet over. But two figures stand out from the welter of personalities who made the medium a reality.

One was Vladimir Zworykin, born in Mourom, Russia in 1889, and trained as an electrical engineer at the Petrograd Institute of Technology. He immigrated to the United States in 1916 and was naturalized in 1924. While he was working as a research engineer with Westinghouse, he invented and patented a device he called the "iconoscope" in 1925. It was a specially treated vacuum tube that formed the basis of the first television camera and was the most immediate ancestor of

the technology at the heart of modern television. Zworykin left Westinghouse to become director of electronic research for RCA (1929–42) and associate director, then director of the RCA Laboratories (1942–47). During this period, he refined his invention and in 1933 was able to transmit a television picture over a radio-wave relay between New York and Philadelphia. It was the first television broadcast.

Zworykin's invention, astounding though it was, did not create the television industry. Six years went by before the first public television broadcast took place in 1939, when NBC aired live video of Franklin D. Roosevelt at the New York World's Fair. Regularly scheduled programs were not broadcast until 1944, and only to a select number of New York-area subscribers, most of whom were engineers. Proponents of early television were faced with a classic chicken-and-egg dilemma: The sets were costly, cumbersome, and terribly finicky. Few could afford to invest in them, and fewer still were willing to invest in an entertainment medium for which there was virtually no programming. Yet there could be no programming until a sizable enough user base of households with television sets had been built up to attract advertisers to sponsor broadcasts. What the country needed was a reason to buy television sets.

The man who provided that reason was Milton Berle, the second stand-out figure in the development of television. Born Milton Berlinger in New York City on July 12, 1908, the young comic changed his name when he went into vaudeville. His big break came when the National Broadcasting Company (NBC) tapped him in 1948 for a show originally titled "The

Texaco Star Theater," premiering on September 21, 1948.

It soon became apparent that Berle had found his medium, and the medium had found the star it so desperately needed. The nation fell in love with Berle, who was dubbed affectionately "Uncle Miltie" and, more accurately, "Mr. Television." He dominated the medium from 1948 to 1956. People dropped whatever they were doing every Tuesday evening to watch the hourlong program that mainly featured the vaudeville antics of Berle, who was often done up in very homely drag. Entire families left the dinner table to watch—and soon began to bring their plates with them. Television was on its way to becoming a ubiquitous guest in American homes and a mass medium more influential than books, movies, and radio put together.

Bell Laboratories Scientists Invent the Transistor (1948)

The event: Walter Houser Brattain, John Bardeen, and William B. Shockley developed the transistor, a "semiconductor" device that can control the electrical current that flows between two terminals by a voltage applied to a third terminal, thereby enabling the creation of a vast range of small, lightweight, cheap, and dependable electronic devices.

UNTIL 1948 all electronic devices—from radios to television to the first fully electronic computers—depended upon vacuum tubes to transmit electronic impulses. Such tubes were called radio tubes or just plain tubes. They were wonderful devices, but they suffered from several drawbacks: they were relatively large, very fragile, prone to failure, generally shortlived even under the best of conditions, energy-hungry, costly, and required a warm-up

and stabilization period. Few devices containing tubes could be made truly portable. For example, the 1946 ENIAC computer required 18,000 tubes and weighed in at thirty tons!

Then, in 1948, three Bell Labs physicists—Walter Brattain, John Bardeen, and William Shockley—discovered the remarkable properties of a new kind of crystal "grown" in a laboratory, which consisted chiefly of the element germanium. It was a "semiconductor"; that is, it was capable of conducting electricity better than an insulating substance such as wood, glass, or rubber, but was not as good a conductor as, say, copper or silver. By adding certain substances to the germanium crystal, the semiconductor could be made to serve the same purpose as a vacuum tube, regulating, rectifying, or amplifying a current in a controlled manner. When silicon, abundant and cheap, was found to be an adequate replacement for germanium, the transistor emerged as an inexpensive, more dependable, far lighter, far smaller, far more energy-efficient, and much longer-lived alternative to the vacuum tube for virtually any electronic application.

The invention transformed the second half of the twentieth century by giving rise to a veritable galaxy of sophisticated port-able electronic devices, ranging from transistor radios to electronic medical equipment to advanced computers. Moreover, research into semiconductors continued beyond the further refinement and perfection of the individual transistor. Transistors began getting smaller and smaller, resulting in a trend toward the miniaturization of even complex electronic devices. By 1960, it became possible to etch very tiny transistors into small, thin wafers of silicon, called chips. Each chip, then, functioned as an "integrated circuit." Since 1960, manufacturing techniques have made it possible to etch millions of microscopic transistors onto a single one-inch-square chip, making feasible such devices as extraordinarily powerful and extremely inexpensive desktop computers, aircraft guidance systems, and portable cellular telephones.

China Becomes a Communist Nation (1949)

The event: Late in 1949, after forcing the Chinese nationalist army under Chiang Kai-shek to flee to the small island of Taiwan, Mao Tse-tung and his fellow communists declared China's vast mainland to be the People's Republic of China, an event viewed in the capitalist West as a major "defeat" in the rapidly developing Cold War. U.S. politicians overestimated the cohesion of the so-called "Communist bloc" for some three decades and stubbornly denied recognition of a government that, for the first time since the fall of the ancient Qing (also called Manchu) dynasty at the beginning of the twentieth century, had truly united the massive Chinese population.

THE ROAD TOWARD a Communist state on the Chinese mainland began in and around the port city of Shanghai, a wide-open town that housed White Russian refugees from the Soviet Union, American soldiers of fortune, Japanese and Bolshevik spies, British "diplomats" always ready to double-deal in the interests of a fading empire, and masses of desperately poor Chinese washed up from years of brutal civil warfare among China's cutthroat warlords. During the summer of 1921, a number of radical Chinese students held a series of clandestine meetings, which culminated in weeks of sessions aboard a boat moored on a lake outside the city. It was the only place that the delegates to what was being called the First Party Congress felt safe from the surveillance of Shanghai's corrupt police. From such humble beginnings would grow the twentieth century's largest, most powerful, and longest lasting Communist Party.

Five years earlier, in 1916, China's first Republic, founded by Sun Yat-sen, had fallen prey to the ambitions of a number of regionally powerful warlords, and the vast country had reverted to a particularly bloody form of feudalism. The warlords, many of them not much better than Asian land pirates, constantly fought among themselves, forming a bewildering series of alliances, always supposedly in the name of a united republic, but always collapsing into another round of bitter feuds. Many Chinese had developed a passion for revolution, none more than the students who had made up a majority of Sun Yat-sen's early supporters and who had, therefore, enjoyed a strong draught of freedom during the heady years of China's nationalist revolution against the aged and creaking Manchu dynasty under the boy-king Pu-Yi, China's last emperor.

Loath to let go of the fragile victories in modernization gained under Sun Yat-sen, the students filled the void left in Chinese leadership with radical talk inspired by the success of the Bolsheviks, whom the young Chinese radicals wished to emulate. Recognizing an opportunity, V. I. Lenin sent envoys from the Comintern, the Communists'

vehicle for world revolution, to help China organize the country's disparate socialist groups into a coherent Marxist party.

Arriving in China flush with advice from the Comintern, Chen Duxiu—co-founder of the Chinese Communist Party (CCP)—led the effort to recruit new members and set up schools to train Chinese radicals in the fine art of revolution. A new generation of young Chinese radicals sprang up. In Hunan, a twenty-seven-year-old school teacher named Mao Tse-tung started a Communist group in his home province; in Paris, a sixteen-year-old student named Deng Xiaoping joined the French Communist Party; Zhou Enlai, twenty-two and also living in Paris, founded a branch of the CCP. In Shanghai they all came together and focused their thinking and their goals.

First, they hooked up with Chiang Kai-shek, who had taken over China's Nationalist Party, the Kuomintang (KMT), after the death of Sun Yat-sen. The KMT was China's bourgeois revolutionary party, and to the perceptive few, Chiang was himself not much more than a warlord. But he had an army, and he had been with Sun Yat-sen, and with his help the Chinese Communists organized their own Red Army, which they used to pay back the Bolsheviks by joining their fight against the White Russians, who had been occupying Mongolia for almost a year, and helping the Soviets to win the Russian Civil War in 1923.

Like all his fellow CCP members, Mao Tse-tung had joined the Kuomintang in 1923, and he was chosen as an alternate member of the KMT's Shanghai Executive

Committee in 1924. But Mao could not get along with the imperious Chiang.

Born in Hunan in 1893, the son of a landowning and prosperous peasant family, Mao had received a classical Confucian education before he left school in 1911 to serve briefly with the revolutionary forces of Sun Yat-sen. Shortly after entering the ranks of the KMT, Mao set about organizing unions of laborers and peasants. In 1925, he fled to Canton to avoid arrest for his radical activities, and it was in Canton, protected by the nationalist army, that he moved into Chiang Kai-shek's inner circle, as head of the propaganda section of the KMT. Almost immediately, Mao and Chiang argued, and Chiang fired the young radical in 1926. Mao immediately joined the Peasant Movement Training Institute, a far-left CCP group.

In March of 1927, the CCP organized a strike in Shanghai, which paralyzed the city, leaving it open to Chiang Kai-shek and his revolutionary army. Chiang swept into Shanghai and took the city without firing a shot. The Kuomintang and the Chinese Communist Party controlled most of the country, the long Chinese civil war seemed to be drawing to a close, and the Communists were getting most of the credit. Only Manchuria, ruled by the warlord Zhang Zoulin, remained outside Chiang's and the Communists' sphere of influence.

In Russia, the new Communist Party leader, Josef Stalin, locked in a bitter dispute with Leon Trotsky over the future direction of the Bolshevik government, was beside himself. Moscow interpreted the Communist victory in China's civil war as a victory for Stalin, who was already dreaming of the things he could do with the world's most populous country in his camp.

Chiang, however, had other ideas. In April, a month after taking Shanghai, Chiang double-crossed his radical young allies. He moved his troops against the trade unions in Shanghai, purged the Kuomintang of Communists, outlawed the CCP, proclaimed a Nationalist Republic of China, and named himself its president. The jilted Moscow broke off diplomatic relations, and as Chiang's anti-Communist rhetoric heated up, Comintern agents fled for the Russian border. Stalin quickly engaged in some unseemly revisionism, claiming through tight lips that the former hero Chiang was, like Trotsky, a traitor. Chiang himself turned his attention to Manchuria, launching a campaign against Zhang Zoulin. A year later, the warlord lay dead, assassinated by his son and successor, who made peace with Chiang. China once again was unified, this time under Chiang Kai-shek and his Kuomintang.

Meanwhile, Mao retreated underground and, independently of the CCP, organized a revolutionary army in August, which he led in the Autumn Harvest Uprising in Hunan from September 8th to the 19th. When the uprising collapsed, Mao was ejected from the CCP. He responded by gathering his remaining forces, retreating to the mountains, and allying himself with another CCP outcast, Chu Teh, to form a peasant army called the Mass Line in 1928. Mao and Chu established their own renegade CCP republic, the Kiangsi Soviet, which by 1934 numbered some 15 million people. In doing this, the pair defied not only Chiang Kai-shek's KMT, but also the Russian-dominated international Communist Party, which ordered would-be Communist revolutionaries to concentrate on capturing cities. Mao's policy was also a distinct break with Marxist orthodoxy, for he and Chu turned their attention not to the urban proletariat, as Marx prescribed, but to the rural peasants.

Between 1929 and 1934, using guerrilla tactics, Mao and Chu defeated four KMT attempts to wipe out the Soviet. In 1930, however, the KMT executed Mao's first wife, Yang K'ai-hui, and after the KMT's fifth assault on the Kiangsi Soviet in 1934, Mao set off on the famed Long March out of Kiangsi, leading some 86,000 men and women in a 6,000-mile mass evacuation to the province of Shensi. In October 1935, at Yen-an, his followers numbering a mere 4,000 of the most faithful, Mao established a new party headquarters. He had not been wiped out, and he emerged from the epic ordeal of the Long March more determined than ever to impose his brand of Communism on China.

When, in December 1936, the Japanese invaded China, the CCP and KMT again joined forces. Mao launched the Hundred Regiments offensive against the Japanese from August 20 to November 30, 1940, but mainly used the war years to strengthen the CCP position in northern China and further consolidate his own leadership of the party. Mao worked vigorously to organize peasants, and he also directed a ruthless program

of purges through which he secured, in April 1945, election as permanent chairman of the party's central committee. The CCP had begun the war years in 1937 with 40,000 members. It emerged in 1945 with 1,200,000.

The conclusion of the war also ended the truce between the CCP and KMT, and a bitter full-scale civil war erupted. Mao's forces repeatedly defeated the armies of Chiang Kai-shek from 1946 to 1949, and the Nationalists were forced to flee to the island of Taiwan, where they set up a government in exile. Late in 1949, Mao and his fellow Communists declared the creation of the People's Republic of China on the vast mainland.

The most populous nation on the face of the planet was committed to Communism. When the United States rejected Mao's overtures to establish diplomatic relations, he allied his country with a Soviet Union firmly under the yoke of Stalin; but it was an uneasy alliance. Mao, as much the strongman in China as Stalin was in Russia, found it no easier to share the limelight with Uncle Joe than he had formerly with Chiang. But the West, particularly the United States, was too busy blaming—then purging—the China experts in its State Department for the "loss" of the mainland to notice. As far as the West was concerned, China and Russia had formed a Communist bloc implacably opposed to what the United States and its Western European allies were now calling the Free World.

The USSR Tests Its First Atomic Bomb (1949)

The event: On September 23, 1949, President Harry S Truman announced the detonation of "Joe I," the first Soviet A-bomb, sparking fears of a potential nuclear holocaust that fed the anti-Communism of postwar America and led to a second "red scare" (presided over by Senator Joseph McCarthy) and a nuclear arms race of massive proportions.

AMERICANS HAD PLENTY to worry about in the postwar world, but they took comfort in the belief that it was Uncle Sam and not the Soviet's Uncle Joe who had "the Bomb."

That all changed on September 23, 1949, when President Truman announced that the Soviets had tested a nuclear device. The public, as well as the political and scientific communities, were shocked. No one had expected the Soviets to develop an atomic weapon so quickly. The mystery was explained in February 1950, when Washington learned that for seven years the Soviets had been receiving atomic secrets from Klaus Fuchs, a veteran scientist of America's development of the atomic bomb, called the Manhattan Project.

In the recent past, a weapon capable of destruction on a scale so massive that its potential had to be measured in kilotons, with each kiloton unit the equivalent of the destructive force of one thousand tons of TNT, would be considered an "ultimate weapon." Actually, as America's nuclear scientists were aware, the A-bomb was only the *penultimate* weapon of the twentieth century's brave new world. Many months before the first test, called Trinity, on July 16, 1945 in New Mexico's Alamogorrlo desert proved the A-bomb would work, one of the Man-

hattan Project scientists, Hungarian-born Edward Teller, was already thinking about the next weapon, based on hydrogen isotopes, which he called the "Super." Whereas an atomic bomb explosion could be measured in kilotons, the hydrogen bomb would yield forces measurable as *mega*tons—millions of tons of TNT.

In October 1949, the United States began a program to step up production of uranium and plutonium, a necessary first step in the creation of the H-bomb. Next, Edward Teller and other scientists—including J. Robert Oppenheimer, the principal architect of the atomic bomb—Secretary of State Dean Acheson, Secretary of Defense Louis Johnson, President Truman, and others met in secret to discuss and debate the potential of an American hydrogen bomb program. Among the scientists, Oppenheimer was as reluctant to create the "Super" as Teller was hungry for it. The debate proceeded, but, on January 31, 1950, President Truman announced that he was in favor of developing the hydrogen weapon.

Thus the international arms race was put on a truly apocalyptic footing. Teller pushed the project forward, while Oppenheimer continued to express reservations. Soon, the government began to subject Oppenheimer to surveillance, and, in 1954, based on illegal FBI wiretaps and a biased hearing board, the Atomic Energy Commission declared him a security risk. By then, however, it was almost anticlimactic. On November 1, 1952, the first hydrogen bomb—code named Mike—was detonated at Eniwetok atoll in the Pacific. The test was so secret that it wasn't reported to the public until February 2, 1954, when President Eisenhower made a statement. On March 24 of that year, a hydrogen bomb test in the Marshall Islands exceeded all estimates of its power. The U.S. monopoly on the hydrogen bomb was, however, even briefer than the one it had enjoyed with the atomic bomb.

The Soviets tested an H-bomb on November 23, 1955. The thermonuclear arms race had reached critical mass and had become self-sustaining, with the U.S. and USSR matching one another "device" for "device." Communist China and the French soon joined the race on a smaller scale. From the mid-1950s until the collapse of the Soviet Union brought the Cold War to an end early in the 1990s, the superpowers expended untold billions in order to stockpile weaponry sufficient to destroy life on the planet many times over. Humankind had at last succeeded in producing the ultimate weapon: the instruments of a thermonuclear suicide pact.

The Diners Club Introduces the Credit Card (1950)

The event: In February 1950, Frank X. McNamara founded the Diners Club on the idea that one charge card could be used in many establishments, changing not only the way consumers paid for goods, but the very nature of the marketplace itself.

IF PLASTIC IS *the* preeminent manufacturing material of the twentieth century, one of the century's most important plastic products is undoubtedly the credit card. Credit, of course, is hardly new: the great fortunes of the Italian Renaissance were amassed by money lenders who extended credit to the crowned heads of Europe. In the very early 1900s, a number of hotels in the United States offered customers cards with which they could charge a room and services. The idea was to keep patrons coming back to the same hotel. By the beginning of World War I, many large department stores issued "charge plates" to special customers, dog-taglike metal plates stamped with the customer's name. (The term *charge plate* stuck—even well into the era

of plastic cards.) By 1924, gas stations were issuing credit cards.

When the Depression hit, the interest customers paid on one-store-only credit cards plummeted so that most establishments stopped honoring them. Credit card purchasing was replaced by layaway plans and cash-only business. Credit cards were just coming back into general use when World War II put restrictions on credit purchasing, and, once again, card use slumped.

After the war, department store charge cards returned with a vengeance. Frank X. McNamara ran a small loan company and, one day, took note of the fact that a certain customer of his had a great many department store charge accounts. He would lend the cards to friends, whom he would charge for the use of them. He borrowed from McNamara to pay off the outstanding debt and then pocketed the profits. It was a nice way to pick up some extra cash—until one of the lendees turned out to be a deadbeat, and the whole operation evaporated, sending McNamara to lunch with his lawyer to consult about collection options.

That's when the idea hit him: Instead of lending a bunch of cards to a bunch of people, why not develop a single card that could be used in a wide variety of places and market that card to a large number of people? Perhaps because the idea hit him at lunch, McNamara decided that restaurants would be the best group of businesses to deal with. Putting up $25,000 of his own money and talking his attorney, Ralph Schneider, into parting with an additional $15,000, the pair opened an office in the Empire State Building in February 1950. They signed up twenty-two New York City restaurants and a single hotel, and they called the new enterprise the Diners Club.

Year one resulted in a $58,000 loss. Year two saw $6 million in business, on which the after-tax profit was $60,000. By 1958, the Diners Club was so successful that new cards began to sprout up: American Express entered the travel-and-entertainment card business in a big way, and Carte Blanche came a short time later. By the mid-1960s, several banks were issuing revolving credit lines made available by card, and by the late 1960s, the idea of the bank card had taken hold, made possible by the pooled resources of a network of financial institutions. The new cards were *master charge cards,* usable for purchases at a great

many stores, hotels, and restaurants; for that reason, the first and best-known of the cards was christened Master Charge in 1967. By 1968, the Interbank group—the banks behind Master Charge—had 16.7 million cardholders who could make purchases at some 400,000 merchants.

As the century draws to a close, it is difficult to imagine a world without credit cards. Plastic has encouraged a nation of consumers to consume even more—not necessarily when they have the money to make a purchase, but whenever the "need" to buy strikes. The result has been a nation—a world—of borrowers, some of whom consume credit as an alcoholic consumes liquor, and with remarkably similar consequences. Whatever the emotional and moral dimensions of credit cards, they are part of a much greater trend in the business of exchange.

The widespread use of "master" credit cards would be impossible in the absence of sophisticated electronic computers, so the cards are very much products of their age. They are the plastic keys to a vast economic system. They are "virtual" money, making those wrinkled greenbacks and tarnished silver disks all but obsolete. But if the key admits the bearer into the system, it also admits the system into the cardholder's life, allowing merchants, banks, and the government to monitor spending habits, travel habits, the types and quantities of purchases, and the promptness or tardiness of payments. With each swipe of the plastic through the little machine on the merchant's counter, the cardholder simultaneously exercises and relinquishes a certain amount of freedom.

Billy Graham Becomes America's Most Prominent Christian Leader (1950)

The event: In 1950, evangelical preacher William Franklin ("Billy") Graham, Jr. established The Billy Graham Evangelistic Association, a media-conscious center of a new popular religious awakening in the United States and much of the world that made Graham the undisputed leader of popular Christian revivalism.

MANY PEOPLE THINK of the twentieth century as a period of intense, rapid, and all-consuming industrial, technological, and scientific advancement that created a world in which religion was not merely displaced, but was rendered largely irrelevant. Moreover, of all nations in this century, the United States has emerged as the most industrially, technologically, and scientifically driven. Yet, in vivid counterpoint to this, a number of evangelical personalities have emerged, successfully exhorting the nation to "revivals" of religious belief.

America has a tradition of emotional, individually focused religious inspiration. In 1734, for example, the fire-and-brimstone sermons of the great Jonathan Edwards sparked a religious fervor from Maine to Georgia known as the Great Awakening. Similar movements resurfaced throughout the nineteenth century, and at the turn of the century, William Ashley ("Billy") Sunday, a former professional baseball player, emerged as an extraordinarily popular evangelical preacher.

Evangelicism has long appealed to Americans, who cherish religious freedom and who characteristically don't like to be told what to believe and how to believe it. Yet such non-orthodox religiosity also pre-

sents a dark side of fanaticism, irrationality, and, ultimately, self-centered intolerance. In the twentieth century, many Billy Sunday imitators preyed upon the religious hunger of gullible masses and swindled tent-revival audiences out of hard-earned money. Thus evangelical Christianity fell into disrepute in many circles.

Enter Graham. He was born in Charlotte, North Carolina, on November 7, 1918, graduated from Wheaton College in Illinois in 1943, and became pastor of the First Baptist Church of Western Springs, Illinois, as well as a leader in the national Youth for Christ movement. In 1947, Graham—now calling himself "Billy Graham"—assembled a traveling revival team in the style of Billy Sunday. Two years later, after he and his group appeared in Los Angeles, several prominent Hollywood personalities came to him to convert to Christianity. The next year, 1950, he founded the Billy Graham Evangelistic Association.

Through the association, Graham promoted many crusades and, most remarkably, made extensive use of the very technologies many considered downright "godless": radio and television. Through the force of his personality, Graham almost single-handedly rehabilitated the image of the popular evangelist—although many of his fellow revival-style personalities have fallen from grace, convicted of everything from swindling and embezzlement to general debauchery. In 1969, Graham was so universally admired that Richard M. Nixon asked him to offer a prayer at his presidential inauguration. The two subsequently became close friends, and Graham served Nixon informally as a spiritual advisor. He presided over the former president's funeral in 1994.

Despite his intense evangelicism, Graham is a religious moderate. Yet he is often linked to the so-called Christian fundamentalist movement, a politically right-wing, moralistic, and often narrow-minded popular response to the many pressures, challenges, and tensions of life in a twentieth-century technological democracy.

The U.S. Senate Opens Hearings on Organized Crime (1950)

The event: In 1950 and 1951, the U.S. Senate Subcommittee to Investigate in Interstate Commerce, known popularly as the "Kefauver Committee" after its chairman, Estes Kefauver, U.S. Senator from Tennessee, began to look into the dealings of urban gangsters. The hearings ultimately concluded that there existed in the United States a conspiracy of organized criminals that cost the nation billions of dollars annually, corrupted police forces and governments in almost every section of the country, and reached into the highest ranks of American society.

THE FACT THAT some sort of organized criminal activity existed in the United States was hardly a surprise to Estes Kefauver or anyone else. The Mafia had been part of the nation's popular lore since the assassination of New Orleans Police Chief David Hennessey on October 15, 1890, the last in a series of some forty murders between 1888 and 1890 committed by a group of loosely associated criminal societies.

The previous century had been plagued by such organizations, which fought among themselves, robbed a few honest citizens, looted the waterfronts of various cities, held up banks now and then, owned a gambling establishment here and there, fielded an army of prostitutes, and turned for protection to the urban political machines and their bosses in exchange for delivering vote-getting muscle in their neighborhoods come election time. With the coming of Prohibition, turf wars between rival gangs became endemic, and waves of public outrage and reform occasionally threatened the gangs' existence and livelihood. At the same time, the development of the extremely lucrative illegal traffic in liquor required intercourse between mobs in different cities in a way that the local urban gangs of the nineteenth century could never have imagined.

Two men, John Torrio and Arnold

Rothstein, played key roles in the way organized crime developed in America from the immense potential Prohibition offered the faction-ridden underworld. Chicago's Torrio, a former New York gangster born in Italy, dreamed of making crime into a big business, and he was one of the first to realize that there were immense profits to be made from bootlegging once Prohibition went into effect. Ruthless and brilliant, Torrio imported a tough young Brooklyn native, Alphonse Capone, who like him had been a member of the Lower East Side's infamous Five Points Gang. With Capone's help, Torrio organized Chicago's multi-ethnic gangs into a city-wide syndicate, which he argued was the best way for everybody to make millions and, more importantly, live to enjoy them. Those who refused to join, Torrio attacked. A series of multi-sided, duplicitous wars ensued, which became a nationwide scandal, and almost got Torrio himself killed. After a bungled attempt on his life, Torrio retired to New York, turning his criminal empire over to Capone, who embarked on a ruthless program of exterminating his foes, culminating in the bloody St. Valentine's Day Massacre of 1929.

All of this was watched carefully from New York by the Sicilian-born Charles "Lucky" Luciano and the Polish-born Jew Meyer Lansky, who were students of the infamous gambler and criminal master-mind, Arnold Rothstein. Famous as the man who had fixed the 1919 World Series and as the model for F. Scott Fitzgerald's Meyer Wolfstein in *The Great Gatsby*, Rothstein had recruited Luciano and Lansky (along with Benjamin "Bugsy" Siegel and Frank Costello) from the vicious street gangs of their youth and taught them to approach crime as if it were just another business. Like Capone, Luciano and Lansky had worked to eliminate their major rivals. Unlike Capone, however, they realized when enough was enough. Capone may have "owned" Chicago, as he boasted, but his slaughter of the rival North Side Gang led by Hymie Weiss and George "Bugs" Moran on Valentine's Day, in which Capone henchmen dressed as policemen lined up seven men against a wall and mowed them down with submachine guns, had created a national outrage that threatened the entire bootlegging business.

Advised by the retired John Torrio and inspired by the dead Arnold Rothstein, Luciano and Lansky called a "conference" of gangsters from across the country to be held in Atlantic City, where they hoped to achieve on a national scale what Torrio and Rothstein had always dreamed of achieving in New York and Chicago. The idea of an underworld "syndicate" that would apportion geographical regions and criminal activities to various gangs and Mafia families, and serve as a clearinghouse for the inevitable disputes that would arise, was something new under the sun.

Though the loose-knit organization Luciano and Lansky put together included elements of the old Italian Mafia and Comorra societies imported from Sicily and Naples, it was not synonymous with them. In fact, it sought to avoid the intense loyalties that characterized all gangs, and in particular the "family" values of the Italian gangsters, instead favoring strictly business relationships based on a more-or-less rational ap-portioning of illegal markets. While the na-tional syndicate was never so monolithic as it was later portrayed, resembling more a chamber of commerce than a corporation, it nevertheless provided a forum for the under-world to get together and air its grievances; it also provided enough cohesiveness for the gangsters to make decisions based on busi-ness needs rather than on strictly personal and ethnic loyalties. For example, when Bugsy Siegel later began to embezzle funds invested by other mobsters to build a casino in Las Vegas, a town Siegel almost single-handedly turned from a desert stopover for G.I.'s into a gangster's notion of heaven, the syndicate prevailed on Siegel's boy-hood friend Meyer Lansky to have him murdered.

Organized crime, then, was not a matter of Mafia cabals and blood-spilling initia-tions, but of business opportunities in illegal markets ruthlessly exploited by men inter-ested in profit, not honor—in making money, not settling vendettas. That it was dominated by Italians and Jews was an acci-dent of history, since Italians and Jews were the main occupants of the urban ghettos when Prohibition came along, and it was their gangs of ruthless young men who were engaged in crime when crime began to re-ally pay. Had Prohibition come, say, half a century earlier, it would have been the Irish and the Germans who dominated, and when a situation similar to Prohibition—the explosion of the illegal traffic in drugs, principally cocaine—developed half a century later, it was the Hispanics and the blacks who dominated the trade

and organized their own national and inter-national networks.

After the 1929 meeting in Atlantic City, the syndicate continued to hold national conferences from time to time. Now and again, such meetings accidentally received the kind of publicity that was anathema to the organization, as in Havana in 1946, when the popular young Italian-American singer Frank Sinatra's presence created an unwanted stir, and at the so-called Appala-chian Convention in 1956, when the New York police discovered the meeting and staged an impromptu raid. The trial of Al Capone for income tax evasion, his 1932 conviction, and the attendant publicity, also gave the public a peek at the power and ex-tent of organized crime in America. Some still denied it existed, chief among them the nation's top cop, FBI director J. Edgar Hoover, who contented himself with track-ing down, to great fanfare, the petty bank robbers and individual psychopaths who comprised his "Public Enemies" list. If nothing else, the existence of a popular genre of motion pictures, the gangster film, indicated that by 1950 the question that faced Tennessee Democrat Estes Kefauver was not whether he needed to prove there was a nationwide, organized crime net-work, but how effectively he could expose its far-reaching influence. Kefauver's Sen-ate hearings paraded the leading lights of the underworld before the national audi-ence of the new public medium, television. As the Senate committee traveled from city to city, exposing local corruption in New York, New Orleans, Chicago, Los Angeles, and others, Americans saw not only minor hoods and major mobsters, but also crooked politicians, mayors, and even governors who were controlled by the mob. Racketeer after racketeer refused to testify, invoking the U.S. Constitution's protection against self-incrimination under the Fifth Amendment and making the phrase "taking the Fifth" a part of the American vocabulary.

Kefauver's hearings catapulted him into national prominence and forced J. Edgar Hoover to take face-saving measures to compensate for his strange and stubborn refusal to accept the existence of organized crime. By the end of the decade, the FBI was in an all-out war with the underworld, a war that continued through the series of investigations and committee hearings launched by the U.S. Congress in the following decades. A federal witness protection program was established, which brought testimony from any number of insiders and left little doubt that organized crime not only existed, but exercised much power and influence over local governments, as well as police forces, labor unions, and a growing number of "legitimate" industries, stretching into the highest reaches of American government and society.

Senator Joseph McCarthy Launches a Twentieth-Century Witch Hunt (1950)

The event: In 1950, Joseph R. McCarthy, an undistinguished Wisconsin senator looking for a political future, stunned his audience at the Women's Republican Club of Wheeling, West Virginia, by declaring on February 9 that he held in his hand a list of 205 card-carrying Communists in the United States State Department, launching a twentieth-century "witch hunt" that to this day makes his name synonymous with character assassination by innuendo and guilt by association.

NO ONE EVER actually saw the "list" McCarthy held up from the podium, but, in the bitter and anxious atmosphere of the early Cold War, mere assertion and accusation were more than sufficient to fuel a sweeping witch hunt that, for the next four years, ate into American life, leaving democracy deeply scarred. McCarthy and a troop of hangers-on, all looking to carve out political futures, exploited the nation's fear of Communism by making reckless, usually groundless, accusations at every opportunity.

The tragedy of McCarthyism—as it came to be called—was that, by abrogating major democratic rights, it destroyed individual lives, almost, it seemed, at random. Two early victims were Owen Lattimore, a China expert and professor at Johns Hopkins University, and John S. Service of the State Department. At Senate hearings chaired by Millard Tydings of Maryland, no evidence was offered to support McCarthy's claims that these men were Communist spies. Yet the accusations themselves were sufficient to instill lingering suspicions about these men and others, whose "soft" stance on Communism, according to McCarthy, had contributed to the "loss" of China after the war. The Senate refused to brand Lattimore and Service as Communists, but McCarthy was undaunted. Gaining the chairmanship of the Senate Subcommittee on Governmental Operations, he launched investigations of the Voice of America and the U.S. Army Signal Corps. Astoundingly, he pointed an accusing finger at General George C. Marshall, former chief of staff of the army during World War II and now secretary of state, the distinguished architect of the Marshall Plan, which not only soothed European suffering, but was as effective as any action the United States took to check the spread of Communism.

McCarthy and his aides, most notably a young and ruthlessly opportunistic lawyer named Roy Cohn, next launched investigations of high-profile figures, including prominent celebrities, among them Hollywood stars, writers, and producers. The Hollywood witch hunt and similar campaigns undertaken against other industries were especially destructive, because the force of accusation and innuendo were more than enough to wreck careers by enrolling the accused on a "blacklist" that effectively put him off-limits to employers, investors, customers, clients, and business partners.

In time, McCarthy fell victim to the injustice and stridency of his own campaign. He became increasingly oblivious of the changing political realities around him.

Even after his own Republican party won control of the White House and Congress in the 1952 elections, the Senator continued to attack the government, which he claimed was "infested" with Communists. In the spring of 1954 he accused the entire U.S. Army of being infiltrated with Communists, and that was quite enough for President Dwight D. Eisenhower, a career army man and former supreme allied commander during World War II. Eisenhower discovered that McCarthy had tried to coerce army officials into granting preferred treatment for a former aide, Private G. David Schine. Armed with this information, the president encouraged Congress to form a committee to investigate McCarthy's manipulations. The result was the so-called "Army-McCarthy" hearings, televised between April and June 1954.

As it would time and time again throughout the balance of the century, television cast the brightest possible light on a figure who was best served by darkness and secrecy. The nation was stunned to see that the "crusading" McCarthy was a blustering, blundering bully. Discredited before the public, McCarthy was censured later in the year by the senatorial colleagues who had only recently feared him. Always a hard-drinking man, McCarthy retreated deeper into the bottle and died within three years, a weak and thoroughly mediocre figure who had nevertheless wielded fear over the nation as a grim sword for four shameful years, undermining its citizens' most cherished rights.

The United States Goes to War in Korea (1950)

The event: After Communist-backed forces crossed the thirty-eighth parallel dividing North from South Korea, the United States called for United Nations sanctions against the North, an action that committed America to a war the U.S. government euphemistically called a "police action," which served as something of a dress rehearsal for the war in Vietnam.

O N JUNE 27, 1950, in response to the invasion of South Korea, President Harry S Truman, concluding—incorrectly—that the Soviet Union had directed the assault, committed American military supplies to South Korea and moved the U.S. Seventh Fleet into the Formosa Strait, a show of force meant to intimidate a China Truman assumed to be a Soviet puppet. Truman acted with neither a declaration of war nor the advice and consent of the Senate, though he simultaneously had the United States appeal to the United Nations for sanctions against the North.

Within a month, a U.S.-dominated United Nations coalition was formed to come to the aid of South Korea. It was commanded by General Douglas MacArthur, hero of the Pacific theater of World War II, who was already in charge of the American Far East Command, based in Japan and including four army divisions, the Fifth Air Force, and parts of the Seventh Fleet.

MacArthur concentrated first on holding the southeastern portion of the Korean peninsula, especially the port of Pusan. His ground troops were aided by American air power, which effectively crippled the North Korean supply lines. From September to November 1950, U.N. forces made an amphibious assault at Inchon and progressed toward the Yalu River. The assault was highly successful until China, which, preoccupied with internal problems, had stayed out of the war, suddenly sent masses of its troops to reinforce North Korean forces. MacArthur's troops were once again pushed below the thirty-eighth parallel. From January to April 1951, the U.S. Eighth Army, under the command of General Matthew Ridgeway, countered by driving the North Koreans and Chinese north of the parallel.

From April 1951 until the end of the conflict, fighting was concentrated near the thirty-eighth parallel, particularly in the "Iron Triangle" and the "Punch Bowl" regions immediately north of the line. The U.N. forces engaged in major battles at Heartbreak Ridge in September and October 1951 and at Pork Chop Hill in April 1953, where they were successful in driving back the Communists, but at great cost.

While negotiations for peace began in July 1951, the war ground on for two more years, until July 27, 1953, when an armistice was signed. The cease-fire satisfied no one—not the United Nations, not the United States, not South Korea, not North Korea—and the Korean peninsula remained tensely divided along a line near the thirty-eighth parallel.

The war was immensely unpopular with the American public. Of the 1.8 million Americans who served in the so-called police action that was in reality the Korean War, 54,200 were killed and 103,300 wounded, with 8,200 classified as missing in action. The casualty list had a great impact on the United States, still wearied from World War II, which had ended only five years before the commencement of the Korean conflict. The war also had a major effect on the U.S. armed forces, prompting their desegregation, an important step forward for African-Americans in the military and, by extension, in civilian life. In addition, the war brought a popular president, Harry S Truman, into direct conflict with a popular war hero, Douglas MacArthur. When MacArthur proposed bombing bridges over the Yalu River, which would have meant attacking Red China directly, Truman objected, and MacArthur, in turn, protested, loudly and publicly, the strictures imposed upon him. President Truman relieved MacArthur of his command, replacing him with General Ridgeway. Also, the inconclusive and expensive war cost the Democratic Party the White House, and Dwight D. Eisenhower was elected in 1952 promising that he personally would go to Korea and end the fighting. The Korean War also heightened the anti-Communist hysteria of the McCarthy era, and reshaped international politics by prompting the United States to form a counterpart of NATO for the Pacific region. The Southeast Asia Treaty Organization (SEATO), was another step in American Cold War policy that would ultimately lead to the senseless tragedy of the war in Vietnam.

Rashomon Wins Top Prize at the Venice Film Festival (1951)

The event: When Japanese filmmaker Akira Kurosawa's *Rashomon* won the Venice Film Festival in 1951, the West was introduced to the riches of contemporary Japanese culture and presented with a film that many consider the greatest ever made.

IN ITS FIFTY-PLUS-YEAR history up to the early 1950s, film had emerged as a political and entertainment medium that not only interpreted the century to itself, but often served to shape its attitudes, beliefs, and mores. Multimillionaire actors, actresses, directors, and movie moguls proved that audiences were willing to pay well for the kind of entertainment that movies offered. The extensive use of cinema by Joseph Goebbels and other Nazis showed how film could, for better or worse, mold ideas, beliefs, and values, as well as motivate action. And with films like *Rashomon*, the medium laid claim to being a serious art form—one as valid as literature, painting, sculpture, or music.

Rashomon is a visually overwhelming study of a crime of violence told from four different points of view. It is rich in ambiguity, rich in symbolism and psychological insight, and, like most great works of art, poses questions about the very nature of truth. The film combines timeless narrative skill with the look of traditional Japanese art, state-of-the-art filmmaking, and a keen awareness of modern existential philosophy to produce a work of cinema that was regarded as among the very greatest ever produced when it was released in 1950, and has stood the test of time ever since. Moreover, it introduced the West to the traditional and contemporary culture of Japan, the nation that had so recently conspired to plunge the world into oppression and war. *Rashomon* and the recognition it received did much to rehabilitate the Japanese image and to reintegrate that country into the world family of nations.

Its director, Akira Kurosawa, has an eye for beauty and a penchant for economy of expression that makes him a master in all genres, styles, and even cultures. *Rashomon*, for example, inspired two American remakes, including *The Outrage*, set in the American West, and a made-for-television version of the original in its medieval Japanese setting. Another of Kurosawa's well-known films, *The Seven Samurai* (1954), was imitated by the Hollywood western, *The Magnificent Seven*, which even borrowed its title from the alternate title of the original. The classic "spaghetti western" *A Fistful of Dollars* was inspired by Kurosawa's *Yojimbo* (1961). In turn, Kurosawa's *The Hidden Fortress* owes much to the John Ford tradition of the western, and three of Kurosawa's most notable films are adaptations of European classics: Dostoyevsky's *The Idiot* (1951), Maksim Gorky's *The Lower Depths* (1957), and Shakespeare's *Macbeth* (adapted into a medieval Japanese setting as *Throne of Blood* (1957)). In addition to his other accomplishments, Kurosawa signaled a still-growing trend in the twentieth century away from provincialism and toward world culture.

David Ogilvy Creates the Hathaway Shirt Man (1951)

The event: On September 22, 1951, *The New Yorker* ran the first Hathaway shirt ad featuring the "Hathaway shirt man," touching off a demand for Hathaway shirts that rapidly outstripped the factory's ability to produce them and radically changed advertising from a small-time industry into a pervasive force in American life.

IT HAPPENED LIKE THIS: David Ogilvy was born near London in 1911, a shy, frightened little boy who grew up in the shadow of an overbearing father, older brother, and older sister. He managed to get good enough grades in boarding school to earn him a scholarship to Oxford, from which he was ultimately expelled after flunking chemistry. He took a job in the kitchen of a great Paris hotel, then became a door-to-door salesman of cooking stoves in Scotland. At this he excelled, wrote a pamphlet called "The Theory and Practice of Selling the Aga Cooker," and got a job with Aga's

London-based ad agency, Mather & Crowther. Fascinated with America since childhood, Ogilvy persuaded the agency to send him abroad "temporarily." The sojourn developed into permanent residence, and Ogilvy persuaded Mather & Crowther to help him and some partners establish the Hewitt, Ogilvy, Benson & Mather advertising agency in New York in September 1948.

The agency was successful in a modest way, promoting upscale clients like Helena Rubinstein and Guinness, but when the small Maine shirt-manufacturing firm of Hathaway signed on, Ogilvy orchestrated an elaborate campaign designed to surround the moderately priced shirts with an atmosphere of class and high-tone mystique. His art director found a distinguished-looking male model, who bore a resemblance to William Faulkner, and, as Ogilvy was strolling to the first photo session, he impulsively purchased a black eye patch. George Wrangell, the model, was photographed with it. The

patch, Ogilvy casually observed, would make him "look like a very real and interesting person, instead of a conventional dummy. . . . It is a small matter, but it may make a big difference."

And it did. Not only did the "Hathaway shirt man" become one of the most familiar images in American advertising, the campaign launched a new era in the advertising industry. No longer would ads be based primarily on product information and catchy slogans. The business of advertising would now be the art and science of creating an image, an atmosphere, a context of desire and desirability. Businesses now routinely invest as much or more in advertising their products as they do in developing and producing them. The industry has become gigantic and pervasive, many would say all-consuming, driving all aspects of American life and, indeed, dictating—or at least mediating—the desires of a majority of the world's population.

B. F. Skinner Publishes *Science and Human Behavior* (1953)

The event: In 1953 noted psychologist B.F. Skinner published *Science and Human Behavior*, his second major work. A statement of radical behaviorism, a distinctly twentieth-century psychology, it not only opposed the dominant Freudian model of mind of the time, but declared that the concept of "mind" itself is mythical.

PLAGUED BY UNPRECEDENTED levels of violence and spiritual crisis, the twentieth century has clamored for science to deliver the keys to human behavior. Sigmund Freud offered a concept of largely unconscious and sexual motivation, an idea that

provoked immediate hostility followed by such widespread acceptance that partially understood "Freudianism" became a common popular belief by mid-century. However, by no means were all psychologists interested in the unconscious. Early in the century, the American psychologist John B. Watson identified himself as a "behaviorist," declaring that psychologists must study behavior, because consciousness is private and subjective rather than public and objective. In effect, mind is invisible and, therefore, literally unavailable for study. Only the product of mind, behavior, can be observed and, therefore, analyzed.

Burrhus Frederic Skinner came across the writings of Watson in college and enrolled himself as a doctoral student in psychology at Harvard University. After taking his Ph.D. in 1931, Skinner remained at the university through 1936 to do research into the nature of learning processes, inventing his famous and elegantly simple tool for conducting behavior experiments on animals, the Skinner Box, and writing his groundbreaking work, the highly influential *Behavior of Organisms* (1938).

With his reputation as an animal behaviorist firmly established, Skinner turned to human beings and developed his provocative view that "mind" is mythical. Rejecting all reference to nonconscious mental states, Skinner held that behavior was controlled by the environment (including the private "environment" of consciousness itself), not by internal, unconscious forces. Had Skinner confined himself to theory and basic research, his ideas would have been controversial enough. For, as many saw it, Skinner's behaviorism robbed humankind of complexity, spirituality, imagination, and even humanity itself. But Skinner actively promoted his work as the basis for changing society. Following World War II, he wrote a novel, *Walden Two* (1948), a utopian vision

meant to show how radical behaviorism could improve the lot of humankind. This was followed in 1953 by *Science and Human Behavior*, the most comprehensive exposition of his psychology. Other influential works followed, the most deliberately disturbing of which was *Beyond Freedom and Dignity* (1971), which suggested that the salvation of humankind lay in applying the scientific method to social problems and in abandoning many traditional concepts of freedom and dignity.

Skinner drew fire not only from psychologists, but from spiritual leaders and politicians, who—misguidedly—saw him as advocating schemes for the totalitarian control of society and the use of pain—torture, mind-control—in behavior therapy. He was, in fact, a gentle utopianist, opposed to oppression, tyranny, and violence, yet unflinching and unrelenting in his advocacy of radical behaviorism. Even those psychologists who do not share his absolute faith in the social uses of the scientific method employ the techniques of "behavioral conditioning" that he pioneered to enhance psychiatric therapy, to correct such disorders as drug and other addictions, and to enhance learning. Yet these techniques of behavioral modification and manipulation, many feel, are also available to less scrupulous "professionals," ranging from the creators of advertising to those who would control governments and peoples.

For this reason, the work of B. F. Skinner, like most advances in knowledge during this or any other century, offered both promise and foreboding, declaring hope as its public goal, yet producing disquietude and even fear in the political arena. For better or worse, few working in the fields of psychology or psychiatry today, with their drug-loving cures for mental illnesses assumed to be mostly due to chemical or genetic imbalances, could honestly lay claim to being much more than die-hard behaviorists.

The CIA Backs the Shah of Iran (1954)

The event: In 1954, responding to Iran's nationalizing of the country's vast oil deposits, the intelligence agencies of the British and American governments helped to oust Iran's highest elected official via covert action in support of their "client," the Shah. Operation Ajax was the first of a series of such cloak-and-dagger meddlings in the affairs of other countries that would characterize the newly created CIA run by Allen Dulles.

THE FAMINE AND bankruptcy in Persia—long a locus of the imperial aspirations of Britain, Germany, and Russia—that followed World War I ripened into political upheaval. Late in the war, German and British interests within Iran had struggled mightily for control of the Majlis, Persia's not particularly powerful parliament. When the British Army, exhausted by the war, quit the area in 1919, the road to Persia's ancient peacock throne was cleared for Reza Khan, an officer of the Persian Cossack Brigade. In 1921 he staged a coup d'etat, and in 1925—despite strong opposition from Islamic clergymen—he overturned the Qajar Dynasty and established his own, taking the name Pahlavi and styling himself, as had the Qajars, the "shah." Like Turkey's Mustafa Kemal Atatürk, whom he emulated, Reza Khan Shah Pahlavi attempted to modernize his country. He reformed ancient Islamic divorce laws, making them more favorable to women, and he threw out Muslim veil requirements, ordering both sexes to adopt European dress. His reign engendered the country's first railroad and brought improvements in education and public sanitation. He even managed to negotiate more equitable oil agreements with the British and American oil firms, loosening the foreign grip on Persia. In 1935, he asked everyone to call his nation Iran, not Persia.

But Reza Khan was a ruthless man, and greedy. He had a bad habit of seizing large areas of land for himself. His biggest mistake, however, was backing Hitler in World War II. In 1941, Britain and the Soviet Union—fearful for their oil supplies—moved in on the tough, vulgar, self-made army sergeant, plucked him off the Peacock Throne, drummed him into exile, and replaced him with his son, the callow Muhammed Pahlavi.

The United States had already become a player in the region, courtesy of the war. From 1942 to 1948, Colonel H. Norman Schwarzkopf, an able ex-New Jersey cop turned U.S. Army officer, reorganized Iran's imperial police force and set up a secret police organization—SAVAK—to back up the shaky inexperienced ruler and suppress the country's Communist Party, the Tudeh. American aid programs, pushing war surplus weapons, picked up the slack as England trimmed her military involvement throughout the still strategically vital Middle East. What was beginning to worry both the British and the Americans, however, were the liberal programs then being bandied about in the Iranian Parliament by the left-wing National Front, which had come out of World War II with a much enhanced prestige and a workable majority in parliament.

The National Front was led by a semi-invalid named Dr. Muhammed Mosaddeq, an emotional man, who in 1951 rammed through the parliament a bill to nationalize Iran's oil fields, including the vast holdings of the Anglo-Iranian Oil Company. The bill would revoke a fifty-year-old concession that gave Britain virtual monopoly on Iran's oil. Mosaddeq's decree shook Britain's Labor government, and when the Conservatives returned to power under Winston Churchill, he launched a worldwide British boycott of Iranian oil, sending cruisers to patrol the Iranian coast. For two years the stubborn Iranians refused to come to terms. Luckily for the British there was an oil glut, and they could safely vent their outrage for the moment. But by 1952, the British were getting nervous; Mosaddeq wouldn't budge, and the oil was running out.

That was when Sir John Cochran, "a very senior man in [British] Intelligence" in charge of the operations in the Middle East, approached his CIA counterpart, Kermit "Kim" Roosevelt. The Harvard-educated grandson of Teddy Roosevelt (who had cut his spy teeth in King Farouk's conspiracy-ridden Egypt), listened as Sir John offered him "access to their principal Iranian

friends" (i.e., spies) and proposed a joint covert action to shore up the Shah, bump Mosaddeq out, if not off, and share the oil. Though Mosaddeq sometimes talked like a Marxist, he steadfastly refused to legalize the Tudeh or accept cooperation from the Communists. Instead, he spoke in parliament about the sickly, childish, indecisive Shah and how his weakness was derailing the campaign to take Iran's oil fields back from the foreigners. When he began whipping up his minions to take to the streets and demand Pahlavi's abdication, the Shah packed up his bags and got ready to flee the country.

Roosevelt rushed back to the states to seek approval for his version of the British plan to get rid of Mosaddeq. Calling it Operation Ajax, he hoped to light a fire under the Shah and persuade him, with the U.S.'s tacit support, to force a showdown with the unpredictable old landowner running the parliament, then back up Pahlavi with a mass uprising of mobs from the bazaar. Roosevelt told the Dulles brothers—the elder John Foster now ensconced as secretary of state and Allen at the CIA—he was convinced that both the people and, more importantly, the Schwarzkopf-trained SAVAK and the core of the army would dig in behind the Shah. Operation Ajax was approved.

Roosevelt flew back to Teheran and began to set up intermediaries with the Shah, testing their loyalty with polygraphs. Schwarzkopf flew in to drop off several million dollars at the U.S. Embassy for Roosevelt to disperse. The Shah, who doubted from the beginning that the plan could succeed, unexpectedly fled to his summer palace after Mosaddeq began calling for a referendum to depose the ruler in response to Tudeh charges that he, Mosaddeq, was the tool of the "brainless agents of international reaction." Roosevelt sent an intermediary to talk the Shah into signing a decree dismissing Mosaddeq in favor of General Fazollah Zahedi, an aging Nazi sympathizer the British had thrown in jail during the Second World War. When the Shah finally signed the decree, Mosaddeq responded by declaring himself prime minister and the new head of state. The once and future Shah darted off for Rome. Riots swept Teheran just days after Roosevelt slipped out of the city and drove to Baghdad.

The CIA's new senior man, William Herman, used his embassy cover to put official pressure on the aging Mosaddeq, while the mayhem in the street paid for by Roosevelt escalated. He swung by the embassy to pick up $100,000 to distribute among his designated strike leaders. Meanwhile the U.S. ambassador cornered Iran's new prime minister and nastily threatened to evacuate all American citizens, which would certainly mean that the United States would cut off its aid to the beleaguered country just when its oil revenues had all but dried up. Mosaddeq allowed the police to restrain the extremists among his sympathizers, and SAVAK cleared the streets of Teheran. On cue, a few hundred muscle-bound supporters of the Shah poured into the empty avenues and marched toward Mosaddeq's house flanked by friendly army tanks. A two-hour battle ensued, and the loyalists won. Now Mosaddeq decamped—for Paris—and Allen Dulles flew

into Geneva to follow the progress of the counterrevolution at close hand. Days afterward, when the Shah once again sat on the Peacock Throne, Roosevelt stopped over in London for a brandy and congratulations all around with Winston Churchill.

As the headlines on the "crisis" died out in Western newspapers, their governments visited a geopolitical reckoning on Iran and their hapless client king. In August of 1954, the Iranians agreed to market their oil exclusively as a consortium formed under the guidance of the U.S. State Department. Anglo-Iranian got a 40 percent market share. The five big U.S. oil companies garnered 40 percent among them. Fourteen percent went to Shell Oil. Even the French got a piece, 6 percent to Compagnie Française des Pétroles. A secret "participants agreement" limited the amount of oil each member of the consortium could pump according to a complicated quota system. The intent, however, was clear: the industrial West planned to keep Persian oil production low, and hence its payments to the Shah's government low as well, as long as they could get oil cheaply somewhere else. Iranian oil would be the West's lever for keeping the Arab sheikhs in line. The postwar Middle East had become completely dominated by the politics of oil, and the new CIA—chartered to gather and interpret intelligence—had become the secret weapon of American corporate interests and addicted to covert action, both of which were reflected in the spying business's new jargon. The agency was called the "Company." Those it bribed, blackmailed, or extorted into lifetimes of betrayal were dubbed its "assets." Even the term used for the occasional murder it prac-

ticed in the name of democracy stank of the board room: "executive action."

The U.S. Supreme Court Strikes Down Racial Segregation (1954)

The event: In a landmark decision, handed down on May 17, 1954, the Supreme Court ruled segregation illegal in *Brown v. Board of Education of Topeka*, which launched the twentieth-century struggle for civil rights in earnest.

IN 1896, THE U.S. Supreme Court ruled on *Plessy v. Ferguson*, sanctioning segregation (chiefly in the South) by upholding as constitutional the principle of "separate but equal" public accommodations and facilities for blacks. Backed by the force of law, schools, public conveyances, restaurants, hotels, and other public facilities were rigidly segregated throughout much of the nation. Beginning in the mid-1930s, the National Association for the Advancement of Colored People (NAACP) brought a series of lawsuits against various segregated school districts. In these early cases the Supreme Court essentially upheld its 1896 ruling, declaring that because the "tangible" aspects of schools for blacks and those for whites were equal, the laws providing for segregated schools were constitutional. In

the later case of *Brown v. Board of Education*, however, the NAACP lawyers, among them future Supreme Court Associate Justice Thurgood Marshall, mustered a battery of experts to testify to the debilitating effects of segregation. This time, the high court held that segregated school systems were inherently unequal because of "intangible" factors, and in 1956 the Supreme Court issued guidelines to be used in desegregating the nation's school districts.

In and of itself, *Brown v. Board of Education* was a great step toward equality. By example, it also inspired thousands of African-Americans, especially in the South, to rise up against other laws and traditions that violated their civil rights, and the modern civil rights movement was born.

Disneyland Opens in Anaheim, California (1955)

The event: Walt Disney, creator of animated film fantasies for children, opened Disneyland, a 160-acre real-life incarnation of fantasy in the dreary California town of Anaheim.

IN SEPTEMBER 1959, when Soviet premier Nikita Khrushchev made his first visit to the United States, what he most wanted to

see was Disneyland. The Secret Service and other officials were not amused, but the press and public were. Yet it was not a frivolous request. For Disneyland, 160 acres in what was then the sleepy California town of Anaheim, lay at the very heart of postwar America.

Certainly, America's first "theme park" came from the heart of Walter Elias Disney. He was born in Chicago on December 5, 1901, but much of his childhood was spent in Marceline, Missouri, the epitome of small-town America, existing as a time and place remote from such twentieth-century challenges as foreign immigration, race relations, war, technology, and Communism. Its main street doubtless inspired the nostalgic centerpiece of Disneyland: "Main Street, U.S.A."

After a move to Kansas City, Missouri, Disney met Ub Iwerks, and the two established a modest animation studio, which failed in 1923. Disney and Iwerks started a new studio in Hollywood, and in 1928 released "Steamboat Willie," not only the first cartoon to feature sound, but the debut appearance of Mickey Mouse—whose squeaky voice was supplied by Disney himself—destined to become the single most popular, universally recognizable, and profitably marketable animated character of all time. Disney and Iwerks went on to create a series of innovative cartoons, featuring a veritable zoo of mischievous and cuddly characters that children and adults adored: Donald Duck, Goofy, Pluto, and so on. In 1937, Disney gambled the whole works on creating the world's first feature-length animated film: *Snow White and the Seven Dwarfs*. Doomsayers predicted the extravagantly expensive cartoon would torpedo Disney, but it proved a stunning box-office success and was followed by many more full-length animations, all of which were highly profitable.

Disney seemed to have a magic touch. He instinctively knew what American audiences wanted to see. While Hitler and Mussolini were menacing Europe in 1933, Disney offered *The Three Little Pigs*, in which the solid American work ethic easily triumphs over the Big Bad Wolf. But there was a distinctly darker side to Disney. A political conservative, he was xenophobic and some accused him of being anti-Semitic. Virulently anti-union, he paid his artists and animators poorly, ran his studio like a factory, and allowed a 1941 strike to nearly wreck his studio rather than allow his employees to unionize. Disney became personally known to FBI director J. Edgar Hoover as a 100 percent loyal American, and Hoover enlisted his aid as a SAC—a special agent contact—asking him to infiltrate and monitor a number of Hollywood organizations suspected of having left-wing affiliations.

Almost out of spite, following the animators' strike, Disney turned to the production of live-action features, including *Treasure Island* (1950), *20,000 Leagues Under the Sea* (1954), and *Mary Poppins* (1964), along with well produced but sanitized and sentimentalized nature films. In the 1950s, Disney also produced live-action films for television, most notably the Davy Crockett series, which had millions of American boys and girls clamoring for the fake-fur coonskin caps that Disney licensees were highly willing to purvey. Disney's enormously popular "Mickey Mouse Club" revived the old theatrical cartoon characters for the television generation.

But, in the postwar years, the project that most consumed Disney was Disneyland: a full-scale, three-dimensional incarnation of the fantasy worlds Disney had served up in film. The first stop, just within the great gates, with a sign welcoming visitors to the "happiest place in the world," was Main Street, U.S.A., and the last stop was Tomorrowland, U.S.A.—both utopian visions of America, past and future. In between was the cowboy-and-Indian West of Frontierland and the fairy tale realm of Fantasyland. It was as all-American as the circus or the carnival, but with none of the gaminess of the former or the tawdriness of the latter.

A shrewd student of marketing strategies, Disney reasoned that if handled correctly, his outdoor park would help to sell his films and television shows, just as his movies and TV episodes would lure families to Disneyland. In a novel—but successful—twist of logic, Disney hired scriptwriters to plan his park. Then he hired architects, engineers, and city planners to build the writers' plans. Disneyland was "dedicated to the ideals, the dreams, and the hard facts that have created America . . . with the hope that it will be a source of joy and inspiration to all the world."

Once inside the gates, Disney made sure visitors were joyful. Nothing was left to chance. The workforce, which in the first 15 years of operation increased five times, was carefully coached in how to act, what to say, and how to manage crowds. A bench for resting was never more than a few steps away. Even if the lines for amusement rides and concession stands seemed long, staff dressed as Goofy or Minnie or Donald Duck entertained the visitors as they waited. Whatever else visitors *oooed* and *ahhhed* at, all were singularly impressed by the cleanliness of Disneyland—even as nearby Los Angeles choked with automobile-produced pollution and its inner city, like those all across the country, decayed.

Disneyland certainly served up what American families (and Soviet dictators) wanted. The enterprise became the first of a new breed of theme parks, the first to lure Americans—all across the country—from their suburban homes and urge them to hop in their cars and use some of their leisure time for family vacations. In its first year of operation, Disneyland entertained 4 million visitors; in later years, it drew as many as 10 million visitors annually. Disney himself, a heavy smoker and hard drinker, died of lung cancer in 1966, amid new plans that would ultimately spread his dream of a clean, homogenous, conflict-free, firmly programmed adult version of his never-never land first to Florida (Disney World), and then the world (Disney theme parks in Japan and France).

Ray Kroc Founds the McDonald's Corporation (1955)

The event: In 1954, salesman Ray Kroc persuaded the McDonald brothers, owners of some successful hamburger stands in San Bernardino, California, to make him their licensing agent and the following year created the McDonald's Corporation.

THE VASTNESS OF the American landscape, its democratic form of government, and the diverse backgrounds of its mostly immigrant population might have yielded, in the twentieth century, a nation of infinite variety . . . but it didn't.

The forces of diversity, randomness, choice, and change, often as not, produced an equal but opposite reaction: a move toward homogeneity, orderliness, standardization, and uniformity. America in the 1950s was a land of cities sprawling into far-flung suburbs—often populated by those in flight from an inner city that was now the home of nonresidential corporate development on the one hand and African-American, Latino, and other minority groups on the other. Suburbia was knit together not by the walking-distance proximities of the traditional American small town, but by roads and the newly emerging system of interstate highways, expressways, and freeways. It was also woven into a kind of culturally seamless fabric by mass media and the mass production of a host of "name-brand" goods. All of this developed against a background of disquieting urban change—postwar immigration, the migration of rural African-Americans into the cities, especially those of the North, and the emerging civil rights movement that threatened familiar (if ultimately unjust and intolerable) cultural patterns. Even more frightening change was taking place abroad: the Cold War, the seemingly relentless spread of Communism, and the Damoclesian sword of impending thermonuclear annihilation.

Into this world stepped Raymond Albert Kroc. Born in Chicago in 1902, he was a high school dropout who had served as a sales manager for Lily-Tulip paper cups and plates and a promoter for a milk shake mixing machine. Both put Kroc in touch with the mass food-service market, in which he took an increasing interest. In 1954, one of his customers, the McDonald brothers, owners of a hamburger stand in San Bernardino, California, started ordering an inordinate number of Kroc's milk shake mixers. Any ordinary salesman would just have written up the orders, happily pocketed the profits, and given the matter no more thought—but Kroc was not your ordinary salesman. Hard-working, politically conservative, and unflappably optimistic, he had a deep admiration for "old-fashioned" American virtues and an uncanny sense of mainstream American culture. All of these qualities and instincts converged on the McDonald brothers, who, he discovered, had drawn a large, growing, and loyal following among San Bernardinians by making good hamburgers (and the shakes to go with them) at a low price. Nothing unusual about that, except that the McDonald brothers did this with an unvarying consistency by using assembly-line-style techniques, assigning specific preparation tasks to each of their low-paid high school-age workers, each of whom was thoroughly trained in the precise performance of one simple step in the process. Furthermore, unlike any number of ramshackle hamburger joints across the country, the McDonalds kept theirs scrupulously clean.

Kroc also noticed that the McDonalds had even used their local reputation for quick service, good quality, low prices, and dependable products to franchise a few other restaurants nearby, but they were not aggressive marketers. Kroc proposed to act as their exclusive agent in marketing licenses to others to use the McDonald's name and methods, and, in 1955, he established the McDonald's Corporation to do just that.

Kroc opened his own McDonald's in the Chicago suburb of Des Plaines, Illinois, and used it as a kind of laboratory to demonstrate to potential licensees the profitability of the format he developed. He introduced to the practice of franchising an absolute strict-business format; that is, licensees, while they owned their own businesses, had to agree to conform to detailed operating rules, build their restaurants in strict accordance to prescribed plans, pay a royalty on the food and drink they sold, and purchase supplies from approved vendors. In return, the franchisees benefited from the acquisition of a tested, extremely cost-effective method of production and a growing (soon to be vast) advertising and marketing network.

As the corporation grew, Kroc acquired an associate, Harry Sonnenborn, who developed a scheme whereby the McDonald's Corporation acquired real estate, which it leased to franchisees for their restaurants. This greatly added to corporate revenues and attracted bank investments. In 1961, the corporation bought out the McDonald brothers' interest in the company at the price they dictated.

While it was *their* price, the brothers soon realized that it was too low. By the beginning of the 1990s, McDonald's had sold more than 65 billion burgers and operated some ten thousand restaurants, and, while the political, economic, and production philosophy behind the restaurants remained "all American," outlets were opened in about fifty foreign countries. The giant plastic "Golden Arches" symbol that graces all McDonald's restaurants became an American corporate icon as familiar worldwide as the logos of Coca-Cola or Ford.

Rosa Parks Refuses to Give Up Her Seat on a Montgomery, Alabama Bus (1955)

The event: On December 1, 1955, Rosa Parks, an African-American woman living in Montgomery, Alabama, boarded a city bus. When she refused to relinquish her seat to a white person, she was arrested and jailed. The episode became a seminal event in the struggle of African-Americans for civil rights.

SOMETIMES HISTORY and social circumstances work together to invest the smallest action with great courage and consequence. Such was the case with Rosa Parks, who lived in a time and place that made taking a seat on a bus an event of particular consequence. Following Parks's arrest and incarceration, civil rights activists called for blacks to boycott the city's buses. They did, with devastating effect on bus revenues. Some took advantage of car pools organized to take them to work. Others walked wherever they needed to go. Despite hardship on both sides, the boycott lasted for more than a year, demonstrating the effectiveness of organized, nonviolent activity in the civil rights movement.

The Montgomery boycott was the action that brought the Reverend Martin Luther King, Jr., to the forefront as a dynamic civil rights leader. Advocating nonviolent means to attain racial equality, in

1957 King was elected president of the Southern Christian Leadership Conference, an organization that was to become increasingly active in the civil rights struggle. Over the next decade, the movement produced other organizations equally dedicated to nonviolence. The Student Non-Violent Coordinating Committee, founded in 1960, focused on the rural South, and the Congress of Racial Equality and the Mississippi Freedom Democratic Party worked in Mississippi to enlist rural blacks in the civil rights struggle.

Some of the early protests were marred by violence, but it was not until the 1965 march on Selma, Alabama, the founding of the Black Panther Party during the late 1960s, and the deaths by assassination of Malcolm X and King himself that some black civil rights protesters deliberately turned away from the nonviolence epitomized by Rosa Parks.

The U.S. Government Approves a Vaccine for Polio (1955)

The event: In 1955, the U.S. government approved a vaccine developed by Dr. Jonas Salk to fight polio, thus launching the campaign that all but wiped out one of the world's most dreaded diseases.

WHILE STUDYING MEDICINE at New York University's Medical School, Jonas Salk became interested in immunology and took up research on vaccines under Dr. Thomas Francis at the University of Michigan. Disease-causing unicellular microorganisms had been yielding to antibiotics since Fleming's discovery of penicillin in 1928. But viruses, such as the one that caused the dreaded killer and crippler polio,

proved harder to isolate and treat. It was at the University of Michigan that scientists had produced the first killed-virus vaccine effective against influenza. Before the influenza vaccine was developed, medical theory held that vaccines prepared from dead bacteria were effective in immunizing against bacterial infections, but that immunization against viruses required live-virus vaccines—and these carried the grave risk of infecting the patient they were supposed to immunize. The work at Michigan proved that theory wrong.

Convinced by the evidence that killed-virus vaccines could be effective, Salk became head of a viral research laboratory at the University of Pittsburgh, where he focused his attention on developing a vaccine against polio. He financed his research project with funding from the March of Dimes Foundation, which was dedicated to fighting and treating a disease that most characteristically attacked children. By 1954, Salk had begun testing a killed-virus vaccine for polio, and the following year Food and Drug Administration authorities declared it safe and effective.

Salk was hailed as a savior by millions of parents, who, throughout the polio-scourged early 1950s, had faced each summer (when risk of infection was at its highest) with dread. His vaccine was used universally throughout the United States and much of the world until 1962, when Dr. Albert Sabin persuaded many physicians to switch to his live-virus vaccine, which was administered orally rather than by injection. The Sabin vaccine is now preferred, but it was Salk's pioneering work that rid the nation and the world of one of its cruelest afflictions. Until his death at the age of 80 on June 23, 1995, Salk had been engaged in research to develop a vaccine for another, more recent plague, no less cruel but even more deadly, AIDS.

The Suez Crisis Erupts (1956)

The event: On July 26, 1956, the new Egyptian president, Gamal Abdel Nasser, nationalized the Suez Canal. Britain and France, Egypt's former imperial overlords who were dependent on the canal for oil, secretly conspired with Israel to take back control of the Suez by force. Shortly after ten Israeli brigades invaded Egypt on October 29, 1956, and routed Nasser's army, the two European nations, on schedule and according to plan, demanded that both Israel and Egypt withdraw from the canal zone and announced that they intended to intervene and enforce the cease-fire already called for by the U.N. But when Soviet Russia threatened to put a stop to the nonsense and Dwight Eisenhower, president of the United States and furious with England, France, and Israel, indicated that he would let the Russians bomb them to kingdom come if it came to that, first the French and the British, then the Israelis meekly abandoned their adventure. Nasser emerged from the crisis not merely a victor, but a national hero and leader of the so-called Third World of nonaligned nations.

MODERN EGYPT achieved nominal independence in 1922 after centuries of foreign rule. Until Britain invaded and occupied the country in 1882, the land of the pharaohs had been—except for a brief period of occupation by Napoleon's army—a self-governing province of the Ottoman Empire. In 1914, as Ottoman rule collapsed in the wake of a series of petty Balkan wars, Britain deposed the Turkish lackey of a viceroy (called the "khedive") who ran Egypt and put his uncle, Husayn Kamil, in charge. Calling Kamil the "sultan," the British imposed martial law to protect the strategically vital flow of oil from the Middle East for the duration of World War I. Kamil died in 1917, and his ambitious brother Ahmad Fuad became sultan at a time when, fueled by British wartime repression and war-spawned deprivations, Egyptian nationalism was reaching a fevered pitch. The Ottoman Empire disappeared during the war, and afterward Egypt proposed sending a nationalist delegation to London to petition His Majesty for autonomy. Not only did Britain reject the delegation out of hand, they arrested and threw its leader—the charismatic Zaghlul Pasha—in jail. In response, the nationalists launched industrial strikes against the British colonial government and terrorist attacks against its personnel. Lord Allenby—the general who had ripped Palestine from the cold dead hands of the Ottomans—finally negotiated a settlement and declared Egypt independent "with reservations" in February 1922. The reservations were that Britain still intended to protect foreign interests, meaning the Suez and the oil companies, and to supervise Egyptian defense. Sultan Fuad became King Fuad I and Egypt became a constitutional monarchy, at least on paper; given that British troops remained in the country and Fuad remained the same autocrat he had always been, the changes did not mean much at all.

Nasser was four years old at the time, having been born in January 1918 to a middle-class family in the village of Bani Morr in the Upper Egyptian province of Asyut. Nasser began his rise to power in 1937 when he entered the military academy.

During a short stint in the army as a second lieutenant, he met and befriended two other recent graduates, Zakaria Mohieddin and Anwar al-Sadat, who, with Nasser, would become prominent in the Nazi-backed Free Officers movement. After his army service, he returned as an instructor to the academy in 1941, where he recruited members for the Free Officers Corps. During the 1940s and early 1950s, deep social unrest spread through Egypt under the rule of the sybaritic King Farouk, Fuad's successor. Land was concentrated in the hands of the rich, malnutrition and disease were rampant, and peasants fled the dismal rural areas for the cities, where prices and unemployment were driven steadily higher. The time was ripe for action by the Free Officers. Two thousand troops led by 200 officers stormed army headquarters in Cairo during the night of July 22–23, 1952. By morning, Farouk was dead and a new political order was in place with Major General Muhammed Naguib at its head. Nasser remained in the background as the Revolutionary Command Council took control, but in the spring of 1954, in a reaction against left-wing radicalism, Naguib was deposed, and Nasser emerged as the self-proclaimed prime minister.

Land reform was Nasser's first order of business, but he knew that land reform was not enough to shake Egypt out of its downward economic spiral. A special stimulus was needed as well, and Nasser seized on the construction of the massive Aswan High Dam on the Nile as a vehicle for economic recovery. He first negotiated with Britain and the United States for financial backing for the project. Uneasy about Nasser's courting of Eastern bloc and Soviet support (he had signed an arms deal with Czechoslovakia in 1956), Britain, the United States, and the World Bank withdrew from the project. Undaunted, Nasser nationalized the Suez Canal, whose proceeds had previously gone to European bondholders, and stated that usage fees would be dedicated to constructing the new dam, predicting they would pay for it in five years. Fearing that the unpredictable Nasser might close the canal and cut off oil to western Europe, Britain and France began making their plans to get it back and, if possible, depose Nasser. When diplomatic efforts appeared unlikely to settle the crisis, they struck.

As Nasser's reputation soared after the Suez crisis, he proceeded with the construction of the Aswan High Dam, aided now by the Soviet Union, and he set out to realize yet another goal—the unification of Arab countries. In 1958, the government of Syria merged with Egypt to form the United Arab Republic. It was Nasser's goal to recruit all of the other Arab countries into the fold. The republic was short-lived, however. Not only did the other nations fail to join, but Syria

withdrew in 1961. Nevertheless, Egypt did become a haven for Arab radicals and anti-colonial revolutionaries as Nasser welcomed political refugees from other Arab countries. Even as he embraced foreign radicals, he cracked down on civil freedom in his own country. The end seemed to come in 1967, when Nasser called for the withdrawal of United Nations Emergency Force troops from the Gaza Strip and instituted a blockade of Eilat, precipitating a brilliant preemptive war by Israel that destroyed Egypt's air force on the ground. On June 9, 1967, Gamal Abdel Nasser appeared on Egyptian television to announce his resignation. Hundreds of thousands of Egyptians took to the streets to demand that Nasser remain in power. While some of the demonstrations may have been engineered by Nasser himself, it is undeniable that some were indeed spontaneous. A hard-liner against Israel and the West, and supremely repressive at home, Nasser—from his assumption of power in 1954 until his death from a heart attack on September 28, 1970—was the most popular and influential Arab leader in the world.

Hungary Revolts Against the USSR (1956)

The event: On October 24, 1956, Hungary's prime minister Imre Nagy defied the USSR by announcing an end to one-party rule, thereby igniting the movement to remove itself from the Soviet sphere of influence established in Eastern Europe at the end of World War II, a movement the west came to call the Hungarian Revolution.

THE TREATY OF VERSAILLES that ended World War I not only penalized Germany, but dismembered the tottering Austro-Hungarian empire, leaving Hungary a

nation greatly reduced in size. The Treaty of Trianon, which followed the Versailles document in 1920, stripped the empire of nearly three-quarters of its territory.

Between 1920 and 1944, Admiral Miklós Horthy, the Magyar regent of Hungary, worked to regain the nation's former lands, securing from Germany some revision of its frontiers in exchange for an alliance in World War II. The territorial gains were short-lived, and the alliance meant that Hungary went down to defeat with Germany and, like other eastern European nations, was overrun by a Soviet occupation force.

Following the war, an uneasy coalition government was formed for three years, after which the Communists established a one-party dictatorship under Mátyás Rákosi—which they, of course, called the Hungarian Revolution. In Stalinist fashion, the party imposed forced collectivization of farms and a program of industrialization, both enforced by terror tactics and the secret police. Rákosi, however, was forced out after the death of Stalin in 1953 and replaced by Imre Nagy, who introduced more liberal policies. The "thaw" was brief: in 1955, Rákosi returned to oust Nagy and reintroduced unalloyed Stalinism.

But the brief breath of democracy emboldened the Hungarian resistance to Communism, and opposition to Rákosi mounted. On October 23, police fired on a peaceful student demonstration in support of the June anti-Soviet Polish revolt. Street fighting broke out and soon spread across the country. Within a few days,

revolutionary elements had seized control of many important institutions and facilities, including the radio stations. Soviet troops pulled back, withdrawing from Hungary, and Nagy (who had been reinstated as prime minister on October 24) announced an end to one-party rule—a second Hungarian "Revolution" in little more than a decade.

Despite the United States' stance on the "containment" of Communism as expressed in the Truman Doctrine, the Eisenhower government declined to intervene in the anti-Soviet revolution, and—much to the shock of the Hungarians—announced that it would offer no aid to the new government. Accordingly, the Soviets attacked on November 4, and despite impassioned radio pleas to the United States, no help was forthcoming. Within weeks, the revolution was liquidated, and Hungary, barely recovered from the devastation of the world war, was in shambles. The Soviets had killed tens of thousands, and had imprisoned more. Almost a quarter of a million Hungarians fled the country.

The 1956 Hungarian Revolt was one of the earliest indications that the Soviet juggernaut was not unstoppable, but it also tested—and found wanting—the West's resolve to act against a Russian superpower armed with nuclear weapons. To many in the West, after 1956 the Iron Curtain seemed more impenetrable than ever.

Congress Passes the Interstate Highway Act (1956)

The event: In 1956 Congress approved the biggest public works program in world history, passing the Interstate Highway Act, the high-water mark of a half-century of frenzied road building at government expense that ensured the supremacy of the automobile as an instrument of commerce, technology, and middle-class security.

THE DECISION BY the United States Post Office Department to provide a system of rural free delivery at the end of the nineteenth century spurred the development of the hard-surface roads mail carriers needed to do their jobs. But if the post office hadn't demanded the roads, the public soon would have, as the automobile became the individual American's ticket to freedom, and two-lane blacktops, like the railways before them, seemed capable of making or breaking a community. Good roads became a public passion—and something of a political movement—in the 1920s, accelerating the decline of the small town and the depopulation of the rural countryside already underway. The construction of streets and highways became and remained one of the largest items of government expenditure at every level, often at great cost to everything else, including education.

Spurred by Ford's assembly-line Model Ts, automobiles became the nucleus around which a new consumer society evolved. In 1913, one million automobiles were registered in the United States. Ten years later, that number was ten million. The state of Kansas contained within its borders more cars than either France or Germany, and automobile sales in Michigan outdistanced those of Great Britain and Ireland combined. By the mid-1920s automobiles

ranked first among products valued by consumers, and by 1927 Americans were driving some twenty-six million of them, one car for every five people.

The development of roads and the expansion of the automobile industry fired the economy, making cars the lifeblood of the petroleum industry and a major customer of steel, rubber, and glass factories. In Los Angeles, for example, a cabal of oil and automobile industry leaders managed to ensure that the city abandoned any plans to make its fairly well-developed interurban railways into a functioning public transportation system, and it was no accident that L.A. developed a cult of the automobile even as it gave birth to that most modern of engineering feats, the limited-access cloverleaf. Roads also motivated expansion in outdoor recreation and tourism and their related industries, including service stations, roadside restaurants, and motels. After World War II, the automobile industry boomed to unprecedented heights, and new roads now led out of the city to the suburbs, where two-car families transported their 2.5 children to de facto segregated schools and to shopping malls that sprang up like mushrooms.

The Interstate Highway System, a network of federally subsidized highways connecting major urban centers, was justified, like almost everything else in the 1950s, as a national defense measure, a way of moving men and materiel rapidly in times of national emergency. It also stretched American mobility to new distances, creating hours-long commutes, immense traffic jams, and polluted cities. American roads became part and parcel of the postwar flight from the social problems of the city, symbolized by the "loops" and "beltways" that enabled motorists to avoid going downtown unless absolutely necessary. Highways that had once helped empty the rural countryside now helped impoverish the inner city. Just how inconsequential urban neighborhoods had become was evident every time a new interstate cut through the homes of the poor in the service of tourists and commuters.

Unlike European nations and cities around the world, who almost as a matter of course developed effective subways and interurban transport, the United States treated public transportation as a private business. Between 1945 and 1980, 75 percent of federal funds for transportation were spent on highways, while a scant 1 percent went for buses, trolleys, or subways. The interstate highway system, a magnificent engineering achievement, sealed the fate of decaying urban centers, promoted sprawling, often ugly strip development on the urban perimeters, spawned look-alike suburb after look-alike suburb, and raised the level of environmental pollution to an all-time high.

By the end of the century, America's highway system—like so much governed by American public policy—had about it the taint of racism. Perhaps the world's best road system worked well for a middle class able to afford the latest foreign cars and live in roomy suburbs, and for American business interests that transported their goods at high speeds in ever larger, and ever more dangerous trailer-pulling trucks. At the same time, one of the world's worst public transit systems ill-served the urban—and mostly ethnic—poor, who had to travel to what jobs they could find and do what shopping they could afford on poorly policed and unsafe subways, or in fleets of busses that tax-paying and automobile-driving surburbanites subsidized with much ill-humor. Stewing in bumper-to-bumper traffic, American middle-class commuters no longer may have felt free, but at least they felt safe as they drove from the fortresses of home to lofty offices in expensive corporate skyscrapers that dominated downtowns abandoned by all but the derelict and the dangerous after dark, or to detached and lonely office parks where all signs of life disappeared with the close of the workday.

The USSR Launches Sputnik (1957)

The event: On October 4, 1957, the Soviet Union sent the first artificial earth satellite into orbit, inaugurating the Space Age and the Space Race.

AS THE UNITED STATES and the Soviet Union converged on Germany at the end of World War II, the powers intended not only to control territory, but to grab much of the advanced technology that had created the V-1 and V-2 rockets. Thus, both nations emerged with a handful of "German rocket scientists" and set to work on penetrating outer space.

It was clearly a high-stakes race, though few among the American public could say quite why. For their part, U.S. scientists and government officials spoke of "pure science" and the human spirit restless for exploration and new challenges. But, the fact was that the race to space was largely a military endeavor, and it became increasingly clear that, whatever scientific gains were to be found beyond the earth's atmosphere, getting there meant capturing the century's new high ground. This military advantage would be a commanding position from which any number of tactical and strategic objectives might be met: surveillance, communications, and the development of new weapons systems, to which the V-2 had been but the merest prelude. The space race also became a test of national pride and ideological achievement. In a world in which thermonuclear arsenals had made conquest more dangerous than ever, space was a vast blank field ripe for conquest without retaliatory consequence.

And so it began. But not since the Soviets had exploded their first atomic bomb were Americans so stunned and disappointed to learn that they had been beaten into space by *Sputnik 1*, a 38-pound metal sphere with a radio transmitter launched on October 4, 1957. The United States suffered several failed launches after that date—in-

cluding the Vanguard, christened "Flopnik" and "Kaputnik" when it toppled off its launch pad and burst into flames on December 6—but in January 1958 the United States succeeded in orbiting *Explorer I*. Both nations launched other unmanned satellites, as well as orbiting vehicles lofting dogs and monkeys into orbit. Another blow to the United States came on April 12, 1961, when the Soviet cosmonaut Yuri Gagarin launched on a one-orbit mission, becoming the first human being in space. Less than a month later, on May 5, Alan B. Shepard became the first American in space with a fifteen-minute suborbital flight. It was not until nine months later that Colonel John Glenn made the first U.S. orbital flight.

The American triumph would come at the end of the decade, with the successful lunar landing of *Apollo 11*. But, in its early laps, the space race hurt America's prestige, suggesting that the Soviet way of life turned out people more fit to compete in the modern world. (Others simply concluded that the Soviets had managed to snatch more German scientists than the Americans had.) It also trivialized the profound scientific importance of space exploration on the one hand and, on the other, masked the full dimensions of a potentially lethal contest. For, in developing rockets, both nations were creating increasingly powerful, increasingly longer-range, and increasingly sophisticated vehicles for the delivery of thermonuclear warheads, and the world soon bristled with intercontinental ballistic missiles.

U.S. Federal Troops Force Little Rock, Arkansas to Integrate (1957)

The event: At 12:15 P.M. on September 24, 1957, President Dwight D. Eisenhower ordered General Maxwell Taylor to dispatch army troops to Central High School in Little Rock, Arkansas, in order to prevent defiance of the federally ordered integration of schools pursuant to a decision of the Supreme Court in the 1954 case of *Brown v. Board of Education*.

WHEN GOVERNOR ORVAL FAUBUS of Arkansas called out the state's National Guard and deployed it around Central High School in Little Rock to prevent the entry of about a dozen African-American students who had the constitutional right to attend the school, President Eisenhower did not want to get involved. From his vacation retreat in Newport, Rhode Island, the president remarked about the wrong-headedness of "these people who believe you are going to reform the human heart by law." Faubus, appealing to Ike's well-known sympathy for the South, asked Eisenhower for assurance that he would not intervene, that he would let the state and local governments work out their own problems. Eisenhower sent a telegram to the governor: "The only assurance I can give you is that the federal Constitution will be upheld by me by every legal means at my command." In the meantime, a federal judge set September 20, 1957, as a hearing date on the matter. Before that deadline, however, the President met with Faubus, telling him that a "trial of strength between the President and the governor . . . could [have] only one outcome—that is, the state would lose." Faubus agreed to withdraw the National Guard.

But he did not do so. On September 20,

the federal judge ordered Faubus to stop interfering with integration. However, the situation was no longer within the control of Arkansas's governor. On Monday morning, September 23, an angry mob—estimated at between five hundred and several thousand—gathered around Central High and beat up two African-American reporters. As the police struggled to contain the violence, nine black students slipped into the school. Learning that the black students were inside, the mob stormed police barricades, struggled to get into the school, and screamed "lynch the niggers!" Little Rock Mayor Woodrow Wilson Mann ordered the police to remove the black students from the school. Integration in Little Rock had lasted three hours.

In the meantime, the racist mobs grew, and Mayor Mann telegraphed President Eisenhower directly: "The immediate need for federal troops is urgent." The president gave the order to dispatch a thousand paratroopers from the 101st Airborne Division to Little Rock. Eisenhower was at pains to tell the nation that he was using the troops not to enforce integration, but to prevent opposition to the orders of a federal court. The President appealed for moderation. What he got was the rage of thousands of white segregationists throughout the South protesting a federal invasion. A local Louisiana politician, Leander Perez, called for secession, though his suggestion was met by a half-serious reminder that the "Yankees" these days had nuclear weapons.

On Tuesday, September 24, nine Afri-can-American students entered Central High School under U.S. Army guard. They attended a full day of classes—the first full day of integration in Little Rock, Arkansas, and the beginning of integration for public schools throughout the South.

Chairman Mao Launches China's "Great Leap Forward" (1958)

The event: In 1958, the Chinese Communist Party Chairman Mao Tse-tung announced a program of accelerated industrialization and forced agricultural collectivization, not unlike Stalin's radical economic reforms of the 1930s; and, like Stalin's collectivizing, the "Great Leap Forward" would not only fail to achieve its goals, but also would lead to widespread famine. Before it was over, some twenty million Chinese would die.

HAVING GAINED LEADERSHIP of China and the Chinese Communist Party, Mao relentlessly purged the party of all opponents from 1949 to 1954. He then moved against the nation's agricultural landlords in a program of collectivization that recalled Stalin's "five-year plans" of the 1930s. Mao's early agricultural program, however, was but a prelude to the Great Leap Forward that would come at the end of the decade.

After intervening in the Korean War and following the death of Stalin in 1953, Mao became the preeminent figure in world Communism. Secure in his position, he initiated a self-critical period of examination, professing dissatisfaction with what he saw as the slackening pace of revolutionary change in the Chinese countryside. Mao launched the Hundred Flowers movement in 1956, using the slogan, "Let a hundred flowers bloom, let a thousand schools of thought contend." In stark contrast to other Communist leaders, he encouraged intellectuals to criticize the party and its methods of government and administration, winning the admiration of many world leaders. But the Hundred Flowers movement was not destined to endure very long. Whether by design or out of fear of the extremely hostile tone of the free-flowing criticism he had invoked, Mao used the Hundred Flowers movement *against* the dissidents, and he embarked on a campaign to create a cult of personality focused on himself—again, much as Stalin had done.

As Mao elevated himself, he stepped up the pressure to eliminate private property completely and transform the nation's farmlands into people's communes. He called his radical program, begun in 1958, the Great Leap Forward, and, through it, he meant to show that China could "catch up with Britain" in industrial production in fifteen years, bypassing the Soviet Union in the process and creating a truly communal society. Mao brought the full force of his personality to bear upon the masses, who were exhorted to heroic efforts. Ordinary people built "backyard furnaces" for the production of iron, and farms were collectivized. The collectives were, in turn, merged into vast communes.

Far from catching up with Britain and surpassing the Soviet Union, China was devastated by famine worse than any this perpetually famine-menaced country had ever seen. In a very short time, as many as twenty million Chinese starved to death. Late in 1958, Mao stepped down as head of state and was replaced by Liu Shao-ch'i. Nominally retired and in seclusion, Mao carefully began a campaign against his successor, bursting back into public life in the mid-1960s with a brilliantly orchestrated attack against Liu Shao-ch'i. Borrowing from Trotsky's notions about permanent revolution, Mao proposed a new kind of proletarian-led movement, one that went beyond politics and addressed the notion of Chinese culture as the centerpiece of revolutionary change.

The Cubans Stage a Revolution (1959)

The event: On New Year's Eve of 1959, Cuban guerrillas under the leadership of Fidel Castro fought their way toward Havana. As the populace of the island's capital rose up in support of the "Fidelistas," the brutal Cuban dictator Fulgencio Batista fled to the United States in the early morning hours of New Year's Day. The Cuban Revolution had succeeded.

THE UNITED STATES' intervention in the Cuban struggle for independence from Spain, which resulted in the Spanish-American War of 1898, was in large part motivated by a desire to protect extensive American business interests on the island. Although America officially guaranteed Cuban independence, it had also officially made itself the arbiter of that independence. In truth, of course, business ties and America's "interests" in the fate of Cuba continued to make the island a de facto dependency, and American companies often exploited cheap Cuban labor, engaged in corrupt practices, and encouraged corruption among Cuban government officials.

Cuban leaders, seeking to maintain their personally profitable relationship with United States interests, were characteristically oppressive. Such was Gerardo Machado, who was overthrown in a coup led by Fulgencio Batista and Carlos Manuel de Cespedes. In 1933, Batista led another coup, which ousted Cespedes. In the manner of many Caribbean and Central American "strong men" (the euphemism the American politicians and the American press used for tyrants) Batista was elevated to high military command, serving as army chief of staff, rather than elective office. From his military position, he governed by means of a series of civilian puppet presidents until 1940, when he was finally elected to the office himself. After serving a term, Batista left Cuba to enjoy the fruits of his regime as a retiree in Florida, but returned to Cuba in 1952, and, through a bloodless coup, once again became president.

Batista's second regime was even more repressive and corrupt than his first, making deals not only with American business interests, but with U.S.-based organized crime. Batista's depravity became so blatant that, by the end of the 1950s, President Dwight D. Eisenhower canceled scheduled arms sales to the regime. In the meantime, Cuban opposition to Batista was mounting, and Fidel Castro Ruz emerged as a leader of the movement.

Castro was born on August 13, 1926 (some sources report 1927) on a farm in Mayari municipality, Oriente province, and received a rigorous Catholic education, including training at a Jesuit boarding school, which instilled in him a sense of spartan order and discipline. He obtained a law degree from the University of Havana in 1950 and became active in the social-democratic *Ortodoxo* party, earning a reputation as an eloquent opponent of Batista. On July 26, 1953, Castro led an assault on the Moncada army barracks, a government armory. Captured, he was sentenced to fifteen years' imprisonment, but was granted amnesty in 1955 after serving only two years.

Castro went into self-exile in Mexico, where he founded the 26th of July Movement and prepared to carry out revolution in a Cuba already seething with insurrection. On November 30, 1956, Castro and 81 others, including the charismatic guerrilla leader Che Guevara, returned to Cuba. Met by Batista's forces, the guerrillas were apparently routed, and Castro was reported dead. Actually, he and his followers had set up a secret base camp in the isolated Sierra Maestra Mountains. From there they conducted a highly successful guerrilla war between 1957 and October of 1958, when they emerged from hiding to take the offensive. Batista, his forces in disarray, fled the country on New Year's Day of 1959, and Castro occupied Havana on January 8.

Just the day before, the United States had declared its official recognition of Castro's government, for, at the time, Fidel Castro was not an avowed Communist. He had conducted the revolution in the name of anti-imperialism, nationalism, and general reform—all palatable enough to official Washington. Yet, shortly after taking up the reins of government, Castro became defiant and bellicose, particularly concerning the United States and the degradations it had historically visited on his country. Without a doubt, under Castro the living conditions of the masses dramatically improved, and the Cuban people supported Castro's nationalization of foreign-owned properties and industries, most of them American. Those who resisted Castro's new direction for Cuba found themselves subject to arrest, imprisonment, exile, or execution, and many of them followed Batista's example and fled, most often to Florida.

On May 7, 1960, Castro announced the resumption of diplomatic relations with the Soviet Union (which had been broken off by Batista), and by the middle of the year, he explicitly aligned his nation with the USSR, at which point Soviet Premier Khrushchev warned that he would defend Cuba against American aggression, even to the point of thermonuclear war. Suddenly, an outpost of Soviet-style Communism was a mere ninety miles from the city of Miami.

Castro menaced the United States naval base at Guantanamo Bay, and, on November 1, 1960, President Eisenhower declared that the United States would take "whatever steps are necessary to defend" the base. On January 3, 1961, he severed diplomatic relations with Cuba. Twice afterward, the United States directly challenged Cuba sovereignty—once during the failed Bay of Pigs invasion in 1961, and again during the 1962 Cuban missile crisis. Both events only made Castro more defiant and drove him further into the arms of the Soviets. (He loudly and boldly declared an alliance with the USSR in December 1961.)

In July 1964, when the Organization of American States instituted sanctions against the island, Castro permitted refugees to leave for the United States in a series of what Cuban expatriots and some American officials called "freedom flights" that continued from November 1965 until August 1971, bringing about a quarter of a million Cubans out of the country. When the United States continued to encourage Cubans to immigrate over the next two decades, Castro threw open the gates of the island's jails and allowed not only Cuba's political internees, but its hardened criminals to take off for Miami. Many blamed these "Muriels," named after one of Cuba's toughest prisons, for increased violence in the streets of Miami and the renewed growth of its already healthy drug-trafficking underworld.

Castro gained a large measure of prestige when he was elected chairman of the Nonaligned Nations Movement in 1979, but he generally failed as an economic reformer at home, for which he blamed the United State's continued economic boycott of the island. Despite its financial woes, Cuba became the model for revolutionary movements throughout Central and South America, often supplying ideological guidance and tactical advisors, and occasionally supplying weapons and equipment, mostly Soviet-built, as well. The well-trained Cuban army offered the service of its troops to the socialist factions in Third World hot spots, most famously those fighting a civil war in African Angola. With the decline of the Soviet Union in the 1980s, and its collapse at the end of the decade, Castro lost his principal source of economic aid. Yet, perhaps through sheer force of personality, he continued to hold sway over the island, a considerable accomplishment in the volatile world of Caribbean politics.

Rockefeller Proposes a System of Fallout Shelters (1959)

The event: On July 6, 1959, New York Governor Nelson Rockefeller proposed funding a system of public shelters to protect U.S. citizens against radioactive fallout following a nuclear attack, merely one measure of the anxieties created by the constant threat of atomic warfare during the Cold War.

IN SIMPLER TIMES, home buyers looked for amenities such as a patio or a swimming pool in their dream homes, but by the end of the 1950s, a personal bomb shelter was a good selling point for suburban real estate. In the cities, the streetscape was punctuated with signs identifying public shelters. In schools, shelter often consisted of little more than the "duck and cover" maneuver, which had millions of school children cowering under their desks in anticipation of annihilation.

Bomb shelters were not new to the nuclear age. Londoners learned to use their extensive and, fortunately, deep subway system—the Underground—as public shelter space during the blitz of World War II. They also built so-called Anderson shelters, little more than corrugated metal culverts buried in the backyard, but most people found these too claustrophobic and suggestive of living burial. Atomic warfare presented special problems. Not only was the initial blast far greater than that of any conventional bomb, it was accompanied by tremendous heat, and if you escaped instant destruction, there was the dreaded radioactive fallout.

In 1959, New York's Nelson Rockefeller proposed a national system of public shelters, and, beginning in 1961, the U.S. National Shelter Survey identified sites sufficient for sheltering a total of some 140 million people. The sites included the basements and subbasements of large public buildings, subways, tunnels, and mines. However, a significant number of the shelters identified by the survey were not easily accessible and would require a program of extensive, organized evacuation, which would probably be impractical in the case of impending attack. The government funded supplies for the shelters, which included two weeks' worth of food, water, sanitation kits, and medical supplies, as well as radiological-monitoring equipment. Ventilation systems were provided to eliminate radioactive dust. In the suburbs, a significant minority of homeowners converted their cellars into fallout shelters or dug shelters in their backyards.

Not everyone worked up much enthusiasm for the shelter program. Some believed that nothing less than mass evacuation of the nation's cities would be effective in the event of nuclear attack. Others countered that such evacuation, while effective, would be impossible. Many suggested that the intense heat of a nuclear blast would transform any shelter into a furnace. There were also people who felt that the shelter program hardly went far enough, that only an elaborately planned and fully integrated civil defense program, involving extensive civilian training, a warning network, and a massively scaled shelter construction program would reduce casualties. But those opposed to such a program pointed out that it would send a message to the world that the United States believed a nuclear war could be won, therefore increasing the likelihood of such a war. Finally, there were other people who argued that survival in a post–nuclear-holocaust world would simply not be worthwhile.

By the 1980s, public shelters were less in evidence, but into the 1990s the United States government continued to spend about $100 million annually to restock shelters with food and other supplies, while the Department of Defense estimated that five years and an expenditure of about $230 million would be required to protect 30 million people—less than one-sixth of the U.S. population—adequately.

The Birth Control Pill Is Introduced (1960)

The event: In 1960, orally administered contraceptives were made available in the United States; within a year, more than one million women were using "the Pill." This easy, effective method of contraception gave women more control over their own bodies, leading to the decade's famous sexual revolution.

B IRTH CONTROL IS an ancient practice and hardly peculiar to the twentieth century; but two influential birth-control movements were new, as was a medical breakthrough. The Planned Parenthood organization was founded in 1942 for the purpose of promoting and, where necessary, legalizing contraception. Planned Parenthood asserted that birth control was a means of achieving family stability, and that successful marital adjustment is based on a permissive attitude toward sex without fear of conception. Planned Parenthood remained aloof from the related issues of women's rights and avoided addressing the sexual exploitation of women. Its focus was on sexual freedom within a marital context.

By the early 1960s, Planned Parenthood was the preeminent birth-control advocacy organization in the United States. After oral contraceptives were introduced in 1960—and were immediately popular, with more than a million women taking them during the very first year of their availability—a strong women's liberation movement came into being. The Pill once and for all divorced sex from reproduction,

effectively giving women more control over their bodies. By the late 1960s, the issue of birth control had shifted from Planned Parenthood's focus on promoting family stability to the focus of the women's movement on women's self-determination. The Pill, women's liberationists realized, made men and women—no longer *necessarily* burdened by reproduction—sexual equals. Thus medical technology profoundly influenced the sexual politics of the era.

Feminists soon saw the Pill as a double-edged sword, however, as research concerning the health dangers and other side effects that resulted from interfering with natural reproductive cycles came to light. Many women concluded that the great pharmaceutical houses were exploiting them for profit, even at the cost of their health. Such suspicions resulted in a waning of confidence in the established health system and sparked interest in the creation of a women's health movement, yet another avenue of self-determination.

Apart from the feminist program, the Pill made possible the so-called sexual revolution of the 1960s: an era of relaxed morals or, more accurately, of morality defined in terms of emotional freedom and sexual expression. Whereas earlier generations considered sex outside of marriage immoral, the generation of the 1960s considered immoral the dishonesty and hostility associated with being sexually repressed or, in the phrase of the decade, "uptight." Accordingly, it became very important to rid oneself of inhibitions, and, toward this end, the use of drugs—chiefly marijuana—was widespread and widely encouraged. Not everyone bought into the "permissive society" of the 1960s, though, and the era produced a mighty backlash in the form of a new political conservatism and the development of a powerful religious right wing, which continued to grow in numbers and in political clout from the 1970s onward.

A "Wind of Change" Arrives in Africa (1960)

The event: In 1960, British Prime Minister Harold Macmillan, who had come to office in the wake of a crisis that had resulted in Britain granting Ghana its independence in 1957, spoke to the parliament of the white-ruled South Africa about the new realities in Africa, announcing that a "wind of change" was sweeping the continent. Macmillan's phrase was not typical political hyperbole, since by 1960 seventeen new nations had emerged from the old African colonial states, and from 1960 to 1965 another eleven were to follow, leaving in effect only the white-settler nations in the south as the last outposts of Africa's European-dominated past.

THE CHANGE THAT Harold Macmillan referred to had its most immediate origins in a conference of black politicians held in Manchester, England, in October of 1945. There, a thirty-six-year-old activist from the West African colony of the Gold Coast named Kwame Nkrumah declared that "we affirm the rights of all colonial peoples to control their destiny" and warned Europe that "the long, long night is over." Another speaker, Nigeria's Nnamdi Azikiwe, set a deadline for independence in British-held Africa—fifteen years. And the conference targeted not only Britain's African empire, but demanded independence for all the other European colonies as well, including the French territories that comprised most of the west and center of the continent, the Belgian Congo, Portuguese Guinea, Mozambique, Angola, the independent white-settler state of South Africa with its black majority, and South Africa's own virtual colony, South-West Africa.

Few outside Britain heard the Manchester declaration, and few British officials took the words of Nkrumah, Azikiwe, and the others seriously. Less than a century before, most Europeans had regarded Africa—or at least Africa south of the Sahara—as the Dark Continent, and only a generation or two before, a Europe then at the apex of centuries of imperial expansion around the world had divided the subcontinent among the Western world's great powers. Now all of a sudden a few hotheads—Communists, no doubt—were talking about independence. But the African nationalists were appealing to principles long accepted in the West, and their words would prove prophetic.

The great powers themselves had affirmed the right to national self-determination in the 1918 peace settlements at Versailles. These were plagued, as most of them saw it, by an American president named Woodrow Wilson, who seemed determined to make all the slaughter mean something; that the Great War had made the world safe for democracy and for national governments ruled for and by their peoples. In 1945, the United States insisted that the right of national self-determination become a cornerstone of the Charter of the United Nations. India was well on the way to independence from British rule by then, and in the Far East, new nations were emerging from the chaos of World War II. Little wonder, then, that Africa's black leaders should be seeking nationhood for their peoples, or that some of them should be turning to the revolution-minded Marxist government in Russia.

Conditions in post-World War II Africa seemed ripe for revolution. Both the world wars had exposed the vulnerability of the colonial rulers, and in 1945 the winners and losers in the second one were crippled by its almost mindless destructiveness, saddled with massive war debts, and faced with the awesome task of reconstructing homelands scarred by bombed-out ruins and widespread social dislocations. The economy of the African colonies was more complex, but also ready for change. The war had ushered in a period of booming commodity prices that would last throughout the 1940s and 1950s, raising expectations of widespread prosperity in those countries that were geared to exporting raw materials. In those colonies with large white settler populations, such as Kenya, the immigrants had taken advantage of the distractions in Europe provided by the war to increase their own power locally, and as European-dominated businesses like mining and large-scale farming grew, it was they—and not the indigenous natives—who benefited. Even in West Africa, where independent peasant farmers had prospered because of the booms, Britain organized schemes for monopolies to buy up the land, which caused West African natives to join in the social resentments spreading across the continent. Most provocative, perhaps, was a fresh wave of settlers who descended on postwar Africa at the behest of the colonial governments. These technical experts came for the best of reasons—to work in veterinary medicine, crop development, road building, health care, and welfare programs—but in the long run they only appeared to make white colonial "oppression" more pervasive than ever.

The growing tinderbox first exploded on the Gold Coast, in Britain's richest and best-educated colony. Britain's always small white colony there had long depended on a system of government dominated by traditional tribal chiefs, and in 1946 a new constitution drafted by the whites granted Africans a majority in the ruling legislative council. But political and economic discontent continued to smolder, flaring up especially after the return of Nkrumah in 1947.

By 1948, Africans were rioting and looting in the major townships, and Britain tried to appease them by appointing a new, all-African committee to rewrite the constitution. The Africans called for a general strike in 1950 after Nkrumah demanded immediate self-rule, and though he was jailed for his efforts, the new constitution was more radical than Britain had planned for, placing political power firmly in African hands. In the ensuing national elections, Nkrumah's Convention People's Party won hands down, and Nkrumah himself was released from jail to form a government. Under his guidance, the resource-rich Gold Coast was set on the path to self-government, emerging in 1957 as the first newly independent country south of the Sahara and taking the name of a medieval West African kingdom, Ghana.

In more ways than one, Ghana was to prove a model for the continent as a whole. And as Harold Macmillan tacitly admitted in his 1960 parliamentary address to South Africa, independence could hardly be confined any longer to the relatively rich colonies of West Africa, but would inexorably spread to Central and East Africa as well. The French by then certainly thought the British prime minister's conclusions were accurate. At first they had tried to co-opt the wind of change on the continent. In 1944, Charles de Gaulle's Free French government-in-exile had met in Brazzaville, in the French Congo, to draft a blueprint for French Africa's future, and without consulting the Africans, declared that they all should be partners in a French union, with their own seats in France's National Assem-

bly in Paris, as long as they realized that "the establishment of self-government in the colonies, however far off, cannot be contemplated."

After the war, one of the Africans who had attended that constituent assembly, Felix Houphouët, who added to his surname the sobriquet Boigny, meaning "immovable object," won election to the newly restored National Assembly and traveled to Paris, where within a decade he became a member of the French cabinet and dominated the drafting of a law that gave the vote to all Africans in France's African holdings. By then, France had been forced after a long and bloody war for independence to withdraw from Indochina and was deeply mired in its struggle to hang onto Algeria. At the height of the Algerian crisis, General de Gaulle came to power and offered France's twelve colonies in sub-Saharan Africa the choice between independence and membership in a new French Community that would grant each member internal autonomy. Only Guinea, led by Ahmed Sekou Touré, refused to join, opting for full independence. De Gaulle's response was immediate and draconian; he ordered the instant withdrawal of the French colonial government and everything connected with it, and French doctors, teachers, lawyers, and civil servants left en masse, taking with them all records and equipment, including unplugged generators and telephones literally ripped from the walls, nearly destroying Guinea's infrastructure and its economy. But Touré had become an African hero, and Ghana offered a substantial loan to avert immediate economic ruin, while the Soviet

Union promised long-term aid. Like Ghana, Guinea was quickly accepted into the United Nations, and its sudden prestige emboldened other French-speaking African nations to request formal independence. By 1960, all of the former French colonial holdings in Africa but Somaliland, a small enclave on Cape Horn, were at least technically independent, and the notion of a unified French Community was history.

As was British East Africa. Kenya's powerful white community had firmly resisted any form of majority rule, and in 1945 had even sought to build up its settler population, centered around Nairobi, the capital, located in what they called the White Highlands of the farm-rich Rift Valley. Although the settlers made a feint toward appeasing natives by bringing a few Africans into Kenya's Legislative Council, the tokenism fooled no one, and native discontent began to focus around Jomo Kenyatta. A tall, gregarious Kikuyu, Kenyatta had spent seventeen years in England, where he married an Englishwoman. He abandoned her after returning to Kenya in 1946 and the following year became president of the Kenya African Union, the voice of the country's now rabid nationalism. In the early 1950s, Kenya's colonial authorities charged Kenyatta with masterminding the Mau Mau uprising, a bloody terrorist campaign aimed at Kenya's white settlers. Though Kenyatta vehemently denied being involved, the white government jailed him for eight years. However, it succeeded only in making his popularity with the country's black population reach legendary proportions. The continuing Mau Mau troubles, the revolution in

West Africa, the winning of independence by three other East African colonies (Tanganyika, Zanzibar, and Uganda), all persuaded the British-backed colonials of the impossibility of staying in power. Kenyatta, now called *mzee* ("grand old man") by his fellow Africans, was released from house arrest to lead his country to independence in 1963.

In the rush to independence, few Africans considered the implications of a continent suddenly awash in sovereign new nations. Kwame Nkrumah promoted a continent united by the ideals of socialist internationalism and its own black identity, and some leaders were sufficiently attracted to experiment with linkages into larger economic units. Mali teamed up with Senegal in 1959, and in 1963 Kenya, Tanganyika, and Uganda tried to establish a common customs union, but neither plan worked very well. Africa's new national leaders were more enthusiastic about creating political blocs, one school of a half-dozen following Nkrumah's hard-line rejection of any contact with former colonial powers and his dedication to radical socialism, another much larger group coming together under the banner of moderation, seeking both economic and political stability through collaboration with the erstwhile colonial West. Two years later the schism was resolved when thirty-nine nations joined the Organization of African Unity in Addis Ababa. But despite these displays of Pan-Africanism, most of the African nations were too wedded to their borders and too committed to the concept of nationhood to give up even a little of their hard-won new sovereignty. What they saw happening in the former Belgian Congo only made them more adamant about national sovereignty.

The Congo, a huge country twice the size of any other black African nation, had suffered from the particularly brutal colonial heritage stemming from its days as the personal fiefdom of King Leopold of Belgium. The post–World War II Belgian Congo was flooded with white immigrants who flocked to the mineral-rich Katanga province and tripled the settler population. The Belgians showed no sign of relinquishing power as black unrest rose in the 1950s on the heels of unemployment and white contempt, and the long oppressed, mostly illiterate native population lacked even a nascent black elite to promote the cause of nationhood. Only one man had more than a local following, a former postal worker and now the leader of the radical Congolese National Movement, Patrice Lumumba, and even his influence was dissipated by the hostility of regional leaders. When the Belgian government suddenly abandoned the Congo following rioting in Leopoldville in January 1959, the country collapsed into political chaos. Congolese army officers mutinied against their white superiors, paralyzing the new independent national government and creating a state of anarchy in which local loyalties overwhelmed national sentiment. Katanga declared independence from the Congo, and Lumumba appealed to the UN to come in and restore order. Dag Hammarskjold, Secretary-General of the United Nations, sent troops under his personal direction, and confusion reigned in the ruling circles. Lumumba was arrested by his former aide, army chief

Joseph-Désiré Mobutu, just as the parliament in Leopoldville was voting Lumumba "special powers." Though the UN continued to recognize him as the Congo's legitimate ruler, he was spirited away to Katanga and shot, possibly on the orders of the man he had himself placed in the office of president, Joseph Kasavubu. Kasavubu had Moise Tshombe, Katanga's strongman, arrested for treason, then released. Dag Hammarskjold, flying into Katanga to negotiate with Tshombe, was killed in a mysterious plane crash. The UN marched in, overturned Katanga, and exiled Tshombe, who returned after the UN had pulled out, once more leading Katanga into secession. The country dissolved into civil war, Kasavubu was overthrown in a bloodless coup by Mobutu, and Tshombe fled to Spain, where he was sentenced to death in absentia. Hijacking a plane to Algeria, he arrived only to be arrested and held, awaiting extradition, until he was murdered in 1969. Meanwhile, the military had enforced a precarious peace in the Congo, which it renamed Zaire.

Two other newly formed African countries suffered similar fates. Nigeria, after attaining independence in 1960, fell prey almost instantly to a civil war between the Muslim north and the more developed, primarily Christian south and east that turned into a blood bath, leading to the exposure and starvation of the civilian population in a region called Biafra, which became an international scandal. In Uganda—a nation like many of the new African countries, with no natural political unity, having been created by the British out of a patchwork of rival kingdoms and tribes—the first president, Milton Obote, launched a war on the Baganda people that ultimately led to escalating violence, brutal repression, and economic collapse, ushering into power a corrupt former heavyweight boxing champion named Idi Amin. One of only two army officers in the Ugandan army at the time of independence, Amin had gained a reputation for brutality while serving with the King's Rifles in Kenya in the wake of the Mau Mau uprising. Once in power, Amin more than lived up to his brutal image. By the time Amin was finally deposed by Tanzanian troops in 1979, he had become world-famous as the very definition of a bloody tyrant, having murdered in a number of especially horrifying ways some 150,000 people.

The chaotic sequence of events in the Congo, Nigeria, and Uganda forced the newly linked countries in the Organization of African Unity to assert the primacy of the nation-state over the secessionist demands of various regions, since no nation wanted to risk suffering such brutal excesses. But the British, French, and Portuguese empires had dissolved as differently as they had formed, and the varying geo-political patterns that emerged in the east, west, and center of the continent produced largely artificial frontiers inherited from the colonial past. The emerging nations had to struggle to unite disparate peoples, languages, and traditions in a search for genuine nationhood made even more complicated by the frustrations of their assumption that eventually all of black Africa would be free. Instead, in the south, the intransigent white settlers of Rhodesia and the Republic of South Africa, defining themselves as every bit as native to Africa as the blacks, held on to their minority-controlled governments, affecting the politics of all the emerging nations and dominating the development of the whole southern half of Africa. In these complex crosscurrents were born those seemingly intractable problems that remain unresolved everywhere in Africa as the twentieth century draws to a close.

The Cuban Missile Crisis Unfolds (1962)

The event: United States President John Fitzgerald Kennedy appeared on national television on October 22, 1962, to make a startling announcement: The Soviet Union was building bomber and nuclear missile bases in Cuba, a mere ninety miles off the coast of Florida, and he intended to stop them. When the Soviet Premier Nikita Khrushchev proved just as determined to complete the bases, the world seemed on the brink of a nuclear Armageddon as the two superpowers squared off in what became known as "the Cuban Missile Crisis."

WHEN FIDEL CASTRO came to power in 1959, he faced to his north an economic and military colossus that since the Spanish-American War of 1898 had insisted on protecting its interests in Cuba, chiefly through supporting brutal regimes friendly to the interests of American big business. Castro's attempts to distance himself from his powerful neighbor and its corrupting influence led him to court a relationship with the United States' major rival, the USSR, which only caused American officials—at first inclined to be friendly—to turn against him. As Castro embraced the revolutionary tenets of Marxist-Leninism and nationalized Cuba's industries and sugar plantations, the United States launched a trade war against the tiny island and imposed a full-scale economic boycott. Then, no longer able to tolerate the upstart revolutionary who was becoming a hero to much of Central and Latin America, and fearing that other small countries might follow Cuba's example, the United States decided to get rid of Castro.

The American Central Intelligence Agency devised a plan to overthrow the Cuban leader. Gathering a force of Cuban exiles, the CIA directed an invasion at the Bay of Pigs on April 17, 1961. It was a fiasco. Not only did the Cuban people—most of whom wholeheartedly supported Castro—fail to join the invaders, the United States reneged on its promise to provide the Cuban "freedom fighters" with American air support. Within three days the abortive invasion was over, and JFK, as well as the United States, were humiliated, both for having staged an illegal invasion and for having failed at it.

As for Castro, the Bay of Pigs clearly showed him the need for strong allies and a better defense against U.S. intentions, driving him deeper into the Soviet camp. In retrospect, it is not so hard to understand that he would agree to permit the Soviet Union to construct missile bases on his island. The surprise is that he almost pulled it off. But

his hopes of keeping the construction of the bases a secret long enough for the Russians to deploy their missiles were dashed in October 1962, when an American spy plane photographed the nearly completed bases. President Kennedy demanded the immediate withdrawal of the Soviet missiles and the closing of the bases, ordering a naval blockade of the island on October 24. The world held its breath as each passing day brought two thermonuclear superpowers closer and closer to a shooting war. Anyone who was a schoolchild during this period recalls the daily air raid drills in anticipation of Armageddon.

Kennedy, still reeling from the domestic criticisms of his handling of the Bay of Pigs, stood his ground, and on October 28, Soviet premier Nikita Khrushchev offered to remove the missiles under United Nations supervision in exchange for a promise that the United States would never again attempt an invasion of the island. On the following day President Kennedy suspended the blockade, and by November 2 the missile bases were being dismantled. Since—as both Kennedy and Khrushchev understood—the United States was hardly going to mount another attack on Cuba after the abject failure of the last one, the showdown over the missiles was a triumph for the young American president. Indeed, it did much to erase the humiliation of the Bay of Pigs, though it hardly served to check Castro's defiance. President Kennedy, sobered by the experience, began to talk about summits and peace and ending the arms race as he looked toward a second term in the White House.

Vatican II Convenes (1962)

The event: On October 11, 1962, after four years of preparation, the Second Vatican Council formally opened. Its purpose, in essence, was to bring the largest faith in the world into greater harmony with modern times.

THE SECOND VATICAN COUNCIL was the twenty-first ecumenical council ever held by the Roman Catholic church. In contrast to previous councils, its purpose was not to counter contemporary heresies nor to address disciplinary issues but, as Pope John XXIII put it, to renew "ourselves and the flocks committed to us, so that there may radiate before all men the lovable features of Jesus Christ, who shines in our hearts that God's splendor may be revealed."

Even if Vatican II (as it came to be called) had been of interest only to Catholics, it would have had a significant impact on the world. The world's Catholics amount to some 900 million people, making it not only the largest of Christian sects, but the biggest single faith on the globe. However, as an attempt by a major religious body to come to grips with the many pressing realities of twentieth-century life, Vatican II represented the struggle of traditional faith in a world shaped by science, war, commerce, and skepticism, a world in which humankind was endowed with unprecedented power for creating and for destroying.

The council was announced by Pope John XXIII on January 25, 1959. On October 11, 1962, the council opened, convening four sessions from 1962 to 1965; the last three (1963–65) were presided over by Pope Paul VI, who succeeded John upon his death in June 1963. For the first time in any church council, participants with full voting rights included bishops and other officials of the Eastern as well as the Western rites, and non-Catholic Christian churches as well as Catholic lay organizations were invited to send nonvoting observers.

The council produced sixteen documents on such subjects as divine revelation, the liturgy, and the church in the modern world. The most far-reaching of these documents authorized vernacularization of the liturgy to replace the traditional Latin; called for greater lay participation in church affairs; mandated the need for the church to adapt to the contemporary world; approved an ecumenical approach to worship; and declared the right of people everywhere to religious freedom.

Vatican II strove to keep the church alive and vital by responding more fully to the needs of its followers and by opening itself to a greater variety of beliefs, placing tolerance, not orthodoxy, high on the list of spiritual values.

Rachel Carson Publishes *Silent Spring* (1962)

The event: In 1962, biologist Rachel Carson published *Silent Spring*, in which she described her vision of an Earth ravaged by pesticides. The book launched a new environmental awareness in the United States and around the globe, even as Carson, through the force of her eloquent writing, almost single-handedly shaped modern attitudes about the natural world.

IN THE LATE 1930S while she was working for the U.S. Bureau of Fisheries, marine biologist Rachel Carson discovered her innate talent for graceful, evocative nature writing, producing *Under the Sea Wind* in 1941. Ten years passed before her next work, *The Sea Around Us*, was published in 1951. It became an instant classic, especially popular with younger readers, and the following year Carson left the Fish and Wildlife Service to become a full-time writer, producing *The Edge of the Sea* in 1956.

Back in the 1860s, when President Abraham Lincoln was introduced to the author of *Uncle Tom's Cabin*, Harriet Beecher Stowe, he reportedly greeted her with, "So you're the little lady who wrote the book that made this big war!" A hundred years later, President John F. Kennedy might well have said something similar to Rachel Carson about *Silent Spring*. In fact, he said nothing of the kind, but he made no secret of his admiration for the 1963 book, which many environmentalists still cite as the popular manifesto that started the "big war" against the heedless overuse and abuse of pesticides and, on an even broader front,

launched the contemporary environmental movement.

Silent Spring portrayed a world ravaged by pesticides, especially DDT, which the public regarded as a kind of agricultural miracle drug, not only protecting crops, but controlling yellow-fever-bearing mosquitoes. While Carson's book did draw fire from government agencies and private industry, the public was moved, convinced, and alarmed by its message. Violently attacked, especially by the agricultural chemical industry, *Silent Spring* was officially endorsed by JFK's Science Advisory Committee, the most immediate result being a body of federal restrictions on DDT and other environmentally hazardous pesticides. The National Wildlife Federation presented Carson with its Conservationist of the Year Award in 1963, and in 1969, the Department of the Interior renamed the Coastal Maine Refuge the Rachel Carson National Wildlife Refuge. "A few thousand words from her," said one newspaper editor, "and the world took a new direction."

Andy Warhol Exhibits *Campbell's Soup Can* (1962)

The event: In 1962, Andy Warhol stunned, amused, and outraged the art world by exhibiting a large, beautifully silkscreened image of a can of Campbell's soup in New York's Stable Gallery, a show art historians credit with giving birth to the "Pop Art" movement.

A NEIGHBORING NEW YORK gallery responded to the pricey Warhol work on exhibit at the Stable Gallery by setting up a display of genuine Campbell's soup cans with a sign saying, "Get the real thing for 29 cents." But the humor was uneasy, for Warhol's work, and the Pop Art movement it spawned, was yet one more twentieth-century assault on traditional concepts of art and its "spiritual" or "transcendent" value. Warhol presented, without comment or judgment, the vacant, banal, and bland images of American commercial culture, in effect holding up a mirror to the mass-mediated values and desires of twentieth-century consumer culture. Many of the public laughed, and many of the critics sneered, but Warhol's work would not go away.

Warhol found work in New York as a commercial artist during the 1950s, achieving considerable success and professional recognition. In 1960, he produced the first of a series of paintings depicting enlarged comic strip images, including such characters as Popeye and Superman, which were meant for a commercial window display. The work also marked his transition into fine art. About the same time, Warhol developed a process of transferring an enlarged photographic image to a silk screen that was then placed on a canvas and inked from the back. The technique enabled Warhol to pro-

duce the series of mass-media images—repetitive, yet with slight variations—that he began in 1962. These, the most famous of his graphic works, depict such items as Coca-Cola bottles, Brillo boxes, and the faces of celebrities ranging from Elizabeth Taylor to Mao Tse-tung, and can be interpreted as comments on the combined homogeneity, blandness, and ambiguity of American culture.

Later in the 1960s, Warhol made a series of experimental films, including *Sleep* (1963), *Empire* (1964), and *The Chelsea Girls* (1966), dealing largely with what might be described as the phenomenology of twentieth-century boredom and banality. *Sleep*, for example, is a film of a person sleeping, and *Empire* consists of eight uninterrupted hours of the Empire State Building viewed from the outside.

Warhol's Lower Manhattan studio, called The Factory, became a gathering place for intellectuals, celebrities, and would-be intellectuals and celebrities. Warhol himself declared that, in our media-saturated culture, everyone would be famous for fifteen minutes. Warhol's ironic distance on the phenomena of fame in our times seemed to have collapsed by the 1970s, when he became obsessed with drinking in the flashy New York nightlife and associating himself with jet-setters and trendsetters. Nevertheless, this naturally shy, taciturn, pasty-faced figure not only made a great impact in the art world, but was for a time more effective than any contemporary social critic, student of society, philosopher, or preacher in making the century aware of what drives it: its mores, values, and passions. The great bulk of these, Warhol seemed to claim, were the products of the media—advertisements, movies, television images, and even product labels.

Medicare Is Proposed (1963)

The event: President John F. Kennedy submitted to the United States Congress a plan for medical and hospital insurance to be funded through Social Security.

DURING THE LATE nineteenth century, in the United States and in much of the world, the medical profession grew in popular esteem. Bound by the noble Hippocratic Oath, some 2,400 years old, physicians were seen as valiant crusaders against the ravages of disease and injury. Following such innovations as anesthesia at the beginning of the nineteenth century and aseptic surgery later in the century, physicians were also evolving into effectual healers. When Alexander Fleming discovered penicillin in 1928 and a host of antibiotic drugs followed, it became increasingly routine for the public to expect miracle cures from the medical profession, and, from a technological point of view, such expectations have been fulfilled to a surprising degree.

Yet medical economics has failed to keep pace with medical technology. The lay public mourned the passing of the "old-fashioned" selfless practitioner, who was willing to do absolutely everything to save his patient. The fact is that, until relatively recently, "absolutely everything" wasn't very much. Medicine had comparatively few resources to draw upon, and it cost almost the same to do everything as it did to do nothing. By the mid-twentieth century, however, medicine could offer a wide variety of treatments, many of which were costly. In response, a number of nations, most notably Great Britain and the Scandinavian countries, adopted versions of "socialized medicine," treatment subsidized by the government. In the United States, President Harry S Truman first proposed a program of federally funded health insurance in 1948, but the more firmly entrenched capitalist interests resisted. By the 1960s, it was becoming apparent that rising costs were excluding many people from the best—or any—medical treatment in a nation that boasted the most advanced medical technology.

President John F. Kennedy took the first small step toward government-subsidized health care when he proposed Medicare to Congress in 1963. Government-provided health insurance for the elderly (age sixty-five and older), it was to be operated by the Social Security Administration and financed largely by social security funds. Medicare was not signed into law until 1965, when it became part of President Lyndon Johnson's package of "Great Society" programs. At that time, Medicare was supplemented by Medicaid, a program for the indigent.

Even to the limited extent that it had taken on the financial burden of medical care, the government soon faced staggering costs, which threatened the entire Social Security system. In attempting to control these costs, flat-fee payments based on a system of "Diagnosis Related Groups" (DRGs) were imposed on hospitals in 1983, and the same principles were used in setting fee schedules (1991) for outpatient procedures. Absolute reimbursement limits were placed on each procedure, and only listed procedures would be covered. Moreover, physicians, researchers, and administrators were put on notice that new procedures would be covered only after cost-benefit analyses. The implications of this were stunning: No longer were caregivers expected to do "absolutely everything," but, rather, whatever medical procedures were deemed cost effective.

Even with cost controls—however distasteful and disturbing—in place, a large number of Americans remained outside of the health care umbrella—unable to afford health insurance, but neither poor enough nor old enough to qualify for Medicaid or Medicare. As the twentieth century drew to a close, therefore, American society was faced with a medical challenge as great as that posed by any epidemic disease, with some 41 million men, women, and children living at dire risk from the consequences of disease and injury they could not afford to treat. As the century was poised to turn, the nation was still troubled by runaway costs of a Medicare system that will be bankrupted by 2002 unless reforms are enacted. It is precisely because universal coverage would require profound changes in the practice of medicine as well as in the nature of American democracy and the relation of the government to those governed that the United States, while the richest nation in the world, remains the only industrialized country that does not offer its citizens universal health care.

John Fitzgerald Kennedy Is Assassinated (1963)

The event: John Fitzgerald Kennedy, youngest of America's presidents, was assassinated while riding in a motorcade through the streets of Dallas, Texas, on November 22, 1963.

AMERICANS WERE no strangers to political assassination, yet few Americans were prepared for the assassination of the youthful, vigorous, and dynamic JFK, with his young and attractive wife, his children Caroline and John-John, and the passion with which he seemed intent on leading the nation to an idealistic greatness.

Elected by the slimmest possible margin in 1960 at the age of forty-three, Kennedy established the Peace Corps and bolstered and accelerated the American space program. He went "eyeball to eyeball" with the Soviets over missiles in Cuba and prevailed, and he established the Alliance for Progress with Latin America. But

Kennedy also took heat for bungling the Bay of Pigs invasion, the fiasco that encouraged the Soviet Union to send nuclear missiles to Cuba in the first place. Some accused him of escalating the fighting in Vietnam by first overcommitting himself to President Ngo Dinh Diem and then becoming an accomplice in his overthrow. A mediagenic personality, Kennedy never succeeded in building an effective coalition with Congress, whose members thwarted his efforts to further the cause of civil rights, to increase federal spending on education, and to provide a program of medical care for the elderly.

All ambiguity vanished with the gunshots that ended the president's life, furnishing a martyr and a myth of greatness that propelled the "Great Society" social reforms of his successor, Lyndon Baines Johnson. Kennedy, cut down in his prime, was anointed in legend as a second Lincoln, a great president repeatedly blocked by the short-sighted machinations and private agendas of his political enemies, destroyed before he could make his proper mark on the history of the world.

On the day he was shot, a suspected assassin named Lee Harvey Oswald was arrested by the Dallas police, only to be himself assassinated on national television by local nightclub owner and shady mob fringe figure Jack Ruby. The shocking turn of events prompted President Johnson to appoint a commission, headed by Chief Justice Earl Warren, to investigate the assassination. The Warren Commission report, based on a ten-month investigation, found Lee Harvey Oswald to be the lone assassin,

though certain eyewitness reports and forensic evidence seemed to contradict that conclusion and led many to brand the findings a cover-up. Fueled by an abortive conspiracy trial in New Orleans, by the secrecy surrounding the original investigation, by countless conspiracy theories advanced over the years in some two thousand books, and by the media, Congress produced startling new revelations about the CIA and FBI when the U.S. House of Representatives appointed a special committee to reopen the investigation in 1976. The House committee found that a conspiracy was indeed likely. In 1992, filmmaker Oliver Stone directed a box-office smash dramatizing the conspiracy theory of flamboyant New Orleans District Attorney Jim Garrison. The following year, a lawyer named Gerald Posner wrote *Case Closed*, which argued against the conspiracy theory just as passionately as Stone's film had argued for it.

Clearly, the assassination had transcended its status as an historical event to become a myth—and to function as myths always function, resolving the contradictions of the societies they serve, obscuring and justifying as well as explaining and even celebrating the "reality" they portray and replace. Through the prism of JFK's assassination, Americans were able to take a look at the national security state—with all its repressions, secrets, and lies—that had come to dominate their lives. The postulation of a "right-wing coup," for example, in the Oliver Stone film was one way the myth could explain the historical situation in which Americans found themselves, one that allows policymakers to ignore the public will at the behest of well-heeled special interests, fighting wars no one wants to fight, for example, or refusing to pass legislation that polls show again and again have widespread popular support. The passion with which the American public embraced the theory of a conspiracy to assassinate John Kennedy is a measure of its disenchantment with a system that no longer seemed responsive to those it purported to govern.

The U.S. Surgeon General Warns about the Hazards of Cigarette Smoking (1964)

The event: On January 11, 1964, a committee appointed by the Surgeon General of the U.S. Public Health Service issued the results of a study concluding that most lung-cancer deaths are directly caused by cigarette smoking.

WHEN EUROPEAN COLONISTS arrived in America, they were startled to see the Indians smoking a leafy substance called tobacco. The newcomers shared the weed with the first Americans, who so enjoyed the effects of smoking that they deemed tobacco worthy of export. By 1619, tobacco was the leading export of the Virginia colony.

Still, individuals used relatively small amounts of tobacco, even as late as the end of the nineteenth century. For the most part, it was consumed in the form of snuff, pipe tobacco, and especially cigars. Cigarettes did not appear in America until 1867 and did not provide a major source of revenue until the late 1880s, when a cigarette manufacturing machine was developed. This allowed the tobacco industry to make cigarettes available cheaply and in large quantities, and manufacturers began to advertise the product heavily. From quite early on, the advertising was aimed at creating ideal images of cigarette smokers, particularly men, whom even the early ads depicted as tough and virile. It was not until the

1930s that tobacco companies began marketing their product to women, developing ad campaigns associating cigarette smoking with a world of elegance and glamour.

During the ensuing period of sharply increased cigarette smoking, lung cancer and heart disease rates increased concomitantly. On July 12, 1957, Surgeon General Leroy E. Burney reported that studies showed a "direct relationship between the incidence of lung cancer and the amount smoked," and in 1961, smoking was linked to heart disease. It wasn't until 1964 that the surgeon general reached the far stronger conclusion that most lung-cancer deaths were directly caused by cigarette smoking, which the report also linked to chronic bronchitis, emphysema, and cardiovascular disease. The "Surgeon General's Report" prompted a large number of Americans to quit—or attempt to quit—smoking, although many soon discovered just how addictive nicotine was and found it difficult or impossible to give up the habit.

On June 24, 1964, the Federal Trade

Commission announced that, beginning in 1965, warning labels would be required on cigarette packages. On April 1, 1970, President Nixon signed into law a bill banning cigarette advertising on radio and television, creating a crisis not only for cigarette manufacturers, but also a panic in the advertising and broadcasting communities, which lost substantial revenue. In the meantime, the official health reports became stronger and stronger. On January 11, 1979, Surgeon General Julius B. Richmond issued a report labeling cigarettes as "the single most important environmental factor contributing to early death," and in 1982, the U.S. Institute of Medicine identified cigarette smoking as a leading cause of death, killing some 320,000 Americans each year. More recent figures place the number of deaths at 420,000 yearly, and recent studies indicate that about 53,000 nonsmokers die annually from diseases related to the passive inhalation of so-called secondhand smoke.

Cigarettes not only emerged in the century as a popular means of self-destruction, but smokers became the targets of a raft of social legislation at the local, state, and federal levels regulating just where and when a person could light up. Long associated in advertising with images of freedom—the "Marlboro Man" riding the open range of the American West—by the 1980s, cigarette smoking was banned in many public places, in most public conveyances, including airplanes, and even in the workplace. Moreover, parents were told that by smoking in their own homes, they were exposing their children to potentially deadly secondhand smoke, and some legal decisions actually prohibited adults from smoking in their own homes on the grounds that the activity endangered the welfare of a minor. While militant nonsmokers agitated for increased government regulation and restriction of smoking, smokers complained that their civil rights were being violated, creating a crisis common in democracy when the perceived rights of one group come into conflict with the perceived rights of another.

Beginning in the late 1980s, the government and public focus shifted somewhat from regulating smokers to calling on cigarette manufacturers for accountability. Increasingly, these companies were seen as reaping profits from a product they knew to be destructive to the nation's health, and on June 13, 1988, a cigarette manufacturer was found guilty in the cancer death of a longtime smoker. A federal jury in New Jersey awarded the husband of Rose Cipollone $400,000 in damages in the first of three hundred suits filed since 1954 successfully prosecuted against a tobacco company. In 1994, a congressional committee began investigating charges that numerous cigarette companies engaged in harmful practices, such as deliberately increasing the level of nicotine in cigarettes and in other ways chemically adulterating them in order to make them more addictive. At the midpoint of the century's last decade, the nation seemed poised to begin a muckraking campaign against the tobacco industry on a scale not seen since the pure food and drug reforms of the turn of the century.

United States Congress Passes the Civil Rights Act (1964)

The event: On July 2, 1964, President Lyndon Johnson—in a seminal achievement of his administration—signed into law the Civil Rights Act, banning racial discrimination in all public places in America, outlawing racial discrimination by employers and unions, and withdrawing federal funds from state programs that discriminated against anyone on the basis of race.

POSTWAR AMERICA was torn by racial unrest, especially in the big cities. President Harry S Truman, reluctant to propose civil rights for political reasons, argued in public that no federal law could, by itself, achieve racial equality. During the Eisenhower administration, the Supreme Court ordered the nation's schools desegregated in its *Brown v. Board of Education of Topeka* decision. That decision inspired African-Americans to test other racial barriers as well, and the Montgomery bus boycott led to a Supreme Court decision that barred segregation in public transportation systems and propelled the Reverend Martin Luther King, Jr., to the forefront of the civil rights movement. In 1961, more than seventy thousand demonstrators participated in sit-ins in 112 Southern cities, pressing for the desegregation of restaurants. Others tested the desegregation of interstate transportation in "freedom rides" on segregated buses throughout the South. In August 1963, more than two hundred thousand people marched on Washington and demanded immediate racial equality.

The passage of the Civil Rights Act of 1964, in many ways the legal culmination of the struggle for equality, did not provide true social equality for African-Americans. Moreover, severe repression by state and lo-

cal governments and certain institutions, such as the FBI, within the federal government, the assassinations of Malcolm X and Martin Luther King, and the heated infighting among black militants caused a decline in social protest as the volatile 1960s drew to a close. Nevertheless, the changes brought about by the civil struggles, court decisions, protests, and legislation did leave a lasting mark on American culture and society. Certainly, the more overt, officially sanctioned forms of racial discrimination, the social acceptance of openly expressed bigotry, and the official segregation of public establishments, schools, and facilities all came to an end. African-American politicians ran for office, and won, in communities where once blacks could not even vote. Colleges and universities, even those in the South, recruited black students instead of banning them. Racial violence in the South declined. Commercial television began featuring actors of color and offered shows featuring black families. Perhaps most important, many employers, especially governmental bodies and nonprofit organizations that depended on the largess of the federal government, instituted affirmative action programs. Though such programs sometimes gave rise to white backlash movements and protests of "reverse discrimination," they did bring a large number of African-Americans into the work force in jobs and positions that had historically been closed to them.

While de jure (law-based) segregation disappeared, de facto (end-results) segregation stubbornly resisted being legislated out of existence. Public school systems and the housing market in particular remained strongly segregated, usually separate *and* unequal. Racial bigotry and repression continued to play a significant role in American life, and, if anything, greater inequalities than ever before in wealth and income surfaced in the 1970s and 1980s. To many, the spirit was bled out of the civil rights movement during the decades that followed the 1960s, when African-American communities in America's cities—abandoned by a federal government whose social programs had been slashed by conservative politicians even as white Americans abandoned the cities themselves—were swept by unemployment and despair.

U.S. President Lyndon Johnson Envisions a "Great Society" (1964)

The event: In his bid for election in 1964 to a term as president, Lyndon Johnson called for his fellow Americans to work with him in building a "Great Society . . . that rests on abundance and liberty for all."

IT IS NO EASY THING to follow in the path of a martyr, but such was Lyndon Johnson's lot as president as he succeeded John F. Kennedy. When he ran for election as president in his own right in 1964, Johnson built a platform that was not only worthy of the already heavily mythologized Kennedy, but that evoked the heady days of Franklin Delano Roosevelt.

Johnson called it the "Great Society," and that phrase became a blanket term for a slate of major and highly ambitious social programs. Civil rights was a major part of the Great Society, and in 1964 Congress passed a Civil Rights Act that desegregated public accommodations such as restaurants, hotels, and theaters, and banned job discrimination on the basis of race. The following year a Voting Rights Act guaranteed African-Americans their right to vote in elections at all levels. In 1968 another civil rights act outlawed housing discrimination.

African-Americans were profoundly affected by Johnson's civil rights programs, but a host of social welfare measures also typified Great Society legislation. In 1965, Congress passed a law creating the Medicare program, which helped all Americans over the age of sixty-five pay for medical treatment. The following year, medical coverage was expanded to include welfare recipients of any age in a program called Medicaid.

Great Society legislation also affected American education. The 1965 Elementary and Secondary Education Act provided federal funds to poor school districts across the country. The Higher Education Act of 1965 gave tuition assistance to college and university students, ensuring that millions who could not have afforded to attend college in the past could now earn a degree, the traditional ticket into the American middle class.

Great Society legislation created new cabinet posts, including the Department of Housing and Urban Development and the Department of Transportation, as well as the National Endowments for the Humanities and the Arts, and the Corporation for Public Broadcasting. The environmental field saw passage of the National Wilderness Preservation System and the Land and Water Conservation Act (both in 1964) and the creation of the National Trails System and the National Wild and Scenic Rivers System (both in 1968).

Such laws as these transformed not only the American social political landscape, but also the lives of American citizens. However, the most dramatic—and in many ways the most promising—among the welter of Great Society laws would not prove to have so powerful an effect, and in fact would ultimately fail to accomplish their goals; they were those laws passed as a result of Johnson's declared War on Poverty. In 1964 Congress enacted the Economic Opportunity Act, which created the Office of Economic Opportunity to oversee numerous community programs, including the Job Corps, the Volunteers in Service to America (VISTA), the Model Cities Program, Upward Bound, the Food Stamps program, and Project Head Start.

The great tragedy of the Great Society is that the overwhelming majority of its anti-poverty programs were inadequately funded, largely because the president's other great preoccupation, the war in Vietnam, drew off increasing amounts of precious revenue. Many of the programs were dismembered and discontinued after the Republicans captured the White House in 1968, so the image of Johnson as an obsessed and dissembling commander-in-chief during the long and undeclared war in Southeast Asia rather than his compassionate and inclusive domestic initiatives is what most Americans think of when they recall his presidency. (Aid to dependent children and unemployment compensation, the two main programs that make up the "welfare system" against which conservatives so often rail, were part of the New Deal's social security legislation. The two Great Society programs that still thrive—Medicare and Medicaid—are the only form of health care provided to its older and poorer citizens by a country that, alone among industrialized nations, offers no national health insurance.) Driven by the mystique of JFK and conceived by President Johnson, many of the social policy experiments of the 1960s died, along with some 50,000 American soldiers in the rice paddies of Southeast Asia.

The U.S. Congress Passes the Gulf of Tonkin Resolution (1964)

The event: In response to an apparent attack on a U.S. destroyer conducting espionage activities in the Gulf of Tonkin off the coast of North Vietnam, the U.S. Senate passed the Gulf of Tonkin Resolution on August 7, 1964, giving President Johnson a free hand to prevent further "aggression" by North Vietnam and providing broad congressional support for expanding the war in Southeast Asia.

THE SMALL Southeast Asian nation of Vietnam had known thousands of years of intermittent warfare when, following World War II, Vietnamese nationalists, led by the Communist Ho Chi Minh, fought French colonial forces to a stalemate. As a result of a 1954 Geneva peace conference, the country was divided into North and South Vietnam pending the outcome of free elections scheduled for 1956. Caught up in the Cold War strategy of containing Communism wherever possible, U.S. President Dwight D. Eisenhower, concluding that free elections would result in the unification of the country under Ho Chi Minh, gave American approval and covert support to South Vietnamese President Ngo Dinh Diem when he co-opted the election process and ruthlessly suppressed the opposition. His act prompted the expansion of already existing guerrilla forces, which included Buddhists, Nationalists, and Communists supported by North Vietnam and other Communist nations. The next five years were consumed in guerrilla-led civil warfare, with North Vietnam calling on the National Liberation Front, popularly known as the Viet Cong, to lead the struggle against Diem.

Fearing a Communist takeover, Eisen-hower's successor, President John F. Kennedy, heedlessly, secretly, and without securing the consent of Congress, sent U.S. combat troops to aid Diem, so that by 1962, 15,500 Americans were involved in an undeclared war against the Viet Cong—an involvement justified only after the fact in 1966 by invoking the ambiguous SEATO treaty. In 1963 Kennedy plunged even deeper into Vietnam's affairs by allowing the CIA to plot the murder of the thoroughly corrupt Diem, now perceived as a political liability rather than an asset, in a military coup that led to years of instability, during which South Vietnam had twelve governments, none popular enough to survive on its own. By 1965, Ho Chi Minh's North had essentially prevailed, having killed twenty-five thousand South Vietnamese soldiers and having so demoralized the others that a hundred thousand or so deserted.

Even as the Gulf of Tonkin resolution was being passed, Lyndon Johnson assured the American public that its sons would not die fighting an Asian war. But scarcely was the 1964 presidential election over, when Johnson—faced with withdrawing from or escalating the conflict—chose to commit 22,000 fresh troops. By 1965, 75,000

Americans were fighting in Vietnam; by 1966, 375,000; by the next election, over half a million. Earlier in the conflict, both Kennedy and then Johnson had referred to the troops as "military advisors." By 1966, there was no way to denominate them as anything other than combat troops sent to fight and very possibly to die. As draft calls increased by 100 percent in 1965, young men flooded into American colleges to avoid conscription and service in that "little green country." Starting in February of that year, the United States bombed the North, then stopped to see Ho Chi Minh's response, which was invariably to send yet more leaders, more weapons, and more troops to help the Viet Cong. Over the next eight years the American army in Vietnam would grow to a peak of 542,000, and the economic cost of the war would bleed Johnson's cherished Great Society dry.

By then, too, opposition to the war was mounting in America, as some of its businessmen began to question the astronomical costs and many of its draft-age students the morality of dropping bombs and chemicals to destroy and defoliate the very country their president claimed to be "protecting." An obsessed Johnson and military leaders, acting almost as if they were independent of the publicly stated American policy, no longer bothered to consult citizens or senators while they turned Vietnam into the fourth-bloodiest conflict in American history. Johnson's own secretary of defense, Robert McNamara, admitted in 1967 that the bombing had not stopped North Vietnam's infiltration. Then, in 1968, as if to prove McNamara's point, came the stun-

ning massive and coordinated attack of the Viet Cong in the January Tet Offensive. In thirty-five cities all over South Vietnam, allied troops were surprised by the enemy's ferocity and determination. Though they suffered enormous casualties, the Viet Cong continued the attack for a month, penetrating the United States embassy in Saigon and capturing the ancient capital of Hue, before being forced back into the countryside, where they destroyed hamlet after hamlet during their retreat. Whether the Viet Cong "won" the Tet Offensive or not, it was certainly successful in contradicting Lyndon Johnson's public claims about the war. As 350,000 refugees abandoned their hamlets en masse and poured into the recently besieged towns, the United States began to strong-arm its puppet regime in South Vietnam toward the peace table, and on May 10, 1968, talks with the North opened in Paris.

If Johnson was willing to ignore the growing unrest on American campuses and the perhaps more ominous disaffection for the war among the business community, he certainly could not ignore the challenge to his leadership his conducting of the war brought within his own party. By 1968, it was obvious to everyone that Robert F. Kennedy, who had served as attorney general under his brother John and briefly under Johnson, was searching for a way to run against the incumbent president of his own party. There had been little love lost between the two men even during the Kennedy administration, but their enmity swelled into loathing, especially after Kennedy embraced the antiwar movement.

When Eugene McCarthy showed strongly in the democratic primary in New Hampshire, demonstrating that a mainstream presidential candidate opposing the Vietnam war was viable, Kennedy entered the ring, winning both the Indiana and Nebraska primaries.

Johnson's worst fears were realized: The press despised him; the voters did not trust him; his approval ratings were the lowest in history; the 1968 election was obviously turning into a referendum on America's involvement in Vietnam; and the hated Bobby Kennedy would likely humiliate him by stealing the nomination of the Democratic Party for president. Surprising almost everyone in the world, Johnson went on national television before the California primary and announced he would not seek a second term, throwing the election wide open.

Robert Kennedy's assassination on June 6, 1968, following his sound victory in the California presidential primary, destroyed the potential for the election to become a public referendum on Vietnam. The self-professed Arab nationalist Sirhan Sirhan took more than an individual life that night; he destroyed more than one man's vision of how the nation's problems should be solved. Because Kennedy was clearly trying to mold an antiwar constituency into a true Democratic coalition for withdrawal, his murder deprived the American middle class of the opportunity to vote for or against the war at a national level. This didn't happen until George McGovern's weak campaign of 1972 when Richard Nixon, running for a second term, asked the silent majority for the right to end the war anyway, only at his own pace.

The murder turned the disorienting, violent, and chaotic year of 1968 into a brutally incomprehensible one, virtually ensuring that the United States would be politically incapable of avoiding profound, dangerous divisions in the body politic more serious than any since the Civil War. As the raging Chicago police beat antiwar demonstrators before the eyes of the world at the Democratic Convention, a politically revived Richard Nixon made plans to continue the grim policy, legalized by the Gulf of Tonkin Resolution, of bombing a small country into oblivion to satisfy the ideological lusts of the Cold War once he finally managed to win a seat in the Oval Office.

The Beatles Invade the United States (1964)

The event: On February 1, 1964, "I Want to Hold Your Hand" hit number one on the pop charts, and the four young Englishmen who recorded the song and called themselves the "Beatles" announced an American concert tour. Immensely popular already in Britain, the Beatles received enough attention in America to ensure worldwide fame and wealth beyond imagination. Called "Beatlemania," it was perhaps the purest example of the power of the twentieth century's cult of celebrity spawned by mass communications and the rise of a consumer society.

ROCK 'N' ROLL EXPLODED on the American scene around 1955 in the form of a comet—actually, Bill Haley and his Comets—and a meteor called Elvis Presley, who started recording in 1954, gained widespread notice the next year, and was a teen idol by the time he appeared on television's "Ed Sullivan Show" in 1956. Presley and many of the rockers who immediately followed him brought to the white cultural mainstream the musical—and sexual—energy of what had been called "race" music: African-American blues and rhythm and blues. As "covered" by white artists, the essential black music expressed the drive, desire, sexual energy, and ambition of adolescence. It was a bold affront to the sentimental balladeering of the late forties and early fifties, and teenagers took great satisfaction in the degree to which it offended their parents.

Rock 'n' roll's first phase was short-lived. By 1957, the music was shedding its outlaw energy and retreating into a groove of normality that would soon wear into a rut of dull, dumb music, and many predicted the imminent death of rock 'n' roll as yet another teen fad.

Unknown to Americans, a small group of British teens—working-class kids, mostly, and not from sophisticated London, but blue-collar Liverpool—had also picked up on the early rockers. In 1955, fourteen-year-old John Lennon was already performing with a "skiffle" band, The Quarrymen, when he met thirteen-year-old Paul McCartney at a church social. The two performed with The Quarrymen and sometimes also appeared as the Nurk Twins. In

1958, fifteen-year-old George Harrison, a guitarist influenced by Chet Atkins and Buddy Holly, joined The Quarrymen, which became Johnny and the Moondogs, the Silver Beatles, and, finally (in homage to Buddy Holly's Crickets), the Beatles. The next year, the group was joined by a Liverpool art student named Stu Sutcliffe, and in 1960 drummer Pete Best was added as the Beatles performed in Liverpool nightclubs and in clubs in Hamburg, Germany. In 1961, Brian Epstein began to manage the Beatles. The following year Sutcliffe died of a brain tumor, and drummer Best was replaced by Ringo Starr. By August 1962, the Beatles were recording with London's EMI label, but its American counterpart, Capitol, declined the group's option.

After reaching number twenty-one on the British pop charts with "Love Me Do," the Beatles released "Please Please Me" in January 1963, and it skyrocketed to the top of the charts, suddenly unleashing Beatlemania throughout Great Britain. The album of the same name enjoyed similar success, leading to an American release, *Introducing the Beatles*, which failed to make much of an impression. Then came 1964 and "I Want to Hold Your Hand." It topped the charts and launched Beatlemania in the United States.

Meet the Beatles, the group's second album for Capitol, became the best-selling album in history up to that point. The group's first movie, *A Hard Day's Night* (1964), garnered not only great popular success, but considerable critical acclaim, and an American tour triggered mass hysteria.

Having established a beachhead on the North American continent, a whole British invasion followed, including the Rolling Stones, the Who, the Kinks, and a host of others. The emergence of these "foreign" groups, who brought energetic new sounds inspired by early U.S. rockers, revitalized a foundering genre.

The Beatles' tremendous success through the 1960s opened the way to fame and fortune for other rock groups, American as well as British. Moreover, the group proved to have great staying power, evolving as the decade evolved, releasing in 1967 the first piece of psychedelic rock, "Strawberry Fields Forever," and following it with the *Sgt. Pepper's Lonely Hearts Club Band* album, prompting critic Langdon Winner to

observe the following year that "the closest Western Civilization has come to unity since the Congress of Vienna in 1815 was the week the *Sgt. Pepper* album was released." Everywhere one went, the music was heard: across America and across much of the world.

The music of the Beatles—and a handful of other rock groups—simultaneously upset the complacent cultural status quo even as it brought diverse people together. The breakup of the Beatles in 1970 was received around the world as a seismic event, and when John Lennon was murdered outside his New York City apartment building by Mark David Chapman, a deranged fan, on December 8, 1980, it was as if yet another idealistic world leader had been assassinated.

Ralph Nader Publishes *Unsafe at Any Speed* (1965)

The event: In 1965, lawyer and journalist Ralph Nader rocked the automotive industry with his book *Unsafe at Any Speed*, revealing (as its subtitle said) the "Designed-in Dangers of the American Automobile," and giving birth to the consumer rights movement.

IN THE 1950s, the United States was a country driven by its automobiles. To serve them, a vast interstate highway system was put under construction, cities were paved over, fast food restaurants sprouted, and suburbs became the new centers of American population. In the 1960s, the automobile industry was still riding high, and each year millions of Americans looked forward to the introduction of the new models. It seemed as if nothing could ever stand in the way of the nation's romance with four wheels, shapely sheet metal, and the internal combustion engine.

Then came Ralph Nader, an ascetic, almost priestlike man, a lawyer by training, who had also worked as a freelance journalist and an assistant to Daniel Patrick Moynihan—in 1964, assistant secretary of labor, later the senior U.S. senator from New York—as staff consultant on highway safety. The nation needed such a consultant, since its affair with the car was proving a fatal attraction. The year 1963 brought traffic deaths to an all-time high of 40,804. What both shocked and interested Nader is that, while many of these fatalities were due (as expected) to driver error, a very large proportion were caused by mechanical defects or, even more significantly, design defects. His experience in Moynihan's office provided the background for his 1965 bombshell book, *Unsafe at Any Speed: The Designed-in Dangers of the American Automobile*.

The book's principal exhibit was General Motors' Corvair, which was riddled with deadly safety problems. Nader pointed out that the company, which profited every year to the tune of $1.7 billion, spent a mere $1 million on safety-related issues. As this and other revelations made headlines, GM hired detectives in an effort to get the goods on Nader and open the closet door on a blackmail-worthy skeleton. But the man had no vices. Ultimately GM President John Roche was summoned before a Senate committee to defend his automobiles and to apologize to Nader.

Following *Unsafe at Any Speed*, "Naderism" become the buzzword of a new consumer protection movement, and Nader himself was transformed into something of a folk hero. Nader's testimony before a highly receptive Congress was influential in the passage of the National Traffic and Motor Vehicle Safety Act of 1966, which brought automobile design standards under tight federal regulation. In 1967, Nader turned his attention to the food industry, becoming instrumental in the passage of the Wholesome Meat Act of 1967, and he also agitated for and secured legislation to regulate natural gas pipeline safety and radiation hazards. In 1968, Nader capitalized on student activism by organizing college students into study groups—dubbed "Nader's Raiders"—to investigate the efficacy of government regulatory agencies. The results of these efforts became the basis of an organization Nader founded in 1969, the Center for Study of Responsive Law. Two years later, Nader established a consumer-oriented lobbying group, Public Citizen, Inc., which spawned a series of related advocacy organizations devoted to such broad and diverse consumer issues as tax reform, health issues, Congressional conduct, corporate ethics, and the insurance industry. Nader greatly extended the concept of consumer advocacy, including under that umbrella environmental and labor concerns. In 1970, he was instrumental in the establishment of the Environmental Protection Agency and, later, was active in the creation of OSHA—the Occupational Safety and Health Administration.

By the 1980s, the consumer protection movement was in full swing, and even the big corporations, originally hostile to many issues of safety and value—product "features" they believed to be essentially unsalable—learned to see safety and value not only as ethical imperatives, but as sources of product appeal and profit.

Malcolm X Is Assassinated (1965)

The event: On February 21, 1965, the controversial and highly influential African-American activist Malcolm X was assassinated by three Black Muslims while speaking to a Harlem audience.

WHEN MALCOLM X was gunned down in Harlem's Audubon Auditorium, most white Americans—and even Dr. Martin Luther King, Jr.—saw the murder as the inevitable consequence of the violent rhetoric of racial hatred. Most Americans knew Malcolm X as the fiery advocate of black separatism who had been vocal in his belief that the white man was nothing less than the devil incarnate. But *The Autobiography of Malcolm X*, written with Alex Haley (who would later become famous as the author of *Roots*), published soon after Malcolm X's death, revealed to America and the world a very different figure from the one-dimensional apostle of hate the media and the white press had painted him. The *Autobiography* presented nothing less than the odyssey of a black man in twentieth-century America.

That odyssey began in Omaha, Nebraska, where Malcolm Little was born to a strong-willed Baptist preacher, who urged his African-American congregation to take control of their own lives. Malcolm's father refused to bend to white intimidation, and when Malcolm was six years old, his father was killed by a mob of Black Legionnaires, a white racist organization modeled on the Ku Klux Klan. Malcolm and some of his siblings were placed in foster homes.

From that point on, Malcolm Little was a troubled child. He dropped out of school in Detroit after the eighth grade and joined a series of street gangs. At twenty-one he was convicted of burglary and given a long prison sentence. It was in prison that he first encountered the teachings of the Honorable Elijah Muhammad, leader of the Lost-Found Nation of Islam, popularly known as the Black Muslims. As Marcus Garvey had done at the beginning of the century, the Black Muslims promulgated the doctrine that African-Americans were corrupted by contact with whites, who were incarnations of the devil. Malcolm Little, renouncing his "slave name," became Malcolm X, adopted the ascetic life prescribed by the Black Muslims, studied the faith, and, in conjunction with it, developed his ideas on the best course for black America.

After his release from prison, Malcolm X became minister of Temple No. 7 in Harlem. From his pulpit, with an anger tempered by great eloquence, he condemned white crimes against blacks. So impressive was his message that it reached well beyond the confines of the temple and struck fear into white Americans, who heard in his words a potential for great violence. But Malcolm X was never a simpleminded racist and hate monger. He questioned not only society according to the white man, but the Nation of Islam according to Elijah Muhammad. Over time, Malcolm X came to regard his former spiritual leader as a corrupt womanizer and as a tyrant who demanded absolute and unthinking obedience.

In December 1963, as friction between him and Elijah Muhammad grew, Malcolm X was suspended by the Black Muslims. Malcolm X used the suspension to strike out on his own, traveling to Mecca, where he studied the orthodox Islam religion and discovered that it taught the equality of races. During his Middle Eastern sojourn, he also encountered white members of the faithful, who were certainly no devils. Malcolm X eschewed his earlier belief in the unredeemable evil of whites and returned to America, now calling himself El-Hajj Malik El-Shabazz. He founded the Organization of Afro-American Unity in June 1964 and began leaning toward a form of socialism as a cure for the ills of American society. His organization found adherents among other disaffected Black Muslims, and on February 21, 1965, he was assassinated by three church members, possibly with the knowledge (if not complicity) of federal authorities, who had tapped Malcolm X's phone and generally monitored Black Muslim activity.

The Autobiography of Malcolm X became a powerful catalyst of the "black power movement" of the Student Non-Violent Coordinating Committee (SNCC). But the death of Malcolm X at such a critical time in his development meant that his legacy to the cause of civil rights would forever be incomplete and open to wide interpretation.

Riots Break Out in Los Angeles (1965)

The event: On August 11, 1965, a white policeman on patrol in the predominantly black Watts section of Los Angeles stopped a black motorist on suspicion of drunk driving. A crowd gathered, rumors of police brutality circulated, and, over the next six days, the neighborhood erupted into widespread rioting.

WHILE MARTIN LUTHER KING, JR., the dominant figure in the struggle for African-American civil rights during the 1960s, preached a philosophy of nonviolence inspired by the example of Mohandas Gandi, the decade brought the most violent, widespread racial unrest the country had ever endured. Many African-Americans, facing the violence and despair of the inner city ghetto day in and day out, and profoundly affected by the higher-profile murders and assassinations of the early 1960s, came to regard King's message and methods as passive, conciliatory, and ineffective. Thousands of the disaffected turned from King to more militant organizations, like the Congress for Racial Equality (CORE), organized by Floyd McKissick, and the Student Nonviolent Coordinating Committee (SNCC), led by Stokely Carmichael, who called for "Black Power" and an end to white involvement in the civil rights movement. By the summer of 1965, the civil rights movement was torn in two directions, and the atmosphere was primed for violence.

In Watts, a sprawling, squalid Los Angeles neighborhood, the climate was such that a routine arrest for a traffic violation quickly developed into a major "confrontation"—a word that echoed throughout news broadcasts daily during the decade—and police reinforcements were summoned. The gathering crowd called in its reinforcements as well, and they began hurling stones, concrete blocks, and glass bottles at the officers. The police responded by cordoning off the neighborhood, but the next evening thousands of area residents roamed the streets, hurling Molotov cocktails and looting stores—usually white-owned and, therefore, objects of great resentment.

The National Guard was summoned to aid the Los Angeles police, and the officers, the Guard, and the rioters battled for six days. Thirty-five people were killed and more than a thousand injured. Property damage totaled approximately $200 million.

Watts was the first of the "race riots" that seemed to become a fixture of American urban life year after year, during what newscasters and journalists dubbed the "long hot summer." Many whites had taken comfort in thinking of blacks as a "slow-to-anger people," and they saw Dr. King as a leader who would bring change—but gradually and without violence. Rioting broke out in the summer of 1966 in New York and Chicago. In 1967 Newark and Detroit were the scenes of deadly riots, and in the spring of 1968, when Martin Luther King was assassinated in Memphis, more than one hundred cities across the nation erupted.

After Watts and the death of King, many African-American civil rights organizations began excluding white members and white influence. Some, like the Black Panthers, became outspokenly militant, striking frightened and outraged whites as a cross between a paramilitary organization and a ghetto street gang. A significant number of whites, whose sympathy for the civil rights movement had grown during the early part of the decade, abandoned the cause. Other whites vented resentment against federal and state programs aimed at improving the economic condition of African-Americans. Still other whites turned to violence themselves as the courts ordered the desegregation of neighborhood schools through compulsory busing of students.

By the late 1960s and early 1970s, despite undeniable gains in the attainment and acceptance of civil rights, American society was, if anything, more visibly polarized than ever before.

China Undergoes a Cultural Revolution (1966)

The event: In 1966 Mao Tse-tung and his third wife, Chiang Ch'ing, launched what they called "the Cultural Revolution," and until roughly 1969 they effectively maintained China in a state of perpetual revolution while attempting to create a pure Marxist society. Following Mao's death, the "Gang of Four" briefly renewed this Cultural Revolution.

IN OUSTING LIU SHAO-CHI, Mao and Chiang Ch'ing engaged the Chinese nation in a frenzied debate on its political future. Once Mao regained his post as party chairman and head of state, he embarked on a headlong program to expunge every trace of traditional Chinese government and culture. The so-called Cultural Revolution created a mass army of radical Maoist students known as the Red Guards, who brought perpetual revolution to China. When the activities of the Red Guards assumed the dimensions of anarchy, Mao turned to the military, led by Lin Piao, whose support he recruited by arranging to have him named his successor in the 1969 constitution of the Chinese Communist Party. By 1971, Lin Piao had effectively pacified the Red Guards, but soon afterward was reported killed in a plane crash after having plotted to assassinate Mao.

With the Red Guards in their place and Lin Piao dead, Mao Tse-tung was again in control of China, but the experience had taught him the value of moderation, and the same leader who had wanted to eliminate Chinese tradition on the one hand and Western influences on the other now made overtures to the United States, in hopes of reestablishing diplomatic and economic relations. Mao even received President Richard M. Nixon in Beijing in 1972. These were important overtures, but the aging chairman failed to carry through with them when his health deteriorated rapidly during the early 1970s; he died in Beijing on September 9, 1976.

With Mao dead, the trend toward moderation was stifled for a time. Chiang Ch'ing and her circle of intimates, derisively called the Gang of Four, attempted to seize power from Mao's immediate succes-

sor, Zhou Enlai. The four were arrested and accused of the terrorist excesses of the Cultural Revolution. Tried in 1980 on charges that included attempting to overthrow the state, two "gang" members—Mao's widow and Zhang Chunqiao—protested that they had only done Mao's bidding. Nevertheless, in January 1981, all four were found guilty. In the meantime, the man Mao had designated to succeed him, Hua Kuo-Feng, also had been ousted from the government, and China came under the control of genuine moderates.

The Cultural Revolution had been an astounding amalgam of contradictions. Like the Hundred Flowers Movement, its founding principles were constructive criticism and questioning those in authority, but it produced an almost hypnotic mass personality cult, and the image of Mao Tse-tung was everywhere in both public and private places, while his "little red book"— a collection of *Quotations from Chairman Mao*—was read, studied, and pored over by virtually every man, woman, and child in China. The book, the perpetual revolution (an idea with unacknowledged roots in the writings of Leon Trotsky), and Mao's celebrity (recognized by that most astute student of celebrity, Andy Warhol, in a famous series of paintings) had an impact on left-wing movements worldwide, especially in France and the United States, where posters of Mao became *de rigueur* for student radicals and appeared ubiquitously at public protests.

Bobby Seale and Huey Newton Form the Black Panther Party (1966)

The event: Two militant African-Americans, Huey P. Newton and Bobby G. Seale, created the Black Panther Party in Oakland, California.

T HE MOST VISIBLE civil rights leader of the 1950s and 1960s was Dr. Martin Luther King, Jr. Many whites feared and despised King, but in fact he was a racial moderate. Earlier leaders such as Marcus Garvey had been far more radical and even militant, as was the Lost-Found Nation of Islam, founded in Detroit during the 1930s and dedicated to black nationalism. Any number of King's sixties contemporaries were likewise more militant. Stokely Carmichael, a leader in SNCC (Student Non-Violent Coordinating Committee) had started using what many perceived as a distinctly violent phrase—*black power*—in place of the less disquieting "equal rights," "equality," or "integration," and Malcolm X advocated change for black America "by whatever means necessary"—a phrase as portentous as it was memorable.

While King and the more militant leaders spoke, two radical black leaders, Huey Newton and Bobby Seale, living in the predominantly African-American city of Oakland, California, adjacent to the nation's most radical college town, Berkeley, tapped into the growing mood of quasi-revolutionary protest and combined it with the black power movement to create the Black Panther Party. The Panthers combined community activism with an almost paramilitary orientation. On the one hand, the organiza-

tion received funding from neighborhood merchants and well-to-do sponsors to finance free breakfasts and medical and educational programs for ghetto children. On the other hand, Newton, Seale, Eldredge Cleaver, and other Panther leaders urged African-Americans to arm themselves for combat against their oppressors. Toward this end, the Panthers collected small arsenals.

Tension between the Black Panthers and police officials ran high, and numerous armed confrontations occurred between party members and police. In 1967, Newton was tried and convicted for killing an Oakland policeman, but the conviction was overturned on appeal. In 1974 he was again charged with murder, this time in a street fight, and he fled to Fidel Castro's Cuba. In the meantime, Bobby Seale and other Panthers were accused of torturing to death a former Panther they suspected of being a stool pigeon, but the trial resulted in a hung jury and charges were ultimately dropped.

Another prominent Black Panther, Fred Hampton, met a violent end in 1969, when Chicago police raided a Panther residence early in the morning, killing Hampton in his bed. The police denied that this was an act of political assassination. With the death of Hampton and the exile or incarceration of Newton and Seale, the Panther movement declined amid in-fighting and a waning spirit of radicalism during the 1970s, as indicated by the fate of Eldredge Cleaver.

Eldredge Cleaver was undoubtedly the best known of the Black Panthers, largely on the strength of his remarkable *Soul on Ice*, a collection of essays and letters written while he was incarcerated in California's

Folsom Prison. In 1968 he fled the United States when his parole was revoked for what he considered political reasons. After seven years of living in exile in Algeria, Paris, and Cuba, Cleaver returned to the United States in 1975, resolved his problems with the law, and turned away from radicalism to become a lecturer on Christianity.

The National Organization for Women (NOW) Is Founded (1966)

The event: Betty Friedan, author of *The Feminine Mystique* (1963), which ushered in a new era of feminism, was instrumental in founding the National Organization for Women in 1966 and served as its first president, the premiere champion of women's rights in America.

BETTY FRIEDAN, a free-lance journalist, looked to her own graduating class from Smith College for an assessment of the status of women in the 1960s. She sent her classmates questionnaires, and the responses became the basis of her best-selling *The Feminine Mystique*, published in 1963. What she discovered is that the majority of middle-class and upper-middle-class women were greatly dissatisfied with their lives as narrowly defined by their roles as wives and mothers. Friedan concluded that women were the victims of a collective social myth—what she called the "feminine mystique"—a pervasive belief that women gain genuine satisfaction only through marriage and children and that all other pursuits were, in effect, sublimations of this single imperative.

A community of like-minded women gravitated to Friedan's book, and in 1966 she was one of the founders of the National

Organization for Women (NOW), serving as its first president. NOW focused on obtaining equity for women in the workplace, liberalizing abortion laws, and securing passage of the Equal Rights Amendment, which had been languishing in Congress since it had first been proposed in 1922. NOW grew steadily in membership and influence, helping to create the climate in which Gloria Steinem founded *Ms.* magazine in 1972, which spread the message of feminism to a wider audience.

By the late 1960s, the feminist movement began to splinter into different groups, essentially represented by NOW, which believed in change through the electoral process, including lobbying and legislation, and other groups who believed the issues of "women's liberation" (as they termed it) went beyond official politics and were inherent in Western and American culture and in all male-female relationships within that culture. Indeed, such feminists as Shulamith Firestone, Ti-Grace Atkinson, and Kate Millett spoke of "sexual politics," asserting that all relationships between men and women were political, generally involving the man's cultural imperative to dominate the woman.

The activities of both NOW and the more radical feminists provoked conservative reaction against the women's movement, primarily on the grounds that the movement posed a direct threat to the integrity of the family. As to Friedan, although she did not abandon the fight for equality and women's rights, her 1981 book, *The Second Stage*, represented a dramatic shift, with emphasis on the importance of the family. It reflected the agonizing second thoughts many career-focused women were having as they approached or passed their childbearing years without having begun a family.

The U.S. Supreme Court Rules on *Miranda v. State of Arizona* (1966)

The event: In 1966 the U.S. Supreme Court handed down a decision in *Miranda v. State of Arizona*, finding for the plaintiff and ruling that the Fifth Amendment to the U.S. Constitution, which extended to an individual the right to refuse to testify in court against himself or herself, also applied to individuals in police custody. Hailed by the champions of individuals' rights as a landmark case, the ruling shocked and angered conservative law-and-order advocates, who have yet to cease vilifying the decision.

ONE COULD LOOK to certain scientific advances in crime detection, such as the emerging field of DNA "fingerprinting," for the events that most profoundly affected the nature of crime and punishment in this century. Most American police agencies would argue, however, that the single event that most profoundly affects the day-to-day business of law enforcement in our time is the Miranda decision.

In 1963 a career criminal named Ernesto Miranda kidnapped and raped a teenage girl. After he was arrested and identified during a police lineup, he made a written confession, which included a statement that he had been informed of his rights. During his trial, however, Miranda's attorney argued that the defendant had not been told by the arresting officers of his right to have legal counsel present during questioning. Miranda was nevertheless convicted, but his case was adopted by the American Civil Liberties Union, whose lawyers argued it before the Supreme Court. The court voted five to four to reverse the conviction, ruling that Miranda had incriminated himself because he had been improperly advised of his rights.

The Miranda decision requires law enforcement officers to inform individuals in their custody that they have the right to remain silent, that anything they say can and no doubt will be used against them, that they have the right to have an attorney present before any questioning begins, and that if they cannot afford an attorney, the court will appoint one to represent them. The court held that any statement provided by an individual in police custody before he has been "Mirandized"—that is, advised of his rights—is inadmissible in court. Nor can a defendant's choice to remain silent be held against him in court.

The Supreme Court did not base its ruling entirely on the interpretation of the letter of the law, but, rather, handed down the decision after a thorough examination of police practices. The high court concluded that physical abuse, intimidation, and deception were commonly used to obtain confessions, declaring that "custodial interrogation exacts a heavy toll on individual liberty and trades on the weakness of individuals." The Miranda decision is one of many restrictions law enforcement officers must work under in a democratic society, which, following English common law, regards an accused person as innocent until proven guilty. As for Ernesto Miranda himself, he was subsequently retried on new evidence and convicted.

Israel Fights a Six Day War Against Egypt and Its Arab Allies (1967)

The event: On June 5, 1967, Israel launched an attack on Egypt and other Arab states in the Middle East, fighting a six-day war and capturing the Sinai Peninsula, the Gaza Strip, and the West Bank of the Jordan River. As Israel occupied the captured territories with intentions of turning them into a buffer zone, the outraged Arabs protested to a world startled by Israel's display of military prowess.

ISRAEL, A HOMELAND for the century's most ruthlessly persecuted minority, came through a difficult birth in 1948 and has been in a chronic state of guerrilla warfare with neighboring Arab states ever since. Occasionally, as in the Arab-Israeli War of 1956, the guerrilla and terrorist action flared into outright war. In an attempt to stabilize the region, the United Nations sent an emergency force (UNEF) to Egypt, but withdrew it in May 1967 at the demand of Egypt's president-general, Gamal Abdel Nasser. Once Nasser had secured removal of the UNEF, he sought to strangle Israel by means of a shipping blockade of the Strait of Tiran, closing the principal Israeli port of Elat on the Gulf of Aqaba. With the blockade in place, Egyptian and Syrian forces mobilized along the border, and Israel responded in kind.

It was an all-too-familiar scenario, as both sides apparently braced for another round of guerrilla attacks along the borders. But this time, on June 5, Israel stunned the Arabs—and the world—by launching a massive air attack on some two dozen Arab airfields, destroying more than four hundred Egyptian, Syrian, and Jordanian aircraft on the ground. It was the bulk of the Arab air forces. Simultaneously, under the direction of General Moshe Dayan, a one-eyed veteran of the 1956 war, ground forces invaded the Sinai peninsula, Jerusalem's Old City, Jordan's West Bank, the Gaza Strip, and the Golan Heights, seizing and occupying these areas when an unsponsored cease-fire was declared on June 10, 1967.

Although the guerrilla and terrorist activities continued, and another war would erupt on Yom Kippur, the holiest of Jewish holy days, in 1973, the 1967 Six Day War marked a turning point in Israel's relationship to the Arab world and the world at large. For centuries—and in no century more than the twentieth—Jews had been regarded as vulnerable, as eternal objects of persecution and perpetual victims. The brilliant performance of the Israeli armed forces in the Six Day War, achieving the century's most complete military triumph in proportion to the forces engaged and the length of the engagement, convinced Arabs and others that the Jews were no longer willing to be victimized.

Martin Luther King, Jr., Is Assassinated (1968)

The event: On April 4, 1968, the Reverend Martin Luther King, Jr., was cut down by an assassin's bullet as he stood on the balcony of his Memphis motel room.

WITHIN ITS FIRST FEW MONTHS, 1968 was already the climax of a crescendo of intense racial unrest and massive protest over the Vietnam War. On April 4, a slow-witted white supremacist named James Earl Ray leveled his rifle at Martin Luther King, Jr., the leader of the civil rights movement since the momentous 1955 Montgomery bus boycott. After he pulled the trigger and ended King's life, 1968 became a year like no other.

The year of unrest had begun on January 31 with the Communist Tet Offensive in Vietnam, a massive and brilliantly coordinated attack on American positions throughout that beleaguered nation. Tet demonstrated

to the world that the Viet Cong could strike at will, and, hard as the offensive was on American troops, it annihilated the optimistic propaganda of American military leaders. One month later, on February 29, Defense Secretary Robert McNamara resigned after concluding the war was unwinnable. That very day Los Angeles blacks rioted, and Watts went up in flames a second time. Two weeks later, on March 12, Senator Eugene McCarthy, an outspoken opponent of the war, came close to defeating President Lyndon Johnson in the New Hampshire primary, prompting Robert Kennedy to declare his candidacy for the Democratic nomination four days later on

March 16. Before the month was over, Johnson stunned America by withdrawing from the race on March 31. Within the week, Martin Luther King was dead.

King had gone to Memphis to rally the city's striking sanitation workers, and the night before his death, he delivered his most stirring speech, one that seemed hauntingly valedictory, as if he somehow knew his end was at hand. "I've been to the mountain-top," he declared, and he had seen the "Promised Land." Although, he warned those to whom he spoke that he might not get there with them, he assured those in his audience that they would live to see an American promised land.

In more than a hundred cities across the country, riots, looting, burning, and death followed the assassination of the apostle of nonviolence, who had been powerfully influenced by the teachings and example of Mahatma Gandhi. King had been the leader of the Southern Christian Leadership Conference, and was the most dramatic and impassioned voice of the civil rights movement, forging links of conscience and understanding between whites and blacks. He had led the March on Washington in 1963 and had stirred the nation with his "I have a dream" speech, and he won the Nobel Peace Prize in 1964. Nevertheless, his leadership of the civil rights movement came under attack by more militant African-Americans, including Malcolm X (who called for

black nationalism) and Stokely Carmichael (who called for Black Power).

By the time of his death, King had grown more radical, joining the struggle for civil rights with the struggle to end the war in Vietnam and planning a massive "Poor People's March," at which some who knew him suspected he intended to call a nation-wide general strike. Yet King never abandoned the course of nonviolence, and he remained a strong symbol of the civil rights movement and the nonviolent approach to it even after his death.

Still, the year of King's assassination seemed to mock the very idea of nonviolence. Idealistic presidential candidate Robert Kennedy, younger brother of the president slain in 1963, was himself assassinated on June 6, immediately after winning the California Democratic primary. In Chicago, from August 26 to 29, the Democratic National Convention was torn by what was universally described as police riots. Throughout the year, as antiwar demonstrations grew larger and more frequent, an increasingly aloof and imperial president conducted the war in isolation and secrecy. All of this, and more to come in succeeding years, made it seem as if Martin Luther King's dream for America had been replaced after his death by a nightmare of senseless violence and social injustice.

Americans Walk on the Moon (1969)

The event: On July 20, 1969, at 4:17 P.M. Eastern Daylight Time, two American astronauts landed on the moon, left their craft soon afterward, and walked where no human being had ever walked before.

For most Americans, among the more galling aspects of the Cold War struggle between the United States and the Soviet Union was the so-called "space race." The Soviets were the first to launch an artificial earth satellite, and they were the first to launch a man into space. President Kennedy's goal, set forth in his 1961 inaugural address, of putting a man on the moon before the end of the decade struck many as resoundingly hollow. Indeed, toward the end of the decade, in 1967, the U.S. space program suffered a terrible blow when a launchpad fire killed three astronauts during a test. Yet the lunar program was pushed forward, and on July 20, with half a year to spare before the decade came to an end, astronauts Neil Armstrong and Edwin ("Buzz") Aldrin became the first human beings to walk on the moon.

The National Aeronautics and Space Administration (NASA) had been created in 1958 and, with the Soviet Sputnik I satellite already in orbit, found itself dead last from the start in a two-nation race. The gap closed somewhat on May 5, 1961, when the United States sent Alan B. Shepard on a fifteen-minute suborbital flight in the first Mercury space capsule. This flight came less than a month after the Soviets launched the first human being into space, Yuri Gagarin, who actually orbited the earth. It would

take another nine months before the United States orbited its first astronaut, John Glenn, who came perilously close to dying in the attempt when the heat shield of his capsule partially failed.

Project Mercury was succeeded by Project Gemini, a series of two-crew member missions that provided NASA with valuable experience that led toward a lunar landing. These Gemini astronauts scored an American first: "extravehicular activities" or "walks" in space. They also practiced and perfected in-space docking procedures, and generally undertook flights that were much longer and more ambitious than the Mercury missions.

After astronauts Armstrong, Aldrin, and Michael Collins (who flew the Apollo spacecraft's "command module," which orbited but did not land on the moon) returned from the lunar mission, NASA sent six more flights to the moon before ending the lunar exploration phase of the Apollo program in December 1972. Thereafter, NASA worked on the development and launching of Skylab, an orbiting space station, in 1973; the Apollo-Soyuz Test Project, a joint American-Soviet endeavor in 1975; and the space shuttle program, which replaced the expendable space capsule with a reusable spacecraft meant to open up the military and commercial potential of space flight.

Whereas the previous space vehicles had been designed to fly one mission only, the *Columbia* shuttle was a reusable vehicle capable of carrying equipment and scientific teams to space and returning to earth by landing on a runway like an airplane, rather than splashing down in the ocean as all earlier spacecraft had done. *Columbia* was first launched on April 12, 1981, and other flights followed. But the shuttle program met with disaster on January 28, 1986, when the *Columbia*'s sister craft, *Challenger*, exploded during takeoff, killing its crew of astronauts and civilian mission specialists. For the next two and a half years NASA modified several design components on the shuttle, and in September 1988 resumed shuttle flights with the launch of *Discovery*.

In addition to manned space flights, NASA has launched numerous unmanned satellites and planetary space probes. Pictures transmitted back to earth from the Explorer satellites and the Ranger, Surveyor, Lunar Orbiter, Mariner, and Voyager probes have provided extremely valuable information about the earth, other planets, the solar system, and the universe. In 1990 NASA launched the Hubble Space Telescope, which promised unprecedented views of the solar system and beyond, although preliminary results called several design elements of the equipment into question, and bungled manufacturing threatened—in the wake of the *Challenger* disaster—to tarnish NASA's image irreparably with an already disenchanted public. With the Cold War at an end, NASA no longer had the rubric of national security behind it to hide its mistakes, its frequent delays in programs and launches, and its often massive cost overruns. In fact, in a period when the defense budget itself—almost sacrosanct for nigh unto four decades—faced spending cuts, rumblings began to be heard about abandoning America's space program entirely.

400,000 Gather for the Woodstock Festival in Upstate New York (1969)

The event: Amid much confusion and apprehension, this three-day outdoor rock-and-roll concert was held over the weekend of August 17, 1969, drawing 400,000 fans to Max Yasgur's dairy farm outside of Bethel, New York. It marked the seminal moment in the identity of a generation of protesters.

TWO YEARS BEFORE WOODSTOCK, the first rock music festival was held at the Monterey County Fairgrounds in northern California. From June 16 to 18, 1967, it drew 7,100 paying fans and an additional 50,000 freeloaders. The festival had been a nonprofit event for charity, and, while fans and backers considered it a great success, public officials complained about the "hippie invasion," which had brought massive drug use and frequent public sex. (To add injury to such insults, the festival's bookkeeper pocketed some of the proceeds.) While Monterey said no to any follow-up festivals, over the next two years they were held at other locations across the country.

As in Monterey, not everyone was pleased. The so-called "Establishment" saw youth as a dangerous power bloc, drug crazed, and tending toward revolution as they formed such groups as the Yippies, the Black Panthers, and the SDS (Students for a Democratic Society). And, yes, there was the sex: lots of it, on the lawn, in the open, under the sun, the moon, and the stars. Many communities rushed restrictive "mass gathering" ordinances through their town councils, but the wave was hard to stop.

Indeed, most of the rock festivals were rather ugly affairs, put on by fly-by-night promoters interested in a fast buck and renting the cheapest sites, supplying inadequate sanitary facilities, substandard sound systems, and a raft of no-show acts, so that if patrons (in the phrase of the era) were bummed out by the whole experience, they simply resorted to even more drugs, more sex, and sometimes varying degrees of violence. It was in this atmosphere that Woodstock came into being.

It was originally planned for a site outside of Walkill, near Woodstock, New York, but just four weeks before the festival was slated to start, the town's zoning board revoked the permits, and promoters were left twisting slowly in the wind. An intensive search turned up a dairy farm near the town of Bethel belonging to Max Yasgur, a farmer looking for some fast cash, and the gig was on. Despite the change in location, the festival was still called Woodstock.

Of the 400,000 or so young people who descended upon the farm, more than 100,000 were gate crashers. It hardly mattered, because the promoters stopped checking tickets after the first several hours. Nor could the town—population 2,763—or county provide police protection. But that hardly mattered, either, because the fans policed themselves, after their fashion, and medical volunteers took care of such emergencies as drug overdoses, hangovers, and bad acid trips. It had all the makings of a disaster: food was scarce, drinking water in critically short supply, and heavy rains had turned the ground into soup. While the acts were the greatest rock musicians ever assembled at any time and place, probably only a minority of the audience could actually hear them. But that hardly mattered: The vibes were good.

Sex and drugs there were, but violence and bad feelings there were not. Following years of bitterness, of rioting, of assassinations, and of the ceaseless, senseless slaughter in Vietnam, Woodstock seemed an embodiment of the peaceful, joyous solidarity of youth. It showed that the world didn't have to be like 1968. Woodstock revealed *another way*.

Or so it seemed. While the hundreds of thousands who were *at* Woodstock, and the millions who *said* they had been at Woodstock, and the millions more who *owned* the *Woodstock* record album or who *saw* the *Woodstock* movie remembered the event as the high point of their lives, Woodstock came and went and was never repeated, even in the self-conscious re-enactment staged on the festival's twenty-fifth anniversary. Long before that, the Woodstock generation and the Rolling Stones tried to recapture the event again at the Altamont Speedway in California, about forty miles southeast of psychedelic San Francisco. There the Stones gave a free concert as part of their 1969 tour, drawing some 300,000 fans. It turned into the anarchic nightmare parents and police had warned everyone about from the beginning. There were the usual food, water, and sanitary deficiencies. There were the drugs and the sex. But there was also an air of viciousness and violence.

The Stones had hired a cadre of Hells Angels bikers to serve as a security force, and when a young black man drew a handgun, the Angels converged on him and subdued him—with knives. He died, along with three others. In fact, there had been injuries and deaths at Woodstock, but they hardly mattered, not in the prevailing atmosphere of love and the romance of communal liberation. Altamont, on the other hand, immediately symbolized the end of the counterculture as a positive force in America.

A New Discovery Makes Organ Transplants Possible (1969)

The event: In 1969, a microbiologist from the Swiss pharmaceutical firm Sandoz, on vacation in southern Norway, dug up a soil sample on an isolated plateau that contained an organic compound no one had ever seen before. Dubbed "cyclosporine" by Sandoz, it proved to be the "miracle drug" that at last made heart transplants practical and successful.

THOUGH SOUTH AFRICAN SURGEON Christiaan Barnard was given credit in the popular press for launching the successful, high-tech practice of transplanting human hearts, the procedure itself was perfected by Stanford University Medical Center's Dr. Norman Shumway and his assistant, Dr. Richard Lower. Experimenting with dogs in a primitive laboratory in Palo Alto to find ways of making open-heart surgery safer, one afternoon in the late 1950s Shumway decided—after he and Lower had removed a dog's heart, placed the animal on a heart-lung bypass machine to keep it alive, and cooled the heart in saline solution—to stick the organ back in the dog, reconnect it, and see what happened. As the heart warmed up, it began to beat again on its own: The dog lived.

By then the concept of transplanting organs and tissues was nothing new. Skin grafting, the simplest kind of tissue transplant, had been practiced for centuries, but it only worked when the skin—like the dog's heart—came from the patient's own body. Clearly, the body built up a resistance to foreign skin, just the way it does to diseases. The body's immune system was rejecting the transplants. Then English biologist Peter Medawar discovered that for a brief period early in a baby's life, when its immune system is not yet fully developed, doctors could perform skin grafts using alien tissues that the baby did not reject. Medawar's work—for which he received a Nobel Prize—emboldened a Boston surgeon named Joseph Murray on December 23, 1954, to remove one of two healthy kidneys from Ronald Herrick and place it in Herrick's twin brother, Richard, who was dying because both his kidneys were failing. Richard's immune system did not recognize Ronald's kidney as a foreign body: Both brothers lived and Boston became the world center for transplanting kidneys between identical twins. These surgeons also began to have some limited success with transplants between people whose blood types closely matched, if they crippled the patients' immune systems with radical techniques, such as total body irradiation. Later, they developed a "cocktail" of drugs—mostly steroids—to suppress a transplant recipient's immunological responses.

Back at Stanford, Shumway reasoned he, too, could develop immunosuppressant regimens like those for kidney transplant patients that would allow him to transplant hearts. For nearly a decade, he and Lower conducted exhaustive laboratory research to perfect the surgical procedure and improve the immunological steroid "cocktails" that in kidney patients so often caused mood swings and even brief periods of psychosis, puffed up their cheeks like balloons, and sometimes destroyed bone tissue. By the time Shumway felt confident enough to announce his plans for transplanting a human heart in the November 1967 *Journal of the American Medical Association*, Lower had left Stanford for the Medical College of Virginia. There a South African doctor named Christaan Barnard, visiting to observe kidney transplants, sat in on one of Lower's canine heart transplants. Shumway, meanwhile, had delayed his operation when the first donor's heart proved unsuit-

able for his patient, and a month later—on December 3, 1967—he picked up his morning paper to read the news from Cape Town.

Staring out at Shumway was Louis Washkansky, a fifty-five-year-old grocer, smiling beside the young, handsome Barnard and sporting a new heart taken from a twenty-three-year-old woman killed in an automobile accident. "I'm the new Frankenstein," Washkansky said.

He died eighteen days later.

But it was too late: The operation had fired the public's imagination like no other breakthrough in the history of medicine. Barnard became a world celebrity overnight, and was invited to lunch by the president of the United States and asked his opinion not merely on every imaginable medical matter but also on unrelated political and social issues as well. Barnard, however, was calling Norman Shumway, desperate to learn as quickly as possible how to diagnose rejection of a transplanted heart.

Soon others rushed to perform the procedure. Within a year, the irrepressible and technically acclaimed "Texas Tornado," Dr. Denton Cooley, had in his Texas fashion transplanted more hearts than any other physician in the world, proclaiming his "exhilaration" at being able to "renovate an old carcass." However, within a year, most of Cooley's transplant patients were dead, as were the vast majority—85 percent—of all those receiving transplants. Only Norman Shumway's results were better and, three years later, he had managed to keep only 40 percent—nine of twenty-three people—of his original transplant patients alive.

Shumway was angry at Barnard for

"stealing" his fame, but he was even angrier at the damage he saw Cooley doing to the long-range potential of the new specialty he had pioneered. The operation, he said, was mechanically very simple. If it had been simply a matter of cutting and sewing, everybody would have survived. The real problems came after the operation, with the care provided the patients and their new hearts. Because the mortality rate was so high, most surgeons abandoned heart transplantation, and teaching hospitals and research centers declared the procedure experimental. Shumway continued to transplant hearts in the face of mounting criticism.

Enter Sandoz. Since the discovery of penicillin, drug companies, always on the lookout for bacteria and microbes that would make good antibiotics, encouraged their employees, even on vacation, to dig among the moss and lichen of the world on the off chance that something might turn up. When the dirt containing cyclosporine showed up at the Sandoz laboratory, tests soon proved it was not much of an antibiotic, and the company lost interest. But a Sandoz scientist named Jean-Francois Borel, a Wisconsin Ph.D. who had specialized in immunogenetics, began playing around with the small sample and became intrigued when he discovered that cyclosporine had tremendous power to suppress the immune systems of animals; not only that, but unlike steroids, it did not kill just any immune cell, but wiped out specifically the T lymphocytes, the killer cells a body sends out to destroy foreign bodies that invade it.

Borel immediately realized the implication cyclosporine held for transplants. The trouble was, he could not persuade Sandoz of its potential, and what the little bit he had was every ounce of the substance known to exist in the world. He tried, without success, to interest European doctors in the drug's peculiar properties. Desperate, he gave all he could spare to a few British clinicians, and they managed to achieve encouraging results with the small sample in animal experiments. Borel advertised those results as widely as he could, creating enough of a stir in the medical profession to get Sandoz to commit tentatively to a limited production. After a few false starts, he got a usable version of the compound into the hands of Dr. Tom Starzl—who had pioneered liver transplantation at the University of Colorado—and Norman Shumway for experimental use. They combined cyclosporine with steroids and other drugs and began to achieve amazing results.

By 1983, the Food and Drug Administration approved the use of cyclosporine, combined with steroids, for all transplant patients. By 1989, the number of heart transplants had increased some twenty times; transplant centers were springing up everywhere; organ-procurement organizations were organized; appeals for donors became commonplace in the media; modern science had worked another miracle; and heart transplant surgery had become the pinnacle of the medical profession.

Sony Introduces the Betamax (1969)

The event: In 1969, the Sony Corporation—one of Japan's leading electronics manufacturers—developed and marketed a color videocassette recorder for industrial and home use that transformed not only the entertainment industry, but daily life as well.

LIKE RADIO BEFORE IT, television did much to change—and shrink—the world, as media guru Marshal McLuhan asserted in the 1960s, into a "global village" of shared images, ideas, and experiences. The television McLuhan knew was, from the point of view of the audience, a passive medium. Programming was created and broadcast by large corporate networks, which scheduled each day's programming, often thereby scheduling the lives of millions of habitual viewers.

Videotape technology was under development in the 1950s, but broadcast-quality videotape was not generally available until the early 1960s, and the equipment was large and very costly, requiring special studio facilities and trained technicians to operate it. Japan's Sony corporation was in the forefront of developing a small videotape unit, within the means of businesses and families and operable by nonprofessionals. In 1969, the company introduced the Betamax, carrying a price tag in the low five figures. Over the next few years, Matsushita Corporation introduced its own videocassette recorder in the VHS (as opposed to Beta) format, and, soon many other manufacturers were turning out machines as well. As production increased, prices declined each year, until, by the 1990s, VCRs were available starting at about $200, and most families who owned television sets owned at least one VCR.

Having a VCR meant that viewers could regulate their own entertainment schedules, setting the machine's automatic timer to record programs off the air for playback at will. Or they could rent or purchase prerecorded entertainment at the neighborhood video store, seeing movies soon after their theatrical release or viewing time-honored classics that were not always readily available on commercial broadcast television. Significant as this measure of autonomy was, even more profound in its implications was the availability of small video cameras with portable VCR units and later even more portable camcorders, in which the video camera and VCR were integrated into a single compact unit. Camcorders suddenly transformed the television from a receiver of mass-media images produced by vast corporations to an instrument capable of reproducing family memories—home movies—and even personal creative endeavors.

As the century came to a close, the impact of the camcorder as an instant witness to history was increasingly evident. Although television was preeminently a visual medium, standard network news—despite the constant criticism by the politicians upon whom it spent so much of its coverage—had never been very effective at capturing unplanned events, especially those like police brutality, political coups, and state-sponsored repressions commonly hidden from the light of public scrutiny. Traditionally, only when an event, or, more often, its consequences, had forced the networks to suspend the normal time and content controls—exercised over tightly produced and artificially compressed "segments" of their nightly news programs—had they had historical impact. Some examples are television coverage of wars, riots, politically charged public hearings, or even terrorist actions staged for the camera.

Television did not, for instance, uncover the Watergate scandal, whose clandestine operations and secret White House plottings took place out of the range of the network's huge and cumbersome news-gathering apparatus. But when diligent and dogged work of individual reporters forced the scandal into the public arena, television was quite effective in bringing the extremely complicated story of the coverup before the American people simply by giving over its time to the Watergate hearings. Similarly, John Kennedy's assassination was an event powerful enough to disrupt network scheduling, with the unexpected result that the world saw Jack Ruby murder Lee Harvey Oswald on live television, probably the medium's single most unforgettable moment of raw news coverage.

But, as the amateur videotapes of the March 3, 1991, Los Angeles police beating of motorist Rodney King demonstrated, camcorders threatened to make such moments as the Oswald killing less a fluke of timing. The advent of cable television as well as the proliferation of video equipment among the citizenry had changed the rules, and "real-life" coverage of significant events, once beyond the reach of cameras, had become increasingly common. Just as cable ripped control of prime-time programming from greedy network hands, widespread video-recording equipment challenged network supremacy over the "news," undermining the network's ability to satisfy the public with slickly produced prepackaged snapshots that fit neatly between commercial messages. Law enforcement agencies were among the first to recognize the potential of videorecorders, and in the last decades of the twentieth century, viewers were treated to such sights and sounds as United States Senators accepting bribes, a major automobile industrialist trafficking in cocaine, and the mayor of Washington, D.C. smoking crack.

The networks responded with "reality-based" programs (during which, for example, camera crews followed police on raids) and with ever more coverage of the kinds of events and private stories that had once been the province of sleazy tabloid journalism, raising in the process questions about what was coverage and what was creation of the news. A fascination with the weird and the horrifying seemed to be the result, and television talk shows and tabloid-format electronic "magazines" proliferated, constantly eroding individual privacy.

If television had recreated the world as a global village, the evolution of video technology had given that village its insatiable appetite for apparently infallible electronic gossip, an appetite as corrosive to the media—and to American life—as widespread video equipment was liberating.

The U.S. Department of Defense Launches the Internet (1969)

The event: In 1969, the U.S. Department of Defense established the Advanced Research Projects Agency Network (ARPANET) to provide a secure communications network that could survive an outside attack for organizations engaged in defense-related research, the seed from which grew the so-called information superhighway's Internet.

SOON AFTER THE Department of Defense set up ARPANET for those who had contracted to do defense-related research, researchers and academics in other fields began to make use of the computerized network, which had a common addressing system and communications protocol called Transmission Control Protocol/Internet Protocol (TCP/IP). Around the same time, the National Science Foundation (NSF) had created a similar and parallel network called NSFNet, and it made sense to combine the two. At length NSF took over much of the TCP/IP technology from ARPANET and established a widely distributed network capable of handling far greater traffic. NSF called this network the "Internet," and from its creation in 1983 the Internet grew rapidly beyond its primarily academic origins into an increasingly commercial and very popular medium.

By 1995, the Internet connected more than two million computers in more than one hundred countries. It served somewhere in the neighborhood of 25 million users, with no end in sight to the number who wished to log on and travel what U.S. Vice President Al Gore first called the "information highway." Many commercial computer networks and data services, such as Compuserve, America Online, et. al., also provided at least indirect connection to the Internet. Everyday users logged on to send electronic mail, which in the jargon-filled world of computers they called "e-mail," to transfer files using a file transfer protocol label (ftp), to hook up with other users for long-winded gossip sessions or for trading information of every ilk on the ubiquitous computer "bulletin boards" and/or "newsgroups," and to gain access to remote computers. Businesses as well as individuals found the Internet a good marketplace for their wares, such as books, magazines, and video and audio broadcasts. Executives found video-conferencing on the Internet a cool means to while away a morning. Services were delivered to the Internet through a bewildering number of media—amateur radio, cable television wires, spread spectrum radio, satellite, fiber optics, you name it. Networked games, networked money transactions, virtual museums—all were quickly developed for the Internet by entrepreneurs imagining unlimited profits from a wild collection of new customers unreachable in any other way. Promises of ever more integration through an ever-growing number of home computers boggled the minds of people the world over, as users both serious and fun-loving invented ever new ways to extend the network's utility and test the limit of its technology.

At the same time, members of the U.S. Congress heard rumors that some people were using adult language on the Internet, and, not understanding the technology, immediately began debating legislation calling for the monitoring and censoring of Internet communications, criminalizing the use of dirty words on the information highway, and tracking down child molesters who found their prey on-line, all of which, given the very nature of the medium, is practically impossible, not to mention wrongheaded and probably unconstitutional.

NSF continued to maintain the backbone of the network, but the development of the Internet protocol was taken over and governed by the Internet Architecture Board, and the Internet Network Information Center (InterNIC) administered the naming of computers and networks.

It is clear that the Internet augurs much for the future, though just what it augurs is pretty vague at times. And, like much of modern-day technology, the Internet owes its very existence to government investment, particularly Defense Department spending. Both the information highway and the Interstate Highway system began with a concern for national defense against an attack that never came from a government that no longer exists, for reasons that never made much sense in the first place.

Chemists Create a Synthetic Gene (1970)

The event: In 1970, a team led by Indian-born American chemist Har Gobind Khorana put a gene-like molecule together from scratch, forever changing the nature of life and non-life.

HAR GOBIND KHORANA shared a Nobel Prize in 1968 for his work in elucidating the "genetic code," that is, explaining just how genetic information—the very keys to life—are passed from DNA to proteins. Born in poverty, Khorana attended Punjab University at Lahore, India, and the University of Liverpool, England, on government scholarships, obtaining his Ph.D. from Liverpool in 1948. He first began working with nucleic acid in 1951 at Cambridge under Sir Alex Todd, and by early the 1960s had synthesized small nucleic acid molecules whose exact structure he did not recognize. Nucleic acids carry the genetic information in the cell and, when combined with the proper materials, Khorana could get his synthetic nucleic acids to synthesize proteins, just as a cell does. Actually, he was heading a research team that, in 1970, created a gene-like molecule using nucleotide proteins. By comparing his synthesized proteins with his nucleic acid molecules, he was able to determine which portions of the nucleic acids contained the "code" for each part of the protein.

In effect, Khorana and his colleagues had synthesized a gene—the basis of life— and, in 1976, they took the process a giant leap further by introducing an artificially created gene into a living cell. Within the cell, the gene functioned perfectly. To fellow scientists, Khorana's work was nothing more or less than practical proof of what had already been surmised in theory about the structure and operation of genes. To many laypersons, however, the creation of what amounted to an artificial animal gene was either nothing short of a miracle, holding immense promise for a better life in the future, or a kind of blasphemy, a usurpation of something divine, presaging Frankenstein-like experiments in genetic engineering and control.

However one interpreted the event, it was clear that the borders separating life from non-life—and the human-made from the natural realm—were, in fact, no longer clear at all.

The United States and the Soviet Union Establish "Détente" (1972)

The event: On May 22, 1972, Richard M. Nixon became the first U.S. president to visit Moscow. There he proposed to the secretary-general of the Communist party, Leonid I. Brezhnev, a policy of détente, to which Brezhnev at length agreed, creating a period of relaxed hostilities in the ongoing Cold War.

DÉTENTE, the French word for a release of tension, entered the American vocabulary beginning in 1971 and was heard frequently in the spring of 1972. With some justification, cynics said that President Nixon's trip to Moscow, like his earlier trip to China, was an election-year political tactic to deflect criticism of his conservative domestic policies and his continuation of the war in Vietnam. Whatever his motivation, the results of the meetings with Brezhnev were historic and profound: Seven agreements were signed, among them the prevention of accidental nuclear attack; arms control, pursuant to recent Strategic Arms Limitation Talks (SALT); unprecedented cooperation in scientific research, particularly in space exploration; and expanded trade. When Brezhnev returned Nixon's visit in June of 1973, coming to the United States for Summit II, the symbolism was unmistakable. The Soviet Union, menaced now by China, with whom relations had gone increasingly sour, was in no mood for flogging the old, familiar ideological differences separating Communism from capitalism.

Unfortunately, the millennium that seemed at hand did not come to pass. Relations at Summit III, held in June 1974, were cool to chilly, and the ongoing SALT talks came to a grinding halt. In the meantime, Congress blocked several of the commercial agreements concluded with the USSR because of human rights violations against Soviet Jews, and President Nixon, beleaguered by the Watergate scandal, had neither the attention span nor the energy to fight for the preservation of détente.

President Jimmy Carter tried to pick up

the pieces with SALT II, but Brezhnev balked at the depth of missile cutbacks demanded, even while Carter pressed forward with a military buildup and a morally superior human rights campaign. Cooling U.S.-Soviet relations were plunged into the deep freeze by Carter's successor, Ronald Reagan, who adopted a bellicose military stance and referred to the Soviet Union as the "evil empire."

Terrorists Strike at the Munich Olympics Village (1972)

The event: On September 5, 1972, Palestinian terrorists belonging to the "Black September" group infiltrated the Israeli dormitory at the Munich Olympic Village, killing two Israeli athletes and taking nine others hostage. A botched rescue attempt ended in a shootout that killed five of the eight terrorists and the nine hostages.

IT WAS IN THE SHADOW of nuclear Armageddon—where the state seemed to hold a monopoly on organized violence and possessed unlimited resources for repression and where a few nuclear powers arrogantly divided the world into ideological camps—that existentialist author Albert Camus argued in *The Rebel* and elsewhere for the authenticity of the terrorist, for the individual so engaged in a cause that he or she was willing to take responsibility for specific violence, even at the cost of his or her own life. The all-pervasive and ever-growing influence of the mass media in the twentieth century, with its immense potential for political propaganda and its commercial cousin, advertising, also held the potential to make terrorist acts quite effective. Hence the twentieth century saw the rise of the cult of personality in the era's great tyrannies and the cult of celebrity in its great consumer societies, and it also witnessed conflicts waged for the television camera and terrorist acts staged to attract a wide audience. The modern terrorist took Andy Warhol at his word, and in the fifteen minutes of fame garnered by this explosion or that assassination hoped to rivet the attention of the world on a problem it was ignoring. The message of all terrorism was that it was dangerous not to pay attention; the hope of all terrorists was that, in paying attention, the world would do something about it.

The Arab-Israeli conflict of 1948 was typical of much warfare in the latter half of the century. It hardly resolved the question of Israeli-Palestinian coexistence in the Middle East, and the result was not only a series of outright wars, but a long and sporadic train of terrorist actions that came to seem the hallmarks of the 1960s and 1970s. In the aftermath of the Six Day War, the world's attention had indeed been fixed on Israel and its struggle for survival among hostile neighbors who refused to even recognize its existence. A kind of admiration, often grudging, had grown up for Israel's military prowess, and certainly the United States seemed enthralled with its feisty ally. Palestinian Arabs, who believed that the Jews had stolen their "homeland" from a country that by rights belonged to those now suffering an Israeli occupation, also felt that other countries either did not understand the situation or chose to ignore the oppression of Palestinians in the occupied territories. That led the Palestinians to the decision to export some of the terrorism practiced by both sides that had plagued the region since the 1920s—to the Olympic Games.

In the tense years following World War II, the Olympic Games emerged as a symbol of international friendship, cooperation, mutual respect, and coexistence. The summer Olympics of 1972, held in Munich, West Germany, were especially intended to be marked by friendship and openness. The presence of Israeli athletes on German soil was in and of itself a healing gesture. In this spirit, security was minimal, and even the dormitory buildings were unlocked. Yet the event that would shock the world began an hour before dawn on September 5, 1972. Eight members of Black September, an extremist cadre of Yasir Arafat and Abu Jihad's Palestine National Liberation Movement, or al-Fatah, scaled a six-foot, six-inch fence surrounding the Israeli compound in the Olympic Village. The Black Septemberists crossed the sixty yards from the fence to Building 31 on Connollystrasse, climbed to the second floor, and knocked on the door that led to the Israelis' rooms.

Two Israelis were killed in the initial assault, but they managed to warn their countrymen and others in the building, many of whom managed to flee. But nine were taken hostage, herded onto a couch, their hands tied behind them, and bound together by ropes around the waist. Initially, the Black Septemberists demanded the release of two hundred Palestinian guerrillas imprisoned in Israel and safe passage for themselves back into the Arab world. A noon deadline was set, at which time, the terrorists announced, they would begin executing their hostages, one by one.

Traditional terrorism was enacted in seclusion and secrecy, with the terrorists content to let the acts speak for themselves as they were reported afterward. By Munich, however, even the darkest acts were televised worldwide, as people sat down nightly to watch men killed in rice paddies halfway around the world. The terrorists, seduced by the power of the medium, decided to act on camera, using masks and disguises to maintain their anonymity, and so the world shared the experience of seeing the tragedy unfold. The Israeli government refused to meet the Palestinians' demands, but German officials offered "unlimited" ransom, some even proposed themselves as stand-ins for the captive Israelis. But it was to no avail. A new deadline was set, and German antiterrorist units took up positions to lay siege to Building 31.

Bizarrely, some of the games went on—the Olympic Committee decided to suspend competition, except for events in progress. Russia and Poland played volleyball not a hundred yards from Building 31. With the hostages bound together, there was no way to storm the building without touching off a mass execution. Therefore, after about nineteen hours of waiting and watching, German authorities allowed the terrorists and their captives to board a bus for a short ride to three helicopters waiting to take them to the airport and a Lufthansa 727, which they had demanded. The plan was for sharpshooters to ambush them at the airport.

But the plan went awry. To begin with, the German authorities believed there were at most five, not eight, terrorists, and so they had only five sharpshooters positioned. For five snipers to hit all eight targets would have taken nothing less than a miracle. Worse yet, the snipers opened fire when only four of the eight terrorists were visible—which meant that four gunmen were still with the hostages. Two of the terrorists had been killed by the snipers and one

wounded. What followed was a tense hour of silence and inaction, ended by bursts of gunfire. The Black Septemberists had executed all of the hostages. The German police killed another three terrorists and captured the remaining three. One German police officer was also slain.

It did not take long for Israel to retaliate, launching Phantom and Mirage jet fighter attacks against guerrilla bases and naval installations in Lebanon and Syria, and the cycle of violence continued in a time when war knew no fronts, made no distinction among soldiers and civilians, and recognized no one as innocent.

American Psychologists Declare That Homosexuality Is Not a Disease (1973)

The event: In 1973, the American Psychological Association's committee on nomenclature voted to remove homosexuality from its diagnostic manual of psychological disorders and diseases.

BEFORE THE END of the nineteenth century, the idea of "homosexual rights" would have been met in most quarters not so much with revulsion or outrage as with utter incomprehension. In 1897, a homosexual Scientific-Humanitarian Committee was founded in Berlin, which sponsored rallies and campaigned for legal reforms on behalf of homosexuals throughout Germany, Austria, and the Netherlands. Committee founder Magnus Hirschfeld was a sponsor of the World League of Sexual Reform, which held congresses from 1921 to 1935, when Adolf Hitler's regime ended the movement.

Throughout the twentieth century,

other homosexual advocacy movements, organizations, and forums were established, but the organized movement did not reach the United States until Henry Hay founded the Mattachine Society in 1950 in Los Angeles. Nevertheless, for the heterosexual majority—and, doubtless, for most homosexuals as well—the idea of homosexuals as a minority entitled to the same democratic rights as any other minority did not begin to take shape until the era of intense civil rights activism during the 1960s. Indeed, most social historians date the birth of the homosexual rights movement very specifically: About three o'clock on the morning of June 28, 1969, when New York City police officers raided a gay bar, the Stonewall Inn, at 53 Christopher Street in Greenwich Village. Such raids were nothing new. But, in the past, bar patrons would have accepted the situation—and whatever abuse was doled out—passively. On this occasion, some two hundred homosexuals fought back, taunting police officers and igniting a forty-five-minute riot that resumed on succeeding nights before developing into a series of more organized protest rallies. From that point forward, homosexual rights organizations proliferated, succeeding in gaining the repeal of many laws against homosexuality and in securing civil rights protection for homosexuals. In many states, homosexual domestic partnerships have been legally recognized and put on the same footing as conventional marriages.

An important gain in the battle for full recognition of rights was the removal of the stigma of disease. Officially, the battle was won when the APA committee on nomenclature removed homosexuality from its manual of diseases and disorders. At last, psychologists seemed willing to admit publicly what most homosexuals had always known about themselves, that they were normal people who worried about jobs, money, mortgages, and being liked by those they met; people who read books, went to movies, and cursed politicians. The true differences lay with what others saw when they looked at an avowed homosexual, not what he or she saw in the mirror.

The U.S. Supreme Court Rules that Women Have a Right to Abortion (1973)

The event: In the case of *Roe v. Wade*, the United States Supreme Court ruled that a woman's constitutional right to privacy includes the right to abort a fetus during the first trimester of pregnancy, a controversial decision the implications of which have yet to be fully accepted.

IN ONE OF ITS MOST controversial decisions, the Supreme Court determined that the right to privacy, guaranteed by the Constitution, extends to a woman's right to abort the fetus she carries. The high court also ruled that this right applies only during the first three months of pregnancy, beyond which the fetus must be considered "viable"—able to live outside of the womb—and the state, therefore, has the responsibility of protecting it.

The case was first filed by Norma McCorvey, who sued the state of Texas for denying her the right to an abortion. When the case reached the Supreme Court, few people expected the justices to overturn Texas law, especially since the court had become increasingly conservative with the appointments by President Richard Nixon of Chief Justice Warren Burger and Justices Harry Blackmun, Lewis Powell, and William Rehnquist; and the retirement of liberal Chief Justice Earl Warren and the deaths of Hugo Black and John Marshall Harlan II, both judicial liberals. Yet the court overturned Texas, with Justice Blackmun writing the majority opinion, which extended the "right to privacy" implied by the First and Ninth Amendments. Dissenting from the majority ruling were Justices Rehnquist and Byron White.

The ruling barred the states from prohibiting abortion in the first trimester, and it gave rise to opposing movements, one to preserve women's right to have abortions ("pro-choice") and the other to limit or deny that right ("right-to-life"). Beginning in the early 1980s, the right-to-life movement called for a constitutional amendment to ban abortions except in cases of rape, incest, or threat to the mother's life. Right-to-life actions have included everything from lobbying, to picketing abortion clinics, to threatening and even murdering physicians who perform abortions. Pro-choice actions supported pro-choice political candidates, staged demonstrations, arranged escort protection for women entering and leaving abortion clinics, and filed lawsuits against right-to-life groups when necessary.

Roe v. Wade was challenged in 1976 by the Hyde Amendment, which prohibited federal funding for abortions, and in 1989 by *Webster v. Reproductive Health Services*. In ruling on the latter, the Supreme Court upheld its fundamental decision in *Roe v. Wade*, but urged the states to seek new solutions to the problems engendered by abortion policy.

Abortion is hardly new to the twentieth century. Under colonial and early American law, for example, abortion was legal, provided that it was carried out before movements of the fetus could be felt—generally about midway through pregnancy. By the 1830s, abortion was widespread as a method of birth control; newspapers and magazines carried advertisements for abortionists, and women freely discussed the topic with their doctors. By the 1860s, doctors estimated that women had abortions at the rate of one for every four live births. But at that time, however, the newly created American Medical Association began a campaign to outlaw abortions, except when deemed necessary by physicians themselves. A wave of legislative reform followed, most of it wrapped up with regulations concerning the licensing and qualifications of medical practitioners. These new laws sent abortionists underground, but substantial numbers of women continued to have abortions throughout the nineteenth century and into the twentieth.

What did come about in this century was a movement to repeal state laws banning abortions. The drive began in the 1950s, not in the context of preserving a woman's choice, but out of a professed concern over the postwar "population explosion." Supporters of the movement included a more powerful women's constituency; individuals fighting against the inequality that existed between wealthy women, who could afford safe abortions, and poor women, who could not; and physicians themselves, 87 percent of whom favored liberalized abortion laws in 1967. Opposed to such liberalization were the Roman Catholic Church and various fundamentalist and evangelical Protestant groups.

The Supreme Court's *Roe v. Wade* ruling meant that all states were directed to lift their bans on abortion, though many resisted doing so, seeking to find a legal formula to avoid the court's clear intent. As an alternative, opponents of abortion began actively to seek nominees to the court who would overturn the decision, and a potential justice's opinion about abortion fast became a litmus test for the U.S. Senate in giving its consent to a nomination. By late in the century, even an otherwise perfectly well-qualified candidate for the federal post of Surgeon General, Dr. Henry Foster, found his nomination blocked essentially because he had, as an obstetrician, performed abortions.

Roe v. Wade, important a decision as it was on its own merits, also raised issues about the American judicial system and the federal government and its role in the most private affairs of its citizens. The debate over abortions seemed quite naturally to lead to questions concerning the degree to which the government could legislate the most private and fundamental issues of life and death, including the questions of when life begins and when it ends, questions often challenged by scientific, technical, and medical advances, and continually debated by scientists, moralists, and theologians. Little wonder they were questions that also proved to be political dynamite.

Chile's President Salvador Allende Dies in a Military Coup (1973)

The event: On September 11, 1973, in the midst of a United States-backed coup staged by the Chilean military, Marxist President Salavador Allende shot himself in the presidential palace, bringing to a close a brief and precarious revolution in many ways typical of the volatile nature of South American politics in the twentieth century.

FOR MOST OF THE twentieth century, the incredibly diverse and culturally rich South American continent lived in the shadow of its powerful and jealous neighbor to the North. Occasionally, as with the rise to power in Argentina of the populist demagogue Juan Peron or the coming to office of Salvador Allende in Chile, South America seemed poised to break free of U.S. influence. But, more often than not, the mask of good neighbor promoted by North American presidents slipped to reveal a nation bent on maintaining its hegemony over the Western hemisphere.

Allende, a scion of Chile's upper middle class who held a medical degree from the University of Chile, was one of the founders of Chile's Socialist Party. Elected to the chamber of deputies in 1937, he served in the left-leaning coalition of President Pedro Aguirre Cerda in the late 1930s and 1940s before running for the Senate in 1945. During his four successive terms as a Chilean senator, Allende would enter the presidential race twice before finally becoming Chile's chief executive on November 3, 1970. Though Allende was never as openly anti-United States as Argentina's Juan

Peron, he also did not turn his back on the left once he gained power as Peron did. An avowed Marxist, Allende immediately began to restructure Chilean society along socialist lines, while retaining the democratic form of government and respecting civil liberties and the due process of law. As different as one can imagine from the dictatorial strongmen Washington seemed to favor throughout Latin America, Allende expropriated without hesitation or compensation the U.S.-owned copper companies in Chile, which put him at odds with the hemisphere's major power and shook foreign investors' confidence in his government.

Still, determined to be independent of U.S. influence, Allende established diplomatic relations with Cuba and China, both arch-foes of the United States. Chile's leader began purchasing privately owned businesses in the mining and manufacturing sector, took over large agricultural estates and turned them into peasant cooperatives, authorized huge wage increases, and froze prices, all in an attempt to redistribute the wealth of the country before he ran out of time. He paid for his structural changes by printing copious amounts of unsupported currency to cover the huge deficits run up in his purchase of basic industries. The results

were stagnant production, a fall-off in exports, a loss of private-sector investment, exhausted financial reserves, widespread strikes, rising inflation, food shortages, domestic unrest, and foreign intrigue. The United States made sure that Chile was cut off from international lines of credit, and Allende's own inability to control his radical left-wing supporters ensured that he incurred the hostility of the Chilean middle-class from which he had sprung.

Through it all, Allende retained the support of most workers and peasants, and his electorial coalition won 44 percent of the vote in the March 1973 congressional elections. It was all too much for the United States-trained and CIA-backed Chilean generals, who staged a coup on September 11, 1973. Though Allende shot himself during the military's concerted attack on the presidential palace, Chile never publicly acknowledged his suicide, which was not confirmed until his body was exhumed from an unmarked grave in 1990 and given a formal and public burial. Meanwhile, Allende, along with other martyrs to the cause such as Che Guevara, had become a hero of the Latin American left and an object lesson in the dangers of standing up to *El Norte* for South American political leaders.

OPEC Embargoes Oil to the West (1973)

The event: On October 17, 1973, the Organization of Petroleum Exporting Countries (OPEC) declared an embargo on oil exports to nations that had supported Israel in its war with Egypt.

FOR AMERICANS, the automobile has long embodied personal freedom: the ability to get up and go without asking permission

or giving the matter much thought. But Americans have learned that, like just about every other freedom they enjoy, this one comes with a price, including roads that usurp the beauty of a landscape, internal combustion processes that pollute the air, and accidents that take more lives than most diseases. In 1973, they learned that the pursuit of freedom had bound their nation to the economic and political whim of a group of nations distant from America both geographically and culturally.

Between 1950 and 1974, American oil consumption doubled. With 6 percent of the world's population, the United States consumed one-third of the world's energy—precisely why the OPEC oil embargo hit Americans hard. Gasoline prices, which had been (on average) 38.5 cents a gallon in May 1973, shot up to 55.1 cents in June 1974. Americans immediately cut their consumption of petroleum products by about 7 percent, but shortages and gas station lines that stretched down the street and around the block were commonplace for several months. Motorists weren't the only ones affected. In some cases, factories requiring large quantities of fuel oil had to curtail operations, and that meant layoffs or reduced hours for thousands of workers.

The short-term effects of the OPEC oil crisis were severe, but the long-term consequences, still felt today, have most affected American life. For the first time since the Great Depression, average Americans had a taste of what it was like to do without. They learned that, at the threshold of the last quarter of the twentieth century, the United States—and, indeed, the world—faced an "energy crisis," an object lesson on energy as a finite resource. The realization may, in fact, have been a healthy one, especially for the environment of the planet. But the OPEC embargo produced another, more dangerous result. Since 1973–1974, the United States has regarded any threat to its supply of oil as a threat to national security. The policy has figured in repeated brushes with armed conflict—and, in the case of Saddam Hussein's Iraq, one full-fledged war—involving oil-producing nations of the volatile Middle East.

Muhammad Ali Regains the World Heavyweight Title (1974)

The event: Muhammad Ali knocked out the formidable George Foreman in the eighth round of the "Thriller in Manila" on October 30, 1974, regaining for Ali the undisputed heavyweight title, which he had lost not to another fighter but to the boxing commission, when as a Black Muslim he refused to submit to the draft for service in the armed forces.

SINCE JULY 4, 1910, when Jack Johnson, the first black heavyweight champion, beat Jim Jeffries—the "Great White Hope"—in fifteen rounds fought in Reno, Nevada, boxing has been one avenue in which African-Americans have sought, literally, to fight their way to the top. Cassius Marcellus Clay, Jr., born on January 17, 1942, in Louisville, Kentucky, was no exception. He first attracted attention as an amateur, when he won the Golden Gloves and the Olympic Games light heavyweight championships in 1960. He became world heavyweight champion for the first time on February 25, 1964, when he knocked out Sonny Liston, and between 1965 and 1967 he successfully defended his title nine times. In 1967 he gained universal recognition as champion after beating World Boxing Association champ Ernie Terrell on February 6, 1967.

Clay was a defiantly colorful figure, handsome, fast, and graceful in the ring, and given to the spontaneous composition of doggerel outside the ring. "Float like a butterfly, sting like a bee," he said, boasting: "I am *the* greatest!" Clay's white fans enjoyed such brilliant flashes of personality, but many were outraged when he joined the Nation of Islam (Black Muslims), adopting the name Muhammad Ali, then refused to submit to induction into the armed services on religious grounds in 1967. Convicted of violating the Selective Service Act, Ali was stripped of his title and reviled as both a draft dodger and an arrogant black militant.

In 1970, Ali resumed boxing, defeating two title contenders, but losing a fifteen-round decision to heavyweight champion Joe Frazier on March 8, 1971. In that year, however, the Supreme Court overturned Ali's conviction, and, for the next three years, he took on all title contenders, finally winning a decision over Frazier on January 28, 1974. This brought him up against George Foreman on October 30, 1974, whom he knocked out in the eighth round, once again becoming the undisputed world heavyweight champion.

Ali defended his title successfully six times before losing to Leon Spinks on February 15, 1978, but he regained the WBA title in another meeting with Spinks seven months later, becoming the only boxer in history to win the world heavyweight championship three times.

Muhammad Ali fought two more major bouts, with Larry Holmes in 1980 and Trevor Berbick in 1981, losing both. It was revealed in 1984 that Ali was suffering from chronic encephalopathy of boxers—the "punch drunk" syndrome—and he retired, perhaps the single best-known sports figure in the world and one who had earned universal respect.

Richard Nixon Resigns as President of the United States (1974)

The event: The nation and the world were stunned on August 8, 1974, when Richard M. Nixon made a televised announcement that he would resign as president of the United States on the following day.

THE EVENT THAT CAUSED the scandal forcing Nixon to resign occurred on June 17, 1972, when a security guard summoned police to a burglary in progress at Washington, D.C.'s Watergate apartment and office complex. The five "burglars" they arrested had broken into the Democratic National Committee's headquarters, located in the Watergate, and were found to be employees of the Committee to Re-elect the President (better known by its remarkable acronym, CREEP). The five men were attempting to "bug" the telephones of democratic leaders and obtain political documents outlining the democratic campaign strategy. They were all members of the "Plumbers," a covert unit the Nixon White House had organized to plug "leaks" after the publication of the Pentagon Papers had demonstrated just how embarrassing a leak could be. The Plumbers included anti-Castro Cuban refugees (veterans of the ill-fated Bay of Pigs invasion), former FBI agents, and a former CIA agent who had helped plan the Bay of Pigs. One of the former FBI men, G. Gordon Liddy (a rabid rightwinger with a penchant for quoting untranslated Nietzsche) and the former CIA man, E. Howard Hunt (a "spook" who wrote second-rate spy novels in his spare time) were in charge of the group. Liddy was the "counsel" for CREEP, and both men had been previously on the White House payroll.

The Democrats failed to stir up enough interest in the Watergate burglary to derail the Nixon reelection campaign, but, shortly after Nixon began his second term, more details of the scandal appeared in the *Washington Post*. The press coverage led the Senate to form a select committee to investigate the incident, to be shown in special televised hearings. Not since the Army-McCarthy hearings had been televised in the early 1950s had Americans been so shocked by

the conduct of their government. It was evident to the millions who watched the hearings that not only had Nixon, his aides, and his reelection committee conspired to sabotage the Democratic challenger's campaign, but that the White House was deliberately blocking the Watergate investigation itself, a criminal offense known as obstruction of justice.

Nixon bowed to public pressure in May 1973 and appointed a special prosecutor to investigate the case. Distinguished Harvard professor Archibald Cox, working with a federal grand jury presided over by Judge John Sirica, subpoenaed secret tapes of presidential meetings and phone conversations. Nixon refused to produce the tapes, citing national security as his reason and invoking the doctrine of executive privilege as his authority. Cox persisted, and in October 1973 the president directed Attorney General Elliott Richardson to fire Cox. In response, Richardson resigned rather than carry out the order, and his second-in-command did likewise. Nixon found a Justice Department staffer who would obey his orders, but public indignation forced Nixon immediately to appoint a new prosecutor, Leon Jaworski, who simply renewed the legal battle for the tapes.

By July of the following year, Jaworski's grand jury named Nixon as an unindicted coconspirator in the obstruction of justice for having attempted to block the Watergate investigation. The House Judiciary Committee adopted three articles of impeachment on similar charges. The Supreme Court rejected Nixon's claim of executive privilege, and Judge Sirica once again ordered that the tapes be produced. Nixon, so consumed by the case that he had virtually ceased functioning as president, released eight transcripts of the tapes, portions of which had apparently been intentionally erased. Yet there was enough to demonstrate that Nixon had been lying; that he knew about the cover-up, and he knowingly broke the law.

Rather than face an impeachment trial, Nixon resigned on August 9, 1974, the first U.S. president ever to do so. He was, however, pardoned the following month by his successor, Gerald Ford, for all offenses he had—or might have—committed during his presidency. Nevertheless, all of the Watergate conspirators, save Nixon, were convicted, and all of them, save Nixon, went to jail.

Nixon's political life was finished, yet he remained visible as a public figure and, through the succeeding decades, greatly rehabilitated his image; after all, it had been Nixon, once an ardent "Cold Warrior," who opened up the avenues of diplomatic communication and détente with the Soviet Union and Communist China. Yet Watergate revealed to the nation a president who held himself above the law and the Constitution he had sworn to protect and defend. He had refused to obey the legal rulings of the legitimate branches of government, including his own Justice Department. Nixon and his later supporters often expressed amazement at the intensity of the reaction against Nixon and the grave consequences of Watergate. What they failed to appreciate is that the Watergate break-in and even Nixon's desperate obstruction of justice were only moments in a pattern of domestic spying, of misuse of campaign funds and government agencies, and of abuse of power, all of which Richard M. Nixon cloaked under a blanket of "national security." If the consequences the president suffered were grave, so were the injuries done to the government: a corruption of the legitimate electoral process, an attempt to usurp unconstitutional power for the presidency, and a concerted effort to undermine the American legal system itself. Finally, there was the damage done to the office of the presidency, for after Richard Nixon, many Americans never truly trusted a chief executive again.

Personal Computers Are Introduced (1975)

The event: In January 1975, *Popular Electronics* magazine and the MITS company introduced a $400 build-it-yourself computer for hobbyists called the "Altair 8800," the first "personal computer."

AN "EXCLUSIVE" ARTICLE in *Popular Electronics'* first issue of 1975 began: "The era of the computer in every home—a favorite topic among science-fiction writers—has arrived!" It went on to describe the Altair 8800: "not a 'demonstrator' or souped-up calculator, [but] the most powerful computer ever presented as a construction project in any electronics magazine."

Programmable through a series of

switches on the front panel and producing its output through an array of light-emitting diodes (LEDs), the Altair sported at most eight kilobytes (8,000 bytes) of random access memory. Compared to the personal computers of today—which run a bewildering spectrum of sophisticated software, display their output on full-color monitors and sophisticated printers, and use as much as 128 *mega*bytes (128 million bytes) of random access memory—Altair was indeed puny. But its makers suggested that it could do such things as perform scientific calculations, automate ham radio stations, provide the brains for a sophisticated intruder alarm system, serve as a digital clock with time-zone conversion, control an automatic pilot, convert printed matter to Braille, or serve as the brain for a robot. And all within the privacy of your home. That is, of course, if you could figure out how to assemble the machine, then how to program it in the absence of commercial software, and, finally, how to hook it up to a burglar alarm, airplane, or robot.

Despite what must have been a formidable learning curve, the Altair proved more popular than anyone thought it would be, and by 1977, new companies such as Apple and Commodore were producing more sophisticated personal computers that employed a relatively simple programming language (originally developed for large "mainframe" computers) called BASIC. Other, larger companies got into the lucrative, but limited "niche" market, including Radio Shack and Heath.

The traditional computer companies—most notably IBM—took a wait-and-see attitude, most executives believing that there would never be much of a market for home computers. Then, at last, in 1981, IBM brought out the personal computer—the "PC"—and the revolution began in earnest.

There was one kink, however. As IBM invested heavily in creating the personal computer industry, it spawned not only a giant software development and publishing industry, but also a vast number of manufacturers who built "IBM clones," which soon competed directly with IBM. The computer giant, suddenly fearful that the desktop monster it had created would destroy its long-profitable mainframe business, pulled back briefly from the PC. By this time, more and more people were eager to command the kind of power—access to data and the ability to manipulate numbers, images, and words—that, less than a decade earlier, had been the exclusive province of research institutions, governments, and big business. IBM's competitors got the jump on the company reverentially called Big Blue, and in the mid-1980s the computer giant began to suffer not only the worst losses in its history, but some of the worst losses any American business has ever incurred.

Still, the PC, which continued to increase in power and decrease in price, had transformed the way the world does business and, indeed, the way the world thinks. Millions of homes and offices could be linked to one another and to virtually limitless stores of data. The proverbial man on the street—or the humblest middle manager—could access much of the same information available to the most august head of state or the highest-paid corporate CEO. By the last decade of the twentieth century, many PC users would insist that the machine that evolved from the "nerdy" Altair had done as much to further the cause of democracy as the Bill of Rights and universal suffrage—maybe more.

Saigon Falls (1975)

The event: In April 1975, the American forces remaining after the last ground combat troops withdrew from Vietnam on August 12, 1972, evacuated Saigon just ahead of the advancing National Liberation Front army, bringing the United States' involvement in Vietnam—and the existence of South Vietnam itself—to an end.

THE VIETNAM WAR COST $140 billion and 58,000 American lives—750,000 lives on all sides. At its height in 1968–69, more than half a million American troops were fighting in it. And that was hardly the total cost of America's longest war.

To begin with, there was what the war in Vietnam cost Lyndon Baines Johnson's "Great Society," a set of visionary social programs intended to end poverty and inequality in America. The funding stream for these programs was diverted to Vietnam, a trickle at first, then a roaring torrent. Then there was the physical and emotional cost to the soldiers and airmen and sailors who fought a war their countrymen learned to despise them for fighting, a war without a front, a war with an all-but-invisible enemy, a war against a regime defined as some vague evil and in support of a regime weighed down by incompetence, corruption, and outright larceny. There was the cost to America as an entity—a country deeply divided by a war on the verge, it seemed, of open rebellion, morally exhausted by the self-realization that what it was doing in Asia was fruitless at best and wrong, terribly wrong, at worst. Finally, there was the cost to Vietnam itself—hundreds of thousands dead; hundreds of thousands more wounded, homeless, and starving; its cities in ruin; its countryside napalmed to a crisp; its village culture destroyed.

By the time Richard Nixon took office, radical opposition to the war was growing vehement. Nixon turned most of the fighting over to the highly reluctant South Vietnamese army. Calling for the support of the "silent majority" of Americans, he began massive—at first secret and always illegal—bombings of Viet Cong supply operations in nearby Cambodia to buy time for an American withdrawal. In June of 1971, the *New York Times* launched a series of articles on a government study called collectively "The Pentagon Papers," which revealed that for three decades the United States government had not only bungled its handling of Vietnam but had, intentionally and as a matter of course, deceived the American people about its foreign policy.

Officially entitled *The History of the U.S. Decision Making Process in Vietnam*, the secret study ordered by Secretary of Defense Robert McNamara, a Kennedy appointee, before his resignation from the

Johnson administration in 1968, traced through its two-million-word collection and analysis of documents, telegraphs, memos, and position papers a tale of confusion, conflict, and covert action in the policymaking of every administration from Harry S Truman to Lyndon Johnson. Courtesy of a conscience-stricken MIT professor named Daniel Ellsberg, who had been a member of the Rand Corporation team that conducted the study, and the *Times* reporter, Neil Sheehan, to whom Ellsberg "leaked" the papers, Americans learned for the first time that their government had helped plan the ouster and execution of another country's head of state—South Vietnam's Prime Minister Diem. They discovered that the Gulf of Tonkin resolution, supposedly a response to North Vietnam's attack on the U.S. destroyer *Maddox*, had been drafted months in advance of the incident. And they learned that one of their presidents, Lyndon Johnson, had been clearly lying to them in his public pronouncements that he had no long-range strategy for the war.

President Richard Nixon, at first delighted to see past Democratic administrations come under attack, soon realized that to let the leaking of classified documents go unchallenged established a dangerous precedent, especially when those documents proved to be official confirmation of what the most radical antiwar activists had been claiming for years. Even before the publishing of the Pentagon Papers, more and more Americans—especially students—had been listening to the radicals. In October of 1969, half a million protesters had congregated in Washington, D.C., to

demonstrate against the war. Then, when Nixon had announced the U.S. invasion of Cambodia in his silent-majority speech of April 1970, students across the country had poured onto the grounds and quadrangles of colleges and universities to protest. At Kent State University in Ohio, protesters set fire to the ROTC building. In response, the governor called out nine hundred National Guardsmen, most of them inexperienced "weekend warriors," twenty-eight of whom opened fire on a crowd of students, killing four of them and wounding nine more. A photograph of a bewildered and grief-stricken young woman kneeling beside the body of a slain student, which appeared in *Life* magazine, seemed to sum up the tragedy of the times in a single, horrific image. There had been other such images—newsreel footage of a Saigon policeman summarily executing a suspected Communist sympathizer by shooting him in the head; a *Newsweek* photo of a naked girl crying into the camera in the middle of a hellish road—that had turned the world against the U.S. adventure in Southeast Asia. But the *Life* photo captured the sense that the "war" had come home to the streets of America.

That sense was underscored in May 1971, two months before the Pentagon Papers were published, when once again a horde of protesters descended on Washington, D.C. Nixon, barricaded in the White House behind specially requisitioned school buses and unable to sleep, made a surprise 4:00 A.M. visit to protesting students before frantic aides located their president and whisked him away. Before it was over, the police and the National Guard had moved in, dispersing the crowds with tear gas and locking up thousands in hastily-erected chicken-wire pens, where they stood, glaring out at news cameras and looking like prisoners of war. By then, the President's Commission on Campus Unrest had investigated the Kent State shootings and issued a report calling them "unnecessary, unwarranted, and inexplicable," but no legal action had been—nor would be—taken against the Guardsmen. It was shortly after the May Day demonstrations that Ellsberg, like McNamara a former "hawk" who had lost his enthusiasm for the war and quit his job and—unlike McNamara—decided to go public with what he knew, became one of the most famous and effective "whistle-blowers" in history.

Once Nixon realized the implication of what Ellsberg and the *Times* were doing, he sent Attorney General John Mitchell to threaten the newspaper with charges of espionage, and when that failed, got a temporary injunction from the federal courts blocking further publication. By then, both the *Washington Post* and the *Boston Globe* had also begun publishing the papers, and they, too, were restrained until June 30, 1971, when the U.S. Supreme Court ruled six to three in favor of freedom of the press under the First Amendment to the Constitution and against prior restraint by the national security state. Congress, responding to public outrage at the four deaths at home, the three-quarters of a million deaths in Vietnam, and the shocking revelations of the Pentagon Papers, voted to cut off funds for the war. With no legal money to continue the fighting, with the antiwar protests esca-

lating with every escalation in the conflict, Nixon and his negotiator Henry Kissinger decided to settle with the North Vietnamese, regardless of the consequences, in 1973.

All of which reinforced the "bunker mentality" of the Nixon White House, and a vengeful Nixon's response was to try Ellsberg for treason. With hopes of discrediting Ellsberg personally, Nixon set up a special "unit" run directly from the White House by a former CIA special agent, E. Howard Hunt, and an ex-FBI agent, G. Gordon Liddy, under the tutelage of Special Counsel Charles Colson. The unit was called the "Plumbers" because it was supposed to plug leaks, and it was the same group of men who—beginning with a burglary of Ellsberg's psychiatrist's office—went on to bug Democratic Party headquarters at the Watergate complex, engendering the scandal that would lead to Nixon's resignation.

The publication of the Pentagon Papers damaged America's security credibility and perhaps some of its intelligence operations, while immensely strengthening its First Amendment guarantees to the press and providing the Vietnam protest movement with respectability and new vigor. This led Nixon, in effect, to declare victory, which he called the "peace with honor" of the January 1973 Paris accords, and withdraw from the war. Ellsberg's act of conscience hastened the end of a war that had for nearly a decade bitterly divided the country, and the revelations about the Plumber's burglary during the series of Watergate investigations would get Ellsberg's case thrown out of court. The antiwar sentiment would spill over from the end of the war to fuel the Watergate investigations, which—like the Pentagon Papers—would reveal to Americans that its president was lying to them, costing not only Richard Nixon his job but public disillusionment with government as well. Within two years from the time Nixon left office in disgrace, Saigon fell. North Vietnam had defeated the South and reunited a country that almost everyone admits would have come under Ho Chi Minh's control, minus the spilling of so much blood, in 1956 had the United States allowed its people to conduct legitimate, free elections.

Karen Anne Quinlan Falls into a Coma (1975)

The event: After drinking a few gin and tonics and possibly taking some drugs, twenty-one-year-old Karen Anne Quinlan lapsed into a coma on April 15, 1975. In what her doctors called a "persistent vegetative state," she became the focus of a legal battle to remove her from the medical equipment purportedly sustaining her in such a state, triggering a long, continuing controversy over the "right to die."

OPINIONS ON EUTHANASIA—painlessly putting to death persons suffering from painful and incurable disorders—goes back at least to the days of Plato and Socrates. But, in the twentieth century, when medicine had provided the means of sustaining life (or, at least, basic life processes) even in hopeless cases, the issue of euthanasia centered on whether or not a person has the right to die. Wracked by war and cruelty, the century produced an infinite catalog of ways to kill and ways to die. But it also brought undreamed-of advances in medical science, all aimed at staving off death. Life support systems, especially ventilation and respirator devices connected to electronic monitors, could sustain the basic processes of life, even in cases of hopeless coma.

Yet physicians, medical ethicists, and the families of victims asked, "At what cost?" At what cost in dollars and cents, in emotional anguish, and in human dignity? On the other hand, if the means to sustain life exist, who has the right to make a decision *not* to make use of these means?

In the case of Karen Anne Quinlan, physicians, ethicists, and lawyers argued over whether or not she was, in any significant sense, alive. Her apparently drug-and-alcohol-induced coma was profound, and her brain was damaged beyond repair or recovery. There was little doubt that, sustained by a respirator, she was condemned to exist in a "persistent vegetative state," yet, because other medical equipment—an electroencephalograph (EEG)—detected traces of electrical activity in her brain, she was not "brain dead." To most physicians and the legal system, that meant Karen Anne Quinlan was technically alive, albeit the signs of life she showed were only detectable by a machine.

Quinlan's parents, after consulting their parish priest and wrestling with their consciences, determined that their daughter had a *right* to "die with dignity" and began a precedent-setting legal battle to gain guardianship of her in order to effect her removal from life support. After Quinlan had lain in a coma for seven months, her parents lost their bid in the New Jersey Superior Court to have the respirator turned off, the court ruling that she was not brain dead. Quinlan's court-appointed guardian, attorney Daniel Coburn, declared, "This is not a court of love, of compassion, but a court of law. You can't just extinguish life because it is an eyesore." The New Jersey Supreme Court, however, overturned the lower court's ruling, and on March 31, 1976, Karen Anne Quinlan was removed from life support. Much to the surprise of everyone involved, she continued to exist in a coma for years, and so did the controversy she had triggered.

The case of Karen Anne Quinlan and others initiated a shift in medical science and medical ethics from the mere sustenance of life to the quality of the life sustained. It prompted many people to write "living wills," directing their families not to sustain their lives by heroic medical measures in the case of a hopeless condition. While these principles have gained acceptance in the medical and legal communities, in the 1980s and 1990s Michigan physician Jack Kevorkian opened a new ethical frontier not by passively allowing patients to die by removing them from life support, but by actively assisting them to commit suicide when they felt incurable illness had made their lives too painful to bear. For his trouble, Kevorkian was repeatedly—and unsuccessfully—prosecuted in the Michigan courts, at one point staging a hunger strike while in jail.

Once again, twentieth-century technology had challenged basic notions about life and living, and once again a legal and political system fashioned from precedent and historical experience struggled to answer that challenge.

"Roots" Airs on Network Television (1977)

The event: For eight consecutive nights in 1977, some 130 million Americans were riveted by the television story of a black family's passage from Africa, through slavery in America, to freedom. Based on Alex Haley's novel, the mini-series "Roots" captivated a nation.

ONE HARVARD SOCIOLOGIST compared "Roots" to the aftermath of John Kennedy's assassination as a major television event, and some black leaders called it the most important civil rights event since the 1965 march on Selma, Alabama. Vernon Jordan, director of the National Urban League, said it was "the single most spectacular educational experience in race relations in America."

It started when Alex Palmer Haley, born in Ithaca, New York, in 1921, began writing to break the boredom of long voyages while he was serving with the United States Coast Guard between 1939 and 1959. In 1965, Haley worked with Malcolm X on *The Autobiography of Malcolm X*, which achieved wide acclaim and is considered a classic of American autobiography. But the author's greatest success came when he looked at his own background, becoming interested in stories related by his maternal grandmother. The family stories led him to genealogical research, which took him from his grandmother, to the National Archives, to the Gambian village of Juffure, to which Haley had traced his ancestral roots through seven generations. Using his research, Haley wrote *Roots: The Saga of an American Family*, a 1976 novel that gained instant popularity and was quickly transformed into the television miniseries.

The tremendous appeal of "Roots" was a combination of good storytelling, the pervasive power of the television medium, and the intense humanization and particularization of the black experience. It was not told through the abstractions of history texts or through lectures, however impassioned, on right, wrong, inequality, and injustice, but by following the story of that most basic of human units, the family. For it was families—of all races and religions—who gathered before their television sets to watch, and it was families who came to understand what it meant to grow up in a certain land, to be taken forcibly from that land, to be transported as a slave to a strange land, and, above all, to lose your family, then to fight for the freedom that allowed you to regain your family. In the 1960s, media theorist Marshal McLuhan had predicted that television would transform the world into a "global village." "Roots" went a long way toward proving him right.

A Cult Commits Suicide in Jonestown, Guyana (1978)

The event: On November 18, 1978, in a Guyana compound called Jonestown, the self-proclaimed messiah and leader of the People's Temple religious cult, the Reverend Jim Jones—fearing retribution for several murders he had ordered—commanded his followers to drink cyanide-laced punch "or be destroyed from the outside." Nine hundred and thirteen people died in what came to be called the "Jonestown Massacre."

IN A CENTURY lived under the threat of instant and mass destruction, it is hardly surprising that millions turn to religion for solace, nor that apocalyptic cults should flourish. Especially as the millennium approaches, the astounding growth of cults appears as inevitable as the revival of Shiite fundamentalism or evangelical Christianity. The Jonestown massacre, so shocking at the time, had by the end of the twentieth century come to seem merely the beginning of a trend.

James Warren Jones, born on May 13, 1931, in Lynn, Indiana, combined the qualities of the early American evangelists with those of the 1960s gurus. During the 1950s and early 1960s, he gained a reputation as a charismatic preacher in a church he established in a poor Indianapolis neighborhood. He moved his church to northern California in 1967, settling first in Ukiah and then in San Francisco in 1971. The People's Temple, as he called it, attracted a dedicated following who came to believe in Jones as the messiah. The temple attracted the attention of the press, and many journalists referred to it as a cult. Moreover, certain journalists began reporting stories that Jones was embezzling church funds for his own use. In the face of mounting criticism, Jones and many of his followers immigrated to Guyana in South America in 1977, setting up an agricultural commune, Jonestown, in the jungle. The Jonestown compound was remote from other settlements, and Jones not only seized his followers' passports, but gained control of millions of dollars' worth of their assets. His spiritual leadership was reportedly enforced with threats of blackmail, beatings, and death. From time to time, he instructed his followers in rituals of mass suicide, all the while indicating to them that he, they, and their community faced destruction from outside forces.

In the meantime, the families of the Jonestown cultists prevailed upon U.S. Representative Leo Ryan of California to investigate conditions in the Guyanese compound. On November 14, 1978, Ryan and a group of newsmen and relatives of the cultists arrived in Guyana. Four days later, as Ryan's party, together with fourteen Jonestown defectors, were preparing to leave from an airstrip near the compound, Jones ordered their assassination.

Representative Ryan and four others—three of them newsmen—were killed, but the others escaped. Fearing that the survivors would send the authorities, Jones put into action his well-rehearsed plan for mass suicide. The Jonestown followers were summoned to the compound's central pavilion, where they were given Flavor-Aide punch laced with a mixture of cyanide and tranquilizers. Most apparently drank the "potion" (as Jones called it) voluntarily. Others did so at gunpoint, coerced by Jones's armed security force. Mothers coaxed their children to drink, and hypodermic syringes were used to spray the poison into the mouths of infants. When it was over, 913 cultists, including 276 children, lay dead. Jones died of a gunshot wound to the head—apparently not self-inflicted.

The Jonestown tragedy hardly put an end to religious cultism. Indeed, cults began to flourish to the extent that a minor "deprogramming" industry developed, consisting of persons paid (usually by family) to retrieve cult members and wean them away from cult domination. In 1993, Vernon Howell, calling himself David Koresh (an Anglicized form of the Persian Cyrus) and proclaiming "I am the lamb," led his followers—the so-called Branch Davidians—to their deaths in the cult's fortified compound outside of Waco, Texas. Acting on information that Koresh and his followers had amassed a large arsenal of weapons, federal officials raided the compound—called Ranch Apocalypse—on February 28, resulting in the deaths of four agents of the Bureau of Alcohol, Tobacco, and Firearms, and six cult members. A fifty-one-day siege followed, ending in a tragically inept assault on April 19 that prompted cult members to set fire to the compound and immolate themselves, including their children.

A "Test-Tube" Baby Is Born (1978)

The event: On July 25, 1978, Lesley Brown gave birth to a child conceived outside the womb through in vitro fertilization, the world's first "test-tube" baby.

A CENTURY THAT SAW the boundaries of death tragically expand in wars and state-decreed programs of genocide also saw the frontiers of life pushed to new scientific and ethical limits. In the past, couples who suffered from infertility—usually blocked fallopian tubes in women and low sperm count in men—could not hope to have children. For many years, the technique of in vitro (literally, "in glass") fertilization was used in animal breeding. But it was not until 1978 that doctors Patrick Steptoe and Robert G. Edwards of London's Oldham Hospital succeeded in performing a human in vitro fertilization that resulted in the birth of a healthy child.

Using a surgical instrument called a laparoscope, the physicians extracted a mature egg from the mother's ovary and transferred it to a culture dish containing the father's sperm and a nutrient solution. The fertilized egg was then placed in another solution and began to divide. When it had divided into eight cells, it was placed in the uterus through the cervix, using a plastic tube called a cannula. Some days later, the growing ball of cells (called a blastocyst) implanted itself in the uterine wall, and the fetus began to develop normally.

In vitro fertilization was widely hailed as a modern miracle of science, especially by infertile couples, whose numbers grew by the thousands as baby boomers postponed establishing families until they were in their thirties or later. Many others, however, raised ethical and moral objections to the procedure. The Roman Catholic Church opposed in vitro fertilization on the grounds that embryos not used for implantation were destroyed; that someone other than the husband could serve as a sperm donor, thereby removing conception from the marital context; and that severing reproduction from the conjugal act was inherently sinful. Others predicted that in vitro fertilization would lead to genetic experimentation and manipulation of Frankensteinian proportions. Still others simply found the notion of fertilization outside the body freakish, bizarre, and somehow wrong. Related techniques, especially the freezing of ova, sperm, or embryos for future implantation, would soon come to pose even more complex personal choices and moral challenges.

Egypt Makes a Separate Peace with Israel (1978)

The event: On September 17, 1978, Israeli prime minister Menachem Begin and Egyptian president Anwar Sadat, after holding talks hosted by U.S. President Jimmy Carter at Camp David, Maryland, concluded agreements paving the way for a peace treaty between Israel and Egypt and a broader plan for peace in the Middle East. The "Camp David Accords" and the peace process that grew out of them won the Nobel Peace Prize for both Sadat and Begin and an important place in the history of the twentieth century.

EVEN IN A CENTURY of tremendous, rapid, and continual change, there are certain conditions of existence that are taken as given and unalterable. One such was the implacable enmity between Israel and Egypt, rooted in Old Testament times, but, in the modern world, a direct result of the United Nations having carved Israel out of Arab lands in 1948. Since that year, Egypt and Israel had been in a continual state of war.

It took the foresight and courage of Egypt's president, Anwar Sadat, a former army officer who had served at a high level under no less a figure than Gamal Abdel Nasser, to make the first steps to alter the unalterable. During November 19 to 21, 1977, in a daring—almost breathtaking—political move, he became the first Egyptian head of state to visit Israel, coming to Jerusalem to address the Knesset (Israeli parliament). This visit gave rise to a series of negotiations between Sadat and Begin, which reached a deadlock in 1978. At that point, United States president Jimmy Carter invited both heads of state to Camp David, the rural Maryland retreat established by Franklin Roosevelt in 1942. (Called Shangri-La back then, it had been renamed Camp David in 1953 by President Dwight

D. Eisenhower after his grandson.) At Camp David, Carter mediated negotiations between Sadat and Begin, and, following twelve days of talks, the three emerged with two documents: a framework for a peace treaty between Israel and Egypt, and an outline of a program for peace throughout the Middle East.

The first document called for a phased withdrawal of Israeli troops from the Sinai, occupied since the Six Day War of 1967. In return, Egypt pledged the safe and unrestricted passage of Israeli shipping through the Suez Canal. The second document called for Israel to phase in self-government for the Palestinians in the Israeli-occupied West Bank and Gaza Strip. On March 26, 1979, Israel and Egypt concluded a definitive treaty that embodied the Camp David Accords.

Peace, however, remained an uncertain commodity in the Middle East. On October 6, 1981, as Sadat was reviewing a military parade commemorating the Arab-Israeli War of 1973, he was assassinated by Muslim extremists for his role in bringing about the accords. Nevertheless, all provisions, except for Palestinian self-rule, were fulfilled on schedule. After a historic White House meeting between Israeli foreign minister Yitzhak Rabin and PLO president Yasir Arafat, mediated by President Bill Clinton in 1993, the process of returning the West

Bank and the Gaza strip to the Palestinians got underway in 1994, though violence continued to plague the long-disputed areas even as they were being granted self-rule.

Ayatollah Khomeini Becomes the Ruler of Iran (1979)

The event: In 1979, after returning from exile in Paris, the Ayatollah Ruhollah Khomeini led a successful Islamic revolution against the Shah of Iran, who had fled the country. After lending support to the capture of ninety American diplomatic hostages on November 4, 1979, an event that led to the political downfall of President Jimmy Carter, Khomeini was made the *faghi*—"Supreme Religious Guide," that is, the absolute ruler for life—of the new Islamic Republic of Iran.

THE SHAH OF IRAN, Muhammad Reza Pahlavi, one on America's long list of autocratic, repressive, even tyrannical anticommunist allies, was forced into exile by revolutionary activity during January 1979. The shah left Iran as his longtime political and ideological enemy, the Ayatollah Ruhollah Khomeini, returned to Iran from the exile the shah had imposed on him.

Khomeini was born in Khomein, Iran, in 1900, the son of an ayatollah (literally, "reflection of Allah," a learned priest) of the fundamentalist Shiite Muslim sect. Young Khomeini devoted himself to the study of theology and by 1962 had become one of the six grand ayatollahs of Iran's Shiite Muslims. As a Shiite, Khomeini was also a nationalist who opposed the shah, not only for his repressiveness and corruption, but for his alliance with such western powers as the United States. Khomeini was exiled in 1963 for leading religious demonstrations against the shah, and in 1978 moved to France. There, far from his country, he or-

ganized and led a rapidly growing anti-shah movement, which finally resulted in the ouster of Pahlavi.

The shah lived for a time in exile and then was stricken with cancer. Terminally ill, he was admitted into the United States for medical treatment in October 1979. Many Americans welcomed the shah, to the outrage of religious radicals who controlled Iran, and the next month, on November 4, 1979, some 500 militants stormed the U.S. Embassy in Teheran, seizing ninety American hostages. Khomeini supported, perhaps inspired and even instigated, this action. In December, he was made *faghi*.

As an act of revenge for America's longtime support of the shah's regime and, in particular, for President Carter's support of the shah in his illness, the hostage-taking was highly effective. Not only were Carter's ability to govern effectively and his chances for reelection destroyed, his inability to free the hostages and his much-publicized abortive rescue mission came to symbolize American powerlessness—to the extent that hostage-taking became a popular tactic in the Middle East's domestic politics. Khomeini's rise to power also signaled a turn to Muslim fundamentalism that caused trouble throughout the Middle East, as conservative tribal and traditional societies tried to come to terms with the "modern" values the industrial west had been trying to introduce for almost a century.

The Sandinistas Oust Nicaraguan Dictator Somoza (1979)

The event: On July 17, 1979, the longtime president and brutal dictator of Nicaragua, Anastasio Somoza Debayle, resigned his office and fled before the advancing revolutionary army of the Marxist Sandinistas.

THOUGH AMERICANS LIKE to think of themselves as champions of democracy and human rights, the United States has often sacrificed these values to its big businesses' imperialistic hunger for huge profits. Such was the case in the opening act of the long and complex drama of relations between the United States and the Central American nation of Nicaragua.

For about a century after Nicaragua became independent in 1838, the nation was torn by a power struggle between Liberals and Conservatives. The Conservatives were especially friendly to outside business interests, including American-owned fruit producers. In 1893, the Liberals regained power, but under threat by the United States were forced to yield to the Conservatives in 1909. To back up the new government and to protect American business interests in Nicaragua, a Marine detachment was dispatched to the scene. It remained until 1925, when its withdrawal sparked an outright civil war between Liberals and Conservatives. In 1927, the United States sent thousands of Marines to put down the Liberal insurrection. However, two elections held under U.S. supervision resulted in the election of Liberal presidents in 1928 and 1932. After training the Nicaraguan National Guard to maintain order, the Marines withdrew in 1933, leaving a handpicked man, Anastasio Somoza Garcia, in charge of the Guard.

The Liberal government of the early 1930s was far more moderate than earlier Liberal regimes; however, one important "radical" leader remained, Cesar Augusto Sandino, whose radicalism consisted of leading a resistance movement not only against the Conservatives, but one opposed to the U.S. presence as well. Somoza Garcia, knowing the United States would support him if he made a bid for power, took his chance and invited Sandino to a peace conference, but arranged to have him abducted and murdered by the National Guard. With Sandino out of the way, Somoza Garcia rallied support for the ouster of President Juan Bautista Sacasa in 1936, after which he was elected president. Among his first acts was to extend the presidential term from four to six years, and he served two terms before allowing his 1936 political opponent,

Leonard Arguello, to be elected in 1947. Less than a month after Arguello was inaugurated, Somoza declared him "incapacitated" and took over the government, returning to the presidency officially in 1950 and serving until 1956, when he was fatally shot by a nationalist poet.

During his long tenure, however, Somoza laid the foundation of a modern dynasty, appointing his family members to the highest government posts and manipulating government policy to facilitate his amassing a fortune in money and land. Following Somoza Garcia's assassination, his third son, Anastasio Somoza Debayle, was named commander of the National Guard, while his older brother Luis became president. When Luis died in 1967 of a heart attack, he was succeeded by Rene Schick, whom Somoza Debayle deposed that same year in order to become president himself.

The new leader transformed the National Guard into a private palace army under his personal control. He struck a deal with the opposition Conservative Party to succeed himself as president in 1971 in return for giving the Conservatives 40 percent of the legislature. Then came a sudden windfall in the form of the devastating 1972 earthquake, which destroyed a large part of the capital city of Managua and brought in millions of dollars in foreign aid, mostly from the United States. Somoza engineered personal control of the funds, diverting much of the money to finance his family's vast catalog of business interests, including real estate, construction, finance and insurance companies, food processing, fisheries, retail outlets, recording firms, ports, the state airline and merchant shipping line, hotel chains, newspapers, radio and television stations, banks, and plastics and chemical factories. By then, the Somoza family also held half of the nation's land deeds and owned outright a quarter of the best arable land.

Not only did American firms have many dealings with the Somozas, but more importantly, the United States came to regard the regime, distastefully arrogant and distressingly repressive though it was, as a bastion against Communism in a chronically unstable Central America.

Throughout the 1970s, opposition to Somoza Debayle's political and business dealings mounted. After his election to a third term in 1974, the Sandinistas, a leftist guerrilla force named in honor of Augusto Cesar Sandino, stepped up their attacks, which included the abduction of high-ranking members of the Somoza government. The president waged a two-and-a-half-year counterinsurgency campaign, which killed thousands. Nevertheless, the Sandinistas made steady gains, and, on July 17, 1979, Anastasio Somoza Debayle resigned as president, fleeing two days later first to Miami and then to Paraguay, where he was assassinated in a September 1980 bazooka attack.

The new Sandinista government nationalized all of the Somozas' holdings, and while it expanded ties with many non-Communist nations, it established particularly close relations with Cuba. President Ronald Reagan took this as evidence of an expanding Communist presence in Central America and not only cut off economic aid to

Nicaragua, but authorized some $20 million to arm former members of Somoza's national guard now living in exile in Honduras and El Salvador to fight the Sandinistas. Reagan justified his actions by pointing to the fact that the Sandinistas were building a huge army themselves and, so he claimed, were acting in concert with Cuba to destabilize the government of neighboring El Salvador.

By the mid-1980s, the Contras—as the counterrevolutionaries came to be called—numbered about 15,000 soldiers. The Sandinista government responded by a further military buildup. President Reagan wanted additional backing for the Contras, but there was a problem. Congress did not want to fund the Contras, who in their raids into Nicaragua had lived up to the reputation for brutality and atrocity they had formerly had as Somoza's soldiers. In 1987, it voted against supplying further military aid to the Contras. This led to one of the century's more bizarre presidential scandals, which cast a cold, hard light on the tangled web of world diplomacy and government in the later twentieth century.

In 1979 Reagan organized a covert operation run by a right-wing zealot and Vietnam vet on his national security staff named Oliver North, in which the United States would sell Iran weapons it desperately needed for its ongoing war with Iraq in ex-change for American hostages held by the followers of the Ayatollah Khomeini. North would use the money from the arms sales to fund the Contras behind the back of a Congress that had banned all such aid. North recruited former CIA and military men to help him, and soon he was talking about expanding the operation into a permanent, off-the-shelf covert enterprise always ready for use in circumventing legitimate congressional oversight of secret missions. That was when the press found out what was going on and exposed the plan. A major scandal followed, which included Watergate-style hearings, that virtually derailed Reagan's presidency and got North fired and indicted. Though convicted of lying to Congress, North was pardoned, became a right-wing hero, and later ran for the U.S. Senate.

Meanwhile, without massive U.S. aid, the Contras were quickly defeated and demoralized by the Sandinistas, who in 1990 held open and free elections, just as they always said they would. Their country in economic tatters, mostly owing to U.S. meddling, they lost the election to the U.S.-financed National Opposition Union candidate, who took office peacefully and negotiated a cease-fire with the Contras. It seemed that at last true democracy had come to Nicaragua, no thanks to Ronald Reagan and Ollie North.

Russia Invades Afghanistan (1979)

The event: Late in December 1979, the Soviets sent troops into Afghanistan to install and support a new Marxist government under leftist prime minister Babrak Karmal, launching what many called the USSR's "Vietnam War."

EVEN IN AN AGE of instantaneous global communications and weapons systems that, it seemed, could deliver destruction from any point to any target, no matter how remote, ancient issues of strategic location continued to play a key role in the fate of nations. So it was with Afghanistan. A crossroads in Central Asia since time immemorial, Afghanistan had been exposed to repeated conquest.

In the nineteenth century, Afghanistan became the object of European imperialism, as the British and Russians fought over control of the nation as a buffer between their two empires, giving rise to the Anglo-Afghan wars of 1839–42 and 1878–80. The British then subsidized an Afghan ruler until 1921, when Amanullah Shah negotiated an end to British involvement in the country and embarked on a program of modernization, which brought such vehement tribal opposition that he fled the country. His successor, Zahir Shah, ruled from 1933 to 1973, when further attempts at liberalization resulted in a bloodless coup by Muhammed Daud Khan, who ruled as president from 1973 to 1978, when he was assassinated by Marxists. Their leader, Noor Muhammed Taraki, brutally reformed traditional Islamic educational and social institutions, touching off a violent backlash.

The Soviets, who were looking to create an economically dependent buffer state against Pakistan (which had developed uncomfortably close ties with China), intervened, but despite their growing support, the Taraki regime was crumbling. In September, Taraki was ousted—and subsequently killed—by his trusted lieutenant, Hafizullah Amin. With the nation on the verge of outright anti-Marxist revolution, the Soviet Union invaded, executing Amin, and replacing him with a handpicked puppet, Babrak Karmal, long a foe of both Taraki and Amin.

Soviet air and land forces—more than a hundred thousand troops—sought to crush resistance in a single stroke. What they encountered, however, was a widespread and grimly determined national resistance spearheaded by the *mujahadin* (Islamic warriors), who received aid from the United States as well as Pakistan. Despite the assistance, the mujahadin were poorly equipped, yet they consistently prevailed against the vast Soviet forces. The Soviet situation in Afghanistan was repeatedly compared to the American situation during the long Vietnam War: the state-of-the-art forces of a modern imperialist power stymied by a comparatively primitive, but absolutely committed, indigenous opposition.

In 1986, as the war ground on, the demoralized Soviets withdrew support from Karmal, who resigned and was replaced by Sayid Mohammed Najibullah, former head of the much-feared secret police. In the meantime, in January 1987, an international Islamic conference petitioned the Soviet Union to remove its troops, and Najibullah simultaneously announced plans for a cease-fire. Seven of the mujahadin groups rejected the cease-fire, demanding direct negotiation with the USSR, not its "puppet government." Militarily, the Soviet position continued to deteriorate, and in November 1987, Najibullah called a summit of tribal leaders, who approved a new constitution and elected Najibullah president. In April 1988, an international agreement was concluded for the withdrawal of Soviet troops, and half were withdrawn by August 15, 1988, the remainder by February 15, 1989.

Yet many of the mujahadin continued to fight, and Najibullah declared a state of emergency from February 1989 to May 1990, when the constitution was amended to allow multiple political parties. The reforms, however, did not stop the fighting, and in April 1992, mujahadin forces occupied Kabul, sending Najibullah into hiding and bringing about his resignation.

The West followed the war in Afghanistan with emotion often approaching glee as the Soviets were repeatedly confounded and mired in an unpopular and costly war. But while Americans may have wanted to view the struggle as one of democracy versus Communism, it was never that simple, and in the vacuum created by the Soviets' departure, various ethnic, military, and religious factions continued to fight.

Ted Turner Launches the Cable Network News (1980)

The event: On Sunday, June 1, 1980, the colorful and controversial billionaire, Atlanta businessman, and America's Cup sailor Ted Turner launched the Cable Network News (CNN), the world's first twenty-four hour all-news television channel, which ultimately changed not only the way viewers watched television coverage of news events, but the way political leaders the world over approached the political initiatives that often created those events.

THE NOTION OF AN all-news cable television channel was certainly in the air in the late 1970s, but of all those talking about launching a twenty-four hour news station the outspoken, yacht-racing, irreverent Ted Turner seemed in many ways the least likely candidate to do so. The son of a self-made billionaire, Turner had built a small financial empire by turning his local television station into a low-rent "super-station"

broadcast over the new medium of cable television, and using the advertising revenues to purchase two professional sports teams, the National Basketball Association's Atlanta Hawks and the National Baseball League's Atlanta Braves. A brash populist, Turner was driven to both success and displays of his wealth and power. While he was perhaps America's best-known rich businessman and something of a celebrity, what he was known for was his pursuit of the America's Cup, his public carousing, and his occasional controversial statements that seemed deliberately aimed at outraging someone. In fact, Turner's Atlanta Superstation was primarily remarkable for two reasons: its broadcasting of second-rate and badly edited Hollywood movies, and its questionable news coverage. Much of the superstation's news programming was an intentional parody of network news, revealing what one might characterize at best as Turner's lack of interest in the news, and at worst his scorn for it.

But Turner was a cable pioneer and he understood the medium better than most. When it originated in 1949, cable television was never intended to compete with the emerging broadcast networks. It was simply an alternative means of transmitting the available broadcasts to areas where the conventional television signal was weak. As such, cable spread quickly in rural municipalities, which negotiated franchise agreements with cable operators. During the mid-1970s, cable began to emerge as an alternative to the fare offered by the three big networks, CBS, NBC, and ABC, as well as local broadcast affiliates. By late 1975, a system of privately financed communications satellites made it possible to increase the range of cable offerings. Centralized production and broadcast facilities could originate a program, send its signal to a satellite, then retransmit it back to earth, where it could be picked up by cable receiving stations and sent, via cables, to local viewers. The Home Box Office (HBO) company was the first cable programmer to contract

with RCA for domestic satellite delivery of its fare—chiefly, recently released movies. Cable's special quality was its ability to accommodate special-interest "narrowcasters," offering programming suited to the interests of a particular audience.

It took a certain kind of genius to see in "narrowcasting" the potential for an all-news channel that could be far more influential than merely a news-junkie's wildest dream. Turner announced publicly that he would begin broadcasting within a year, started negotiating with subscriber stations, arranged for the sale of one of his more desirable television and radio stations in North Carolina to finance the start-up, and went to the banks for a loan to cover the rest. Subscribers were few, and the banks turned him down.

No one, it seemed, believed Ted Turner could do it. Which was, without a doubt, the best way to ensure that he did. Turner hocked everything he owned, including his Gone-with-the-Wind-ish Atlanta mansion. Against all odds—the satellite he planned to use disappeared when it was launched into space, and Turner had to threaten a lawsuit he couldn't afford to get more space temporarily on a current satellite; the commercial networks attempted to create a rival cable news network, and Turner had to bluff them out of the business; the unions began organizing his work force, and Turner had to play a financial game of chicken to defeat the certification election—he pulled it off. Going on the air with a bunch of rejects from the major news media and a slew of very underpaid and inexperienced newcomers, CNN's gaffe-ridden, tacky coverage was at first scorned as "the Chicken Noodle

News." Turner's CNN would never be able to attract more than a tenth of the audience held by the commercial networks, it was said, but what an audience: By the 1990s, many of the world's political leaders regularly monitored the network for information unavailable elsewhere. Boris Yeltsin relied on CNN for news during the short-lived coup by Communist hard-liners in Moscow during 1991, and the U.S. military turned to the service as part of its intelligence-gathering during the Persian Gulf War in 1992.

Commercial television had always had its greatest impact on world events when it suspended the tight programming constraints imposed by the need to make money. After President John Kennedy's assassination, Americans remained glued to their set for four days, as the networks ran for a short time what was in effect a twenty-four-hour news operation. CNN had the potential to do that daily, and as a matter of course; the millions who watched the O.J. Simpson trial as a substitute for soap operas later proved this was true. In times of crisis, CNN could offer full coverage without worrying about offending its sponsors, since they were advertising on an all-news channel in the first place; at other times, it could rely on the proven cable dynamics of narrowcasting. It attracted news addicts and those with a need to be completely up to date—political leaders, for example, and corporate executives, many of whom left the television running all day long in their offices, tuned to CNN.

And CNN's news coverage soon became equal if not superior to that of the commercial networks. Not only did CNN

weave together a seamless narrative of live coverage from around the world, it redefined news coverage itself, making it into a narrative of compelling immediacy. Ted Turner had changed the way we looked at the world, a fact that became evident on Wednesday, January 16, 1991, at 6:35 P.M. Eastern Standard Time, when the battle opened in the Persian Gulf, America's—and the world's—first electronic war. It was not merely that those in the White House and the bunkers of Iran, and the American viewing public became equally fascinated by the odd phenomenon of a live, real-time war unfolding on the screen as it happened, but also that they—like the reporters covering the war—used CNN for information gathering *and to pass information and disinformation to each other.* CNN was not only providing the first rough draft of history, it was helping to write it. More than a recorder of events, it became a player in them. As Anthony Lake, an assistant for national security affairs to President Bill Clinton, said: "Our foreign affairs policy seems to be increasingly driven by where CNN places its camera."

CNN also ensured the staying power of cable. Throughout the 1980s, a host of specialized cable networks appeared, including Arts and Entertainment, Black Entertainment TV, Christian Broadcast Network, the ESPN sports network, Financial News Network, Nickelodeon (a children-oriented network), the Weather Channel, and many others. Of all the cable networks, including CNN, it was perhaps MTV, introduced in 1981, that most dramatically demonstrated the benefits narrowcasting had as a vehicle for advertisers to target a specific market, rather than the much less focused, non-targeted conventional broadcast channels. With CNN demonstrating the potential political power and MTV the massive commercial opportunities of cable narrowcasting, it was fairly clear that the days of a broadcasting system controlled by a relatively small number of executives operating a limited number of major commercial networks were doomed. But if commercial network television had always carried with it the potential for a "Big Brother" control over our lives, cable broadcasting opened the door to a potentially just as destructive "village gossip" intrusion into our homes and our outlook on the world.

Solidarity Strikes the Gdansk Shipyards (1980)

The event: On September 22, 1980, the Independent Self-Governing Trade Union Solidarity—better known simply as Solidarity—became the first independent labor union in a Soviet bloc country and faced down Poland's Communist government during a strike at the Lenin Shipyards in Gdansk.

MARX AND, following his lead, Lenin rightly believed that the seeds of revolution would be sown by and among the workers, and so the Communist revolutions began. But when Communism no longer served the needs of labor, once again it was the workers who brought about change. Solidarity's origins are to be found in the Workers' Defense Committee (Komitet Obrony Robotnikov, KOR), formed in 1976 by dissident intellectuals after thousands of striking workers had been beaten and jailed throughout Poland. KOR supported the families of those imprisoned, worked for the prisoners' release, and disseminated news through an underground communications network. Its 1979 "Charter of Workers' Rights" helped spark a new round of general strikes throughout Poland in 1980, principally in protest of rising food prices. The shipbuilding town of Gdansk became a focal point of the most intense protest activity, and in the summer of 1980, some 17,000 workers at the Lenin Shipyards went on strike and barricaded themselves within the facility.

Their leader was an electrician, Lech Walesa, who not only assumed leadership of the action at Gdansk, but formed an Interfactory Strike Committee to coordinate strikes throughout the country. By mid-August, the committee presented a list of demands to the government, which was based largely on the KOR charter. On August 30, the government, under General Wojciech Jaruzelski, agreed to allow the formation of free and independent unions with the right to strike. The government also made concessions granting greater freedom of religious and political expression. On September 22, Solidarity was officially formed, and an agricultural union, Rural Solidarity, followed on December 14. Within a year, Solidarity had a membership of ten million, virtually the entire Polish work force.

The humble, unassuming, and charismatic Walesa gathered support not only in Poland but throughout the world. Soon, teenagers in England, France, America, and elsewhere were wearing T-shirts emblazoned with the Solidarity banner. Emboldened, Solidarity made greater and greater demands on the government throughout 1981, often over the objections of Walesa, a political moderate who favored more gradual change. Pressured by Soviet hardliners, Jaruzelski imposed martial law on Poland on December 13, 1981, declaring Solidarity illegal and arresting its leaders.

The Polish parliament (the Sejm) formally dissolved the union in 1982, but it continued to function as an underground organization for the next six years until 1988, when a new wave of strikes paralyzed Poland. Among the strikers' demands was the recognition of Solidarity. In April 1989, labor and the government reached an agreement allowing a legalized Solidarity to participate in free elections. In June, Solidarity swept the newly formed Polish Senate (upper house), taking 99 out of a hundred seats, and claiming all 161 Sejm (lower house) seats available to the opposition. Jaruzelski had no choice but to nominate a Solidarity member as prime minister and selected Taduesz Mazowiecki, who formed Poland's first non-Communist government in forty years. Jaruzelski resigned as Poland's president, and Lech Walesa easily won election to the office in 1990.

Iraq Goes to War with Iran (1980)

The event: On September 21–22, 1980, Saddam Hussein launched Iraqi warplanes and troops on an invasion of Iran in an attempt to topple the regime of the Ayatollah Khomeini.

IRAQ AND IRAN had long disputed control of a 120-mile-long tidal river, the Shatt al-Arab, which flows past the important Iraqi port of Basra and Iran's Persian Gulf port of Abadan. Following the Iranian Revolution of 1979, which overthrew the Shah and elevated the fundamentalist Shiite Ayatollah Ruhollah Khomeini to power, the dispute grew into a holy war of terror aimed against Iraq's president, Saddam Hussein. Members of the Iranian terrorist group Al Dawa ("the Call") targeted Saddam and also made an attempt on the life of Iraq's deputy premier. Iran backed civil disturbances in Baghdad, attacked Iraq's embassy in Rome, attempted to incite Iraq's Shiite minority to rebellion, and shelled Iraqi border towns, killing civilians. At last, on September 21–22, 1980, Saddam Hussein launched fighter planes and ground troops against Iran, hoping for a quick victory, which would bring an end to the Khomeini regime.

Initially, Iraq did deal Iran severe blows, sinking gunboats in the Shatt al-Arab and destroying airfields and oil refineries. But Khomeini, whose revolutionary nation was by no means unified behind him, saw the attacks as an opportunity to bring his people together against a common threat. Accordingly, Khomeini called for an all-out military response, including suicidal attacks on the more technologically advanced Iraqi forces, which were equipped with the latest Soviet-built tanks, missiles, and artillery as well as French-made fighter planes. The Iraqi military, however, with some 500,000 men under arms, was vastly outnumbered by the Iranians, who mustered an ill-equipped army of two million.

The result was neither the quick victory Saddam had hoped for nor the overwhelming victory Khomeini had urged, but a long stalemate that evolved into one of the bloodier, more extended, and more futile wars ever fought in this volatile region. The Iraqis soon found themselves on the defensive, hunkered down behind fortifications of earthworks and sandbagged bunkers stretching across a three-hundred-mile front as Iran threw wave after wave against them, using everything from regular army troops to teenaged Revolutionary Guards, inflicting heavy losses while incurring even heavier ones. A measure of Iran's fanaticism came in March 1984, when ten thousand children were roped together and sent into an Iraqi minefield ahead of assault troops. Iraq responded with chemical warfare, launching mustard gas shells against the children—something that had not been used (except by Iraq against rebellious Kurdish tribesmen) since World War I. Two years later, Iraq used nerve gas as well as mustard gas against the Iranians.

Since neither side proved capable of mounting a decisive offensive, the war settled into a contest of attrition and great suffering. But it was precisely in the attrition that Saddam Hussein found his secret weapon: It was, quite simply, the willingness to endure substantial losses and take great punishment while, in the meantime, exhausting the enemy. Saddam's military was like some third-rate boxer, outclassed but able to take punishment until his opponent fell from sheer exhaustion.

In the meantime, the United States, with some trepidation, sold military equipment to Iraq, hoping, like Saddam, that the Khomeini regime would fall. The quasi-alliance between the two countries was tested in May 1987 when an Iraqi fighter struck an American destroyer, the USS *Stark*, with a French-made Exocet antiship missile. While the United States officially accepted Iraq's explanation that the attack had been an accident, President Reagan soon acted to "reflag" Kuwaiti oil tankers leaving the Gulf—temporarily giving them U.S. registry—to legitimate armed escorts. The result was a buildup of U.S. warships in the region. On April 14, 1988, one of the vessels, the USS *Samuel B. Roberts*, escorting a reflagged Kuwaiti tanker, struck an Iranian mine. In response, President Reagan authorized Operation Praying Mantis, a combined raid by army helicopters and Marine commandos, supported by naval gunfire and air strikes, against Iranian oil facilities and military installations. The Iranians threw their small naval forces—four combat ships and a few patrol boats—against the United States fleet in the Gulf. Following a ten-hour battle, Iran lost three of its principal ships and suffered severe damage to the fourth.

Defeated on the sea, Iran launched a missile attack against Baghdad, using sixty Soviet-made "Scud" medium-range ballistic missiles. Iraq retaliated by launching more than two hundred Scuds in what came to be called the Battle of the Cities. The missile battles and the earlier naval losses were the prelude to a campaign the Iraqis called "Tawakalna Ala Allah," a final offensive in which Saddam supplemented his regular troops with 100,000 crack Republican Guards in a deep invasion of Iran beginning on April 17, 1988. Within four months, the long and costly war was over.

Officially, both sides claimed victory, but, in fact, Iran emerged from the conflict with its armed forces shattered and its people exhausted, whereas Iraq, despite the heavy losses it had incurred, was strengthened in its resolve to prevail at any cost. Tactically, Saddam Hussein had lost the war, yet, for all practical purposes, he had prevailed, and what that taught him was a species of international thuggery that would prompt him to invade Kuwait and touch off the Persian Gulf War of 1991.

American Automobile Production Hits a Twenty-Year Low (1981)

The event: In 1981, Detroit turned out 6,200,000 passenger cars, a twenty-year low; automakers reported record losses, a grim message about the growing industrial might of Japan, as Americans seemed increasingly to prefer purchasing high-quality imports, even at relatively high prices, than to pay for what were becoming second-rate goods from an ailing American industry. No longer could arrogant auto manufacturers carelessly boast that what was good for General Motors—or Ford or Chrysler—was good for the country.

THE UNITED STATES emerged from World War II as the strongest nation on the planet and basked in the glow of being the country that saved the free world. Through the 1950s and into the 1960s, the nation's heavy industries, led by steel, produced more and more goods for a population who wanted more and more of everything—especially cars to fill their suburban two-car garages. Prosperity, however, led to complacency, lack of efficiency, and a superficial view of the marketplace. This was especially true in the auto industry,

which was run on the principle of planned obsolescence, introduced by General Motors chairman Alfred P. Sloan, Jr., in 1920. Planned obsolescence was not aimed at continually revising and improving the basic engineering of the automobile, but at introducing essentially cosmetic changes designed expressly to make owners dissatisfied with their present car so that they would be prompted to buy a new one. As a marketing strategy, planned obsolescence worked for a long time; but the 1970s brought an energy crisis, an environmental crisis, and a general recession, all of which made the big American cars seem like dinosaurs. Worse, the 1970s saw a crisis in quality control in the Detroit product, which convinced many buyers that American cars were just no good.

What they started flocking to, beginning in the 1970s, were Japanese automobiles—something that would have been not merely unthinkable a decade earlier, but downright laughable. But by 1981, Japanese automakers, offering a smaller, cheaper, more fuel efficient, and more dependable product, had captured more than one-quarter of the United States market. Almost weekly, during the late 1970s and early 1980s, came announcements of autoworker layoffs and plant closings. By 1980, 28 percent of the United Auto Workers membership was on layoff. Worse, one in seven American jobs was tied directly or indirectly to the auto industry, which meant that the layoffs rippled through the entire economy.

It was a hard lesson for the auto industry and an even harder lesson for American industry in general, but it was a lesson they took to heart. From the early 1980s, a new approach to design, efficiency, and productivity began, which made planned obsolescence obsolete. Slowly, through the 1980s, America became competitive again.

But the auto industry's crisis signaled a more basic transformation as well: from a manufacturing-based economy to a service-based economy. Detroit's slump heralded nothing less than the end of the Industrial Revolution, which had begun in the late eighteenth century, and the beginning of the postindustrial age, in which fewer people would earn their living *making* things and more would live by *handling* things, chiefly processing and providing information.

Deng Xiaoping Initiates Economic Reforms in China (1981)

The event: Ostensibly deputy prime minister of China, but, in fact, effectively head of the Chinese government, Deng Xiaoping peacefully purged hard-line Maoists from power and instituted sweeping liberal economic reforms that opened up the largest potential market in the world to foreign investment and that held the promise at least of a democratizing of China's vast bureaucratic state.

WHEN, IN THE YEARS immediately following World War II, the world suddenly crystallized into two irreconcilably opposed ideological spheres, the Communist countries and the democratic capitalist nations, the enmity promised to be all-encompassing—or so the superpowers of the United States and the USSR wanted the world to believe. One side or the other must eventually triumph, they claimed, as they edged the earth toward a third possibility—the annihilation of both sides in a brief series of thermonuclear blasts. Of all the communist countries, none seemed more intractable than China, which some even called the "mad dog" of world politics. But such a conclusion was based on a perception of China as monolithic and immune to change, a perception that was fostered by the virtual deification of Mao Tse-tung and by his attempts to "out-do" Russia in revolutionary zeal and nuclear brinksmanship. When Mao died in 1976, China began a remarkably rapid transformation.

At the heart of that change was Deng Xiaoping. Born in 1904, Deng became active in the Communist movement when he was a student in France in the early 1920s. He visited the Soviet Union in 1925 and, after returning to China, became a key participant in the Jiangxi Soviet, the Communist enclave Mao Tse-tung established in southeast China. When the People's Republic of China was formed in 1949, Deng was elevated to vice-premier and, two years later, he became secretary-general of the Chinese Communist Party. By 1955, he was a full member of the ruling Politburo. Despite his rise and his close association with Mao, Deng split with the chairman over economic policy. Mao was resolved to impose his agrarian version of Marxism on China, but Deng advocated such quasi-capitalist expedients as material incentives and the formation of technical and managerial elites.

During 1967–69, in an atmosphere of escalating tension, Deng was removed from his high party posts and vanished from public view entirely until 1973, when Premier Zhou Enlai named him deputy premier. When he became vice chairman of the party's Central Committee, a member of the Politburo, and chief of the general staff in 1975, he was effectively head of the Chinese government.

But not for long. When Zhou Enlai died in January 1976, the radically Maoist "Gang of Four" removed Deng. Deng's ouster, however, was followed by Mao's death in September 1976 and the fall of the Gang of Four. Deng was restored to his high government posts in July 1977, and in 1980 and in 1981 his hand-picked candidates, Zhao Ziyang and Hu Yaobang, were named premier and party leader. With Deng pulling the strings, China plunged headlong into a reformation. Wages were tied to workers' output, small-scale free enterprise was encouraged, and the Chinese economy and marketplace was opened to the West. The latter step was not only a profound change for China, it came at a timely moment for the West, which was struggling to emerge from the long recession of the 1970s. By the beginning of the 1980s, it appeared as if the long Communist experiment was coming to an end in China and a new nation—and world—was emerging as a result.

Researchers Identify the AIDS Virus (1983)

The event: In 1983, a virus that attacks certain white cells—T4 lymphocytes—was separately discovered by Robert Gallo at the U.S. National Institutes of Health and Luc Montagnier at France's Pasteur Institute.

THE OLD TESTAMENT and even earlier human records are replete with visitations by deadly plagues. During the thirteenth century, Europe was devastated by the bubonic plague pandemic, which may have wiped out as much as half the continent's population. At the beginning of the twentieth century, an influenza epidemic claimed at least twenty million victims worldwide. But since an effective polio vaccine had been discovered, tested, and widely dispersed, bringing an end to the dreaded crippling summers of the 1950s, most people had complacently settled into thinking of serious epidemic illness as a scourge of the world's poor and primitive populations. Adequate sanitation and modern medical science, it was believed, had made epidemic disease a thing of the dark and distant past.

Then, in the late 1970s, certain very puzzling and quite rare cancers, as well as a spectrum of gravely serious infections, were recognized in increasing numbers of previously healthy persons. Although the disorders were diverse, they had one quality in common: they hardly ever threatened persons with normally functioning immune systems. By the end of the decade, an additional pattern had become apparent: the cancers and immune-deficiency-related disorders predominantly affected homosexual and bisexual men. AIDS—Acquired Immune Deficiency Syndrome—was first formally described in 1981. Publicized widely as the "gay cancer" or the "gay plague," it was soon detected as well in intravenous drug users, hemophiliacs, and recipients of blood transfusions, irrespective of sexual orientation.

However, in the early 1980s, as far as the public was concerned, AIDS was a homosexual disease, and many in the "straight" population remained apathetic at best and cruelly moralistic at worst. Conservative president Ronald Reagan did not mention AIDS publicly until April 1987, six years after the epidemic began. While federal agencies, notably the Center for Disease Control and the National Institutes of Health, researched the disease, funding was limited. Nevertheless, researchers were able to determine that AIDS is transmitted through the blood and certain body fluids, and that AIDS patients showed dramatic depletion of certain white blood cells called T4 lymphocytes. These cells help coordinate the body's immune defenses against invading disease organisms. In 1983, a virus that attacks T4 cells was separately discovered by Robert Gallo at the U.S. National Institutes of Health and Luc Montagnier at France's Pasteur Institute. At first given a variety of names—human lymphotropic virus (HTLV) III, lymphadenopathy-associated virus (LAV), and AIDS-associated retrovirus (ARV)—it soon was officially called human immunodeficiency virus (HIV). (A second strain, HIV-2, was later identified, but it appeared to be rare outside of Africa.)

While the discovery was a crucial scientific breakthrough, a perception of official inaction provoked a grass-roots political response to the epidemic. Urban gay men, already a politically sophisticated and organized group, created service, information, and political organizations. In the face of irrational public fears, which threatened to put AIDS sufferers in a kind of "untouchable" caste—shunning them, barring them from public facilities, and firing them from their jobs—and in the context of the

Reagan administration's reluctance to engage a crisis involving homosexuals, these grass-roots organizations developed a high degree of sophistication and effectiveness. They even served as models for organizations concerned with other health issues, especially breast cancer. The gay groups, in addition to advocacy by a large number of high-profile celebrities (most notably the actress Elizabeth Taylor) and the public's growing awareness that AIDS claims victims of all kinds—including heterosexuals, women, infants, children, and potentially anyone who receives blood or blood products for medical purposes—helped increase federal funding for AIDS from an initial $5.6 million in 1982, to over $2 billion in 1992. Moreover, the 1990 Americans with Disabilities Act included protection from discrimination for people with HIV, and the Ryan White Comprehensive AIDS Resources Emergency Act—named for a teenaged hemophiliac who contracted the disease and became a courageous public spokesman for sufferers like himself—was passed to provide funds to American cities hit hard by the disease.

Yet, as the century drew to a close, no cure or even conclusively effective palliative treatment had been found for AIDS.

The disease, 100 percent fatal, also carried a huge private and public price tag and threatened basic civil rights. In 1993, for example, the lifetime cost of treating a person with AIDS from infection to death was approximately $119,000. However, HIV-positive individuals experienced great difficulty obtaining health insurance coverage, and the leading treatment drug, AZT, cost about $6,000 per year. The epidemic also introduced a new level of intrusive bureaucracy into daily life, as AIDS tests were now required in the military services, and many proposals began to appear for mandatory screening of other vocational groups, especially those in health care. Immigrants to the United States were now tested, and, in many school districts throughout the nation, efforts were made to isolate school-aged HIV-infected children.

Perhaps even more profound—as the number of U.S. AIDS victims since the disease was first defined in 1981 topped 315,000 at the end of 1993—was the failure of federally funded medical science to "conquer" the disease. Since at least the New Deal days of Franklin Roosevelt, Americans had looked to their government to "fix things," if for nothing else. In every way possible, the AIDS crisis severely tested such an attitude.

Crack Cocaine Appears on the Streets of America's Cities (circa 1985)

The event: By 1986, "crack"—smokable cocaine, cheap, plentiful, and intensely addictive—was in wide use across the United States at the apogee of a drug epidemic.

OPIUM WAS WIDELY USED in the United States as early as the eighteenth century, not only recreationally, but in a panoply of home and patent medicines. By the early nineteenth century, morphine had been isolated from opium and was generally available in the United States by the 1830s. It was the basic ingredient of a wide range of patent pain relievers, including medications designed to relieve menstrual cramps and to tranquilize overactive children (one brand was called "Mother's Helper"). Heroin, derived from morphine, was introduced by the Bayer Company in 1898. By the mid-1800s, the addictive properties of morphine and other opiates were recognized. Little was done, however, to regulate the use of these substances in readily available patent remedies. Worse, with the introduction of the hypodermic syringe in the 1860s, physicians mistakenly believed that injecting morphine (and, later, heroin) was a protection against addiction because the amount required to relieve pain was smaller. By the 1890s, opiate use per capita was higher in the United States than ever before, or than it would ever again be until the 1970s.

In 1860, a Viennese chemist extracted cocaine from coca leaves, and the Italian beverage maker Angelo Mariani created Vin Mariani, a popular elixir made from cocaine and hailed by celebrities as diverse as Thomas Edison and Pope Leo XIII. In 1886, an Atlanta druggist named James Pemberton partnered with Asa Candler to produce Coca-Cola, a version of Vin Mariani, but made alcohol-free in deference to the temperance movement active in the United States. In its purer forms, cocaine became immensely popular as a casual tonic.

At the turn of the century, drugs of all kinds fell under the scrutiny of Progressive reformers, and many Americans became concerned about the use and overuse of blatantly addictive narcotics. This anxiety was augmented by anti-Chinese prejudices, and reformers as well as the popular press conjured up sensational images of Chinese opium smuggling and opium dens, which were said to be widespread in American cities. The Pure Food and Drug Act of 1906 was intended, in part, to regulate the inclusion of addictive narcotics in patent medicines by requiring clear and adequate labeling. The Harrison Narcotic Act of 1914 went even further by restricting the availability of narcotics, but it was struck down by the Supreme Court in 1919 as unconstitutional. In the meantime, states and municipalities enacted their own antidrug legislation, and Congress fortified the Harrison Narcotic Act in 1924. By the 1930s, fear and intolerance of drugs had reached a height approaching popular hysteria, and a Uniform Narcotics Drug Act was passed in 1932.

During the 1930s, drug use in America was associated with the inner city and was thought to be especially prevalent among urban African-Americans. However, parents were increasingly concerned that their children would be induced to addiction by "drug pushers," and the subject of illegal narcotics figured in popular literature and movies.

With the social protest movement of the 1960s, drug use penetrated inward from the social margins to the mainstream, as many believed drug use expanded the mind and brought new levels of insight and pleasure. Favored drugs included marijuana—which, while illegal, was often smoked openly—and hallucinogenic substances, especially LSD (lysergic acid diethylamide). LSD was popularized by such figures as Harvard psychology professor Timothy Leary—"Tune in, turn on, drop out," he advised—the novelist Aldous Huxley, and the hipster novelist Ken Kesey. By the end of the decade, a full-fledged "drug culture" had developed, along with an active movement to legalize or decriminalize drugs, marijuana in particular.

The "psychedelic" culture of the 1960s waned before the decriminalization movement achieved its ultimate objectives, but the clash between harsh drug-abuse laws on the one hand and widespread recreational use of drugs on the other did result in a general softening of drug penalties on the federal level, as evidenced in the Comprehensive Drug Abuse Act of 1970. Social and legal tolerance of much drug use continued throughout the 1970s, but by the end of the decade, in the midst of an economic recession, a new mood of conservatism swept the country, and the public and lawmakers alike began to reverse their tolerant stance. In large part, this was due to a perception that the nation's cities were being destroyed by a mounting tidal wave of crime largely driven by traffickers and users of drugs.

Worst of all, the police and the federal government seemed powerless to make even a small dent in the drug trade. The best the Reagan administration seemed to be able to offer was First Lady Nancy Reagan's antidrug motto: "Just say no." In this climate of fear and perceived impotence, the American public first heard about crack cocaine. Whereas powdered cocaine,

usually inhaled, was expensive and used primarily by upper-middle-class whites seeking a momentary thrill, crack cocaine could be smoked, was cheap, plentiful, and highly addictive—more addictive than either cocaine or heroin. Crack threatened not only to overwhelm law enforcement departments, but social services providers also, as addiction problems soared. Inner-city neighborhoods, already avoided by the white American mainstream, were written off altogether, and many saw themselves living in a nation at war.

The ravages of drugs like crack cocaine are obvious and devastating. Less apparent is the corrosive effect of drugs on basic democratic freedoms, as law enforcement agencies are granted a broader spectrum of authority and power, all in the name of fighting the "war on drugs." The crack epidemic has even profoundly affected U.S. foreign relations, most dramatically in the raid against Panama by United States troops during December and January of 1989 and 1990, which resulted in the capture of the nation's dictator, Manuel Noriega, who, brought back to the United States, was tried and convicted of cocaine trafficking. Thousands of Panamanian citizens were killed in this unprecedented, but tragically clumsy, military operation.

Meanwhile, back in America, tough but under-funded cops did not truly battle evil, rich inner city drug-lords and youth gangs in a never-ending war of clear moral extremes. Nor were the souls of our children truly at risk because they were confused innocents bewitched beyond our control by the all-powerful appeal of drugs. In reality, the cops were on the take, the dope flown in by rich foreign capitalists with fancy high-priced lawyers, the money laundered through politically protected autocrats, and the only kids who were dying in significant numbers were kids from the inner cities. For crack cocaine was more than a drug, it was a desirable commodity, one that produced such a high rate of return on the international market that hard-nosed businessmen considered the risk worth taking. So much money flowed from the sale of crack that the business had the potential to corrupt almost everyone it touched, from bankers to law enforcement agents to the dopers themselves puffing on pipes in the dark rooms of well-guarded and empty houses.

Lethal Gas Escapes a Pesticide Plant in India (1984)

The event: In history's worst industrial accident, poison gas leaked from a Union Carbide pesticide plant in Bhopal, India, on December 2, 1984, killing 2,500 people and injuring some 200,000 others in what should have served as a wake-up call about the conditions and dangers in the industrializing Third World.

FOLLOWING WORLD WAR II, underdeveloped countries sought to relieve their chronic poverty by rapidly industrializing, and many of the giant corporations of the West were eager to build plants in these lands of incredibly cheap and abundant labor, where government taxation and regulation were at a minimum. For the nations involved, such development was a step up from absolute want. For the corporations, it was a production bonanza.

In many other cases, the combination of twentieth-century heavy industry, cheap labor, outmoded techniques of labor, and nonexistent regulation has produced a Third World industrial landscape reminiscent of Charles Dickens's evocations of early nineteenth-century England's "Coketowns," but on a scale so vast as to conjure up nothing less than Dante's vision of hell. Such exploitation would not be tolerated in the industrial cities of the United States or the European nations, but, tucked away in the remoteness of the Third World, it was long one of the dirty secrets of postwar civilization.

Then came December 3, 1984. It was an unusually cold night for central India. At the Union Carbide pesticide plant, which loomed over the shantytowns of industrial Bhopal, a worker detected a problem. An indicator showed a dangerously high pressure reading on a storage tank holding MIC—methyl isocyanate—an active ingredient in pesticide production. The worker alerted his supervisor, who sounded an alarm.

It came too late. A cloud of white gas was already spreading over Bhopal—forty-five tons of deadly poison vapor—and people began running in panic, defecating and vomiting uncontrollably, collapsing, dying. "It was like breathing fire," one survivor recalled.

Before the gas dissipated, some 2,500 people had perished and another 200,000 were injured—perhaps as many as half of them permanently, suffering from such horrors as blindness, sterility, kidney disease, liver infections, tuberculosis, and brain damage.

Subsequent investigation confirmed what many had suspected: This Third World plant was understaffed and operating with substandard safety procedures. Nor was it the first accident at the plant. On October 5, 1982, a flange joining two pipes split, releasing gas into the shantytowns and touching off a small-scale riot. Leaks were also reported in 1983, and a plant worker died in January 1984. The Indian government, anxious to keep the plant operating, largely ignored these incidents. In 1989, the Indian Supreme Court ordered Union Carbide to pay $470 million in compensation. To many, Bhopal was a cautionary event, a warning of the consequences of haphazard development and general global neglect.

Gorbachev Initiates Reforms in Russia (1985)

The event: In 1985, USSR Premier Mikhail Gorbachev announced a program of "restructuring" (in Russian, *perestroika*) designed to rejuvenate the Soviet system by allowing a greater degree of democracy, free enterprise, and normalized relations with the West. The program was closely linked with a new "openness"—*glasnost*, a free sharing of ideas and information—that Gorbachev hoped to introduce even to those critical of the system.

THROUGHOUT THE 1970s and 1980s, the Soviet economy, artificially insulated from the world marketplace, was deteriorating, a process accelerated by the Cold War, which compelled the Soviets to spend disproportionate sums on the arms race with the Western powers, particularly the United States. Faced with the growing crisis of an increasingly dysfunctional Soviet society, Premier Mikhail S. Gorbachev split with hard-line Communist Party members by introducing a series of reforms, falling under the general categories of *perestroika* and *glasnost*.

Perestroika included a restructuring of the central government, genuine multiple-candidate elections, and an end to the Communist Party's power monopoly. In the area of economics, Gorbachev introduced limited private enterprise along with more flexible price structures determined in some measure by the marketplace rather than by government decree, and generally decentralized economic decision making. Foreign policy was also profoundly affected. In 1989, Gorbachev formally renounced the "Brezhnev Doctrine," under which the Soviets had claimed the right to intervene militarily in Warsaw Pact countries. The Soviet system of maintaining buffer "satellite" states in Eastern Europe was essentially dismantled, resulting in a rapid thaw of Soviet-American relations and, ultimately, an end to the Cold War. Gorbachev was awarded the Nobel Peace Prize in 1990.

Along with perestroika came a new policy of "openness" or "publicity," called glasnost. Censorship was largely lifted, and freedom of speech invited. Soviet totalitarianism had depended in part on the control of information through the manipulation of the media in what amounted to a program of rigid thought control. Starting in 1985, Gorbachev instituted broad tolerance of criticism and encouraged the rewriting of Soviet history.

Gorbachev's reforms were intended to revitalize Soviet society and to bring an end to tensions with the West. The second objective was certainly attained, and, for the first time since the end of World War II, the world had taken substantial steps back from the edge of the thermonuclear abyss. At home, however, Gorbachev worked vigorously not merely to change policy, but to reshape Soviet society, introducing restrictions on the use of alcohol—a very serious problem in the Soviet Union—and to increase labor productivity, eroded by decades of central authority and guaranteed employment. In effect, Gorbachev attempted to turn

his country on its head. Under the old system, authority and initiative came from above. Gorbachev wanted it to come from below, replacing edicts with individual initiative and the forces of the marketplace.

A series of crises—the nuclear accident at Chernobyl in 1986, a cataclysmic earthquake in Armenia in 1988, and the nationalist fervor of many of the republics that made up the USSR—derailed the reform process or, rather, transformed it from a project of revitalization to one of deconstruction. Amid hesitant implementation of economic reforms, which led to strikes and severe shortages of consumer goods, Gorbachev's popularity eroded. Suddenly, his leadership was being challenged by the even more radical Boris Yeltsin, president of the powerful Russian republic, the largest of the Soviet states within the Union.

The Chernobyl Nuclear Reactor Explodes (1986)

The event: On April 26, 1986, reactor number 4 at Chernobyl, near the city of Kiev in the Soviet Union, exploded, sending a cloud of dangerous radioactive gas over part of the Ukraine and into Europe.

REACTOR ENGINEERS were conducting an experiment with the graphite-moderated reactor at the Chernobyl plant, some eighty miles outside of Kiev, the USSR's third most populous city. Although the reactor was new, having been completed in 1983, its technology was outmoded and inadequate. Even more critical, the plant's emergency water-cooling system had been turned off. As the experiment proceeded, miscalculations soon became terribly

apparent. A neutron buildup began in one area of the reactor core, and there the nuclear reaction suddenly went out of control, producing a power surge. The power surge combined with another, steam-induced explosion and literally blew the roof off a reactor that had an inadequately designed containment unit. A third chemical explosion followed. Fragments of superheated material ignited numerous fires.

The Soviet press was not forthcoming

with information about the explosion. The government issued a terse, four-line statement, reporting that "only" two persons had died and fewer than two hundred had been injured. The Soviets provided no data on radiation contamination. Even as Swedish diplomats in Moscow unsuccessfully pressed for information from the secretive Russians, Soviet diplomats in Stockholm and Bonn sought expert advice on extinguishing a graphite fire. The United States made offers of technical assistance, but the USSR rejected these.

Only after several days did Soviet authorities admit that the initial explosion had actually killed thirty-one persons and had injured at least five hundred more. Persons living within nineteen miles of Chernobyl were evacuated, but the force of the explosion and the intense graphite-fueled fire that followed sent radiation to high altitudes, spreading it across the Northern Hemisphere, with significant levels of fallout descending on the western Soviet Union and parts of Europe. The western nations took emergency steps to protect food and water supplies from contamination, and the Soviets moved vast amounts of contaminated earth from the vicinity of the site. Authorities later acknowledged, however, that—as of 1990—millions of people were still living on contaminated ground, where thyroid cancer, leukemia, and other radiation-related disorders occurred more frequently than normal.

While the Soviet government entombed Chernobyl reactor number 4 in vast amounts of concrete, they also—astoundingly—put two of the facility's three remaining reactors back on line. A series of additional minor accidents prompted Ukrainian officials to press for a complete shutdown. Without an alternative source of electric power, however, the USSR kept Chernobyl in operation.

Radioactive contamination was not the only fallout from Chernobyl. In the Cold War atmosphere of the 1950s, American backers of nuclear weapons were eager to develop a positive image of atomic energy in an "Atoms for Peace" public relations campaign. Physicist Edward Teller, a senior member of the Manhattan Project and the prime mover behind the development of the hydrogen bomb, experimented with small nuclear devices for demolition and excavation work. To be sure, the bombs dug big holes. The excavated earth, however, was contaminated with deadly radiation. A more promising peacetime use for nuclear energy appeared to be as a means of generating electrical power, and the United States as well as other nations committed vast resources to developing nuclear plants. By the 1970s, in the face of a growing ecological awareness on the one hand and a growing distrust of government-supported science and technology on the other, a powerful international antinuclear movement had developed. On March 28, 1979, an accident occurred in the United States at the Three Mile Island nuclear power plant near Harrisburg, Pennsylvania, in which a deadly reactor core meltdown was narrowly avoided and millions were put at risk. The Three Mile Island near-disaster fueled the growing controversy over the safety and economic feasibility of nuclear power. The far more grave Chernobyl disaster seemed unmistakably to vindicate the antinuclear activists, and the building of nuclear power plants—a priority of the 1960s and early 1970s—ground to a standstill.

But Chernobyl had even more profound consequences: It served to undermine an already faltering Soviet economy and government. Mikhail Gorbachev, champion of the new Soviet policy of *glasnost*—openness—had been secretive, even misleading about Chernobyl. That in itself was an internationally recognized indictment of Soviet-style business as usual, and the relatively primitive design of the reactor was an equally scathing indictment of Soviet technical know-how. Beyond that, Chernobyl revealed the scientific hubris on which so much of the century's civilization was built.

Europeans Act to Unite Europe (1986)

The event: The European Single Act (ESA) was signed on February 26, 1986, increasing the powers of the existing European Parliament and paving the way for a plan to eliminate all trade barriers among participating European nations, effectively transforming Europe into a single, unified market.

THE EUROPEAN CONTINENT is big, but, throughout its long and troubled history, it has never proved quite big enough to contain—peacefully—its diversity of peoples, languages, national laws, ambitions, jealousies, hatreds, and greed. Limited by geographical realities, the continent obviously could not be enlarged, and, therefore, in the years following World War II, many European leaders began to look for ways in which to create out of a jarring and fractious welter a harmonious European community, which, nevertheless, respected individual national identities.

The result was the European Community (EC), formerly called the European Economic Community (EEC), and also known as the Common Market. It was an intergovernmental organization of twelve Western European nations (Belgium, Denmark, France, Germany, Greece, Ireland, Italy, Luxembourg, the Netherlands, Portugal, Spain, and the United Kingdom) aimed at creating a united Europe through peaceful means in order to promote economic growth, social cohesion among the European peoples, and general cooperation among governments.

A plan for a united Europe was first proposed after World War II by Jean Monnet, a French statesman. Another French official, Foreign Minister Robert Schuman, proposed a plan that resulted in the creation of the European Coal and Steel Community (ECSC) in 1952, which pooled resources and coordinated industrial policies and activities in the coal, iron ore, and steel industries of France, West Germany, Italy, Belgium, the Netherlands, and Luxembourg. A customs union and a free-trade area were created for these economic sectors, which operated free from national regulations or restrictions.

The establishment of the ECSC required a treaty, the Treaty of Paris (April 18, 1951), which led to another, the Treaty of Rome (March 25, 1957) that established the European Atomic Energy Community (EURATOM) and the European Economic Community (EEC or Common Market). EURATOM pooled research and regulation of atomic energy, while the EEC broadened the common market concept to most of the nations' other industries and economic sectors. The Merger Treaty (April 8, 1965) created common governing institutions for the Common Market: the Council of Ministers, the European Commission, the European Parliament, the Court of Justice, and the European Council.

The European Single Act (ESA) of February 26, 1986 (entering into force on July 1, 1987) greatly extended the powers of the European Parliament and paved the way for a grand plan designed to create a true, barrier-free European community—for economic purposes, in effect, a single, unified Europe. In December 1991, the

Maastricht Treaty was drawn up, providing for the eventual creation of a single European currency, a European Central Bank, and Community-wide citizenship. Put to a popular referendum vote, Denmark rejected the treaty in June 1992, but approved it in 1993, after engineering certain exemptions from some of its provisions. Another holdout, Britain, after much debate—a debate that ultimately led to the downfall of England's prime minister, Margaret Thatcher, an adamant foe of full unity with Europe—approved the treaty in August 1993. Delay in final approval upset the program's schedule, and planners found the creation of a single currency to be fraught with more problems than anticipated, principally because the German mark was so much stronger than other European currencies. Nevertheless, faced with economic competition from the United States, Japan, and other Asian nations, the European Community seemed determined, in the mid-1990s, to enact the provisions of the Maastricht Treaty, creating a Europe more unified than at any time since the height of the ancient Roman Empire.

Montreal Conference Calls for a Ban on Chlorofluorocarbons (1987)

The event: In September 1987, representatives of twenty-four nations gathered at a unsponsored international conference in Montreal, Canada, and agreed in principle to a treaty calling for limiting the production of chlorofluorocarbons (CFCs), used widely in such modern conveniences as aerosol sprays and air-conditioning equipment, which damage the Earth's ozone layer.

BEFORE THE LATE 1970S, few people knew about the layer of ozone that en-

velopes the earth at the level of its troposphere, but at about that time, scientists began to detect decreases in ozone concentrations in the envelope, a fact that received much attention in the press. High-altitude flights by U-2 "spy planes"—modified as ER-2 research craft—confirmed the decreases, especially over Antarctica, where ozone concentrations decline naturally each spring. Now, however, scientists suggested something more than nature was affecting the ozone: a "hole" seemed to have appeared in the ozone layer, and its size was measurably increasing. A similar hole also appeared to be developing over the Arctic as well.

Ozone (O_3) is created when oxygen (O_2) molecules are bombarded by solar ultraviolet rays and some of the free oxygen atoms recombine with O_2 to form O_3. Unlike the two-atom oxygen, the three-atom ozone absorbs ultraviolet light and therefore protects the oxygen beneath it in the atmosphere, also absorbing most of the harmful, high-radiation ultraviolet rays before they reach the earth.

Depletion of the ozone layer was dangerous because it allowed oxygen to be lost and admitted higher levels of ultraviolet radiation, which could cause eye damage and skin cancer in human beings and other animals. Of even greater concern, however, was the so-called greenhouse effect. The naturally occurring gases of the lower atmosphere—water vapor, carbon dioxide, and methane (CH_4)—keep ground temperatures at a global average of about sixty degrees Fahrenheit by trapping solar radiation reflected from the heated surface of the earth—much as the glass roof of a greenhouse admits sunlight, but does not allow the lower-frequency infrared radiation to escape and therefore maintains a higher temperature within the greenhouse. Insofar as the ozone layer was compromised, more high-energy ultraviolet radiation would reach the earth and warm its surface, producing higher-than-normal amounts of infrared radiation, which would be trapped not only by naturally occurring atmospheric gases, but by a host of human-generated pollutant gases. The result may be a rise in average surface temperatures that could lead to a partial melting of the polar icecaps and a major rise in sea level, which would bring cataclysmic floods along with other severe environmental disturbances.

Studies concluded that chlorofluorocarbons—CFCs, used widely as aerosol propellants and refrigerants—were most directly responsible for damaging the ozone layer. Technological advances that had greatly eased life on earth were threatening perhaps to destroy it, causing not merely a rip in the atmosphere but also in international relations. Countries most addicted to the scientifically spawned gadgetry of the twentieth century were the most culpable for the era's environmental degradation, and Third World nations were loath to give up the potential improvements in their standards of living to help correct the excesses of the economically advanced. In that context, the Montreal resolution was a remarkable instance of international cooperation directed toward averting ecological disaster. Manufacturers of such substances as "freon" quickly began to develop alternatives that would not harm the atmosphere. Most major Western industrial nations also pledged to stabilize or reduce the emission of carbon dioxide, a gas that greatly increases the greenhouse effect. While the United States, without a well-developed public transportation system and hooked on the internal combustion engine, did promise to reduce CFC manufacture and use, it made no promises regarding carbon dioxide production.

The Montreal Conference was one of the earliest and perhaps the most successful international conference to deal specifically with "green" issues. Much of its success could no doubt be traced to the narrowness and clear definition of its purpose, and to the general agreement among the participants about the facts surrounding chlorofluorocarbons. Nevertheless, the conference did inspire other meetings, the most significant of which could well have been the 1992 "Earth Summit" held in Rio de Janeiro.

In spirit, Earth Summit was epoch making. Most of the nations of the world—some

118 countries—assembled in the belief that, despite the exclusivity of their political borders, they all shared the same planet and, therefore, had a profound common cause. However, most of the resolutions arrived at were voluntary, nonbinding, and so vague as to be open to a wide range of interpretation. Most disappointing was the role of the United States, which—operating under a president, George Bush, at odds even with the delegates his government sent to the conference—seemed to participate in the summit grudgingly and abrogated much of its traditional leadership role in environmental matters. Approaching re-election, his popularity foundering in a stubborn economic recession, Bush was loath to take any action that might cost American jobs. Still, the historical thrust of the summit was profound: For the first time ever, most of the nations of the world pledged to take into account global environmental concerns when creating internal economic policy.

China Suppresses the Prodemocracy Movement (1989)

The event: On June 4, 1989, following two months of large-scale prodemocracy demonstrations in Beijing and other cities, People's Republic of China leader Deng Xiaoping stunned the world by ordering the Chinese army to crush the student-led protests centered around Beijing's Tiananmen Square.

IT WAS A HOPEFUL WORLD that watched the events unfolding in China. Under Deng Xiaoping, the country had been swept by an unprecedented liberal tide, not only internally, but in foreign relations as well. For two months in the spring of 1989, students had been leading demonstrations designed to push the spirit of reform across the line

into full-blown democracy. Such activity would have been unthinkable under Mao Tse-tung, but Deng restrained his response—until June 4.

The heart of the prodemocracy demonstrations was in Tiananmen Square in the capital city of Beijing. There protesters defied the government with nonviolent protest that had the whole world watching. Martial law was decreed, but some ten thousand students stood their ground at Tiananmen, erecting a plaster and plastic foam "Goddess of Liberty," which resembled the American Statue of Liberty. On June 3, the army intervened—mildly—by sending mostly unarmed soldiers wading into the protesters. At some point, the demonstrators turned violent, hurling rocks. The army came back, and this time they came with tanks. The world, courtesy of CNN, was treated to one of history's greatest images of individual protest against an all-powerful totalitarian state, as a lone Chinese student stood his ground against the approaching tanks of the People's Liberation Army. This time, too, the Chinese soldiers were greeted with rocks and Molotov cocktails. The soldiers withdrew, only to return shortly after midnight on June 4, when they opened fire—mercilessly. Between five hundred and a thousand students were killed, and the democracy movement was suppressed.

Immediately following the Tiananmen Square massacre, party hard-liners made themselves visible, many of them sporting the severe button-up uniforms of the most orthodox Maoist days. Within the next several months, it was becoming apparent that China—with the example of the Soviet Communist Party coming apart at the seams—wanted economic expansion without the ideological changes that the West thought would follow. The Fourteenth Party Congress, held in October 1992, endorsed accelerated economic reforms, yet it maintained a very hard line against political dissent. China—at least for the time being—was not about to accept democratic reform with economic reform, and the West learned to navigate the new political seas more warily.

U.S. President George Bush Bails Out the American Savings and Loan Associations (1989)

The event: In 1989, at the urging of U.S. President George Bush, Congress voted $166 billion to save the corrupt and capsizing savings and loan industry. The Financial Institutions Rescue, Recovery, and Enforcement Act was the biggest federal bailout in history.

SAVINGS AND LOAN associations were the mom-and-pop stores of America's financial network, small-town and neighborhood places, where hardworking families could safely deposit their savings and borrow mortgage money for a first home. These institutions were not unlike the high-minded but folksy "Building and Loan" at the center of the 1946 Jimmy Stewart movie, *It's a Wonderful Life*. They trundled along, making low-risk home loans and paying what was, by the late 1970s, the very modest passbook interest of 5.5 percent, a ceiling mandated by law. In the face of the period's runaway inflation, depositors began flocking to institutions and investments that paid higher returns. The federal government, fearful that the S&L industry would die, deregulated the industry in 1980, permitting S&Ls to pay whatever interest rate was necessary to compete and raising the federally backed FSLIC insurance limit per depositor from $40,000 to $100,000, thereby increasing the taxpayers' exposure two-and-a-half times. Two years later, the Federal Home Loan Bank Board, charged with overseeing the S&Ls, removed its 5 percent limit on brokered deposits, unleashing a flood of deposits from brokerage firms.

Suddenly, the mom-and-pop "thrifts" were transformed into big, aggressive financial corporations, and their CEOs and principal investors grew instantly and fabulously rich. But the price was extravagantly high, as the newly competitive institutions waged a cutthroat rate war on one another to attract business. Soon, most S&Ls were paying double-digit interest rates on deposits even while they were still earning single-digit rates on their long-term home loans, which still constituted the bulk of S&L assets. Late in 1982 the so-called Garn-St. Germain Act gave S&Ls permission to make high-risk acquisition, development, and construction loans. Added to this was federal regulation permitting the S&Ls to lend 100 percent of appraised value on projects—which meant that, if a borrower secured a "cooperative" appraiser, he could secure a loan for 150 percent or more of what he actually paid for a project.

In this climate of deregulation, S&Ls made thousands of reckless loans, especially in Texas and California, and it was a great party—while it lasted.

But it didn't last long. In Texas—and, to a lesser extent, in California—the bottom fell out of the real estate market, and the S&Ls found themselves with huge debts on which they hadn't a prayer of collecting. Regulators suddenly rushed in to close the proverbial barn door after the proverbial horse had decamped. Congress recapitalized the FSLIC to keep it from buckling under an avalanche of failed and failing S&Ls. Then the Federal Home Loan Bank Board took a leaf from the book of the industry it was trying to rescue. Realizing that it had to do *something* with the thrifts it was bailing out, the bank board did what the S&Ls themselves had done: shuffled losses in order to avoid taking them. The bank board cobbled together a series of hasty mergers to create a few "superthrifts," which would be placed under new management.

Shifting losses, of course, did not make them disappear, and that is when President Bush, Republican champion of free enterprise and deregulation, prevailed upon Congress to rescue a drowning industry and its depositors. Committing $166 billion to bail out the S&Ls, Congress created a program that would cost each taxpayer an additional $3,000 per year. Some five hundred S&Ls were closed down or merged as part of the program, and depositors were paid off from a $50 billion federal bond fund. While the $166 billion program was the most expensive financial rescue in history, most experts predict that the total cost of the bailout will actually surpass $300 billion over thirty years.

The Berlin Wall Comes Down (1989)

The event: In the fall of 1989, the Berlin Wall, separating Communist East Berlin from democratic West Berlin, was literally and symbolically chipped away piece by piece by Germans determined to end the politically enforced partition of their country that began after World War II and reached its apotheosis with the construction of the wall in 1961.

A T THE END OF WORLD WAR II, the Allied powers agreed to divide Germany and its capital, Berlin, into two sectors in order to weaken forever the nation that had started two world wars. One sector would be controlled by the United States, Great Britain, and France; the other, by the Soviet Union. For those living in West Berlin, located deep within Soviet-occupied East Germany, life was especially difficult.

The divided city presented problems for the Communists as well, since residents of East Berlin were slipping across to West Berlin at every opportunity. If Communism was so desirable a form of government, why were so many leaving? Doubtless, East Germany's Soviet puppet leader Walter Ulbricht knew the answer, but he was only interested in stopping the highly embarrassing hemorrhage of East Berliners into the West. First he gave border patrols shoot-to-kill orders, then, when the flow of refugees failed to stop, he directed the construction of a concrete-and-barbed-wire wall in 1961.

Of course, the Berlin Wall served a much larger purpose than containing the citizens of East Berlin. For Ulbricht and his Soviet masters, it was an act of defiance directed against the West. For most of the rest of the world, it was a symbol of oppression, of the antithesis of freedom.

By 1989, with Soviet premier Mikhail Gorbachev making overtures of reconciliation with the West, the Berlin Wall had outlived its usefulness. Of late, it had been poorly maintained and generally allowed to crumble. Now East Germans eagerly dismantled it, brick by brick. Within a year, the two Germanies would be politically rejoined as well.

The destruction of the Berlin Wall was a joyous part of the Cold War's end. The reckless national security system it engendered, in which two superpowers, armed with weapons capable of destroying the planet many times over, had divided the world as surely as the Wall had Berlin. And the two hostile worlds had struggled for influence over unaligned Third World countries, even as they poured tremendous resources into holding one another at bay.

Yet the end of the Cold War hardly brought unalloyed rejoicing. In its wake, the Cold War left a somehow murkier world—with one superpower in a state of virtual disintegration and the other, the United States, no longer quite sure of its place, feeling on the one hand it had somehow "won," but on the other thinking that perhaps the winner had been Japan. The Cold War destroyed the Soviet economy and put the United States deeply into debt, leaving it with troubled inner cities, unserved by the social programs that might have been, and now burdened with a massive and unwieldy national security apparatus.

Ethnic Wars Erupt in Yugoslavia (1990)

The event: Yugoslavia, once the most independent of Soviet-allied nations, began to break apart in a bloody storm of nationalism and ethnic hatreds.

THE MODERN NATION of Yugoslavia came into being following the dissolution of the Austro-Hungarian Empire at the end of World War I. But until World War II, Yugoslavia was not so much a single nation as it was a collection of strongly nationalistic, ethnically diverse, and ethnically irreconcilable factions. They were briefly united in opposition to the German-Italian invasion of World War II. The Yugoslavs were led by Josip Broz—known as Tito—a Communist, who, after expelling the invaders, instituted a Marxist regime by the end of the war. Tito's government was unique in Eastern Europe in that it was maintained independently of Soviet military and economic support and even provoked Josef Stalin to expel Yugoslavia from the Communist bloc in 1948.

Remaining true to his vision of Communism, Tito opened up reasonably cordial relations with the West and forged Yugoslavia into a genuinely unified nation. That all ended with Tito's death in 1980, as if to prove that Yugoslavia had been held together by the force of its remarkable leader's personality. The Croatians and Slovenes, the largest nationalist groups in the country, developed separatist movements. In January 1990, the Communist Party voted to relinquish its constitutional mo-

nopoly on power in Yugoslavia, but this did not satisfy the Slovenes, who walked out of the conference. Later in the year, both Slovenia and Croatia unilaterally declared their independence from Yugoslavia and proposed a new, decentralized union. Slobodan Milosevic, the Communist leader of Serbia, another Yugoslav republic, opposed this plan, and Croatia's Serbian minority rose up against the Croatian government. At this point, the Serbian-led Yugoslav army moved in to support the Croatian Serbs.

The civil war soon lost all pretense of being a political struggle and emerged as ethnic warfare among three groups, the Serbs, the Croats, and the Moslems. The United Nations imposed a truce in January 1992, but it proved short-lived, as Bosnia seceded in March 1992, and the Serb population of that republic rebelled. Bosnia was soon reduced to anarchy, and the capital city of Sarajevo was under continual siege and bombardment while the U.N. and the European Community made repeated attempts to negotiate a settlement, but, for the most part, stood by, deliberating action in what seemed a hopelessly murky eruption of human passion. Atrocities and the deliberate targeting of civilian populations were carried out in the name of "ethnic cleansing," the Serbs' systematic expulsion of Muslims and Croatians from Serb-controlled areas. It seemed an agenda worthy of Adolf Hitler, and by late 1993 ethnic cleansing had created some 700,000 refugees, who clogged western Europe.

The struggle in what had been Yugoslavia demonstrated the folly of thinking the world could be structured according to simple oppositions equated with good and evil. The death of Communism did not bring a millennium of bliss, but ushered in a world of greater complexity than ever before, challenging all nations to decide just how to align themselves. American foreign policy following World War II had been motivated chiefly by the strategic doctrine of containing Communism. Hot spots like Bosnia, the African country of Somalia, and Haiti, however, presented no clearcut ideological "good guys" to aid in fighting the "bad," who seemed to be plentiful on all sides. With the implosion of Communism, foreign policy was adrift and rudderless.

Communist Hard-liners Stage a Coup in Moscow (1991)

The event: On August 19, 1992, conservative Soviet hard-liners in the KGB and the army detained Premier Mikhail S. Gorbachev and his family in their vacation home and staged a coup d'etat in Moscow, which ultimately failed when the Soviet military refused to participate, effectively bringing down some seventy-five years of Communist rule in Russia.

MIKHAIL GORBACHEV'S sweeping changes in the Soviet Union sparked a gradual economic and political revolution as old social structures were dismantled in the absence of anything new to replace them. After Gorbachev repudiated the "Brezhnev Doctrine"—which had given the USSR carte blanche to intervene militarily as necessary within the Warsaw Pact nations—many of the Soviet republics declared themselves sovereign or independent. Gorbachev was compelled to renegotiate Moscow's relations with the fifteen Soviet republics, nine of which agreed to a new union treaty. However, the negotiation process was cut short by the conservative Communists' coup attempt, and Mikhail Gorbachev was placed under house arrest in his *dacha* (summer home) while Soviet troops in light and heavy tanks rolled through Moscow and laid siege to the parliament building of the Russian republic.

Many in the international community who watched events unfold in Moscow assumed that the coup would succeed, and the USSR's democratic reforms would go the way of China's in the wake of the Tiananmen Square massacre of 1989. French President François Mitterrand even made a television announcement acknowledging coup instigator Gennady Yanayev as the "new leader" of the Soviet Union and assured his countrymen that France could "do business" with the new hard-liners. Indeed, on the face of it, the odds did not look good. Boris Yeltsin, president of the Russian republic, had barricaded himself and his followers in the parliament building, which was defended by planks, paving stones, and a few hundred ardent champions of reform.

By the evening of the 19th, however, the barricades had been reinforced with disabled trucks and heavy pipes, which sympathetic construction workers had transported to the site by crane. Thousands of ordinary Soviet citizens encircled the building, forming a human chain. At the center of it all was Boris Yeltsin. Born in 1931, Yeltsin had come to power as a party member and special protegé of Gorbachev. In 1985, he became head of the Moscow Communist party organization, but was removed two years later when he broke with Gorbachev. Yeltsin wanted faster and more sweeping reform than his mentor, and in 1989 achieved election to the Congress of People's Deputies. From this position, he quickly built a new and independent political power base, resigned from the Communist Party, and was elected president of the Russian Republic in May 1990.

While his differences with Gorbachev were bitter, Yeltsin insisted on the safe release and return of the premier. Under Yeltsin's leadership, the human chain around the parliament grew deeper and deeper. Many army units had refused to participate in the coup in the first place. Others defected from its ranks, including the crews of the tanks that had been sent into the capital's streets. Moscow militiamen—in effect, the Moscow police force—openly sided with the defenders, distributing gas masks and instructing them in the tactics of civil disobedience. Within days, in the face of military defection and lack of popular support,

the coup collapsed, and Gorbachev was released and returned to Moscow.

The failure of the coup brought about the dissolution of the Communist Party and catapulted Boris Yeltsin into a position of prestige and power as Gorbachev's authority steadily eroded. After Russia and most of the other republics formed the Commonwealth of Independent States to replace the Union of Soviet Socialist Republics, the premier found himself without a party or a nation and resigned on December 25, leaving the new association of former republics in the hands of his savior and rival, Yeltsin.

Yeltsin faced balancing a need for a degree of authoritarian rule with democratic reform. Soviet institutions had been dismantled, but little as yet existed to replace them. Converting the giant nation's economy to the market system would predictably bring a period of great economic hardship, which might easily trigger a reactionary backlash. Moreover, there was the vexing question of just who would control the former Soviet Union's vast military assets, including its thermonuclear arsenal.

Yeltsin moved quickly to secure financial assistance from the West, and he was instrumental in forming the Commonwealth of Independent States. With the Ukraine, he reached a compromise on the potentially disastrous conflict over who would control the great Black Sea nuclear fleet, and in January 1993, Yeltsin met with U.S. President George Bush to conclude the epochmaking START II arms reduction treaty. In the meantime, however, the Commonwealth endured the throes of economic meltdown, and in March 1993, Yeltsin narrowly survived a motion for impeachment in the Congress of People's Deputies. After securing the support of 58 percent of the electorate in a national referendum on confidence in his leadership, Yeltsin dissolved the Congress and called for new elections. When opponents in the parliament refused to dissolve the legislature, Yeltsin employed the military to attack the very parliament building he had recently defended.

Yeltsin instituted elections for a new parliament on December 12, 1993, and submitted a new constitution to the voters. Calling for a strong chief executive, the constitution was narrowly approved, yet parliamentary elections saw a heavy vote for ultranationalist candidates diametrically opposed to Yeltsin's political and economic reforms. At the end of the century, the former Soviet republics were suspended between radical democratic reforms and the forces that would return to the old ways. The Bolsheviks had opened the twentieth century with a ten-day revolution that shook the world. Now, a new "revolution"—less violent, yet also less definitive, more tentative, more diffuse, resembling less the October Revolution than the collapse of the Ottoman Empire—was closing it.

A U.N. Coalition Goes to War with Iraq (1991)

The event: Between January 17, 1991, and April 10, 1992, the United States led a coalition of twenty-eight nations against the army and air force of Saddam Hussein's Iraq, which had invaded and occupied oil-rich Kuwait.

AFTER PREVAILING in an eight-year war against Iran so costly that it nearly led to a military coup in Iraq, Saddam Hussein invaded and attempted to annex the small, oil-rich nation of Kuwait. During his occupation of the country, he plundered it and brutalized the population. The United States sought and received a sanction from the United Nations to act against Iraq and joined twenty-seven other nations to launch Operation Desert Shield, a massive military buildup in Saudi Arabia, near the border with Iraq. President George Bush demanded the immediate withdrawal of Iraqi forces from Kuwait, to which Saddam responded with defiance alternating with vague promises of compliance. At 3 A.M. on the morning after a January deadline for the withdrawal, massive air strikes were launched against Iraq.

Although Saddam promised the United States the "mother of all battles," his air force and ground forces were quickly defeated, and the so-called Persian Gulf War proved a brief affair. Iraqi armed forces inflicted minimal damage against military targets, but they did launch numerous small-missile ("Scud") attacks against civilian targets in noncombatant Israel. Saddam hoped to provoke Israel into a military response that would wreck the participation of Arab nations in the coalition arrayed against him. Israel, however, restrained from launching a counterattack and Saddam's ploy failed.

In the meantime, Iraqi forces in Kuwait

terrorized citizens and laid waste some three hundred oil fields, setting numerous cataclysmic blazes. Indeed, the oil-field fires were the worst legacy of the war, burning through 1991 and into 1992. In addition, Saddam committed unprecedented acts of ecological terrorism by creating massive and deliberate oil spills in the Persian Gulf, hoping to foul Saudi desalinization plants, which produce drinking water for the nation. Despite Saddam's bravado, the Iraqi military defeat was decisive. Losses were estimated to be in excess of 80,000 men, with overwhelming loss of materiel and severe damage to the civilian infrastructure. A cease-fire was concluded on April 10, 1992, and Saddam withdrew from Kuwait. Varying degrees of civil unrest followed in the wake of the ruinous war, especially in outlying provinces and particularly in chronically rebellious Kurdistan. Yet Saddam Hussein managed to maintain power and, throughout 1992, indulged in bouts of defiance against sanctions levied by the United Nations.

The Persian Gulf War appeared to many Americans to be the first "good" war the United States fought since World War II. In an era marked by ambiguity of motives and murky options that often amounted to attempting to determine the least of any number of manifest evils, here was a conflict that seemed a simple matter of choosing to defend good over evil. There were a number of voices raised in the United States—both among the public and in Congress—protesting the exchange of "blood for oil," but to most Saddam appeared the devil incarnate—a stark contrast to the head

of the Coalition forces, the American general, H. Norman Schwarzkopf, who was soft-spoken, frank, and professional (and bore an uncanny resemblance to the benign television comic Jonathan Winters), and to the head of the American joint chiefs, the clear-thinking, politically astute African-American general, Colin Powell.

The pleasure that most Americans took in the victory over Saddam Hussein is evident in the adulation accorded Schwarzkopf and Powell, and in the unprecedented ninety-plus popular approval rating President Bush garnered during and immediately following the Persian Gulf War. To be sure, Saddam Hussein was a tyrant, but the century had seen many, many tyrants far worse—in terms of body count—than he: Stalin, Hitler, Mao, Idi Amin, Pol Pot, and others. The difference was, never had so many people seen a tyrant up close, as the CNN cable television news network covered the war in detail so thorough and intimate that Powell, Schwarzkopf, and others admitted to using the broadcasts as valuable supplements to "official" intelligence. Vietnam had been reported on television—and the effect was powerful—but television audiences nationwide not only got reports on the Persian Gulf War, but they saw it unfold even as the commanders did.

It was a late twentieth-century war, creating around it an electronic community, and, in the process, for better or worse, translating complex moral and political issues into a real-life television drama, a miniseries depicting the triumph of good guys over bad. George Bush began bold talk about a "new world order" based on this first post-Cold War conflict, which would see a confluence of world powers policing "outlaw" nations and protecting the globe from the threat they represented. But even as the smoke continued to billow into the atmosphere from sabotaged Kuwaiti oil wells, ethnic conflicts in Africa and the Balkans raised issues that seemed to befuddle a world united against Saddam, calling into question just how much the Gulf War had to do with humanitarian rescue, and how much with fossil fuels.

Even though George Bush tried to make Desert Storm into the internal antidote for America's so-called "Vietnam syndrome," he could not maintain his popularity when the war degenerated into something of a personal squabble with Saddam after the fighting was over. Even as a worsening domestic economy ate into his political power base, Bush found himself attacked for sending Saddam the confused diplomatic signals that encouraged the Iraqi dictator to invade Kuwait in the first place, for saving a country only to turn it back over to a few incredibly wealthy and arrogant oil autocrats, and for floundering in his immediate responses to Saddam's territorial piracy and flouting of U.N.-imposed sanctions and peace conditions.

Bush's telegenic military commanders, however, fared much better. Schwarzkopf had become a media darling by the time he retired, conducting a well-received and enriching speaking tour and producing a bestselling autobiography centered on his Gulf War experiences. Colin Powell, his authority swelled by the success of the war, proved a thorn in the side of the new U.S. president, Bill Clinton, blocking Clinton's attempt to integrate openly gay men into the military and frustrating Clinton's efforts to make drastic cuts in the defense budget shortly after he assumed office. As an African-American who enjoyed tremendous prestige and great popularity, Powell seemed poised to run for political office himself as he resigned early in the Clinton administration.

Nelson Mandela Becomes President of South Africa (1994)

The event: On May 9, 1994, black South African leader Nelson Mandela, after spending much of his adult life in a white South African jail, became president of the Republic of South Africa, bringing for the first time majority rule to a country long torn by racial strife and mutual suspicion between African aborigines and white settlers, both of whom considered themselves natives to their African homeland.

WHEN THE FORMER European colonies of sub-Saharan Africa began to gain their independence in the late 1950s and early 1960s, one assumption they all shared was that black African self-rule would eventually become continent-wide, spreading inexorably southward and eventually penetrating the very heart of white supremacy, South Africa. Since 1910, following a brutal colonial war with Great Britain,

South Africa had had self-government, but its independent commonwealth status benefited only its two-and-a-half million white citizens at the expense of its overwhelmingly black majority. Indeed, political power had increasingly fallen into the hands of the Afrikaners, white Africans of Dutch descent who had formerly been called Boers (meaning "farmers" in Dutch), and who zealously promoted the white supremacist ideology that had developed out of their settler origins, their frontier history, and their patriarchal, Calvinist heritage.

In 1948, the Afrikaners assumed full political command of the Republic when the Afrikaner-dominated National Party was elected on a program of formal racial segregation the South Africans called "apartheid," literally "separateness." The Afrikaners had done some soul-searching before coming up with apartheid, trying as the conscientious Christians they imagined themselves to be, to find a means by which they could protect a white-dominated society without denying, or at least appearing to deny, all human rights to the nation's blacks, whom they called in public Bantus and in private Kaffirs. The solution, so much resembling the kind of segregation once practiced in the former slave-holding states of the American South, pleased them more than it did the blacks.

In 1952, the African National Congress (ANC), South Africa's black opposition party, began advocating passive resistance to apartheid by calling on blacks to use the public amenities reserved for whites. The Afrikaner government responded by announcing a state of emergency, giving the government dictatorial powers. From that point forward, black resistance and white oppression fed on one another. Afrikaner Prime Minister Hendrik Verwoerd engineered the passage of a law called the Promotion of Bantu Self-Government Act in 1959, granting the black community full citizenship in assigned areas of the country called "homelands," which could work toward nominal independence and therefore allow South Africa to declare to the world that it was, indeed, decolonizing. Nobody, inside or outside South Africa, was much fooled by what looked suspiciously like the system of Indian reservations introduced by the United States in the American West a century before. For one thing, the homelands made up less than 13 percent of the country, and most of that consisted of South Africa's poorest land, yet they were supposed to house the bulk of a black population which outnumbered the whites four to one. For another, blacks were expected to give up all political rights in South Africa outside the homelands.

In reality, cheap black labor remained essential to the South African economy, necessitating on the one hand a humiliating pass-law system that severely restricted blacks' freedom to move about in white areas and, on the other, the forcing of urban black populations into huge, impoverished townships, easily surrounded in times of trouble. As it developed, the Afrikaner political state was a virtual formula for violence. All opposition to apartheid, white or black, the government labeled as Communism, a term of abuse justifying even more repression. In 1959, the year South Africa announced its Bantustan policy, radical factions of the ANC staged demonstrations against the pass laws in the village of Sharpsville, where South African police opened fire on retreating protesters, wounding 178 and killing 69, two-thirds of whom had been shot in the back. Further repression followed after a referendum gave Prime Minister Verwoerd a small majority, and criticism of apartheid by other countries in the British Commonwealth gave him the excuse he needed to withdraw from the commonwealth. A law allowing the state to detain its citizens for ninety days without trial, which could be renewed indefinitely, was used to silence internal critics of the government, many of whom fled to avoid arrest. The Afrikaners banned black opposition parties. In 1962, they arrested a former Johannesburg lawyer and ANC leader named Nelson Mandela and threw him in jail, where he remained for nearly thirty years. For opponents of apartheid, few if any courses of action remained outside armed struggle.

Meanwhile, conditions in southern Africa's other white-ruled countries—Rhodesia, Angola, and Mozambique—deteriorated and by 1977 all three were under black majority rule, with Northern Rhodesia now called Zambia and Southern Rhodesia renamed Zimbabwe.

South Africa became a fortress of white supremacy under siege from all sides. The cycle of violence continued internally throughout the 1970s, growing if anything more heated. In 1976, the South African government decreed that Afrikaans, the Dutch Boer dialect, would become the only

official language, throwing out English as the other, and that only Afrikaans would be used in the public schools. The move made speaking Afrikaans a symbol of official oppression and triggered major riots throughout all the black townships of Natal, most significantly in Soweto, a sprawling urban complex of shantytown slums outside Johannesburg, where several hundred demonstrators were gunned down by police. As Sharpsville had once done, Soweto aroused the conscience of the international community. Some countries threatened sanctions, international corporations began to divest themselves of their South African holdings, and the Afrikaners republic became something of a de facto outlaw nation.

Given such threats to its economic well-being, South Africa started slowly to abandon aspects of apartheid and adopt more liberal policies in the hopes of conciliating world opinion. Even conservative white politicians suggested a relaxation of minor racial restrictions—so-called "petty apartheid"—and more liberal leaders moved for an end to apartheid altogether. Outside South Africa, the events in Soweto drew worldwide censure of the nation's racial policies. They were helped in their cause when the United States and Great Britain actually levied economic sanctions in 1985. Black labor unions were legalized, anti-miscegenation laws were repealed, and so were segregation laws for public transportation. By 1991, South Africa's last white prime minister, F. W. de Klerk, oversaw the writing of a new constitution removing any legal basis for apartheid, and freed Nelson Mandela. Free general elections in which all South Africans could vote were held on April 26, 1994, and the results were announced on May 6. Three days later Nelson Mandela took office as the leader of a new South Africa.

California Voters Pass Proposition 187 (1994)

The event: In the anti-incumbent and culturally conservative mid-term national elections of 1994, the American voters sent a Republican majority to both the U.S. House of Representatives and the U.S. Senate. In tune with the election, Californians passed an initiative labeled Proposition 187, called more popularly by its proponents "S.O.S." for "Save Our State." A draconian proposal that cut off education and all social services but emergency health care for illegal aliens, Proposition 187 required in addition that teachers and doctors turn such residents into the proper authorities. Its passage signaled the return of one of the country's perennially divisive political issues: whom to let in and whom to keep out of what Americans were having an increasingly difficult time defining as their nation.

NOT FOR THE FIRST TIME was immigration proving a problem for Americans. In the 1920s, white-glove Progressives and Know-Nothing nativists began to worry about the impact that swarthy, dark-haired southern and eastern European immigrants were having on the "Anglo-Saxon" culture of "true" Americans. The same United States that had welcomed the immigrants a generation before when it desperately needed laborers for its expanding factories now moved to limit that number by overlaying a complicated quota system on its immigration laws. Then, beginning in the 1930s, immigrants from Mexico swept into the Southwest and California through the United States' porous southern borders. The immigration laws of the previous decade strictly limited the number America would accept legally for potential citizenship after seven years of residency. Consequently, many of the immigrants simply moved illegally to *El Norte*, as they called the United

States, and quietly took up residence. They joined any number of Mexican-Americans, whose culture resembled theirs and whose ancestors had been inhabiting the American Southwest certainly as long as, and probably longer than, those who arrived in the *Mayflower*.

Except for a period during World War II when an alliance between Mexico and Nazi Germany seemed a distinct possibility, Mexican immigrants were mostly welcomed, if not with open arms, at least with a steady eye on the potential surplus value of their labor. Taking jobs in American factories, or becoming migrant workers in the ever-more centralized agricultural sector, or accepting low-paying positions as domestics in the prosperous homes of the Southwest, the industrious Mexican immigrants flourished. They certainly lived better than they had back in Mexico, which one of their proverbs mourned as "poor Mexico" because it was so far from God and so close to the United States. Some grew wealthy and joined the established Mexican-American communities. Others fared less well, crowding together in the barrios that were equivalent to the ghettos of the early Jewish immigrants, the Little Italys of the Italians, or the urban slums of America's internal immigrants, the African-Americans. There they got by the best they could. They saved a little money when possible, saw to the education of their children, and dreamed of future prosperity for their family. Some took up a peripatetic life, working for a while in the United States, then returning to their families in Mexico. Occasionally some would bring their wives and children north to share in their seasonal work.

In the language of the American federal bureaucracy they were called Hispanics, a category that included resident Mexicans, American citizens of Mexican descent, Cuban refugees, and immigrants from the Central and South American countries. They might call themselves Chicanos or perhaps, in Texas, Tejanos, but in the complicated and portentous American notions of "race," they were begrudgingly considered white, after the manner, say, of Italian immigrants in the late nineteenth and early twentieth century. Theoretically, at least, there were no absolute barriers to their climb up the American ladder of success. They did not have to attend segregated schools, or eat in segregated restaurants, or sleep in segregated lodgings, as African-Americans were once required to do by law, though local prejudice often dictated differently. On the other hand, they could qualify as an ethnic minority and enjoy some of the benefits of the post-civil rights era emphasis on equal opportunity. After changes in the immigration laws in 1965 repealed quotas based on national origin, the number of Hispanics in the United States swelled, and they began to garner some political clout. They elected their own representatives to local office and to Congress, demanded recognition for their own cultural traditions and historical accomplishments, and even forced bilingual schools on the dominant Anglo culture.

Frictions between Hispanics and Anglos did exist, and many suffered the kinds of indignities engendered by true bigotry. Nevertheless, by the late twentieth century, recent Mexican immigrants and long established Mexican-Americans seemed to be headed for eventual assimilation into the mainstream political culture, much like the Irish, the Jews, and the Italians (and unlike African-Americans) before them. The apparent upward mobility, however, depended on the long wave of economic prosperity that followed World War II. The situation changed dramatically when an Arab oil embargo in the 1970s brought the wave to an abrupt halt. Another long wave began, this time headed downward. As the American economy went into gradual decline, the Southwest and California—long addicted to extractive industries and federal largess in defense spending and public services—became openly xenophobic. A taxpayers' revolt that began in the wealthy suburbs of southern California spread throughout the country, further eroding the public sector's formerly dominant role in the area's economy. Suddenly

Hispanics were less white than brown, their cheap immigrant labor less a blessing than a curse.

In the 1980s Congress began to address the newly defined "problem" of the massive illegal alien population in the Southwest by passing a muddled piece of new legislation aimed at providing legal status and official protection to longstanding illegal residents and temporary workers, most of whom were Mexican, while somehow slamming the door shut on future illegal aliens. It tried to accomplish the latter by punishing employers for failing to keep track of their employees' immigration papers, which led first to discrimination against anyone with a "foreign-sounding," i.e., Hispanic, name, then—once the new law proved itself virtually unenforceable—to widespread noncompliance.

By the time California's Republican Governor Pete Wilson was ready to run for a second term in 1994, the lines were more clearly drawn and the tactics more carefully considered: Don't punish the employers, punish those who work for them at shamefully low wages. In California, getting tough on illegal immigrants was smart politics in an election year when the poor were being blamed for being poor and the well-off were being touted as virtuous for denying them food stamps and, indeed, any kind of subsistence income drawn from public coffers. Hence, Proposition 187, with its promise to save billions in tax dollars by restricting government aid of any kind (but life-saving health care in the direst of physical emergencies) to the estimated 1.7 million illegal aliens who lived and worked in California.

The proposal was too much for a couple of nationally recognized Republican leaders who came to prominence in the Reagan years. Understanding, perhaps, what the mass desertion of Hispanic voters might mean in the long run to the party, former housing secretary Jack Kemp and former education secretary William Bennett, both with impeccable conservative credentials, in a joint statement attacked California's anti-immigrant fervor as pernicious, un-American, and dangerous. An incensed California GOP struck back, basically calling the two traitors to the cause. The academic cultural wars that had been raging for a number of years between mostly left-wing multi-culturalists and mostly right-wing democratic universalists had finally hit the streets.

The multiculturalists saw America not so much as a nation, but as a home for five national communities, defined by race—white, black, Hispanic, Asian, and Native American. The universalists, on the other hand, conflated the notion of nation and the concept of government to define America as an idea created by a unique set of laws without reference to race or ethnicity. The voters clearly lined up with the latter, passing Proposition 187 with a healthy 61 percent of the votes cast. Because, among other things, the new law required teachers and doctors to act contrary to their codes of ethics, and because it forthrightly violated long-established federal policy, the legality of the new law immediately became a subject on which the courts would rule.

Meanwhile some new rifts portended by its passage had become even more apparent in the American body politic. Shortly after the mid-term elections, Republicans in Congress began a move to cut off *legal* aliens from social welfare programs. The problem no longer centered around who was trying to become an American citizen, but that they might want some of our money in the seven years before they made the grade. The famous nation of immigrants, whose motto was *e pluribus unum*, "out of many, one," no longer saw immigrants as a source of pride and strength. As far as Californians were concerned, the aliens came to their state because, first, California paid them slightly more than they made at home (and, incidentally, slightly less than it would have to pay "true" Americans), and second,

because the state let them sponge off its welfare system. In other words, the worry was no longer primarily or exclusively one of mongrelization, but first and foremost one of cost. There were those who saw in this new emphasis a revolt of the rich; they argued that the real danger was not in the Balkanization of America, the usual intellectual justification for anti-immigrant sentiment, but in the Brazilianization of America, the coming into being of an America where the growing gap between the rich and the poor led the former to wall itself off in a secure world of private privilege while the latter were left to shift for themselves in the mean streets of the country's urban wasteland.

A Bomb Explodes at the Oklahoma City Federal Building (1995)

The event: At 9:02 A.M. on April 19, 1995, a homemade bomb exploded at the Alfred P. Murrah Federal Building in Oklahoma City, Oklahoma, killing 167 civilians outright, including thirteen children attending a daycare center in the building, and damaging numerous other buildings in the area. The bombing affected Americans like few other terrorist activities in the twentieth century had, spawning not merely criminal investigations into the attack itself and into terrorism in general, but also philosophical and political reviews of the American polity and the federal government that in many ways went to the heart of America's identity as a nation.

THE TERRORIST ATTACK, like all terrorist attacks, was horrifying in its slaughter of the innocent. The blast came at the height of Oklahoma City's morning rush hour, sending a reddish-orange fireball into the sky over traffic, and raining shards of glass on pedestrians and commuters. The north side of the federal center vaporized, leaving behind a monstrous-looking carcass of a building, dripping cables and concrete onto

the plaza below as puffs of gas, smoke, and dust drifted upward. Ceilings collapsed, doors blew out, windows exploded, and debris of all kinds spewed across the ground. Uprooted parking meters lay among scattered toys and the indifferently mingled body parts of the victims. Survivors, covered with blood and dust and plaster, staggered into the street through the smoke. Many were in shock, some unaware they were even hurt until they felt their shoes filling with blood or their clothes sticking to their skin.

Crowds came running and joined those injured outside the building and those surviving the blast inside it in the search to find and help others as sirens sounded around them summoning medical students, off-duty cops, paramedics, firemen, policemen, nurses, priests, construction workers, rescue squads, structural engineers, anybody who could help, save, advise, and comfort the hurt and the dying. One news magazine even noted that the ubiquitous news media "helped" by keeping out of the way of the rescuers. Rescue teams from the city, county, and eventually the surrounding states swarmed into the area, plunging into the debris, searching for the survivors still in the building.

Soon, the images of the tragedy were broadcast to the world. As the inevitable body count began, President Bill Clinton more or less vowed vengeance against the terrorists, whoever they were, and the national disaster plans designed by the Federal Emergency Management Agency fell into place like a well-ordered drill. At first everyone, including federal law enforcement officials, assumed the terrorists to be from the Middle East, though a few noted the peculiar coincidence that the blast had occurred on the anniversary of the showdown at Waco, Texas, between federal agents and members of the religious cult the media called the Branch Davidians, favored martyrs for the country's growing number of armed and dangerous right-wing survivalist groups. Before too many Muslims could be

threatened and detained, lucky lawmen had in hand a prime suspect who was, indeed, connected to the survivalist groups springing up across the American heartland.

Americans were stunned. Spoon-fed on newspaper, television, and movie images of terrorists as swarthy Arabs tossing bombs in faraway places like Beirut and Jerusalem, they were used to considering terrorism at most as a risk to foreign travel. True, the recent bombing of the World Trade Center in New York had raised the possibility of "domestic" terrorism, but the villains in that case were familiar enough— Muslim fanatics—and it was, afterall, New York. And true, a few radicals back in the 1960s had tried to blow up buildings, mostly on college campuses, but they seldom killed anybody except by accident. In short, terrorists were psychopathic foreign killers, masking their bloodlust with anti-Western revolutionary rhetoric, not a bunch of beer buddies playing soldier on the weekends in what was left of the American wilderness and complaining about too many taxes and too powerful a federal government.

However, the Oklahoma City bombing was but one among a number of local terrorist attacks, including the assassination of outspoken Jewish radio talk-show host Alan Berg in Denver a decade earlier, by the rapidly growing right-wing racist and survivalist groups, some with familiar names, some not so familiar—Ku Klux Klan, Aryan Nations, Neo-Nazis, Skinheads, Posse Comitatus, Christian Identity, the Patriots, the Michigan Militia (and various other militias), the Freemen, and the Order. The Oklahoma bombing seemed to be aimed at exposing two "local" issues that obsessed the groups—the execution of Berg's assassin and the repression of the Waco sect by what the right-wing groups call ZOG, the Zionist Occupation Government, i.e., the federal government they imagined to be controlled by Jews.

Over the course of a few weeks the survivalists received more airtime to parade their political beliefs and goals than they had in years of recruiting one-on-one and plastering the American heartland with pamphlets. For years, ever since a grieving Libyan dictator had threatened to send squads of fanatics to kill President Ronald Reagan in the White House, the federal government had been slowly retreating behind barricades. Now it became even more entrenched. All over the country barriers and checkpoints went up at federal buildings, much as they had years before at commercial airports. Congressional hearings on the incident at Waco commenced, something the right-wing survivalists groups had long been demanding. The President attacked right-wing talk show hosts as purveyors of hate and inciters to violence, and the talk show hosts went right on purveying their alarmist and apocalyptic message. And from the lawmakers on Capitol Hill and the pundits in the press the word went out: if Americans wanted to be more secure, they were simply going to have to give up some of their freedoms, allowing federal law enforcement agencies—and the police in general, one supposes—more leeway in investigating the potentially violent politics of American citizens. Thus did the terrorists begin to create the very condition they condemned: an isolated, inaccessible, intrusive federal government, suspicious of those in whose name it claimed to rule.

Selected Readings

Asimov, Issac. *Asimov's Chronology of Science and Discovery*. New York: Harper and Row, 1989.

Atkinson, Rick. *Crusade: The Untold Story of the Persian Gulf War.* Boston: Houghton Mifflin Company, 1993.

Baker, Carlos. *Ernest Hemingway: A Life Story*. New York: Macmillan, 1988.

Belz, Carl. *The Story of Rock*. New York: Oxford University Press, 1969.

Blair, Clay. *The Forgotten War: America in Korea, 1950–1953*. New York: Random House, 1987.

Bohr, Niels. *Atomic Physics and Human Knowledge*. New York: Wiley, 1958.

Branch, Taylor. *Parting the Waters: America in the King Years, 1954–1964*. New York: Simon & Schuster, 1988.

Bullock, Alan. *Hitler and Stalin: Parallel Lives*. New York: Alfred Knopf, Inc., 1991.

Carruth, Gorton. *What Happened When: A Chronology of Life and Events in America*. New York: Penguin Books, 1989.

Carter, Richard. *Breakthrough: The Saga of Jonas Salk.* 1966.

de Leon, David. *Everything Is Changing: Contemporary U.S. Movements in Historical Perspectives*. New York: Praeger, 1988.

Dickstein, Morris. *Gates of Eden: American Culture in the Sixties*. New York: Viking Penguin, 1989.

Dockrell, Michael. *Atlas of Twentieth Century World History.* New York: Harper Perennial, 1991.

Douglas, Ann. *Terrible Honesty: Mongrel Manhattan in the 1920s*. New York: Farrar, Straus and Giroux, 1995.

Duggan, Stephen and Betty Drury. *The Rescue of Science and Learning*. New York: Macmillan, 1948.

Dyson, Freeman. *Disturbing the Universe*. New York: Harper and Row, 1979.

Einstein, Albert and Leopold Infield. *The Evolution of Physics*. New York: Simon and Schuster, 1966.

Elliot, Emory. *Columbia Literary History of the United States*. New York: Columbia University Press, 1988.

Ellis, John. *The Social History of the Machine Gun*. New York: Pantheon, 1976.

Emery, Fred. *Watergate: The Corruption of American Politics and the Fall of Richard Nixon*. New York: Times Books, 1994.

Fell, Joseph. *Heidegger and Sartre*. New York: Columbia University Press, 1978.

Floyd, Candace. *America's Great Disasters*. New York: Mallard, 1990.

Foner, Eric, et al. *The Reader's Companion to American History.* Boston: Houghton Mifflin, 1991.

Friedman, Jon and John Meehan. *House of Cards: Inside the Troubled Empire of American Express*. New York: G. P. Putnam's Sons, 1992.

Friedrich, Otto. *Before the Deluge: A Portrait of Berlin in the 1920s*. New York: Harper & Row, 1992.

Frist, William H., M.D. *Transplant: A Heart Surgeon's Account of the Life-and-Death Dramas of the New Medicine*. New York: Altantic Monthly Press, 1989.

Gabler, Neal. *An Empire of Their Own: How the Jews Invented Hollywood.* New York: Anchor Books, 1988.

Gabler, Neal. *Winchell: Gossip, Power, and the Cult of Celebrity.* New York: Alfred A. Knopf, 1994.

Gamow, George. *The Thirty Years That Shook Physics.* New York: Doubleday, 1966.

Garraty, John A. *The Great Depression.* Garden City, N.J.: Anchor Books, 1987.

Gentry, Curt. *J. Edgar Hoover: The Man and the Secrets.* New York: W. W. Norton, 1991.

Glaser, Nathan, ed. *Clamor at the Gates: The New American Immigration.* 1985.

Goldberg, Robert and Gerald Jay Goldberg. *Citizen Turner: The Wild Rise of an American Tycoon.* New York: Harcourt Brace and Company, 1995.

Gordon, Michael R. and General Bernard E. Trainor. *The Generals' War: The Inside Story of the Conflict in the Gulf.* Boston: Little, Brown and Company, 1995.

Gordon, Linda. *Woman's Body, Woman's Right: A Social History of Birth Control in America.* Madison, Wisc.: University of Wisconsin Press, rev. ed., 1990.

Gould, Lewis L. *The Presidency of Theodore Roosevelt.* Lawrence: University of Kansas Press, 1991.

Graham, Davis. *The Civil Rights Era: Origins and Development of National Policy.* 1990.

Greenville, J. A. S. *History of the World in the Twentieth Century.* Cambridge, Mass.: Belknap Press, 1994.

Groves, Leslie. *Now It Can Be Told.* New York: Harper and Row, 1962.

Grum, Bernard. *The Timetables of History.* 3d ed. New York: Simon and Schuster/Touchstone, 1975.

Henderson, Robert. *D. W. Griffith: His Life and Work.* New York: Oxford University Press, 1972.

Hentoff, Nat and Albert J. McCarthy, eds. *Jazz: New Perspectives on the History of Jazz.* New York: Da Capo, 1975.

Hersh, Barton. T*he Old Boys: The American Elite and the Origins of the CIA.* New York: Charles Scribner's Sons, 1992.

Hobsbawm, Eric. *The Age of Extremes: A History of the World, 1914–1991.* New York: Pantheon Books, 1994.

Jones, Max, and John Chilton. *The Louis Armstrong Story, 1900–1971.* 1971.

Katcher, Leo. *The Big Bankroll: The Life and Times of Arnold Rothstein.* New York: DaCapo Press, 1994.

Katz, Michael. *The Undeserving Poor.* 1989.

Keegan, John. *The Second World War.* New York: Viking, 1989.

Kenner, Hugh. *The Pound Era.* Berkeley and Los Angeles: University of California Press, 1971.

Knight, Arthur. T*he Liveliest Art: A Panoramic History of the American Movies.* New York: New American Library, 1957.

Kolko, Gabriel. *Anatomy of a War: Vietnam, the United States, and the Modern Historical Experience.* New York: Pantheon, 1985.

Lasch, Christopher. *The New Radicalism in America, 1889–1963.* New York: W.W. Norton & Co., 1965.

Mandela, Nelson. *No Easy Walk to Freedom.* London: Heineman, 1965.

Mandela, Nelson. *I Am Prepared to Die.* International Defense and Aid, 4th ed. 1979.

Manchester, William. *The Arms of Krupp, 1587–1968.* Boston: Little, Brown & Co., 1964.

Montgomery, David. *The Fall of the House of Labor.* Cambridge, England: Cambridge University Press, 1987.

Nieman, Donald G. *Promises to Keep:AfricanAmericans and the Constitutional Order, 1776 to the Present*. Oxford, England: Oxford University Press, 1991.

Nye, Russell. *The Unembarassed Muse: The Popular Arts in America*. New York: Dial Press, 1970.

O'Brien, Conor Cruise. *The Siege: The Saga of Israel and Zionism*. New York: Simon and Schuster, 1989.

Orfield, Gary. *Public School Desegregation in the United States, 1968–1980*. Ford Foundation, 1983.

Parmet, Herbert S. *JFK: The Presidency of John F. Kennedy*. New York: The Dial Press, 1983.

Pearson, Hugh. *The Shadow of the Panther: Huey Newton and the Price of Black Power in America*. Reading, Mass.: AddisonWesley Publishing Company, 1994.

Posner, Gerald. *Case Closed: Lee Harvey Oswald and the Assassination of JFK*. New York: Random House, 1993.

Reimers, David, ed. *Still the Golden Door: The Third World Comes to America*. New York: Columbia University Press, 1985.

Reisner, Marc. *Cadillac Desert: The American West and Its Disappearing Water*. New York: Penguin Books, 1986.

Rhodes, Richard. *The Making of the Atomic Bomb*. New York: Simon and Schuster, 1986.

Ross, Walter S. *The Last Hero: Charles A. Lindbergh*. 1964.

Sergeant, Harriet. *Shanghai: Collision Point of Cultures, 1918–1939*. New York: Crown Publishers, Inc., 1990.

Shepard, Alan and Deke Slayton. *Moon Shot: The Inside Story of America's Race to the Moon*. Atlanta: Turner Publishing, 1992

Sifakis, Carl. *The Mafia Encyclopedia*. New York: Facts on File, 1989.

Smelser, Marshall and Joan R. Gunder. *American History at a Glance*. New York: Harper and Row, 1978.

Speer, Albert. *Inside the Third Reich*. New York: Macmillan Co., 1970.

Takaki, Ronald. *A Different Mirror: A History of Multicultural Americans*. Boston: Little, Brown and Company, 1993.

Teller, Edward. *The Legacy of Hiroshima*. New York: Doubleday, 1962.

Thelen, David and Frederick E. Hoxie (eds.). *Robert La Follette and the Insurgent Spirit*. Madison, Wisc.: University of Wisconsin Press, 1976.

Tice, Patricia M. *Altered States: Alcohol and Other Drugs in America*. Rochester, N.Y.: Strong Museum, 1992.

Tuchman, Barbara. *The March of Folly: From Troy to Vietnam*. New York: Ballantine Books, 1984.

Tuchman, Barbara. *The Guns of August*. New York: Ballantine Books, 1962.

Volkman, Ernest and Blaine Baggett. *Secret Intelligence: The Inside Story of America's Espionage Empire*. New York: Doubleday, 1989.

Williams, Juan. *Eyes on the Prize: America's Civil Rights Years, 1954–1965*. New York: Penguin, 1987.

Woodward, C. Vann. *The Strange Career of Jim Crow*. New York: Oxford University Press, 1966.

Zieger, Robert H. *American Workers, American Unions, 1920–1985*. Baltimore: Johns Hopkins University Press, 1986.

Zinn, Howard. *The Twentieth Century: A People's History. New York: Perennial Library, 1980*.

Index

Charles Phillips is the author of *The Heritage of the American West* and senior editor of the forthcoming four-volume *Encyclopedia of the American West*. He has served as editor of *Higher Education and National Affairs* for the American Council on Education, of *History News* for the American Association for State and Local History, and on the staffs of *Congressional Quarterly* and the *Washington Star*. He co-wrote and produced *Count Me In: Doolittle's Raid Over Tokyo*, which aired on PBS stations around the country and won an award for historical videos from the American Association of Museums. A graduate of the Iowa Writers Workshop, he has taught at the University of Iowa, and is also co-author of *Passion by Design: The Art and Time of Tamara de Lempicka, A Culture at Risk: Who Cares for America's Heritage*, and *The Wages of History*.

Alan Axelrod is the author of *Chronicle of the Indian Wars: From Colonial Times to Wounded Knee, The War Between the Spies: A History of Espionage During the Civil War, Charles Brockden Brown: An American Tale*, and *The Art of the Golden West*, which was the Booklist Editor's Choice in 1990 and won the National Cowboy Hall of Fame Western Heritage Award in 1991. Axelrod holds a Ph.D. from the University of Iowa, has taught at Lake Forest University and Furman University, served as associate editor for the Winterthur Museum *Portfolio*, and edited *The Colonial Revival in America*.

Together Phillips and Axelrod have written *The Environmentalists: A Biographical Dictionary from the 17th Century to the Present; My Brother's Face: Portraits of the Civil War; Dictators and Tyrants; Cops, Crooks, and Criminologists*; and the highly acclaimed *What Every American Should Know about American History: 200 Events That Shaped the Nation*.